MODERN COSMOLOGY
& PHILOSOPHY

MODERN COSMOLOGY & PHILOSOPHY

Edited by
John Leslie

Prometheus Books

59 John Glenn Drive
Amherst, New York 14228-2197

Published 1998 by Prometheus Books

02 01 00 99 98   5 4 3 2 1

Library of Congress Cataloging-in-Publication Data

Modern cosmology & philosophy / edited by John Leslie.
        p.   cm.
    Rev. ed. of : Physical cosmology and philosophy. c1990.
    Includes bibliographical references.
    ISBN 1–57392–250–1 (alk. paper)
    1. Cosmology. 2. Philosophy. I. Leslie, John, 1940– . II. Physical cosmology and philosophy. III. Title : Modern cosmology and philosophy.
QB981.P563   1998
523.1–dc21   98–47273
                                                                    CIP

Printed in the United States of America on acid-free paper

Contents

Preface to the Second Edition

IN THE PERIOD following the appearance of the First Edition, there have been no sudden breakthroughs in cosmology due to new observations, and no startling new theories have revolutionized people's thinking. COBE, the Cosmic Background Explorer telescope, did get heavy media coverage as "proving the Big Bang" and "revealing the Face of God"; yet the Big Bang was already rather firmly established, the Face of God being nothing more than large-scale ripples such as Big Bang theorists had predicted. And although NASA scientists claimed to have found tiny fossils of primitive life in a meteorite originating on Mars, their discovery was widely doubted. Besides, what if they had instead found the bones of man-sized Martians? Would that have shown that life arises easily in our universe? Not neces- sarily. If tiny fossils can ride from Mars to Earth inside meteorites then so, many scientists reason, could primitive living things; or again, they could ride from Earth to Mars; and either way, life could then have developed in both places, even if the odds had been heavily against its appearing in a single one of them.

There has, however, been a growing interest in the philosophy of this exciting field. The Second Edition includes five new Readings which help to show why.

Preface to the First Edition

OF THE TWENTY-ONE Readings collected together here, the great majority are within the reach of the general reader. A few cannot be fully understood without a knowledge of mathematics; but remember, it was their philosophical importance and not their technicalities which earned them their place in this volume, and the Introduction is a guide to the philosophical points they raise.

Two of the Readings—the ones from Richard Swinburne and George Gale—were generated expressly for the volume. The others have all been in print earlier.

As editor, I thank the Research Department of Philosophy, Australian National University, for the period of visiting fellowship during which the Introduction was sketched out. My wife Jill helped prepare manuscript and bibliography and made useful comments, as did Paul Edwards. John Polkinghorne ran an expert eye over the Glossary, but I take all of whatever blame it still deserves.

INTRODUCTION

Looking at developments since 1954, we ask in *Physical Cosmology and Philosophy* four main questions: Was there a Big Bang, and if so, how can we know it? Is our universe "fine-tuned" in ways that make it especially suited to living beings? May there exist many huge, largely separate, and markedly different cosmic regions, perhaps worth calling "universes" and perhaps only rarely having properties that allow living beings to evolve? And finally, how much life is there in the cosmos?

This Introduction will begin with a quick survey of how the contributors to the book reply to the four questions. After that, their contributions will be introduced one by one, in each case with a short summary and some comments.

1. A Big Bang?

Following McMULLIN's philosophical survey, much of it concerned with how cosmologists could ever have good grounds for believing what they do, there are several readings that argue for and against the now common belief that our universe exploded into existence some few billions years ago. The first is from GAMOW, a main developer of the theory of a universe-wide, intensely hot explosion, today known as the Big Bang, in which space itself started expanding. Everywhere—for instance, where your nose is—would be "where the Bang began." The exploding universe could have always been spatially infinite, which is how Gamow sees it, since even an infinitely large space could be expanding, its various regions growing farther apart. Could it also be infinite in time? Gamow says that it is "satisfactory" to conclude that it existed for infinitely long before the Bang. It was then contracting, the Bang being a rebound rather than the springing into existence of new material. It could be of philosophical interest to ask just why he says this if, as his last paragraph suggests, no traces remain of any situation before the rebound.

While similarly favoring an infinite past for our universe, BONNOR replaces Gamow's infinitely prolonged contraction by an infinity of cosmic oscillations: explosions followed by gravitationally produced recollapses, followed by new explosions. BONDI, in contrast, defends a steady-state universe: no Bang, but external expansion, with new matter constantly appearing to fill the widening vistas. And while REES, writing a decade and a half later, in 1976, considers that this has been refuted, we find NARLIKAR still defending it in 1981.

Two further readings may help to explain such disagreements. GRÜNBAUM holds that cosmologists often regard some situation — total emptiness, perhaps, or eternal existence — as the universe's "natural state," and then struggle to bring their theories into line with this. He urges them to interpret the evidence without such preconceptions. ELLIS, on the other hand, thinks that unverifiable assumptions do need to be made if we are ever to interpret any evidence, yet people make them too confidently. In particular, they too often scorn the possibility that mankind views the universe from an unusual place or time, especially hospitable to observers. This view leads us to the next topic.

2. Fine-Tuning?

Recently, many have argued that either reality as a whole, or else the spatiotemporal region which we can see, is "fine-tuned" to life's needs, by which they mean that tiny changes in its basic properties would have excluded life forms of any plausible kind. (Talk of "fine-tuning" does not presuppose a divine fine-tuner.) DICKE looks at various ratios whose gigantic size had encouraged physicists to develop bold theories about all places and times. Instead, he thinks of these ratios as holding during a very special cosmic epoch: the epoch at which physicists can be alive to measure them. Following his lead, CARTER states an Anthropic Principle that "what we can expect to observe must be restricted by the conditions necessary for our presence as observers." A "weak" version says that our location in space and time must (obviously) be such as to allow us to inhabit it. A "strong" one makes the point — once again self-evidently correct — that any universe with observers in it must be observer-permitting.

When they are so very obviously correct, how could such points be non-trivial? Well, Carter sees evidence of fine-tuning in such things as the strengths of various physical forces. Perhaps the strengths are different at different cosmic epochs or in different cosmic regions. At many times or places no observers can exist, the forces being tuned in life-discouraging ways; but whenever and wherever they do exist, everything of course *must be* tuned rightly. This could be important. When huge cosmic domains or epochs, perhaps successive cycles of an oscillating cosmos, are very much separated or have very different properties, they might be said to be separate "worlds" or even "universes." (Cosmologists often talk like that, whereas philosophers tend to use "world" or "universe" to mean Existence In Its Totality so that *two universes* would be as absurd as *a married bachelor*. For various definitions of **universe**, see the Glossary near the end of this book.) Now, imagining an ensemble of such worlds/universes, Carter suggests that his Strong Anthropic Principle may throw light on why we find our world to have physical forces that seem fine-tuned to life's needs.

While equally impressed by the apparent fine-tuning, CARR indicates that there is a second way of interpreting it. God might have chosen to create just the kind of cosmos in which living beings could evolve. SWINBURNE thinks that this is a much better interpretation, since we could have little excuse for believing in domains, worlds, or universes very different from our own.

Not everyone is happy with such maneuvers. PAGELS claims that the Anthropic Principle is not testable — although one might get the impression that he also thinks it has failed various tests by giving us explanations which have proved to be wrong, and that it will in due course fail others: for instance, when we find intelligent life forms less sensitive than humans to possible changes in force strengths. And GOULD, using the words "Anthropic Principle" as if they meant a belief in divine planning or in something similar, claims that there is no evidence to support any such belief; any argument for the existence of that kind of evidence is "historically moth-eaten." As he shows, the year 1903 provided a sad example of moth-food: namely, A.R. Wallace's universe of concentric rings of stars, with Earth in precisely the place (near the center) for whose benefit the whole was designed.

3. Multiple Universes?

Wallace's universe, however, was miniscule by modern standards. It consisted of a single galaxy, whereas over 100 billion are seen by today's cosmologists. And what happens when these cosmologists struggle to get rid of apparent evidence of fine-tuning? — for instance, evidence that the initial cosmic speed of expansion had to be correct to about one part in ten billion billion billion billion billion billion to avoid the rapid recollapse of everything or else its quick dispersion into cold, enormously rarefied gases. The answer is that their struggles involve picturing the early cosmos as having suddenly "inflated" to such an extent that the region which we can now see is only an extremely tiny fraction of the whole. Further, there are signs that nature's four main forces (gravity, electromagnetism, and the nuclear strong and weak forces) would have been closely unified in the earliest, hottest moments of a Big Bang and that there could have been much randomness in the strengths taken by those forces as they split apart. One common conclusion is that we cannot be at all sure that reality is everywhere like the region visible to us or that it must all be hospitable to observers. If we speak of regions well beyond our horizon as "other universes," then what right has anyone to say that life is possible in any great proportion of those universes? (See Glossary: **inflation, nuclear strong force, nuclear weak force, horizons.**)

GALE lists ways of getting many universes: the above-sketched "inflationary" way and many others, some in seemingly strong conflict with common sense. One way is that of Many-Worlds Quantum Theory, which pictures the cosmos — and everything in it, such as you yourself — as forever splitting. Another is presented by **WHEELER** who imagines many cosmic oscillations. Between successive oscillatory cycles the cosmos is squeezed down to such tiny dimensions that it "forgets" its properties. Thus it can start each new cycle with, for example, a very different number of particles.

TRYON, in contrast, describes universes of different sizes springing into existence from empty space, as quantum fluctuations; that is, they come into being without any cause, but in a way permitted by the statistical laws of quantum theory. Smaller fluctuations are already familiar to physicists: they know that even emptiness constantly gives birth to particles which, however, must typically die again very quickly, since the energy needed for their existence is "borrowed" only for the period allowed by quantum uncertainties, a period usually extremely short (see Glossary: **fluctuation, quantum theory**). But Tryon explains that even a very large universe may have a total energy *of zero* when one takes account of its gravitational binding energy which, like other binding energies in physics, *is negative*. It can then survive for indefinitely long.

As the next two readings show, Tryon's ideas are not sheer craziness. In fact, if there is any such thing as a standard cosmos nowadays, then it is one with something much like them at its foundation. **DAVIES** imagines a small quantum fluctuation as inflating enormously before settling down to leisurely Big Bang expansion: when the inflation ends, the fact of gravitational energy's being negative could mean that tremendously many particles had come to exist without any violation of energy conservation. And **LINDE**, developing the same basic tale, suggests that inflation by a factor of $10^{1,000,000}$ (one followed by a million zeros) could well have occurred and that the inflated cosmos might positively be expected to have split into greatly many gigantic domains. Force strengths and other basic features could differ randomly among them.

4. How Much Life?

SHAPIRO and FEINBERG argue that life might evolve almost anywhere, perhaps even inside the sun: so much for lifeless domains/worlds/universes and the "fine-tuning" of our life-containing one! But the final reading, from HART, takes a very different view. Hart expects living things only on Earth-like planets, which he thinks of as extremely sparsely scattered; and even on an ideal planet they will make their appearance only if molecular combinations happen to occur in highly improbable ways. Nonetheless, he says, life could easily appear infinitely often, since the astronomical evidence suggests a cosmos infinitely large.

Cosmology, in short, has been very richly speculative in recent years. Even today, is there any general agreement on so basic a fact as that a Big Bang did take place? On *that* virtually everyone does now agree — yet people can accept simultaneously that the cosmos is in a steady state, on the largest scales at least, because the Bang in question may have been just a local affair. Perhaps the cosmos as a whole is eternally inflating, and we inhabit just one of many tiny "bubble universes" in which inflation has given way to comparatively slow Big Bang expansion. For if there is one thing on which all the experts agree, it is that we can see but a fraction of reality. If the universe ended at our present horizon, then cosmological theorizing would have still greater troubles than if the Bang turned out to be a mere fiction.

That being so, how can our cosmological theories get any grip on reality in its entirety? Might we argue that it must contain many and varied worlds or bubble universes, this alone permitting us to understand how at least one region manages to be fine-tuned to life's requirements? As we have seen, Swinburne believes instead in a fine-tuner, while others suggest that the fine-tuning is an illusion! It is hard to see how disagreements so basic could ever be settled conclusively. Still, it is a mistake to think that the only theories worth having are those that are completely provable. Philosophy of cosmology can show how arguments that are inconclusive can nevertheless be powerful. At the same time it could bring a little more fairness to cosmology's disputes. This book gets rather technical in places but it is not necessary to master every technicality before coming to appreciate that many a confident argument is sadly one-sided, perhaps actually depending on giving quite the wrong interpretation to an opponent's words. *That*, rather than the scientific minutiae, some of them already outdated and others due to suffer the same fate next week, is what the reader should be looking for.

Here are further details, comments, questions, loosely based on successive readings and intended to hack a path through their technicalities.

Reading 1: Ernan McMullin: Is Philosophy Relevant to Cosmology?

Cosmology studies the cosmos as a whole. Labels like "philosophical" were long attached to it, not as compliments. Today, though, its credentials are strong, partly because our universe is far more simple than we had a right to expect. On large scales everything looks homogeneous or smooth: "smoother than a billiard ball" (P. J. E. Peebles). It was probably still simpler some 15 billion years ago when everything was emerging from a very hot Big Bang. Because physics is in many ways more straightforward at high temperatures, the early universe could be a very useful laboratory; but we can see into this laboratory only indirectly, and indirect observation demands philosophical skill. Much progress has been made by seeking the cosmic elegance and even the *necessity* which philosophers have typically sought. Yet although McMullin says we may some day have cause to deny "that the most basic structures of the universe might have been different," he presumably cannot mean that these structures were perhaps dictated solely by logical necessity, the necessity with which husbands must have wives. So far as mere logic is concerned, the universe might have been immensely messy.

Cosmology, McMullin points out, is "as much a testing-ground for the philosopher's theories of science as it is for the physicist's theories of matter." Philosophers are in trouble when they suggest that theories about distant galaxies are "conventions imposed because our minds cannot operate otherwise." And how about the philosophical thesis that it is illegitimate to ask why any physical constant (the proton/electron mass ratio is McMullin's example) is just what it is? Linde (Reading 19) is a cosmologist who thinks he can *answer* such a question. Linde's idea is that a unified force broke up into many forces as the Bang cooled. "Symmetry-breaking" fields, their intensities varying from one huge region to the next, dictated various force strengths and particle masses at this stage. Thereafter these strengths and masses have been constant inside each region. (See Glossary: **unification of forces** and **symmetry breaking**.)

Let me add that some philosophical attempts to fix limits to what is meaningful or true — the philosophical theory, for instance, that the true is what could warrantedly be asserted in the long run — may find it hard to deal with various cosmological findings. Thus, there are **black holes** (see Glossary) whose internal details cannot possibly be known: now, how could this particular philosophical theory deal with speculation about the precise path taken by some individual particle that has fallen into such a hole? How could it accommodate the fact that signals can have traveled toward us over a distance of only a few billion light years while the cosmos may be infinitely large? How could it allow questions, no doubt unprofitable but surely at least meaningful, about just which events occurred just where during the 100,000 years before our universe became transparent to light rays? Again, later readings consider processes which may have produced heaven knows how many universes having little or no contact with ours, with properties fixed largely by chance. If we guessed that 99.7% of them contained no intelligent beings, might not the guess conceivably deliver the truth? But, one might well think, nobody could have good warrant for asserting any such truth.

Cosmology could also test responses to such philosophical queries as, Why is there a cosmos?. "Intuitively," McMullin writes, "an eternally existing universe seems a more plausible candidate for self-sufficiency than one which begins to be." Replace "self-sufficiency" by "not being God-created" and you may gain insight into F. Hoyle's long fight for a steady state rather than a Bang.

Could life and intelligence be signs of God's creative hand? While they evolved in ways made "natural" by nature's actual laws and constants, a theist might still ask, Why are there just those laws and constants?. Some would reply that since we exist to observe it, the universe *must have* laws and constants permitting observers to evolve. In McMullin's eyes that is no answer. If an observer-permitting universe were somehow very improbable, then we could not explain it by invoking "the presumably at least equally improbable presence of observers." So, perhaps we should accept "a Creator who wills that conscious life develop" and chooses laws and constants with this in mind.

McMullin suggests that the main alternative would be that all possible universes obeying general relativity exist; the existence of our life-containing universe could then be unsurprising. I cannot see, though, that the words "all possible" are justified here. To account for the car numberplate "HUMAN-1" it could suffice that *very many* combinations of letters and numbers appeared on cars. That HUMAN-1 should appear on *mine* could then remain very improbable: yet, so would it remain improbable if *all possible* combinations appeared somewhere. And the cosmological case could be seen as one in which cars without such labels as HUMAN-1 or MARTIAN-22 would never be *mine* to any observer. *An observational selection effect* could help to explain my seeing a life-containing universe if various other actually existing universes were lifeless.

One difficulty here is that the meaning of "universe" changes from author to author. The important point is just that there might be many huge regions of reality. These "universes," if that is what we want to call them, might perhaps be in contact at their edges, but an observer near the center of any one of them could never learn of the others by direct observation.

"A Creator" could also have various meanings. If God is real then "his" reality may be as described by neoplatonists. God is then just the principle that the ethical need for a universe or universes *itself creates* that universe or those universes. Swinburne mentions this alternative in Reading 12.

Reading 2: George Gamow: Modern Cosmology

Appearing in 1954, this paper is inevitably somewhat outdated; e.g., in the mere 5 billion years of expansion that it allots to our universe or in its suggestion that all the elements may have been produced in the first half hour of expansion. Yet it remains a good introduction to cosmology. Gamow sees how hard it is to choose the right universe model when the evidence — for instance, the reddening of light from distant galaxies, suggesting that they recede very fast — is divided from its interpretation by long theoretical chains. Faced with the problem that looking to far regions is also looking backward in time, we must (says he) have faith in the "Copernican" philosophical view that things have been basically the same in all regions. Again, we must trust general relativity, which relates the curvature of space to the average density of matter. Observations point to a density too low to "close" the cosmos like the curved surface of a sphere. (In 1954, physicists had not yet dreamed up exotic particles to provide the extra mass needed for closure.) Gamow thus chooses with some confidence a position he finds both empirically adequate and philosophically satisfying: that an infinitely large universe underwent infinitely prolonged gravitational collapse and is now rebounding. But he treats his opponents fairly, finding various philosophical charms in a steady-state cosmos with perpetual creation of new material at a very slow rate. That cosmos, too, is one "circumventing the philosophical question" — Gamow clearly thinks it a philosophical *difficulty* — "as to the 'beginning' of the universe." The main evidence against it, he reports, is that distant elliptical galaxies do seem to have been intrinsically redder at the earlier times at which we see them. (See Glossary: **red shift, general (theory of) relativity, closed universe, open universe, steady-state universe.**)

Reading 3: W. B. Bonnor:
Relativistic Theories of the Universe

Bonnor shows how a simple "cosmological principle"—that at a given time, observers everywhere "would see essentially the same picture"—can be plausible if space expands. Our main observational evidence for this (we are only in 1960) is that distant galaxies look redder and are distributed evenly. May the universe have come into existence some few billion years ago in a state of infinite density? Bonnor regards such infinities as signs of error, while to introduce an infinite-density-creating God to mend matters is "highly improper." A steady state, with particles continually created "out of nothing" to fill the expanding void, is "less unsatisfactory" but still poor: it violates energy conservation. So, says Bonnor, we had best believe in an infinity of cosmic oscillations: explosions, recollapses, new explosions. We can have "knowledge" of the infinitely many oscillations if no alternative can be made elegant.

Bonnor's conception of *knowledge* is liked by many philosophers of today, and much of his paper is surprisingly up to date scientifically. People now approve of its idea that *tension* could make a cosmos explode (see Reading 18). Many theologians direct Bonnor-like frowns at Pope Pius XII's view that a Big Bang helps to prove God's existence. Is Bonnor fair, though, in dismissing any divine universe-creating act as "miraculous"? (Isn't a miracle a breakdown in an *already existing* system?) Further, might not an infinity in one's equations support a belief in God, without God's having to "disappear" when the infinity was no longer accepted? And anyway (see Readings 7 and 17–19) could not a universe-beginning Bang start with a density less than infinite and even without violating energy conservation?

Reading 4: H. Bondi: The
Steady-State Theory of the Universe

Perhaps, says Bondi, the universe is "very different elsewhere or at other times." But—in part because testing simpler theories yields results faster—we ought to prefer a steady-state universe, spatiotemporally uniform. It would have to expand, else we should be "drowned by a flood of light" (an argument, recently challenged by E.R.Harrison, which is based on Olbers' paradox: see Glossary). To fill the expanding space, "new matter constantly appears" at a rate hard to detect: "one hydrogen atom in a space the size of an ordinary living-room once every few million years." While an unchanging amount of matter would be simpler if taken in isolation, cosmologists must not take things in isolation!

The paper is a gem. Continual creation of matter may seem to be rather odd, yet those who are scornful about it while themselves stating that an entire universe appeared all at once might be pots calling a kettle black.

Reading 5: Martin Rees: The 13,000,000,000 Year Bang

Writing in 1976, Rees can speak of a "consensus" for a Big Bang. Looking to ever greater distances (and so to ever earlier times), we see more and more density and violence. Background radiation suggests a "primordial fireball," as do other conditions such as the relative abundances of hydrogen, helium, and deuterium. Steady-state models are thus refuted, the big question now being whether the cosmos is oscillating, with a series of Bangs.

Rees points to the cosmic **isotropy** and **homogeneity** (see Glossary) as a major puzzle. Quantum gravitational mechanisms may have produced this smoothness, he suggests; but here we might well protest that such mechanisms could have operated only at very early instants. Tremendous turbulence might still have been expected later when large regions which had not previously made contact started to interact, becoming visible to one another like ships coming over one another's horizons. (This is just one of several *horizon problems*. Their common theme is that the early universe's parts could be expected to be poorly coordinated because faster-than-light signaling is impossible. Even in a universe starting off microscopic in size this theme could apply, for space itself would be expanding and thus carrying apart regions which were trying to signal to one another across what had started as very tiny gaps.) Such turbulence would have generated enormously much heat and light. As R. Penrose has stressed, this could make the seemingly high ratio of photons (particles of light) to particles of matter look very fortunately *low*. For each particle of matter, the Bang produced about 100 million photons, but, argues Penrose, turbulence could very readily have generated immensely many more of them, making the universe much too hot for galaxies to form. Today, the idea of inflation (see Readings 18 and 19) might at last be able to solve this Smoothness Problem, the puzzle of why the cosmos is so placid.

Note Rees's suggestion that the properties of elementary particles and of much else "are determined by what happened in the initial instants." Would they be determined in the same way everywhere?

Reading 6: Jayant Narlikar: Was There a Big Bang?

Writing five years after Rees, Narlikar attacks his kind of confidence. How could a Big Bang get started? And may not the universe be too old for Big Bang models to be right? Only the red shifts of **quasars** (see Glossary) hint at more than a doubling of the universe's size, and those shifts may well be produced by something other than cosmic expansion. There is no firm evidence that large-scale properties were different earlier, so the universe could be a steady-state one. The background radiation, furthermore, may have the wrong spectrum for Big Bang radiation. And general relativity, on which Big Bang theorists rely, has not been tested in strong gravitational fields; it may be in trouble now that some observations suggest that gravity weakens over time. Again, *Dirac* Big Bang theorists may need a particular version of quantum gravity — of which *no* versions are yet available. Yes, almost everyone accepts a Bang, but views about cosmology in any period are largely determined by "a few strong individuals."

Many would dismiss this as a mere tirade, but Narlikar is making an important point. Cosmological models depend on long chains of reasoning. The elegant consistency of the standardly accepted results might be in part due to our accepting as "actually observed" only what squares with current dogmas. Other models might be equally elegant.

As I mentioned earlier, a steady state may in fact be compatible with a Bang if the state in question is large enough. Today Narlikar holds that a fairly popular version of the inflation story, a version in which an eternally inflating universe contains "bubbles" that evolve in old-fashioned Big Bang style, is essentially the same as the final version of the steady-state story developed by him and F. Hoyle.

Reading 7: Adolf Grünbaum: The Pseudo-Problem of Creation in Physical Cosmology

If matter has a temporal origin then, Grünbaum recognizes, the details of its origination could have great scientific interest. However, he sees here nothing that is *puzzling philosophically* in a way which could justify talk of "a problem of creation." Even to speak of "creation" rather than of "origination" strikes him as unfortunate because, for instance, it suggests an external cause. The steady-state theory would not be in philosophical difficulties merely because of needing new atoms to appear continually. The Big Bang theory would have no evident and extraordinary problem about where all the stuff of the universe came from, even if the Bang did not just reverse an earlier contraction. One might equally well join Descartes in finding a problem in why tables do not vanish, or side with Aristotelian physicists in asking why moving bodies keep moving in "unnatural" Newtonian fashion. Events carry no labels announcing their degree of "naturalness"! Our duty is to find by experience how the world normally operates. A cluster of philosophical blunders underlies the view that a deity must in some ordinary sense have *caused* nature to act as she does, or to exist at all. And matters get still worse when an unordinary sense is invoked, a sense said to pass all human understanding — so that the words humans use when talking of divine causation could only be meaningless noises.

Such points have considerable force, and no short counter-argument can rebut them. Still, a theist might begin by arguing that we cannot get far by relying on experience alone. Grünbaum would not be puzzled even if it could be shown that there was an instant at which the entire universe originated; were that indeed the case, he would say, then it should be judged to be just as natural as eternal existence would have been if the universe had instead existed eternally; and the same would apply to any appearance of new atoms at a constant, very slow rate, as imagined by the steady-state theory. Now, true enough, neither mere experience nor logic could establish his wrongness. But might not the need for consistency put some pressure on him to accept that if cherubs too appeared out of empty space at a constant, very slow rate, then *that* ought to be judged natural and unpuzzling? Or that if the original of a particular book, the Koran, had in fact existed eternally (as some Moslems believe), then this too would require no explanation? Yet, surely we could have reason to see these and other affairs as "unnatural" in the sense of calling for divine explanation, even if they did characterize Nature. Grünbaum's example of tables that do not vanish might itself draw some of its persuasiveness from the common conviction that this is not only ordinary but *understandable*, so that a thing's existence a moment ago makes it utterly inappropriate to ask why it is present now. However, the Koran case could throw doubt on any such conviction.

Again, a physicist might point out that treating the origin of matter as something in need of an explanation, rather than just as an affair to be described and accepted, has led to important new theories: Tryon's, for example.

Reading 8: G.F.R. Ellis: Cosmology and Verifiability

Ellis is known for his non-standard models of the universe. Their main significance is often philosophical, he thinks. They force us to answer why we prefer the standard ones. His own answer is that we must often be content with assumptions that are attractive but unverifiable.

Ellis's criterion of verifiability may be altogether too severe. He suggests that not even fossils truly verify that the universe wasn't created just 6,000 years ago! But even with a milder criterion, cosmology can still need some rather bold assumptions. Thus, our telescopes give the impression that distant regions are inhabited by violent objects, thickly clustered. We "correct" this impression by saying we really see an earlier epoch of dense violence. Things have since calmed down, say we; a steady state is therefore refuted. Yet might not some steady-state model be right, so that distant objects always have been violent and thickly clustered? Couldn't we be at the universe's center, things being isotropic about us (the same in all directions) yet not homogeneous (scattered evenly)? In other papers Ellis shows how places not at the center might be places where observers would be fried.

Ellis considers a man on an island. Do distant islands look smaller because they are farther away, or are they farther away *and smaller*? Our man may at first adopt the "cosmological principle" that all places are much the same. Besides being vague, that involves assumptions about islands beyond the horizon. So he may come to prefer the "Copernican principle" that he is not at the world's center. This, however, leaves unclear whether he is in a place that is *special* although not central.

Reading 9: R. H. Dicke: Dirac's Cosmology and Mach's Principle

Some general remarks may aid in interpreting this paper:

1. Physicists prefer to calculate in *ratios*, "dimensionless numbers." Six pounds of butter are twice as heavy as three, even when measured in kilograms.
2. Advances are often made by a process which, *when it leads to error*, is dismissed as "numerology." As fools look for neat relationships among various measurements of the Great Pyramid, dreaming that properly proportioned little pyramids will sharpen overnight any razor blades that are placed inside them, so do scientists seek tidy connections among various numbers. When this process leads to the truth, then it is called "physics."
3. Cosmology tends to be a science of very rough approximations. The idea that $1 \sim 10^3$ (i.e., that 1 nearly equals 1000) shocks nobody when 1 and 10^3 are being compared to a huge number like 10^{80}, which is roughly the number of protons there are in the visible universe.

Rough approximations persuaded Eddington and Dirac that some very large numbers were intimately related. Dirac held that gravity's immense weakness reflected the universe's immense age: it had weakened over time. He was assuming that various elegant ratios were products not of chance but of necessity. Which sort of necessity, though? Dicke answers that, necessarily, the ratios *hold in any epoch when physicists can be there to observe ratios*. Times are then necessarily late enough for carbon to have been made available for making physicists and early enough for there still to be life-supporting suns. Dirac, says Dicke, has mistaken an observational necessity for a cosmic necessity that dictates the ratios at every epoch.

Reading 10: Brandon Carter: Large Number Coincidences and the Anthropic Principle in Cosmology

Carter's Weak Anthropic Principle is that our spatiotemporal location is "*necessarily* privileged to the extent of being compatible with our existence as observers"; for instance, heavy elements must have had time to form. His Strong Principle is that the cosmos "must be such as to admit the creation of observers within it at some stage."

Carter now kicks himself for having said "anthropic." Not our being instances of *anthropos*, of Man, but our being *observers* is what is crucial. For his purposes, intelligent dinosaurs would serve as well as men. Again, his "must be such as to admit the creation of observers" has misled many. He is not saying that God, or some tie between real existence and consciousness, guaranteed the existence of observers. Instead, from the fact that we observers do exist *it follows necessarily* that observers *are not impossible* in this universe. "Cogito ergo mundus talis est." Since I am thinking, the world clearly *permits* thinking beings to exist. Their actual existence could depend on lucky happenings in some primeval chemical soup or on what chanced to occur when a unified force broke into many forces whose strengths were settled randomly.

"Observers exist only at times and places where observers can exist." Granted that this is all that the Weak Principle says, it is as clearly right as the statement that bachelors aren't bigamists. But despite being trivially true, it can help to explain things; for doesn't it point toward a possible observational selection effect? Suppose you want to know why the present age of the universe and gravity's present strength have a particular numerical relationship. Explanation (1): This relationship holds at all times, necessarily. Explanation (2): It holds just at those times that physicists could observe. Compare the case of two explanations of why distant stars all look very hot: the first, that all of them really are very hot, and the second, that only the very hot are bright enough to be seen.

Could the Strong Anthropic Principle also be explanatory? People have objected that it is as "tautologous" as the statement that bachelors lack wives; but as we have seen, this is a poor objection, for tautologies are implicitly or explicitly hypothetical, IFy–THENy. (If a bachelor, then wifeless.) Like the Weak Principle, the Strong Principle can suggest an observational selection effect which operates IF there exists *a World Ensemble*, i.e., a capital-U Universe split into many domains, small-u universes, with differing properties, AND·IF not all those properties are *observer-permitting* in view of the sorts of being that observers could in practice be. (Not immaterial spirits. Not intelligent machines unless preceded by machine-designing organisms.)

Carter says we might "think in terms of" such a World Ensemble. Still, thinking in such terms yields an explanation only if many worlds/ universes actually exist. (No Observational Selection Effect Without

Actual Things From Which To Select.) So he draws attention to Many-Worlds Quantum Theory in which different properties are seen by observers in different branches of a many-branched cosmos. All these observers, Carter stresses, "are equally 'real'."

Carter's incautious words might suggest that every World Ensemble explanation must propose the existence *of every single conceivable combination* of initial conditions and fundamental constants; but this would be so wrong (see my comments on the numberplate story of Reading 1) that charity forbids us to read him like that. The most one could need would be *sufficiently many* combinations to make observers quite likely to exist somewhere. Again, while Carter says he would be happier if "a deeper mathematical structure" dictated all basic properties, he is too sensible to think that our universe must fit his personal tastes. And anyway, what is to count as "our universe"? Imagine a cosmos split into huge domains characterized by different fundamental constants. Are these domains "different locations" (to which the Weak Anthropic Principle might apply) or "different universes" (and so perhaps food for the Strong Principle)? Here the distinction between the Weak and the Strong is a matter just of how you choose to define "locations" and "universes."

Reading 11: B.J. Carr: On the Origin, Evolution and Purpose of the Physical Universe

Carr emphasizes the Big Bang theory's reliance on a "Copernican" principle (Bonnor and Ellis would call it "cosmological") that "we are not in a privileged position." But even with its aid the theory cannot say whether Space is "open," destined to expand for ever and filled with infinitely many galaxies, or "closed," finite and fated to recollapse. And why is the matter density so near to the "critical" density dividing "open" from "closed"? To be so near today, it must early on have been near to one part in 10^{60}. Such nearness makes Space almost perfectly "flat," whereas all but a vanishingly small range of the Spaces considered by general relativity are appreciably curved. And the flatness seems crucial to our existence. Without it, the cosmos would have flown to bits very fast or recollapsed very quickly.

Again, there is the enigma of the cosmic smoothness. Life-excluding turbulence could have been expected when regions coming out of the Bang came over one another's horizons.

Carr sees that today's *unified theories* (which hold that at the earliest, hottest moments all was simpler, more "symmetrical," with perhaps just a single force and one general type of particle) might solve these puzzles. But they would do so by going against the Copernican principle, their suggestion being that a huge cosmos contains "bubbles" which at early times inflated very fast. Being in such a bubble might mean getting the right density and degree of smoothness, but would itself be being "in a privileged position."

The Copernican principle must anyway fail to some extent, as presumably no observers could exist in the Big Bang's early years. In fact it seems likely that they could exist only at times late enough to see horizons of about the present size or wider. Earlier they would not have evolved. So, says Carr, the Anthropic Principle — that some features of the observed universe "depend crucially on our being here" — could be important, at least if it said *not* that this universe *couldn't exist* if it lacked those features, but only that *it wouldn't be observed* if it lacked them. More evidence of its importance is given by many "coincidences": features which could apparently easily have been otherwise and which combine to make observers possible. For instance, chemistry's complexities seem possible only because the neutron–proton mass difference is about twice the electron's mass.

The paper makes some philosophically controversial moves.

First, Carr's way of defining the Anthropic Principle makes him say that *the weight of the evidence for it* depends on how many "coincidences" there are. Now, we could not say *quite that* about the Principle as defined by Carter. (The wifelessness of bachelors needs no evidence!) Yet not too much hangs on this. What Carr calls evidence for the Anthropic Principle, Carter could call evidence for its *importance*. And here the length of the list of coincidences could be impressive — especially when, in the ever-growing literature on the subject, they often seem to involve extremely accurate "fine-tuning." For instance, red stars neither become **supernovas** (see Glossary) to scatter heavy elements for making into observers, nor have photons energetic enough to encourage photosynthesis, whereas blue stars presumably burn much too fast for life's purposes. To prevent all stars from crowding into just one of those two classes, the relative strengths of electromagnetism and gravity have to be fine-tuned, P. C. W. Davies has estimated, to one part in 10^{40}. Such estimates are hard to reconcile with Carr's remark that "only the orders of magnitude" of physical constants are pinned down by life's requirements. And Carr himself makes points hard to reconcile with it. Recall how he said that the early matter density may have needed tuning to one part in 10^{60}.

Second, Carr says that an attractive background to all this could be an Ensemble of "worlds" with different physical constants, maybe successive cycles of an oscillating cosmos. He could well be right; but he seems wrong when he then classifies variation in constants as food always for the Strong Anthropic Principle, not the Weak. Consider, for example, the huge cosmos of Davies and S. D. Unwin in which a constant needing tuning to one part in 10^{50} varies very slowly from one location to another. On Carr's account, it would now be the *Strong* Principle which assured us that we were in a life-permitting *location*, which might seem flatly contrary to what Carter said. It would be better to recognize that the distinction between Weak and Strong Principles is often unhelpful since (see the closing comments on Reading 10) it changes with how you choose to define "locations" and "universes."

Third, Carr indicates that Wheeler's idea that "the very *existence* of the universe depends upon life" could give an "interpretation" of the Anthropic Principle. You will find no support for this in Carter's paper — and a proliferation of such "interpretations" has made a jungle out of the "anthropic principle" talk which Carter started.

Fourth, Carr makes the Strong Principle say that living beings can exist only if the fundamental constants "satisfy certain observed relationships." Yet how could we ever know *that*? All we need know is that a lifeless universe would have resulted from FAIRLY MINOR changes in AT LEAST SOME OF the constants. The claim that the Strong Principle couldn't be important unless pinning down *every* constant is too queer for Carr to have intended it; and the following story illustrates the other half of my point. A cherry hangs on a wall, while all around it is a large empty area. A dart hits the cherry. This suggests either skill at dart-throwing or that many darts are hitting the wall. Why? Well, *fairly minor* alterations in the dart's position would have meant that no cherry was hit. Other very different walls or distant parts of the same wall might be thick with cherries, but whether or not they are is irrelevant.

Fifth, our world's strikingly simple structure may, says Carr, "be necessary for our existence, although it is also possible that it is a consequence of presently unknown physics." Here the word "although" is a slip because it might be *both* these things. It might be an important slip since perhaps there exist many universes different in their physics. The Anthropic Principle would then remind us that in ours the physics was observer-permitting.

Alternatively there might be just a single universe whose physics God had chosen carefully so that observers could evolve in it. But here we must please speak of a Teleological Principle (or just of God) and not of a new "interpretation" of the Anthropic Principle.

Reading 12: Richard Swinburne: Argument from the Fine-Tuning of the Universe

Swinburne is impressed by the evidence of fine-tuning. Given very slightly different force strengths, particle masses, and "boundary conditions" such as the number of atoms in our universe, life could not have evolved. Yet why fix one's attention on *life* rather than on white dwarf stars or emeralds? A good reason for seeking to explain a thing is that a tidy explanation suggests itself. And God, thinks Swinburne, very tidily explains this universe's life-generating character. Observations improve your grounds for accepting some hypothesis just when its truth would have made such observations more likely. Now, God had abundant reason to bring about beings who were *alive*, beings whose minds were associated with living organisms.

Our lives are based on chemistry, which means *on electromagnetism*. Swinburne more or less dismisses life on **neutron stars** (see Glossary), life in which *the nuclear strong force* supposedly plays an equivalent role. Silicon might conceivably replace the carbon of our bodies, but silicon's existence requires about as much fine-tuning as carbon's. True, all this does not prove the point — suggested by the paper's first sentence — that a universe *very* different from ours would be lifeless. But Swinburne later makes clear (by retelling my dart-and-cherry story: see the comments on Reading 11) that he does not feel committed to exactly that point.

Is it true, though, that the God hypothesis lacks serious competition? Swinburne considers an Anthropic Principle "that laws and boundary conditions must be such that life evolves, for otherwise no one would be observing it." Some people, he says, think this eliminates all need to explain any fine-tuning. They are like the fool who, when missed repeatedly by a firing squad, argues that no explanation is required "because if the marksmen had not missed, he would not be here to observe them having done so." And, after considering alternative versions of "anthropic" reasoning, Swinburne concludes that they all "serve only to obfuscate."

Do they? How about the idea that there exist many universes with different constants and boundary conditions? Carter's Anthropic Principle then reminds us that we must be observing a universe in which living beings can exist. Might not this contribute to a tidy explanation? Swinburne replies that we have no good grounds to believe in other universes unless they are spatially, temporally or causally related to ours. Perhaps, then, they are only other regions of our universe, regions beyond our horizon, or other cosmic epochs; but if so, then simplicity demands that they be much like our region or epoch. The only further alternative "seriously discussed" is, he says, Everett's Many-Worlds Quantum Theory in which the "other universes" are other branches of an ever-branching cosmos; yet this "seems crazy."

Those last arguments could be judged to be too quick. Whatever we may think of Everett, his is not the only further way of getting multiple universes which is currently widely discussed: see Reading 15. Even universes not in causal contact with ours might reasonably be accepted if whatever mechanism made ours — perhaps Tryon's vacuum fluctuation mechanism — could be expected to make others too. And some fairly well-developed theories of "symmetry breaking" (see Reading 19) suggest that different universes or regions, while obeying *the same basic laws*, might have very different force strengths and particle masses. Stable stars, planets, and chemistry would then have no place in them.

However, *multiple universes* and *God* can *both* draw support from evidence of fine-tuning. (Smith is poisoned, on an island whose other inhabitants are Jones and Bloggs. This improves one's grounds for classifying Bloggs as murderous, despite doing the same for Jones.)

Reading 13: Heinz R. Pagels: A Cozy Cosmology

In Pagel's eyes the "cozy" Anthropic Principle "never predicts any- thing" and "is not testable"; "there in no way we can actually go to an imaginary universe and check for life." It is "anthropocentrism," as- suming that life forms must all be very much as on Earth. Matters for which it gave pseudo-explanations are now explained properly by *in- flation* and by *unified theories*. Appeals to it are "the lazy man's ap- proach," abandoning the search for "a truly fundamental explanation."
Replies spring to mind.

1. The Anthropic Principle says only that our observed uni- verse *is life-permitting* rather than that it is "cozy" or — as Pagel's first sentence expresses the point — "tuned for our comfort." Life-permitting situations can be very uncomfortable.
2. We can visit other universes in just the way Pagels visits the early Big Bang to check for inflation and unification. *Thought experiments* suggest that life and observership would not have arisen if, say, our universe had recollapsed within a second, or if it had contained no planets. In search- ing for extraterrestrials, wouldn't interstellar gas clouds or the sun's interior be poor places to start?
3. The line of thought that Pagels attacks *has* led to predic- tions. The prediction, for example, that extraterrestrials will not be found inside the sun; the prediction that physics will some day show that force strengths, and so on, are not dictated by basic principles, so might vary randomly from one huge region to another; the prediction that our uni- verse's origin will be found to be correctly explained by mechanisms that might plausibly yield multiple universes with varied properties. When Pagels tells us that anthropic reasoning "is not testable" and in his next breath that recent science (e.g., inflation and unification) has refuted it . . . !
4. Inflation, as well as itself perhaps needing fine-tuning, may be essential to the Anthropic Principle's importance instead of being a nail in its coffin. Suppose physical constants were settled randomly, probabilistically. Why did the randomly typing monkey type the same series of letters in regions that could seem to have been causally separated — beyond one another's horizons — at the time he typed, the time of the

"symmetry breaking" described by unified theories (the other alleged nails in the coffin)? Well, inflation could take *a single "bubble" in which the monkey had typed in a life-permitting way*, blowing it up until the entire visible universe fitted inside it.

5. The theory that physical constants are settled randomly during symmetry breaking *does* attempt to give "a truly fundamental explanation." (When quantum theory makes the world partly random, probabilistic, must it be "a non-fundamental theory"? Not at all.)

Still, Pagel's paper usefully points out that life's prerequisites may not be at all strict (so perhaps we should look for life in the sun). It usefully encourages us to keep seeking non-probabilistic explanations. And the final paragraph is helpful in its reminder that *divine selection* might replace the Anthropic Principle's *observational selection*. "The reason the universe seems tailor-made for our existence" might indeed be "that it *was*."

Reading 14: Stephen Jay Gould: Mind and Supermind

As Gould points out, Wallace's one-galaxy universe of 1903 is an awful warning of how mistaken one can be about supposed evidence of design. Is Gould at all clearly correct, though, in his claim that Dyson's "The Argument from Design," presented three quarters of a century later, must have got things equally wrong? Dyson maintains that there are many separate examples of how our universe is fine-tuned to life's needs. Gould considers just two of those examples, then giving the standard bridge hand objection against design arguments: that our universe, like absolutely any hand of 13 cards, cannot fail to be "improbable." To which he adds: Would a physical universe indeed have been unworthy of a cosmos-producing spirit if it contained "little more than diprotons"? But here Dyson could answer: Yes, it would. A lifeless universe could very plausibly have been unworthy of anything like God, and the "bridge hand" of the actual universe finds an attractive explanation in designing spirit because it is a hand of 13 spades.

Gould could seem to have a strong reply: namely, that a universe of diprotons might still have contained observers, "chroniclers" as he puts it, albeit not ones "among its physical objects." Might not there have been angels, disembodied minds having no need of a fine-tuned environment? But a counter could be that Dyson need not show that designing spirit would of course have wanted to produce slowly evolving, embodied intelligence by the use of fine-tuning. Like detectives who can account for a murder without claiming that they could have predicted it, Dyson can instead offer to explain embodied intelligence and fine-tuning when he actually sees them.

Besides, if Gould's arguments were right, then we could have no evidence suggesting divine selection of the universe's properties. Yet that is a risky thing to say, granted that Divine Selection and Carter's Observational Selection would very arguably both select for the same kinds of thing: namely, life-permitting situations. Gould comes very near to telling us that Carter's anthropic principle is useless because there never could be any signs that reality was very varied and that we were seeing a rare kind of region whose force strengths and particle masses chanced to be fine-tuned to life's needs. Now, correct though this might perhaps be, he is a long way from having proved it.

Reading 15: George Gale: Cosmological Fecundity: Theories of Multiple Universes

Tracing the history of imagined "worlds" or "universes" beyond our own, Gale distinguishes three categories: *spatially multiple* universes, *temporally multiple* ones, and ones *other-dimensionally multiple*. Early on, absolutely all the universes were thought of as inhabited. Today, in contrast, the inspiration for multiple-universe theories is often a wish to show how life could be expected at least once, even if it depended on fine-tuning.

A contemporary *spatially multiple* scheme is that of Ellis and Brundrit: a capital-U Universe extends to infinity, its far separated regions counting as small-u universes. But simplicity might now suggest that force strengths, particle masses, and so on should remain the same everywhere, only degree of turbulence varying. We might get greater variety in a "superspace" in which radically separated universes jump into being. Tryon has supplied one: in it, universes originate as quantum fluctuations. Alternatively, a universe could give birth to radically distinct daughter universes, each with its own daughters, etcetera. Again, Linde's universe splits into huge domains with different force strengths and particle masses.

Temporally multiple universes are today conceived as successive oscillations, Gale tells us. Increasing heat was once thought to limit the number of oscillations, but ways around this have been suggested.

Other-dimensional multiplicity is grounded in quantum theory. Everett imagines a capital-U Universe as branching, absolutely all quantum possibilities becoming real somewhere. The randomness that people attribute to the realm of the quantum is then just a matter of their inability to see all the branches.

Many-universe theories are, in short, "utterly commonplace."

Are Gale's three categories quite as distinct as he thinks? Maybe not; thus, Wheeler has said Time may break down during Big Squeezes so that cosmic oscillations might be better called *side by side*, not *successive*; yet this seems none too important. A more significant difficulty is of deciding just what to count as "separate universes." Gale may be somewhat inconsistent about whether the Many-Worlds approach to quantum theory involves belief in multiple worlds/universes, or only in multiple parts or aspects of a single one. A main reason for this approach is that people disagree over just when the so-called "collapse of the wave function" occurs. Many-Worlds Quantum Theory holds that it *does not* occur. Sets of possible later events branching off from any given event *never* become firmly split apart, with one branch becoming "our world" or "the actual world" while others become "absolutely non-actual" or "firmly unable to interact with our world's events." Instead branches can jostle one another and there is a continuing possibility — typically becoming much fainter every microsecond — that two branches will suddenly jostle strongly enough to make it seem artificial to count them as separate. They may coalesce entirely. Further, to call vigorous jostling of two branches "only a faint possibility" is not to state entirely straightforwardly that it probably won't happen. Instead it states that its happening will be confined to a tiny range of the sub-branches of those branches. So whether we are to speak of "many worlds" or just of "many very largely distinct *parts* or *views* of one world" is just a matter of taste, I think.

Another tricky point concerns stochastic gauge theories. Gale seems to see these complex theories, or something similar, as essential if the above-mentioned branches are to differ in their physical constants (he gives the mass of the photon as an example). It would, surely, be better to recognize that *virtually any* multiple-universe scenario, and in particular any version of Many-Worlds Quantum Theory, can use the idea of symmetry breaks at early moments, breaks that fix force strengths and particle masses in ways differing from universe to universe.

Reading 16: John Archibald Wheeler: Beyond the End of Time

Wheeler looks at the recollapse awaiting every "closed" cosmos. While classical general relativity excludes a rebound, eternal oscillations could be given us by quantum theory. Near the Planck length of 10^{-33} cm (one billion trillion trillionth of a centimeter) points may have no fixed neighbors. Things might be so fuzzy that a bounce could occur. Not knowing from just which state it was rebounding, the universe could fix on its properties probabilistically. Number of particles, period of expansion, and even, for example, whether the proton has *five* or *five million* times more mass than the electron, may be "reprocessed" at the start of each new oscillation, as may "a thousand other features." A "biological selection of physical constants" would ensure that each observing eye saw an oscillation whose constants allowed eyes to evolve. (Wheeler, though, is not the man to commit himself to just one idea, and alas, he later makes quantum theory suggest that unobserved oscillations would be unreal.)

How plausible is all this?

1. Wheeler's notion that a black hole *can have* only mass, charge, and angular momentum, because nothing else *can be detected from outside*, could seem sadly "verificationist." It has since become clear that black holes have very high entropy ("disorder"), so mustn't they have complex structures?

2. Suppose that in a closed cosmos, as with a black hole, some properties *must be absent or not definable* while others *must take zero values*, as Wheeler says. How could this help properties to vary from oscillation to oscillation? (An absent property cannot vary.) At best Wheeler's remarks seem foreshadowings of such points as that — see the next Reading — exactly the same total energy would characterize universes very different in the number of their particles; the change from a universe with a billion particles to a universe with ninety sextillion might then be easy.

3. How could all observed electrons have the same mass, given that all masses were settled probabilistically and that horizon problems can occur even at very early times? This is better answered by inflation (cf. the "typing monkey" comment on Reading 13) than by Wheeler's quick appeal to Leibniz.

In short, the paper's ideas may be best treated as only those of a pioneer. But Wheeler's pioneerings are among this century's finest.

Reading 17: Edward P. Tryon: Is the Universe a Vacuum Fluctuation?

Tryon proposes that our universe came into existence "from nowhere." Quantum vacuum fluctuations — particles spring into being and then disappear — are scientific commonplaces. The more energy tied up in the particles, the faster must they vanish. Yet, gravitational binding energy being *negative energy* (another commonplace), our universe might be a fluctuation of zero total energy, able to live for billions of years. Most fluctuation universes would be far smaller, no doubt, but any universe in which observers can evolve must be "impressively large."

Comments:

1. The idea that gravitational binding energy *is negative* should not be treated as especially surprising. When stars burn,

proton pairs bind together to form deuterons which are slightly *less massive*, despite how a deuteron can be regarded as the result of one of the protons in such a pair changing into a *more massive* neutron when they bind. The act of binding has added negative mass-energy. Bear in mind that energy can be stored up by compression, that is, by working against forces of repulsion and pushing things together. Negative energy is stored up by instead working against forces of attraction and pulling things apart.

2. The paper predicts equal amounts of matter and **antimatter** (see Glossary). Searches make this unlikely, but today it seems that a universe originating without a matter excess could develop one early on. Again, we could abandon the idea that our fluctuation universe is exceptionally large. Inflation might make something gigantic from practically nothing.

3. Our universe, Tryon proposes, "is simply one of those things which happen from time to time." A very large space–time is here envisaged, with universes popping into being like bubbles in champagne. Wouldn't we soon have all bubbles, no champagne? Not if each bubble had a good chance of recollapsing before merging with others, or if the champagne were expanding very fast.

4. Why, though, would there be a space–time obeying quantum theory's laws? Could this be just a matter of brute fact? Or would it, too, stand in need of an explanation?

Reading 18: Paul Davies: What Caused the Big Bang?

Davies introduces the now fashionable "inflationary" universe. Quantum theory pictures space as a ferment of very short-lived particles. At the Big Bang's first moments space's energy density was enormous: an associated omnipresent tension may have made every region double in size every 10^{-34} seconds. (This is less paradoxical than it sounds, as only *tension differences* — "non-omnipresence" — pull things together.) When the resulting immense expansion ended, space would have become very flat, making it expand at just the speed permitting galaxies to form. Any original great irregularities would have been smoothed away. True, the first models showed inflation as ending in bubbling chaos. Makers of later models said, *So what?* They pictured the entire visible universe as deep inside a single bubble. (Where else could things be cool enough for observers?) The whole process perhaps started as a tiny quantum fluctuation, much as imagined by Tryon. In some sense of the word "energy," more and more energy could be accumulated during inflation and made into heat and particles later. This could seem getting something for nothing; and so perhaps it would be, energy conservation being difficult to define here. But any newly appearing energy would be accompanied by gravitational energy, *negative energy*, so perhaps we could say total energy didn't increase (cf. Tryon's tale).

While controversial, this is getting to be very much the standard story.

Reading 19: Andrei Linde: The Universe: Inflation Out Of Chaos

Inflation must have occurred, Linde thinks. It solves the Smoothness Problem and the Flatness (or galaxy-producing expansion speed) Problem, and one needs it for saving Tryon's vacuum fluctuation cosmos. Only a cosmos measuring about 10^{-33} cm could appear as a fluctuation, for otherwise a horizon problem would prevent its parts agreeing on when they would jump into being. Inflation could expand this tiny region by a factor of maybe $10^{1,000,000}$ even before the 15 billion or so years of more leisurely expansion which led to humankind.

Our present horizon is still only some 10^{28} cm distant. We thus see but a very small fraction of the inflationary universe: perhaps one part in one-followed-by-roughly-a-million-zeros. Moreover, inflation could occur appropriately only in a very unusual region of a still larger cosmos, a region "far from its equilibrium state" and "almost homogeneous" (i.e., already very smooth, so inflation cannot itself entirely answer the Smoothness Problem). And when inflation ended we could expect very many huge domains, "mini-universes" with differing force strengths and particle masses. In ours a unified force "happens to have been broken into the strong and weak forces and electromagnetism." Elsewhere the break might have occurred quite otherwise, and space might even be other than three-dimensional.

Though Linde speaks of the domains as ruled by "different laws of physics" the same fundamental laws supposedly hold everywhere. Scalar fields of differing intensities yield different *derived laws*, since each affects "the properties of all the elementary particles"; "it helps to determine their masses, and the way in which they interact." Uniform throughout any particular domain, a scalar field would mimic emptiness; yet unified theories rely on such fields to "break" (distort) the force-strength and particle-mass similarities ("symmetries") of the Big Bang's earliest moments. (By interacting with a scalar field a particle can gain mass. And *force strength differences* reflect *differing masses*: the masses of force-conveying "messenger particles," of the particles involved in force "screening" and "anti-screening," or of the particles the forces are trying to influence. This tale, basic to the standard picture of how the nuclear weak force split away from electromagnetism, might well be extended to cover further force-strength and particle-mass differences.)

Many scalar fields would be present, each affecting particles differently. And the potential energy of each would have "many minima of roughly equal depth": it could settle into any of these minima as the Big Bang cooled. The possible combinations of force strengths and masses are therefore legion. Now, when water stops looking the same in all directions and takes on the more limited symmetries of ice crystals, you get crystal domains with differently oriented axes. Physicists have enough confidence in unified theories to talk of a Monopole Problem: that of why conflicting domain orientations didn't result in particles so heavy and so numerous that the universe would have recollapsed at once. But, says Linde, the monopole-creating scalar fields could have made the early universe inflate. Now, inflation would have pushed the monopoles so far apart that we could not detect any. Similarly we should be unable to detect domains whose force strengths and particle masses were different.

Clearly, Linde has painted a particularly elegant World Ensemble in which conditions might be expected to be life-permitting in at least a few Worlds. However, his picture contains much that is speculation only.

Reading 20: Robert Shapiro and Gerald Feinberg: Possible Forms of Life in Environments Very Different from Earth

A biosphere, say Shapiro and Feinberg, need not involve multiple organisms and replication. Its intricate activity, life, need not be chemical activity; it could instead be particle movements or molecular rotations. Its power source could be X-rays, nuclear energy, heat differences, or streams of charged particles. Its complexities might be expressed in a simple alphabet; so even if chemical, it would not need the riches of carbon's chemistry. Silicate life might exist in the liquid rock of Earth's interior; plasma life in the sun; or "the ordered patterns of radiation emitted by isolated atoms and molecules in a dense interstellar cloud" could be living, as could molecular patterns in frozen hydrogen. "Carbaquists" who believe that life demands carbon and water are like the peasant convinced that only Chinese is ever spoken.

Must our conclusion then be that life's presence is no excuse for accepting multiple universes or a divine fine-tuner? In their book *Life Beyond Earth*, Shapiro and Feinberg draw precisely that conclusion. People who use the Anthropic Principle or who talk of divine tuning are there likened to the rotifers inhabiting Little Puddle who view the entire universe as designed to ensure the existence of the tiny, muddy home to which they are adapted so well. They are viewed as comparable to men gasping at how the Mississippi threads its way under every bridge.

All this could throw some beneficial cold water on writers like Wheeler, Swinburne, Carr, and John Leslie. Still, we too have water to throw.

1. If life can evolve so easily, then why have we no evidence of extraterrestrials? A reply might be that it is a huge step from mere *life processes* (perhaps something fairly simple in frozen hydrogen) to *intelligent life*. Multiple universes or a fine-tuner could still be needed, to make intelligent life at all likely.

2. I. L. Rozental argues that very small changes in physical constants would have led to a universe without planets, suns, dense clouds, hydrogen molecules, atoms, or perhaps even a history lasting more than a fraction of a second. Even if many strange life forms filled our universe, a universe slightly differently tuned would still be lifeless.

3. There are quite strong grounds for thinking that chemistry is very special in the intricate structures it makes possible. And our sort of life, at any rate, is chemical, while tiny changes would have made chemistry impossible. Would Shapiro and Feinberg hold that this, the only kind of life we know, is highly unusual? That *other kinds* would need no fine-tuning?

Reading 21: Michael H. Hart: Atmospheric Evolution, the Drake Equation, and DNA: Sparse Life in an Infinite Universe

Hart thinks that only very rare planets could avoid runaway glaciation or overheating. Even so, ten million planets in our galaxy might be habitable. Had life appeared on all, then we might expect half a million long-lasting civilizations. Surely at least one would by now have colonized the entire galaxy, a process requiring only a few million years; so why no sign of this? Hart replies that even on a habitable planet the chance that life will develop is probably much lower than one in $10^{3,000}$. Now, there are only about 10^{11} galaxies inside our horizon. The chance of life's occurring even once in this region was negligible. But why are we alive, then? Well, our universe is probably "open" and, very likely, an open universe must have infinitely many galaxies. On each of an infinity of habitable planets, nature "patiently tosses her tetrahedral dice for ten billion years, trying to line up 600 nucleotides in the proper sequence to make genesis DNA." Almost always she fails — but the results of her efforts can be observed only where she has succeeded.

Despite this talk of "genesis DNA" Hart grants that organisms on other planets may be made of something other than proteins and nucleotides; and even if DNA was needed, perhaps only 100 positions in a 600-nucleotide sequence would have needed filling just rightly, he concedes. But he never abandons the assumption that life's beginnings would be forbiddingly complex. Many would call it a wild assumption. A. G. Cairns-Smith thinks life may have begun in clays able to replicate their crystalline structures, only later adopting the intricacies of nucleotide chemistry.

Nonetheless, Hart's main point is strong. Most cosmologists now agree that the universe extends vastly farther than we can see, and we have little idea of how life started. Now, the argument that its chances of getting started *here* must have been quite high, else we should not be here to discuss them, forgets that a selection effect may be present. Unless space travel has carried a being far from its evolutionary cradle, the "here" which it sees must be where its ancestors began. And in any big enough universe the chances could be high that at least a few planets would be "here" to highly evolved beings even if any given planet's chances of being such a place were always very low. (Hart avoids making them *quite so low* that we would better view ourselves as random collections of atoms, rather than as products of evolution. His infinite universe is no invitation to explain *just anything* as "what was bound to happen somewhere.")

An infinite universe can seem unlikely because its parts would have faced such horizon problems when trying to agree on when to jump into existence. (As explained earlier, a finite universe might avoid these problems by originating as a single quantum fluctuation and then inflating.) Yet even if Hart's picture had therefore to be rejected, reality could well contain infinitely much. Practically any mechanism for generating a (small-u) universe, a system of causally interacting things, would look odd if labeled, THIS MECHANISM OPERATED ONLY ONCE. Yet if a mechanism operated twice then why stop there, or anywhere? Hart, it seems, could have his infinitely many planets whether or not ours was a universe which itself contained infinitely many.

Cosmology is built on *indirect observations:* observations made with the help of much theory. Hart shows that developments *in biology,* if tending to prove that life's beginnings involved very improbable molecular combinations, might help us to "see" that the visible universe was just a tiny fragment of the real. And similar points could be made about evidence of fine-tuning. Such evidence might help us to see — very indirectly — multiple universes with very varied properties. Or might we instead be seeing Swinburne's all-creating person or neoplatonism's more abstract God?

We now come to the five Readings added to this new Edition of *Physical Cosmology and Philosophy*. Three are from writers represented in the earlier Readings.

ELLIS now ranges much more widely, surveying many ways in which cosmological theories go beyond the available evidence. LESLIE reviews the literature on cosmic fine tuning, and on the two chief interpretations which could be given to it: namely, (a) that there is *observational selection* of a life-permitting universe, and (b) that there was *divine selection* of such a universe.

DAVIES then argues that theists should be heartened by recent developments in physics and cosmology, while CRAIG attacks Stephen Hawking's famous suggestion that when the Big Bang is seen in the light of quantum theory there is "no place for a Creator." Finally, REES asks whether life could survive throughout an infinitely prolonged future, and whether humans might become extinct through a disastrous experiment at very high energies.

Here are more details.

Reading 22: George Ellis: Emerging Questions and Uncertainties

Our present view of the universe is limited, Ellis notes, by the distance which light can have travelled after the Big Bang cooled sufficiently to give it free passage. Not even telescopes for gravitational waves could probe very much farther. Consider all the galaxies lying inside our horizon. At least as many more lie outside it—unless (which is unlikely) we live in a universe whose space connects up with itself in such a way that light has travelled round it several times, so that what people think are different galaxies are often the same one, viewed at different points in its history. We might be seeing only an infinitely small fraction of a chaotic universe. Gigantic regions, characterized by very diverse conditions, could be separated by disorderly transition zones.

Using the technology of the now-cancelled Superconducting Supercollider, we should need to build something as large as the solar system if we wanted direct tests of the physics of Big Bang energies. This physics, though, is clearly crucial to cosmology. Still worse, distant matter may influence in unknown ways all the physics that we can test locally: Mach's Principle, for a start, suggests that if remote galaxies weren't there, then our automobile crashes would be harmless! Again, in the case of a universe fated to collapse, a universe with both a beginning and an end to its time, the conditions at the beginning and at the end might actually settle how "the arrow of time" pointed. Unfortunately, "by definition there is only one Universe" so that the beginning, for instance, has "happened only once." We therefore cannot test our theories by seeing how well they apply to comparable cases. The choice between them will have to be made on such philosophical grounds as a preference for simplicity and beauty.

Ellis's message is softened by his distinction between "achieving certainty" or "verifying" (which he thinks is usually impossible in cosmology) and "testing." To recognize that philosophical principles enter into one's testing "is not the same as saying that anything goes," he insists. Also, his point that "there is by definition only one Universe," and that there are no "comparable events" to, say, the ones at the beginning of time, has to be understood carefully. Having said "no comparable events," he immediately adds "or at least, none that are accessible to our observations." Ought we to declare that any inaccessible events were in "other universes," using the word "Universe" (with a capital U) to mean the total of what is accessible, which is of course *only one* total? Or should it mean Absolutely Everything? The choice is surely a mere matter of verbal taste. What's important is that Ellis isn't denying that there might be many huge cosmic regions existing side by side or succeeding one another in time, all our observations being confined to one of them. Again, when he suggests that events early in the Big Bang couldn't be "comparable" to others which we can investigate, he is saying far less than an incautious reader might think. He doesn't doubt that quantum physics would be applicable to very early events, quite as much as to the ones we can investigate today. His point is just that if you wanted any direct test of various important details of quantum physics, then you'd need to journey in your time machine to the Big Bang's early instants.

Reading 23: John Leslie: The Anthropic Principle Today

Hume and Kant are often thought to have refuted the Design Argument for God's existence. Perhaps their most forceful point was that the life-containing situation which we see might well not be typical of the cosmos. Pushing further, Carter noted that we living beings could hardly fail to see a life-permitting situation, even if almost all places, times and universes were life-excluding. (The word "universe" here covers any big cosmic region which is separate or largely separate from other such regions.) Carter's "weak anthropic principle" stated that observers, for example humans, can find themselves only in life-permitting times and places. His "strong anthropic principle" was that any observed regions worth calling "universes" would again have to be life-permitting. Divine selection of a universe with life-permitting properties—selection of it as worthy of being created—could thus be replaced by "anthropic" observational selection.

All this became very important because of two things. First, it came to seem likely that many characteristics of our cosmic situation were "fine tuned for intelligent life": tiny changes in them would have blocked the appearance not just of humans, but of observers in general. Second, cosmologists found many fairly plausible mechanisms for generating huge cosmic regions (alias "universes") with widely varying characteristics. Even universes which started off the same could develop very different properties through rolls of various cosmic dice, perhaps the dice of randomized "symmetry-breaking"–a process in which the strengths of Nature's forces, and the masses of its elementary particles, became differentiated.

Many folks have misunderstood how "anthropic" reasoning works. They have interpreted Carter's strong anthropic principle as stating that our universe had been *forced from its earliest instants,* maybe by divine decree, to have properties which would later *not just permit but necessitate* the arrival of observers, or even of humans. Again, they have portrayed Carter as believing idiotically that the existence of a great many universes had somehow made it more likely that the universe which ultimately came to include you and me *would come* to include observers–instead of simply making it more likely that there would be observers in some universe or other. They protested, too, that absolutely any universe would have some unusual characteristics, there being nothing "special" about life-permitting characteristics to justify believing in multiple universes. Here they were overlooking the fact that not *just any* characteristics could give rise to observational selection effects.

Besides exposing such confusions, the Reading shows that anthropic reasoning encourages many predictions. For example, it encourages us to expect that mechanisms for generating greatly varied universes will continue to be plausible despite advances in physics. Also that early cosmic inflation will remain plausible, too. This is because, given such inflation, we could explain how the strength of some physical force (electromagnetism, say) or the mass of some particle (such as the proton) could be identical wherever our telescopes looked, regardless of whether such affairs had been settled by randomized symmetry-breaking. Again, we can be encouraged to expect that our cosmic situation won't be found to be *much more unusual than was needed* for observers to evolve in it.

This last point is like another which Carter has made. Observers shouldn't expect to be very unusually early in the total temporal spread of their species. Taking its inspiration from this, a controversial "doomsday argument" holds that we have systematically underestimated the danger that humans will soon be extinct.

If cosmic "fine tuning" can suggest observational selection, mayn't it suggest divine selection, too? The Reading notes that divine selection could actually have an advantage. It might explain how one and the same force strength or particle mass can be tuned to satisfy *many separate requirements* of intelligent life, without having to be tuned in conflicting ways.

Reading 24: Paul Davies: Our Place in the Universe

While Davies's *The Accidental Universe* (1982) had argued for anthropic observational selection, his *The Mind of God* (1992) favoured divine selection, or something like it. As he remarks in this Reading, words like "purpose" and "design," because they "derive from human categories," may "capture only imperfectly what the universe is about"; but he is convinced "it is about something." Are these words altogether too vague? Perhaps not, for they may cover various attractive alternatives. The neoplatonist principle, for instance, that the universe owes its existence to the ethical need for it, "God" being a name for this principle. Or the Spinozistic theory that the universe is a divine mind which knows everything (including precisely how it feels to be you or me), a mind whose existence could be explained in the same way.

One main reason Davies now has for believing in God (of some sort) is that he sees a problem in the sheer fact that our universe conforms to anything worth calling "laws." He tells us that his God is not "a temporal Being," or in any way "capricious." God acts through unchanging physical principles, avoiding "the occasional supernatural prod." Even "the coming-into-being of the universe" needn't have been a law-violating process, since quantum physics might explain it. (Davies here refers to Stephen Hawking's speculations, which the next Reading will discuss.) The universe's laws are not "any old rag-bag," for randomly selected laws "lead almost inevitably either to unrelieved chaos or boring and uneventful simplicity." As well as studies which indicate that "the existence of life as we know it would be threatened by just the tiniest change in the strengths of the fundamental forces," there are general reasons for thinking that living organisms could appear only in a universe which sat at "the edge of chaos." Sitting there depends on "laws of a very special form."

Although Davies's reasoning is non-technical, it runs into technical difficulties. For instance it is (as the Reading from Craig will show) far from certain that time is, as Einstein thought, itself "part of the physical universe," whose creation therefore couldn't have been due to "a temporal Being." Again, why should Davies expect extraterrestrials to be common, simply because he considers the universe designed (if that's the right word) for producing intelligent life? Why shouldn't God create stellar systems in "profligate overprovision," just to produce intelligent beings on some single planet? Would creating all those extra stars be a strain on God's power? If God wanted lots more intelligent beings, couldn't these be had by creating lots more universes?

Reading 25: William Lane Craig: "What place, then, for a creator?": Hawking on God and Creation

Craig discusses Stephen Hawking's offer to explain the world's existence without introducing a Creator. Suppose we could look backwards towards the earliest moments of Hawking's cosmos. We would see its space-time becoming more and more evidently space-like, and more and more dominated by quantum uncertainties. These would smear out any supposed "point at which everything began." Instead of being like the tip of an infinitely sharp pin, the early Big Bang would be more like the North Pole. Inquiring what happened before the Bang, to cause it, could thus seem on a par with asking what Earth is like *from the North Pole northwards.*

Craig sees little value in any of this. He protests that the notion of a Creator "left with nothing to do" overlooks the standard theological view that divine creative activity is present at every moment, not just at some first moment. He agrees that Hawking's cosmos is in some sense "eternal," but since when has it been unreasonable to ask *why* about all eternally existing things? (As Leibniz commented, an eternally existing geometry textbook could well provoke the question of why it was about geometry, and not some other topic.) Indeed, Hawking himself sometimes treats his theory as tackling only the *what* of the universe, not its *why.* In fact, Craig continues, the theory is absurd through suggesting that "imaginary time," time of a sort really and truly "indistinguishable from directions in space" (Hawking's actual words), is less of a fiction than time as we ordinarily experience it. Although Einstein believed that the past and the future were absent *only relatively,* thereby adopting what philosophers now call "the B-theory of Time," he (i) never gave a successful proof of this, and (ii) never dreamt of denying that time and space are different. What is more, McTaggart's philosophical argument against absolutely flowing, "A-theory" time—the argument, that's to say, that there's a contradiction in any universe describable *first* as possessing various qualities and *later* as not possessing them—is a complete failure.

Hawking's use of many-worlds quantum theory, in which seemingly alternative *possible histories* of the cosmos are treated, one and all, as describing actual occurrences, strikes Craig as fantastic. And things aren't improved when Hawking slides to and fro between talking about *what's real* (for otherwise what sense could there be in his efforts to dismiss a Creator?) and declaring that he's only playing with mathematics and modelling-clay.

Many philosophers, physicists and cosmologists think very much as Craig does. But others would argue that Hawking's theory, whatever its problems in its present form, is an exciting development of Tryon's idea that our universe could have "quantum-fluctuated" into existence without costing anything.

Reading 26: Martin Rees: Toward Infinity: The Far Future

Most cosmologists, Rees reports, expect our universe to live for at least a hundred billion years. Direct observations suggest a cosmic density lower than is needed for eternal expansion. However, arguments sufficiently abstract to be called "philosophical" favour a finitely large universe, and any such universe must collapse eventually. One of the arguments concerns the origin of inertia: why don't objects shoot away when given the slightest push?

Another such argument is that, as explained early in the book from which this Reading is taken, there must be very many universes, for otherwise (or so Rees thinks) there would have been little likelihood that at least one universe would chance to have characteristics which encouraged life to evolve. But, the argument runs, if there are many universes, how could they each be infinite in extent? Philosophers would tend to doubt this argument, though. If a road can be infinitely long, then so can several roads existing side by side. There is nothing essentially problematic in the concept, even, of infinitely many universes, each of them infinitely large.

How long could life survive in a collapsing universe which grew ever hotter, or in one which expanded eternally, becoming more and more frigid? In the case of a collapse, intelligent living beings might become made of stuff which managed to maintain its complex structure as temperatures rose and events moved ever more speedily. The "clocks" appropriate to measuring the events would themselves constantly be speeding up. Infinitely much information-processing (otherwise known as thinking) might thus occur before the collapse ended, so that infinitely much "subjective time" might pass. In an eternally cooling universe, on the other hand, there could be infinitely much time available for thoughts, even if these became ever more sluggish. (They wouldn't *seem* sluggish to their thinkers, would they?) The continual cooling of the cosmos might actually permit infinitely much information to be processed with the help of a limited amount of energy. For as temperatures fell our intelligent descendants—maybe gigantic clouds of atomic particles, their thoughts moving ever so slowly—might need less and less energy for each step in their thinking.

Such gloriously prolonged futures would be lost if we destroyed ourselves during the next few centuries. Besides pointing to the risks of nuclear warfare and suchlike, Rees discusses a strange catastrophe which might befall us. As already touched on, he has an answer to why at least one universe, ours, has force strengths and particle masses, etc., which permitted intelligent life to evolve. It is that these affairs differ randomly from one to another of many universes. The differences would presumably arise during early "phase transitions" comparable to the freezing of a liquid. Now, it may well be that our universe is in a "supercooled" state. Like supercooled water which will change to a frozen mass if you drop in a microscopic ice crystal, our universe might be ruined by even one tiny event whose energy was sufficiently high. The energy in question would be "hundreds of times higher than can be attained by the Large Hadron Collider," the most powerful machine which experimental physicists will have for quite a while. Still, they might some day get something much more powerful, so "caution should surely be urged (if not enforced)."

1

ERNAN McMULLIN*

Is Philosophy Relevant to Cosmology?

WHAT (IF ANYTHING) do philosophers have to contribute to cosmology today?[1] Steven Weinberg, one of the most articulate of the younger generation of cosmologists, makes *his* answer to this question quite clear:

> I have difficulty in understanding the philosophical content that many people seem to find in discoveries in physics. It is true, of course, that many of the subjects of physics — space and time, causality, ultimate particles — have been the concern of philosophers since the earliest times. But in my view, when physicists make discoveries in these areas, they do not so much confirm or refute the speculations of philosophers as show that philosophers were out of their jurisdiction in speculating about these phenomena.[2]

P. C. W. Davies, in a popularization of recent work in cosmology, is even more emphatic:

> It is a striking thought that ten years of radio astronomy have taught humanity more about the creation and organization of the universe than thousands of years of religion and philosophy.[3]

Davies' polemic is admittedly directed more against religious than against philosophical claims to cosmological insight. Indeed, he goes on to ask such questions as "why is the universe so big?" and "why is

*Reprinted from *American Philosophical Quarterly*, Vol. 18, No. 3, July 1981, pp. 177–189, by permission of N. Rescher. Copyright © *American Philosophical Quarterly*, 1981.

gravity so weak?," to which he responds with aplomb by citing the requirements a universe would have to meet in order to produce cosmologists who can ask such questions. We shall come back to this "anthropic principle" later. But Davies himself notes that this sort of response "has a philosophical basis only, and is not a physical theory." By this he means that "it cannot be falsified by experience or observation";[4] it has thus, he says, the status of speculation, not of science. Such speculation is permissible, but it cannot (he insists) attain the status of respectable knowledge unless some method of putting it to empirical test can be devised.

Would this bleak estimate of the potential contribution of the philosopher to current cosmological debate be shared by philosophers? Obviously not by all. Yet a check through the standard bibliography of philosophical articles published in West European languages over the past three years shows that only about a dozen or so out of more than ten thousand entries qualify under the subject-heading of "cosmology." At the very least, one can conclude that it is not a popular topic among professional philosophers. Is Weinberg right to suggest, then, that this is one more instance of scientists succeeding in a domain where philosophers ought never have asserted any claim in the first place? Is there any reason for a philosophy journal to take cognizance of recent work in cosmology other than to let the former proprietors know what others have made of their estates?

I. The Idea of the Universe

A word first about what I assume the idea (or definition) of the universe to be. Scientists ordinarily take the term "universe" to refer to the totality of physical things. These are further assumed to be in causal connection with one another in such a way as to make them accessible in principle to the instruments — and the theorists — of earth. It is an open question whether there might not be a multiplicity of universes in causal isolation from one another. The criterion for such isolation could be expressed in terms of space, time, and cause, but it could be more readily expressed in terms of the reach of scientific inference. If we could infer to the general features of a universe on the other side of the "Big Bang" or of a black hole, for example, it would be generally agreed that such a universe can properly be construed as part of our own. It is an open question also whether in fact all parts of the universe are *at a given time* in principle observable from (in direct causal connection with) earth. On the Big Bang view, there is a "horizon" about ten billion light years from us at which galaxies are receding from us at velocities close to that of light. Since according to this same model many more galaxies lie beyond this horizon, it follows that the greater part of the universe cannot be observed here now. These now-invisible galaxies will gradually become visible from the vantage point of earth only in the course of later aeons. Nonetheless, they are as much part of our universe as our galactic neighbors are. There is much we can say about them, since their existence and something of their overall characteristics can be inferred from an hypothesis which can be validated on other grounds.

How secure an inference is this? Or to put this in the striking (though misleading) wording philosophers have sometimes used: is the universe only an idea? There is obviously an idea of the universe; in fact, there are many different ideas of the universe. But it is a category mistake to say that the universe *is* an idea. The universe of the Big Bang cosmologist has a certain volume and mass; ideas have neither volume nor mass. What is *meant* by asking whether the universe is (only) an idea is whether there is anything corresponding to the universe-idea as it is projected in the Big Bang (or other) model. Thus, someone might have asked early in the last century: is caloric (only) an idea? meaning: does the idea of caloric have any real referent? And this question in turn reduces to: how good a theory is caloric theory? if one assumes a realistic interpretation of scientific concepts.

And so the question: is the universe only an idea? may be translated as: how reliable an insight do the models of contemporary cosmology give us into the structures of the world on the largest scale? This raises all the issues made familiar by the realism–idealism as well as the realism–instrumentalism debates. The idealist would challenge the assumption of an extra-mental real to whose structures scientific theory has to conform. And the instrumentalist would argue that the success of a theory gives no warrant for believing in the existence of the entities postulated in the associated model. We shall have to leave these issues aside here, and ask the reader's indulgence if we take for granted the merits of some form or other of realistic response to them.[5]

Nevertheless, even if one *does* take a realistic line in general, is one entitled to take it where *cosmological* theory is conceived? It is one thing to maintain the existence of molecules. But how about the assertion that the universe has a certain radius or that it is expanding? The problem is not primarily that the Big Bang model is highly speculative. Rather, it is that at this level of generality one might expect theory to reflect as much on the knowing power as on the world. Surely, the objection might go, the formal principles by means of which we organize spatio-temporal events determine the more general features of cosmological theory. How can we claim to see a world not colored by them? Is there not something presumptuous about the universe-claims of so limited a being as man? Do they not testify more to the presuppositions built into them than to objective structures on the almost unimaginable scale of the universe as a whole?

II. The Credentials of Cosmology

These questions, in one form or another, have been debated over and over, but the balance has been shifting in the last decade. As long as Newtonian orthodoxy reigned, there was no way to construct a scientific cosmology, i.e. a scientific account of the universe taken as a whole. Newton's infinite space and time offered no purchase to the would-be cosmologist; the clue provided by Olbers' paradox not surprisingly went unperceived. Kant's warning that the theoretical reason would inevitably become tangled in inconsistencies if it went universe-building was hardly needed. It was only with the construction of the first general theories of relativity in the 1920's and Hubble's simultaneous discovery of the galactic red-shift that a cosmology proper, providing tentative answers to questions about size, total mass, structure, origins, development, seemed for the first time to be in sight.

But there were some who found the claims of the new cosmology over-weaning, even fraudulent. Herbert Dingle, an English philosopher of positivist leanings, launched an onslaught against what he called "cosmythology." His main targets were Milne and Eddington, whom he accused of the doctrine "that Nature is the visible working-out of general principles known to the human mind apart from sense-perception,"[6] a view he picturesquely but quite inaccurately characterized as a "new Aristotelianism." In the language of a crusader, he reminded scientists of the "loyalty" they owed to a "trust" bequeathed them by Galileo, one in danger of being forgotten because of the new "Universe mania," an "idolatry of which The Universe is god." He belabored cosmology with phrases like "spineless rhetoric," "paralysis of the reason," "intoxication of the fancy," and did not hesitate to characterize as "treachery" any sort of sympathy with its pretensions.

Not all the critics were quite as violent in their opposition. But there were two different features of the new cosmology that were almost bound to excite mistrust. One was the *a priori* status claimed for it by some of its most notable protagonists. Eddington thought he could derive the four "cosmical constants," including the number of particles in the universe, from a purely epistemological analysis of the nature of experimental observation. When the meson was first proposed by Yukawa, Eddington had to oppose this new particle, as it would cause his transcendental deductions to crumble by swelling the number of particles in the universe far beyond the "cosmic constant" based on electrons and protons only. And when the fine-structure constant came out a little different than the exact 1/137 his analysis had led him to propose, even his most ardent defenders had to admit that his attempt to transcendentalize physics was at the very least premature.

Most cosmologists were, however, wary of the *a priori* approach, and hence were untouched by the criticisms of Eddington's work. A second objection proved more troubling. The "cosmological principles" of isotropy, homogeneity and observer-equivalence on which the new science rested appeared to many, as they did to Dingle, to be impossibly idealized assumptions forced upon us by our complete ignorance of the cosmos in the large. Yet without them, relativistic mechanics of itself could not generate universe-models. Dingle objected that they "transcend observation and cannot be derived from induction alone," and argued that there was no chance that they ever could attain the inductive status a true "Galilean" should insist upon for the principles of his science. Others, less positivistically inclined than Dingle, still wondered aloud whether such models could tell one about anything other than the obviously over-simplified cosmic assumptions required for their derivation.

What has happened in the interim? For cosmology quite evidently enjoys a different status today. The first factor, of course, is the enormous amount of new observational material, particularly in the rich field of radio-astronomy. More important, however, are the successes of theory, and in particular the resolution of cosmology's first major internal controversy, that between proponents of the Big Bang and steady-state models. The discovery of the 2.7°K cosmic background radiation in 1965, which had been predicted by the Big Bang model and which the other model proved unable to account for, was a decisive moment. Cosmologists could breathe a little more easily, knowing that the familiar criterion of empirical testability *could* be applied to their theories after all. Then there was the prediction of the cosmic abundance of helium at one-quarter of the total cosmic mass, nearly all of it supposedly formed in the first twenty minutes after the Big Bang. Observational evidence for this figure continues to grow.[7] Finally, the much maligned cosmological principles of homogeneity and isotropy are receiving more and more observational support. The most striking testimony to this has come recently from the cosmic background radiation which proves to be isotropic to within 0.1%, so isotropic in fact that cosmologists are rather troubled by the unexpectedly close fit between observation and what began as an optimistic idealization.[8]

Even more significant, perhaps, is the impressive *coherence* of the emerging picture. When, for example, pulsating radio-frequency sources ("pulsars") were discovered in 1967, they were explained in a matter of months as tiny neutron stars only a few miles across, the remnants of supernova explosions. The theory of such stars had been worked out by Zwicky, Oppenheimer, and others in the 1930's on the basis of the quantum theory of terrestrial matter. Despite the fact that nothing remotely like the extreme conditions of energy, gravitation, and density, of the super-nova or the neutron star can be recreated in the laboratories of earth, the hypothetical extension of the basic theories of terrestrial physics to these quite unfamiliar conditions accounts beautifully and convincingly for pulsar phenomena.

It is worth noting that this is not mere induction, not the simple

analogy of Nature that Newton postulated in his Third Rule of Reasoning whereby the qualities found "to belong to all bodies within the
reach of our experiments are to be esteemed the universal qualities of
all bodies whatsoever."[9] Inductive generalization, which Newton
wrongly believed to be the principal method of empirical science, can
only postulate more of the same elsewhere and can be validated only by
endless and uncertain sampling (unless one lays down risky *a priori*
principles of homogeneity). Hypothetico-deductive inference (retro-
duction) can on the other hand establish the existence of structures and
processes altogether different from any that lie within direct reach, and
is limited only by the resources of the scientific imagination and by the
richness of the causal connections between the postulated structures
and the accessible world of our apparatus.[10]

It is on this much more powerful pattern of inference that cosmology
mainly relies. And indeed cosmology could by now be counted as one
of the domains in which this combined mode of validation and explanation has gained its most notable successes. What has impressed scientists most, perhaps, is the growing realization that the future of physics
itself is likely to depend more and more on such extraordinary testing-
grounds as black hole and quasar, as well as on the degree to which the
most general theories of mechanics can provide coherent explanations
of known cosmological data.

In the last decade, much effort has been expended on applying
quantum and elementary-particle theories to the problem of how the
universe developed in the first moments after the Big Bang. An immensely detailed scenario has been developed, and indeed there are
those who have remarked, only half facetiously, that everything of real
interest to physics happened in that first microsecond! Some of this
speculation is merely playful, but much of it can be defended as serious
thought-experiment. There are, of course, good historical reasons to
distrust the applicability of standard theories to extreme conditions.
Furthermore, no adequate theory of quantum gravity has yet been
devised. So there is every reason to suppose that present reconstruc-
tions of the early universe ought not be taken *too* seriously as history.
Indeed, a modern-day Dingle may once again enter the lists to de-
nounce Weinberg's *The First Three Minutes* as dangerous to the purity
of science. . .[11]

Be that as it may, the credentials of mainline cosmology now seem
fairly secure,[12] though complaints about its "peculiarity" and the inor-
dinate passion of its internal controversies are still frequent.[13] The Big
Bang model has demonstrated the sort of resources that qualify it as a
"good" model, one the scientist can rely on. A cosmological model is
dependent on many more auxiliary hypotheses than is the average
model of the chemist or biologist, so that there are many more "degrees of freedom" in the face of anomaly than usual, as the debate

between the Big Bang and Steady State theorists showed. Nonetheless, the Big Bang model would now be accorded a fair degree of reliability. This does not mean that it gives an exact description, nor even that it might not ultimately be replaced by a model as different as the Steady State one. But what it does imply is that one can by now have a measure of confidence that the universe is something *like* what the model suggests. The "something like" of a successful metaphor does not provide the simple reference of a descriptive term. Yet is not a fiction, not "just" an idea, either.

The question of whether or not the universe is finite is now a relatively straightforward one. The resources of non-Euclidean geometry and the explanatory successes of the cosmological models built on it eliminate the supposed antinomy of the finite and the infinite posed by Kant. Another topic once popular among philosophers, the unity of the universe, has now become reasonably straightforward to handle on the basis of the last half-century of cosmological discovery. The success of HD methods when applied to the most distant regions of the universe as well as to the universe taken as a whole testifies quite strongly to its fundamental unity. So far as one can see, it might *not* have worked out this way. When the spectra of distant stars, or the velocities of distant galaxies, continue to be interpretable by schemas derived from terrestrial processes, confidence quite properly grows in the assumption that these schemas are not just conventions imposed for convenience's sake or because our minds cannot operate otherwise, but that all parts of the universe are united in a web of physical process which is accessible through coherent and ever-widening theoretical constructs created and continually modified by us.

III. The Contributions of Philosophy

Now that cosmology has become a respectable pursuit for the scientist, has philosophy anything distinctive to contribute to it? Note that I say "philosophy" rather than "the philosopher." For one of the unfortunate consequences of the deepening professional separation between scientists and philosophers is the assumption on the part of many that philosophy is what (only) philosophers do. But a philosophic issue is a philosophic issue whether it be discussed by a philosopher or by a physicist. It is likely to be discussed more adequately, one would presume, if its true character is recognized. Nonetheless, it must be emphasized that much of the liveliest philosophic writing on scientific topics in our own century has been done by scientists. There are two very good reasons for this. One is that the philosophic problems raised by such developments as relativity theory and quantum theory often require a familiarity with the intricacies of the science beyond even that of the average scientist. The second is that the fundamental con-

ceptual advances made in twentieth-century science have quite frequently involved the challenging of presupposition and the reshaping
of conceptual scheme that is characteristic of philosophy at its most
creative. Einstein's achievement in the special theory of relativity was a
philosophic quite as much as it was a scientific one. Basic science, at its
most innovative, merges into philosophy.

We need not expect, then, to reveal a task for philosophy which is
altogether distinct from anything a scientist might conceivably engage
in. Though a section on the "unity of the universe" has begun to appear
of late in works written by astronomers,[14] this topic is not one that can
be directly handled by the methods of science. Its elaboration does not
of itself constitute a scientific theory; controversy about the unity of
science cannot be decided by testing empirical predictions derivable
from the rival viewpoints. The "doing" of science will not be affected,
not at first approximation certainly, by the viewpoint adopted on the
disputed topic; indeed, one is not required to take up *any* specific
viewpoint in regard to it in order to function as a cosmologist. Yet the
question of the unity of science is clearly an interesting one. And it can
be responsibly debated, with an abundance of coherent (though rarely
conclusive) argument. There can be no doubt, then, of the legitimacy in
this instance of the philosopher's concern.

Besides the question of ontological import, which as we have already
seen, is perhaps the primary topic for the philosopher who concerns
himself with contemporary cosmology, there are two other general
sorts of issue that are also likely to occupy him. One is concerned with
methods, the other with concepts and substantive principles. The properly "scientific" character of cosmology has, as we have seen, been
persistently challenged. The parameters which constitute a particular
piece of reasoning as good "science" are ordinarily taken for granted
by the working scientist, unless a dispute arises about the status of his
work. Boundary areas, like cosmology or psycho-analysis, are especially
likely to give rise to such disputes.

The criteria for theory-evaluation are usually at the heart of the most
intractable disagreements. Ought cosmological theories be straightforwardly falsifiable?[15] How appropriate *is* falsifiability as a criterion of
science? And what precisely does it amount to?[16] The attractive simplicity of Popper's proposal has long ago evaporated; falsifiability is
much too blunt a weapon, if the testimony of history is at all to be
trusted. To say that questions such as these are "philosophical" is in the
first instance to recall that science itself cannot answer them without
begging the question. They cannot, of course, be settled without constant recourse to the history and present practice of science. But they
do raise intricate logical and epistemological issues that ramify into
almost every part of philosophy. Indeed, the fascination of cosmology
for the philosopher is in part due to this; it is as much a testing-ground

for the philosopher's theories of science as it is for the physicist's theories of matter.

A second type of philosophic question that cosmology, more perhaps than almost any other part of science, seems to elicit is one of concept-clarification. Presuppositions (regarding causality or time-order, for example) are made explicit; implications (such as the rejection of simultaneity at a distance) are explored. Consistency is tested. Relations between the most general principles of the theory and the conceptual framework within which the basic observations have to be situated, are worked out. But why should this be called a "philosophical" task? Ought not the scientist take full responsibility for it?

Calling it "philosophical" appears to be meant to draw attention to three things in particular. First, this sort of conceptual analysis is akin to that which elsewhere defines the work of philosophy. Second, it has to take into account the broader context of already-formulated philosophical systems which are likely to be relevant to the questions raised by cosmology. Third, "normal" science can be carried on without troubling much with issues of this sort, where differences of interpretation do not contribute immediately to the construction of alternative theories. Of course, when anomaly or inconsistency become threatening and a radical theory-change is in the making, it is precisely conceptual issues of this sort that can be crucial, as twentieth-century science has often shown.

There is obviously no sharp-cut distinction between the "scientific" and the "philosophic" here; the ultimate unity between the two implied by the older and no longer fashionable term, "natural philosophy," ought be recalled. What may appear "philosophic" at one time may well turn out to be indisputably "scientific" at another, when theoretical reformulations that are in one way or another empirically testable are in the making. When an Einstein reshapes Newtonian mechanics in the light of its conceptual tensions, this will be called a "scientific" achievement. But when a Reichenbach or a Grünbaum explores the conceptual ambiguities and implications of relativity theory, his work is directed to, and is read mainly by, philosophers. In some ways it is reminiscent of the hazy separation between mathematicians and logicians. One group is occupied with the construction of new theories or formalisms, the other with a clarification of their status. To the former, the latter may seem to do no more than tidy up after the "real" work is over. To the latter, their contribution appears as the essential one of determining what the former are really claiming or have really accomplished.

It is not hard to find instances in the recent history of cosmology where philosophic clarification proved to be necessary. The status of Mach's Principle and its relationship with the general theory of relativity is one obvious example. Another would be the familiar one tracing back to the debate between Leibniz and Newton: are we committed to the acceptance of a "real" space – time existing over and above material objects and their spatio-temporal relations? Far from being settled by the relativistic theory of inertial force, this controversy between defenders of the relationist and substantival views has taken on a new intensity. It can be shown now, much more clearly than before, that it *is* a purely "philosophical" debate, but it is obviously not any the less important for that.[17] On the other hand, some intractable cosmological puzzles of the past, notably those surrounding the notion of the infinite, have been resolved or at least clarified, not by further philosophical debate, but by recent advances in mathematical knowledge.[18]

Among the issues broadly termed "conceptual," there are two that have given rise to particularly lively discussion. Neither is new, but both have taken on new forms in recent cosmology. One is the problem of creation, the other concerns the "anthropic principle" favored by some cosmologists who seek to understand why the universe is the way it is. It may be worth outlining these two debates in somewhat more detail in order to illustrate the sorts of questions cosmology can pose the philosopher.

IV. Cosmology and Creation[19]

In the natural philosophies of Aristotle and of Newton, it seemed quite plain that time could have neither beginning nor end. The stretch of time past must be infinite. Yet for those who accepted the Biblical account of cosmic origins, it seemed as though the universe did, in fact, have a beginning. Newton had a relatively easy way to harmonize the two claims: the material universe was brought into being by God at a finite time in the past, but the space and time into which it came to be were alike infinite in extent. Medieval Aristotelians were less willing to separate matter and time; if matter began to be, then so did time.[20]

The classical Augustinian account of origins made creation a single timeless act on God's part, an act through which time itself as well as the changing things of which time is the measure come to be together. By a subtle analysis of the notions of time, cause, beginning, Aquinas endeavored to show, within a generally Aristotelian framework, that although the natural reason could not of itself demonstrate that time had a beginning, there was in itself nothing incoherent about such a claim. Yet the tension between natural philosophy and the Christian world-view was not really dissipated by the efforts of either Aquinas or Newton, and there were many, like Bonaventure and Leibniz, who were emphatic in holding that an Aristotelian (or a Newtonian as the case might be) could not be sincere in his acceptance of the *Genesis* story.

It is against this background that one must view the controversy with which the expanding-universe theories have been surrounded from the beginning. The current Big Bang model postulates a singularity somewhere between ten and twenty billion years ago, from which the expansion of the universe began. For the first time, natural philosophy was led to assert, on its own resources, something that sounds like a beginning of time. No wonder that scientists and non-scientists spoke of this horizon-event as "the Creation," and of the time since it occurred as "the age of the universe."

But these identifications immediately give rise to two sorts of objection. How is one to know (a point made by Lemaître in the earliest debates occasioned by his model) that the Big Bang was not preceded by a Big Squeeze? Why could there not have been an unending cyclical series, like Vico's *Ricorso* on a grander scale? Even though a Big Squeeze would destroy all traces of the history that preceded, some general features of the prior sequence (the period of the cycle, for example) might possibly be inferred.[21] Though one might prefer to speak of the universe that preceded the Big Bang as a "different" universe, there would still be a perfectly legitimate sense in which, because it provided the "materials" for the next stage, it could be called the "same" universe as ours. Thus, the Big Bang cannot *automatically* be taken to be either the beginning of time or of the universe, nor can one take for granted that the lapse of time since it occurred is the "age" of the universe.[22] Even if the progress of cosmology leads us to opt for the "open" rather than the "closed" expanding model,[23] one which makes the universe expand indefinitely instead of endlessly "rebounding," this could hardly be said to rule out the possibility of a preceding stage of matter, to which we simply have no access through the singularity.

Thus, there is no cogent reason to take the Big Bang to mark the beginning of time. On the other hand, there is no compelling reason why it might *not* have constituted such a beginning. Mario Bunge asserts that science requires a "genetic principle" which would exclude such "irrational and untestable notions" as that of an absolute beginning of the universe.[24] His argument is that the "known laws of nature" require that explanation in terms of an antecedent be always available. E. H. Hutten makes a similar claim: the notion of a first event makes no sense (he says) because one can always ask: "what happened before"?[25] The most determined opposition comes, of course, from Marxist–Leninist writers who claim that the notion of an absolute beginning has "idealist" implications, and that in any event it contravenes conservation laws and runs counter to the basic principles of dialectical materialism.

The notion that absolute beginnings of any kind are excluded by the laws of physics recalls the Aristotelian arguments for a similar position which were so warmly debated by medieval critics. The real question is the applicability of these laws to the sort of singularity the model postulates. Hawking is insistent that the laws of "normal" physics ought *not* be expected to apply to a singularity, especially not a singularity which comprises the entire universe.[26] A genetic principle which tells the scientist he ought always seek for an explanation of a particular state by looking to an earlier state, or a conservation principle which directs scientists to try every other alternative before admitting that conservation of a particular sort fails, are in the first instance methodological prescriptions of a highly successful kind. Scientists ought *not* assume that the Big Bang has no antecedent; they ought to do whatever they can to establish a lawlike succession. But this is not to say that there *must* be an antecedent, that the success of these principles demonstrates that an absolute beginning is impossible. A metaphysical claim of this sort would require more on its behalf than an inductive appeal to the success up to this point of the genetic and conservation principles.

Our conclusion is that the success of the Big Bang model for the first time gives a way of construing in scientific terms what a "beginning" of the universe *might* look like from here. But now a second question arises. Suppose the singularity *was*, in fact, an absolute beginning: can it be called "the Creation"? Creation is the act of a creator. A spontaneous uncaused beginning would not be a "creation"; it would be an absolute coming-to-be, nothing more. The term "creation" is an explanatory, not merely a descriptive, one.[27] To say of the horizon-event that it was the Creation is to *explain* it in terms of a cause, a cause which is outside the time-sequence since its action is what brings time itself to be. Clearly, such an explanation is not a scientific one; science of itself could not establish a sufficiently strong principle of causality. Can philosophy do so? Until Hume's time it was generally supposed that it could, but the critiques of Hume and even more of Kant have made philosophers wary of what has come to be called the "cosmological" argument. The matter is still a hotly-disputed one;[28] on one point, however, there is general agreement and that is that the issue is a properly philosophic one.

Does the Big Bang model have any relevance to the issue? If the universe "began" at a point of time, would this give stronger support to the claim that a Creator is needed than if the universe always existed? Intuitively, one would be inclined to answer "yes" to this. An eternally existing universe seems a more plausible candidate for self-sufficiency than one which begins to be. Yet there are enough difficulties about the notion of "beginning" to warn one to treat this inference with caution. What can be said is that *if* the universe began by an act of creation, as earlier Western thought always supposed, then from our vantage-point it could look something like the Big Bang that cosmologists are now talking about. What *cannot* be said is that the Big Bang model somehow validates the "cosmological" argument for the existence of a Creator. The inference does not work in this direction.

It is interesting to note the extent to which philosophic presuppositions have affected the recent development of cosmology. The "Copernican principle" of the non-privileged status of our solar system or of our galaxy quite evidently had the status of a philosophic claim rather than just a convenient working assumption. Perhaps the most striking illustration of this is Fred Hoyle's rejection of the Big Bang model in the 1950's and early 1960's. He was (and still is) convinced that a theory which implies a past time-singularity beyond which the history of the universe cannot be traced, *cannot* be a good scientific theory.[29] What bothered him most was the affinity between the Big Bang model and traditional Western religious thought. His reluctance to abandon the steady-state model in the early 1960's as evidence continued to mount against it seems to have been motivated at least as much by this "anti-theological" principle as it was by the predictive virtues of his own steady-state model.

One recalls in this connection the theological principles which so influenced Newton in the construction of *his* system. That a cosmological theory should rest in part on philosophical or theological presuppositions is not necessarily to its discredit. What *would* be to its discredit would be to leave these presuppositions as simple expressions of belief and nothing more,[30] or to keep relying on their guidance in science even when this guidance continued to prove unhelpful.[31]

V. The Anthropic Principle[32]

One of the liveliest debates in fourteenth-century philosophy focussed on the question: are the principles of physics necessary (as the Aristotelians maintained) or are they contingent (as the nominalists insisted). Might the universe have been other than it is? The Aristotelian view was that physics is a demonstrative science based on intrinsically evident principles. Contingency requires further explanation; if at the cosmological level one finds something that might have been other than it is, then one has to *explain* why it has taken the form it did. Whereas something that is necessary requires no further explanation, and can thus be properly regarded as a scientific principle. The nominalist–voluntarist objection to this was that it limited God's freedom of choice; if God is free, then the universe might not only not have been, but it might have been of a quite different kind, operating in a different manner. To the charge that this left unexplained contingency at the heart of physics, the nominalists' response was two-fold. First, they argued that a demonstrative science of nature is an illusory goal; some kind of likelihood is the best one can achieve. Second, the contingencies of the world *can* be explained, "explained" in a different sense admittedly than the Aristotelian would be willing to concede, in terms of God's will. The world is the way it is, not because it had to be so, but because God willed that it should be so.

A strikingly similar debate goes on around recent cosmological results. In the Newtonian universe, contingency abounded. It was plausible to argue, as Kant did, that the basic laws of Newtonian physics could not be other than they are. But the infinite universe of stars going in all directions was full of "could have been otherwise." The unification brought about in recent cosmology has revived the older question again. In an evolutionary universe each stage is explained by an earlier one. But when one gets back to the Big Bang, what should one expect? A state that could not have been otherwise? An entirely structureless entity? To put it in older terms, how can the Many come from the One, unless there is some multiplicity latent already in the One? And if there is, how is *it* to be explained?

Coming at it from another angle, how is one to decide whether a particular feature of the universe is necessary or contingent, since we have only one universe, and thus cannot fall back on the simplest way to test a claim to necessity, i.e. that it occur in all cases? The argument for necessity will have to be a *theoretical* one. But such arguments are difficult to construct and notoriously open to self-deception, as we have already seen in Eddington's case. The scientist is caught at this point. The case for necessity makes him uneasy; yet settling for contingency leaves him dissatisfied. If so far as one can see, something *could* have been otherwise, it seems fair to expect an answer to the question: well, then, why *is* it this way? Is there a limit to structural explanation, a point at which any further question (like: why is the proton/electron mass-ratio what it is?) is illegitimate? And is there a similar point beyond which genetic explanation cannot be carried, when we get back to a first state that just *was* that way?

In 1973, Collins and Hawking constructed a particularly teasing variant of the old question.[33] The universe is now known to have a very high degree of isotropy; this is no longer, as we have seen, the simplification assumed for the sake of a first calculation that it once was. What initial conditions would have allowed such isotropy to develop? It turns out that hardly any of the (so far as is known) possible initial conditions would have done so. It appears to be extremely difficult to construct a plausible genesis for the observed isotropy. It is not only contingent; worse, it is extremely improbable, "improbable," that is, in the sense, that isotropy is produced only by an *extremely* small fraction of all the permitted ways in which a universe obeying the equations of general relativity might develop.[34]

How, then, explain such an apparently improbable occurrence? Collins and Hawking argue that galaxies can form only in an isotropic universe, and then go on to note that only where there are galaxies (and hence stars and planets) can there be life, and *a fortiori* rational life. If the universe were *not* isotropic, we could not be here to observe it. Since we are here, the universe *must* be isotropic. This is what Carter has called the "anthropic principle."[35]

The "must" here is, however, a hypothetical one. *If* there are to be cosmologists, then if the argument is correct, the universe will have to be isotropic (and also very old, and thus very large).[36] The necessity is the necessity of consequence. But why should there be cosmologists? So far as we can tell, there very well might not have been. Our presence does not, then, explain isotropy, though isotropy might help to explain our presence. The fact (if it is one) that a non-isotropic universe could not be observed, so that we could *expect* the universe to be isotropic if we did not already know it to be so, makes no difference. The presence of observers in a universe may allow one to predict isotropy. But when isotropy is said to be a very "improbable" state, and we seek an explanation for why it should be the case, we cannot invoke the presumably at least equally improbable presence of observers. Why should the joint state: observers plus isotropy have occurred in the first place?

One may simply say: the explanation ends; this just is the way it is, and there is no more to be said. The anthropic principle might, however, be construed as an *explanation* if one or other of two further specifications were to be permitted. If the universe is the work of a Creator who wills that conscious life develop in it, if in other words, the traditional Judaeo-Christian view should be correct that the purpose of the universe is in part, at least, man, then the presence of man in the world *would* explain the isotropy, the size, the age, and all the rest. Note that this is a stronger form of explanation than the medieval one which would explain, say, the presence of elephants or snow in the world by simply invoking God's will. Reasons can be given in the traditional Judaeo-Christian perspective, why God *would* want man in the world. Thus, the explanation is not merely by the presumed fact of choice, but by some presumptive *reasons* for the choice. The anthropic principle, if fortified by the traditional doctrine of creation, does therefore give an explanation, though it is no longer, of course, a scientific explanation.

The second way in which the anthropic principle might be strengthened is to suppose that all the possible universes do, in fact, come to be in isolation from one another.[37] One would no longer ask: but why this (improbable) universe rather than one of the other more likely configurations? They are *all* "there"; that we should find ourselves in the galactic one (rather than in one of the others) can then readily be explained. If all cars bore the same inscription: "HUMAN−1," one would want to know why this significant-sounding phrase had been chosen rather than others. But if all six-symbol combinations of letters and numbers are in fact realized on different cars, seeing "HUMAN–1" on one car will no longer seem so significant (though it will still draw our attention). The analogy is not exact but it may serve to suggest why if *all* possibilities in some domain are realized, the realization of some *particular* one ceases to be a special issue. Of course, one would still ask how, in the cosmological case, one could *know* that all the possibilities are realized. And one might ask, further, why any of them *should* be realized.

The anthropic principle derives ultimately from the claim (1) that the most basic structures of the universe might have been different from what they are; and (2) that the development of rational life in the universe depends on their being more or less exactly what they, in fact, are. Both premises are clearly vulnerable. It is difficult, for example, to exclude the possibility that at some later time cosmologists may be able to show that the cosmical parameters governing the sort of universe in which we find ourselves could not be other than they are.[38] That the efforts of Eddington, Dirac, and many others in this direction have failed, does not mean that success is impossible, only perhaps that their efforts were premature. It must, however, be said that for the moment at least, contingency seems well entrenched.

VI. Regulative Principles for Cosmology?

Is this all there is to be said? Until recently, philosophers were wont to make a far more robust claim. It was widely agreed that the philosopher could formulate some general principles which are prior to science and regulative of it. This would attribute a far more dominant role to philosophy than the contemporary cosmologist would be likely to concede, as we have seen.

How plausible does this claim now seem? Three broadly different types of warrant have in the past been advanced for it; they might be called Aristotelian, Cartesian and Kantian, as long as one keeps in mind that the historical figures from which these familiar labels are drawn were much too complex to be comprised under a single well-defined account.[39] Can any one of these sorts of argument for a philosophical *a priori* carry weight in today's cosmology?

The Aristotelian, or broadly empiricist, approach is to assume that the knower can formulate on the basis of his everyday experience some very general principles in regard to motion, cause, space and the like. Because the categories employed are understood in a non-problematic way and are validated by even the simplest experiences of the world, the principles take on the character of very general truths about the world. The Cartesian, or broadly rationalist, approach is to suppose that an attentive inspection of certain of our ideas will disclose necessary connections between them; the ideas themselves are assumed not to depend on the specificities of experience. The Kantian, or broadly idealist, strategy is to take the most general categories of the understanding and forms of the intuition to be prior to experience and yet constitutive (or regulative) of it. In this way, synthetic *a priori* principles of a necessary sort can be derived from the *possibility* of experience. In each of the three cases, cosmological principles would rest on a different basis: in the first, on the natures of physical things, assumed to be directly known; in the second, on the interconnections between clear and distinct ideas; in the third, on the uniform structures of the human understanding.

Since science takes its origin in observation, its validity must depend on the integrity of that observation. Scientific theory cannot, therefore, call into question the general framework within which claims to "observe" the world are made, a reminder which Bohr felt called on to deliver to quantum theorists in the 1930's. But this of itself does not commit one to a philosophic *a priori*. How specific is the commitment to the epistemic structures implicit in everyday observation? Can these structures remain unaffected by changes in science? Just how prescriptive *is* the commitment to these structures in the scientist's regard?

Those who defend a philosophically-elucidated *a priori* which is supposed to be normative for the cosmologist tend to be committed to a sort of linguistic foundationalism, an assumption that the concepts, categories, forms, in terms of which the general principles governing the physical world (or our conception of, or our experience of, the physical world) are to be formulated, are somehow themselves given to us.[40] They are assumed to be unproblematic, fixed, not in need of validation. Though he tried to be very careful about what he could assume, Kant never adequately clarified the manner in which the content of the terms through which his *a priori* principles are expressed (terms like "time," "matter," "cause") is itself to be determined prior to all experience. It was not as clear in his day as it is in ours that the content of such terms can be altered by the progress of science (as the content of the term "force" had already been in Newton's time), and that this alteration is itself a complex affair, depending *a posteriori* upon the success of the explanatory theories in which these terms occur. In the more developed parts of science, the constructive power latent within the hypothetical procedure allows older concepts to be reshaped or new ones to be formulated.

It is, therefore, difficult nowadays to defend a Kantian distinction between a "pure physics" enunciating principles of the understanding given *a priori* and an "empirical physics" based on induction and thus merely contingent. Science suggests something closer to a continuous spectrum. Philosophers can still propose principles (the determinism of natural process or the impossibility of time-reversal, for example) from one or other of the classical viewpoints. But they have to be willing to allow a certain dialectic with science. The principle may have to be modified or weakened in the light of a challenge from long-term successful scientific theory. Though it is not impossible that the philosopher should validly derive regulative principles "from the essential nature of the thinking faculty itself,"[41] or from the epistemic situation of the observer, it becomes more and more difficult to maintain that a *necessary* claim of potential significance to the cosmologist could be arrived at in this way.

The choice between making science entirely independent of philosophy, making philosophy prior to and absolutely normative of science, and making the two interactive with one another, is one that has bedevilled Soviet science from the beginning. Indeed, the struggle between protagonists of these three approaches was one of the central intellectual preoccupations in the Soviet Union in the 1920's, until it was pre-empted by Stalin's imposition of the "normative" position in 1931.[42] Reverberations of the struggle can be found in Soviet cosmology. It is asserted over and over by Soviet scientists that fidelity to the principles of dialectical materialism accounts for the successful development of theoretical cosmology in the Soviet Union. The principles most often invoked are those of quantitative difference leading to qualitative leaps (so that, for example, the universe as a whole might be expected to have properties not predictable from those of its parts), and of struggle between opposites (suggesting, it is said, the importance of unstable stellar states and the fundamentally evolutionary character of stellar and galactic formation).[43]

Some writers made cosmology entirely subordinate to philosophy on matters of general principle. Sviderskii, for example, argued that finite universe-models are incompatible with dialectical materialism; only an infinite universe is admissible. Others (e.g. G. L. Naan) asserted that philosophy is not prior to, but is in fact derived from science, so that although it is normative in regard to science, it derives its warrant from science itself. It is hard to decide just what influence dialectical materialism *has* had; for ideological reasons it was important to stress its superiority as a philosophy of science.

But either of the options leads to trouble. If it is attributed some sort of *a priori* status, the question insistently puts itself: how can pre-scientific experience warrant principles sufficiently general and sufficiently precise to serve as norms for a science of the universe? If it is made dependent on science, it can easily reduce to science itself, at its most general. More troubling still from the Marxist–Leninist viewpoint, this may make dialectical materialism vulnerable to challenge from science.

The most renowned Soviet cosmologist, A. Ambartsumian, has always insisted on the directive force of dialectical materialism in cosmology. Consistently with this, he has argued that his own reliance on it in the formulation of successful theories, serves to *confirm* its value.

But this is a dangerous move. One of these theories had to do with the evolution of stars, for example; Ambartsumian opposed the view defended by Jeans and Eddington that stars are relatively unchanging even across vast intervals of time. But now suppose the latter had been right? Would this count *against* dialectical materialism? Should the widespread opposition to the Big Bang model among Soviet cosmologists count against the philosophy that inspired it? One need not be a Popperian to believe that an outcome cannot confirm unless its opposite would count against. To say that Jeans and Eddington could not *possibly* have been right, or that the universe as a whole *must* have properties that differ from those discoverable in its parts, would imply that dialectical materialism includes a metaphysics whose warrant is prior to science and is not dependent upon it.

Outside the Soviet Union, there are few today who would attribute to philosophy a directive role of this sort in regard to cosmology. Philosophers like Whitehead and Broad constructed powerful metaphysical systems of "mixed" warrant, that is, relying on both epistemological and more specifically scientific grounds. The problem in the end is one of metaphilosophy, of deciding on the sort of warrant that is appropriate to philosophic and to scientific claims, seen not as two entirely distinct sorts of intellectual pursuit, but as a continuum. What has made the issue more intractable is the pace of development of theoretical cosmology, a pace too rapid of late to allow metaphilosophy the time it needs to take stock.

NOTES

1. A summary version of Sections IV and V of this paper was presented in a symposium on "The idea of the universe" at the XVI World Congress of Philosophy held in Dusseldorf in 1978, and appears in the *Proceedings* of that congress.
2. "The forces of nature," *American Scientist*, vol. 65 (1977), p. 176. See also his *Gravitation and Cosmology*, New York, 1972, and *The First Three Minutes: A Modern View of The Origin of The Universe* (New York, 1977).
3. *Space and Time in the Modern Universe* (Cambridge, 1977), p. 211.
4. *Op. cit.*, p. 192.
5. See, for example, R. Harré, *Principles of Scientific Thinking* (Chicago, 1970); E. McKinnon (ed.), *The Problem of Scientific Realism* (New York, 1972); E. McMullin, "The fertility of theory and the unit for appraisal in science," *Boston Studies in the Philosophy of Science*, vol. 39 (1976), pp. 395–432.
6. "Modern Aristotelianism," *Nature*, vol. 139 (1937), p. 784. All the quotations here are from pp. 784–786. See the responses to this broadside from many of the leading cosmologists of the day in a special supplement to *Nature* a few months later [vol. 139 (1937), pp. 997–1012].
7. See H. L. Shipman, *Black Holes, Quasars and the Universe* (Boston, 1976), pp. 231–232; 251–253.
8. M. Rowan-Robinson, *Cosmology* (Oxford, 1977), p. 137.
9. *Principia*, Motte-Cajori translation (Berkeley, 1966), Book III, p. 398.

10. The inadequacies of the logical positivist account of HD inference are by now well-known. They derived from a defective empiricist theory of meaning on the one hand and a lack of sensitivity to the temporal dimension of scientific theories on the other. See D. Shapere, "Notes toward a post-positivistic interpretation of science," in *The Legacy of Logical Positivism*, ed. P. Achinstein and S. F. Barker (Baltimore, 1969), pp. 115–160; E. McMullin, "Structural explanation," *American Philosophical Quarterly*, 15, 1978, pp. 139–147.

11. At a recent lecture by E. R. Harrison on the early universe, it was interesting to note the quite different reactions from the physicists and the philosophers present. The former were wary and on the whole hostile to a theory they took to be in principle untestable; the latter were fascinated and defended the model's legitimacy as a thought-experiment.

12. See, for example, P. G. Bergman, "Cosmology as a science," *Philosophical Foundations of Science*, ed. R. J. Seeger and R. S. Cohen (Dordrecht, 1974), pp. 181–188.

13. The reviewer of the *Proceedings* of a recent cosmology conference writes: "There is something slightly odd about the tone of discussion in contemporary observational cosmology. It is at once inconclusive and strangely dogmatic. Opinions seem more strongly held than the evidence for them warrants. Some cosmologists seem to live in private worlds and are deeply persuaded by evidence and arguments that seem to their colleagues to be quite unpersuasive. Few make observations whose implications they find surprising . . .", L. Searle, *Science*, vol. 199 (1978), pp. 1061–1062.

14. See, for instance, D. W. Sciama, *The Unity of the Universe* (New York, 1959).

15. As Davies, for example, claims, *op. cit.*, p. 192.

16. For a discussion of this issue in the context of cosmology, see K. Hubner, "Ist das Universum nur eine Idee? Eine Analyse der relativistischen Kosmologie," *Allgemeine Zeitschrift für Philosophie*, vol. 2 (1977), pp. 1–20.

17. For a summary of this debate and of the philosophical reasons supporting each side, see L. Sklar, *Space, Time and Spacetime* (Berkeley, 1974), Chapter 3, especially pp. 225–234; A. Grünbaum, "Absolute and relational theories of space and space-time," *Minnesota Studies in the Philosophy of Science*, vol. 8, ed. J. Earman, *et al.* (Minneapolis, 1977), pp. 303–373.

18. For a good treatment of both the philosophical and mathematical sides of the antinomies of the infinite, see J. Bennett, "The age and size of the world," *Synthèse*, vol. 23 (1971), pp. 127–146.

19. I have discussed the theological implications of this section and the following one in more detail in "How should cosmology relate to theology?," A. Peacocke (ed.), *The Sciences and Theology in the Twentieth Century* (Oxford, 1981).

20. It is ironic to find Davies claiming that the view of space and time as "concrete properties of the material world" is the product of modern science; the "biblical account of creation" (he asserts) assumed that God built "form into a pre-existing but uninteresting space and time," imagining God "reigning in an earlier phase of the cosmos and being motivated to cause the cosmos" (*op. cit.*, pp. 216–217). But this is *precisely* the (Newtonian) view of creation that Augustine, the first Christian theorist of creation, and the legions of medieval philosophers who were influenced by him, were concerned to reject!

21. In her very useful review, "Cosmology: Man's place in the Universe," *American Scientist*, vol. 65 (1977), pp. 76–86, Virginia Trimble assumes that the successive cycles would each constitute a separate universe, and

remarks that "the question: What happened before the Big Bang? belongs to the realm of pure speculation (philosophy?) rather than that of physics. It is rather like putting a car into a steel blast furnace and asking [of] the trickle of molten metal that comes out whether it was a Pinto or VW before" (p. 78). Of course, one *could* ask whether it was a Pinto or a Cadillac; a mass-measurement might well suffice to answer this. Cosmologists who postulate a contraction preceding the Big Bang are not just indulging in "pure speculation," but are assuming that some parameters either remain invariant (total mass?) or are continuously traceable (radius?) throughout. Hawking has, however, raised some doubts about whether even this sort of "information" could come through the singularity ("Breakdown of predictability in gravitational collapse," *Physical Review* D, vol. 14 (1977), pp. 2460–2473).

22. One further complication about the notion of "age" in this context is (as Milne first pointed out in his *Kinematic Relativity*, London, 1947) that it may come out either as finite or infinite, depending on the choice of physical process to serve as basis for the time-scale. Thus, even if one takes the Big Bang to be the event from which the age of the universe is to be counted, that "age" could still come out as infinite. To decide, therefore, whether the Big Bang universe should be said to have had a beginning requires further precisions about the notion of beginning and of time-measurement. See C. Misner, "Absolute Zero of Time," *Physical Review*, vol. 186 (1969), pp. 1328–1333.

23. Gott *et al.* argue in a recent paper that the evidence already favors the "open" model. See "Will the universe expand forever?", *Scientific American*, vol. 234 (1976), pp. 62–79.

24. *Causality* (Cambridge, Mass., 1959), pp. 24, 240.

25. "Methodological remarks concerning cosmology," *Monist*, vol. 47 (1962), pp. 104–115.

26. "Black holes and thermodynamics," *Physical Review* D, vol. 13 (1976), pp. 191–197; "The quantum mechanics of black holes," *Scientific American*, vol. 236 (1977), pp. 34–40.

27. Bondi has argued that the steady-state model brought the "problem of creation" into "the scope of physical inquiry," by proposing a statistical law which the new appearances of matter in that model would follow (*Cosmology*, Cambridge, 1960, p. 140). Whether such a law *explains* the events depends in part on what one thinks of the D–N model of explanation. But even if it does, it certainly does not entitle one to assume that the problem solved is "the problem of creation."

28. See, for example, W. L. Rowe, *The Cosmological Argument* (Princeton, 1975); D. Burrill (ed.), *Cosmological Arguments* (New York, 1967).

29. *Astronomy and Cosmology* (San Francisco, 1975), p. 684. Note that this goes much further than the rejection of absolute cosmic beginning; it would exclude a Big-Bang type of singularity even if it were *not* an absolute beginning. See also Chapter I of his *Ten Faces of the Universe* (San Francisco, 1977), with its highly emotional attack on religion generally and on belief in "beginnings" specifically.

30. In *Ten Faces of the Universe*, Hoyle continually uses phrases like "I believe" or "I prefer." There is, at the very least, something premature about Davies' assurance to his readers that the new cosmology (unlike older world-views) "does not deal in beliefs but in facts. A model of the universe does not require faith but a telescope," *op. cit.*, p. 201.

31. Hoyle has recently proposed a new and ingenious model which explains galactic red-shifts by a steady increase in the masses of elementary parti-

cles over time, galactic distances remaining constant. The model does have a singularity in the past when all particle-masses were zero. But Hoyle argues that one can plausibly postulate a prior cosmic state of negative masses, as well as a far larger universe, homogeneous over time on a scale much larger than even clusters of galaxies (thus escaping refutation from the growing evidence for local inhomogeneity over time). The theory is *ad hoc* to an altogether alarming extent, alarming, that is, to anyone who is not *more* alarmed by an absolute time-beginning.

32. I am indebted to my fellow-panelists at the Dusseldorf World Congress of Philosophy (1978), Professors V. Weidemann and R. Sexl, for their clear delineation of the problem treated in this section.

33. "Why is the universe isotropic?," *Astrophysical Journal*, vol. 180 (1973), pp. 317–334.

34. It should be emphasized that this is not generally agreed. Trimble, though she agrees that the universe is a "delicately balanced" one in regard to the possibility of the development of life, supports the earlier view that galactic formation is an expected development: "The matter at this [early] stage was not perfectly smooth but was concentrated in lumps . . . The cause of the clumps is not well understood, though they are not unexpected, since, when the universe was very young, there had not yet been time for interactions and smoothing to have occurred across large distances. But they must have been there, because we see galaxies and clusters now" (*op. cit.*, p. 78). It is the explanatory force of this "must have been" that is at issue.

35. B. Carter, "Large number coincidences and the anthropic principle in cosmology," in *Confrontation of Cosmological Theories with Observational Data*, ed. M. A. Longair, Dordrecht, 1974, pp. 291–298. Carter uses a similar argument to "explain" why gravity is so weak, by noting that stable stars (and hence planetary life) could not develop were gravity to be a stronger force. B. J. Carr and M. J. Rees marshal a number of other "anthropic" considerations of this sort in their article, "The anthropic principle and the structure of the physical world," *Nature*, vol. 278 (1979), pp. 605–612.

36. Davies, *op. cit.*, Section 7.3.

37. Trimble speculates that they might be "imbedded in five (or higher) dimensional space, existing simultaneously, from the point of view of a five (or higher) dimensional observer" (*op. cit.*, p. 85).

38. Trimble, *op. cit.*, pp. 85–86.

39. For a more detailed account see E. McMullin, "Philosophies of nature," *New Scholasticism*, vol. 43 (1969), pp. 29–74.

40. This "myth of the given" has been very much the center of critical discussion in recent philosophy of science. See, for example, W. Sellars, *Science, Perception and Reality* (London, 1963).

41. Kant, Preface to the *Metaphysical Foundations of Natural Science*. It is in this work, perhaps, even more than in the Transcendental Analytic of the *Critique* that the difficulties of the Kantian "pure physics" become evident.

42. David Joravsky, *Soviet Marxism and Natural Science*, London, 1961, and review article, E. McMullin, *Natural Law Forum*, vol. 8 (1963), pp. 149–159.

43. See L. Graham, *Science and Philosophy in the Soviet Union* (New York, 1972), pp. 156–188, for the material on which this and the following paragraph mainly depend. See also N. Lobkowicz, "Materialism and matter in Marxism-Leninism," *The Concept of Matter in Modern Philosophy*, ed. E. McMullin (Notre Dame, 1978), pp. 154–188.

2

GEORGE GAMOW*

Modern Cosmology

THE SUBJECT OF cosmology is the study of our Universe's general features, its extension in space and its duration in time. With the great 200-inch telescope on Palomar Mountain man today can look over two billion light-years into space and see nearly a billion galaxies, spread more or less uniformly through that vast volume.

It is important to realize that we are looking not only far into distance but also far back in time. For instance, the present-day photograph of the great Andromeda Nebula shows that group of stars as it looked about two million years ago, for it has taken this time for its light to reach us. The most distant galaxies detected by the 200-inch are seen by us in the state in which they were more than two billion years ago.

The view of the Universe that we are seeing at this instant can be represented schematically by a cone-shaped diagram that takes the time factor into account. At the apex of the cone is our own galaxy as it is now; down the surface of the cone are the other galaxies photographed by our telescopes as they were at dates in the past corresponding to their distance from us. A horizontal cross section through the cone would show the Universe as it was at a given date; this is known as a world map.

Theoretical cosmology attempts to correlate the observed facts about the Universe at large with known physical laws and to draw a consistent

*From *Scientific American*, March 1954, Volume 190, No. 3, pp. 55–63. Copyright ©1954 by Scientific American, Inc. All rights reserved.

picture of the Universe's structure in space and its changes in time. In studying the structure we must accept the Copernican point of view and deny to man the honor of a privileged position in the Universe; in other words, we must assume that the structure of space is very much the same in distant regions as it is in the part we can observe. We cannot suppose that our particular neighborhood is specially adorned with beautiful spiral galaxies for the enjoyment of professional and amateur astronomers.

The Paradox of Finite Light

To make clear the nature of the problems with which cosmologists must deal, let us begin with a paradox first pointed out by the German astronomer Heinrich Olbers more than a century ago. If stars are distributed uniformly through space, and if space is infinite, why, he asked, are we not blinded by their light? (Nowadays we must think of space as filled with galaxies, then unknown, but that does not affect the question.) Olbers' argument goes as follows: Suppose we think of space as a series of concentric spheres with ourselves at the center — imagine it as having the structure of an infinitely big onion. Each sphere is larger in radius than the next smaller one by a certain fixed amount; that is, the thickness of the onion layers, or shells, is uniform. Now the volume of each successive shell is greater than that of the next smaller one in proportion to the square of the increase in radius, and the number of galaxies in the shell is larger in the same proportion. On the other hand, the light reaching the center from galaxies farther and farther away decreases in proportion to the square of the increase in radius. Hence the two opposing factors — the increase in the number of galaxies and the reduction in light from each galaxy — cancel out, and we should expect the center to receive the same amount of light from every shell, no matter how near or how far. Therefore in an infinite universe any given point theoretically should receive an infinite amount of light! Actually, of course, the light sources partly screen one another and as a consequence of this interference the illumination could not exceed the surface brightness of an individual star. But this means that our night sky would be as bright as the sun's disk from horizon to horizon! In daytime the sun itself would be practically unnoticeable against the shining background of the galaxies in the heavens.

What is wrong with this reasoning? Early in this century the Swedish astronomer C. V. L. Charlier proposed an ingenious answer to Olbers' paradox. The visible stars in the Milky Way system altogether occupy so negligible a fraction of the sky area, and our galaxy itself is so limited — a droplet in the vast reaches of space — that all the Milky Way's starlight scarcely illuminates the earth at all. And the distances between galaxies are far greater than those between stars in our galaxy. Because of their distance from us and their great dilution in space, the total illumination of our night sky from the billion galaxies within the range of the 200-inch telescope is only a small percentage of the faint light we get from the Milky Way. This still does not invalidate Olbers' argument, if we assume that space is filled with the same density of galaxies for an indefinite distance beyond the range of our telescopes. But Charlier suggested that there may be a limit to this population: that we may be part of a giant cluster of galaxies which is surrounded by empty space at some distance beyond our telescopic range. If this is so, the total illumination at the earth from the cluster would indeed be negligible.

Of course we cannot stop there; we have to assume that there are other giant clusters, and that they are combined in superclusters, and these in turn in super-superclusters, and so on without end. It is apparent, however, that as we take in larger and larger volumes of space, the mean number of galaxies per unit of space becomes smaller and smaller, because of the increasingly large portions of empty space between the clusters and combinations of clusters. Since Olbers' paradox rested on the assumption that the number of galaxies per space unit remains the same no matter how large a volume is considered, Charlier's "hierarchy Universe" neatly solved the puzzle.

Expanding Space

Today we have a more direct answer to Olbers' paradox: namely, the shift toward the red end of the spectrum in the light reaching us from distant galaxies, which weakens or "dims" their light in proportion to their distance from us. The discovery of the red shift has had far more important consequences, however, than merely the solving of old puzzles; it has profoundly changed man's thinking about the cosmos. The chief change was to introduce the notion of the expanding Universe — an idea which has now become firmly established. One should remember that the expanding Universe theory finds support not only in the red shift but also in classical Newtonian mechanics. Because of the gravitational forces between the galaxies, the cosmic system cannot be expected to remain static, just as a tennis ball cannot hang motionless in midair. The system must either contract, under the forces of gravitational attraction, or expand, as the result of some dispersing force overcoming the attraction.

From the observed red shift one can calculate that the galaxies are fleeing from one another with a kinetic energy which is about 50 times as great as the potential energy of gravitational attraction between them. This means that the present expansion of the Universe will never stop, or, in mathematical language, that the expansion of our Universe is hyperbolic. Further, from the observed recession velocity and the distances between the galaxies one can also compute how long ago the Universe began to expand from its original compressed state.

On this basis Edwin P. Hubble and Milton L. Humason calculated a quarter of a century ago that the age of the Universe was 1.8 billion years. Until recently that estimate stood in serious contradiction to the estimates of geologists and astrophysicists, who calculated from the decay of radioactive materials in the earth and from the rate of burning of nuclear fuel by the stars that the Universe must be five billion years old. But the discrepancy was eliminated a little over a year ago when Walter Baade of the Mount Wilson and Palomar Observatories discovered that as a result of new observations the distances between galaxies, and therefore the age calculated on the basis of the red shift, must be multiplied by a factor of 2.8. This correction (2.8 times 1.8) raises the expansion age to five billion years, in perfect agreement with the geological and astrophysical estimates!

Curved Space

So far we have been discussing the properties of the Universe without reference to the so-called relativistic cosmology based on Einstein's general theory of relativity. The essential point of Einstein's general theory is the introduction of the notion of curved space, and the identification of the effect of gravitational forces with the change of free motion of material bodies in a curved non-Euclidean space. After the great success of his theory in predicting the deflection of light rays by the gravitational field around the sun, Einstein proceeded to apply the theory to the Universe as a whole. According to the cosmological principle of uniformity, one should assume that the curvature of space is the same throughout the Universe; in terms of a two-dimensional analogy, our Universe should be round like the surface of a basketball. There are two possible types of curvature for a curved surface: positive and negative. Positive curvature turns inward, like the surface of a ball; negative curvature turns outward, like a western saddle. Between these of course lies the surface of zero curvature, which is perfectly flat.

In complete analogy with these two-dimensional examples, three-dimensional space can be curved positively or negatively, with zero curvature representing ordinary Euclidean space. In Euclidean space the volume of a sphere increases as the cube of its radius. But in a positively curved space the volume increases at a less rapid rate, while in a negatively curved space it increases more rapidly.

Now if the space of our Universe is curved either way, in principle it should be possible to find that out observationally by counting the galaxies within volumes of space of successively greater radius from us. If the number of galaxies increases more slowly or more rapidly than the cube of the distance, this would indicate a positive or a negative curvature. During the past two decades the late E. P. Hubble carried out such counts at the Mount Wilson and Palomar Observatories, but unfortunately with very indefinite results.

The difficulty is that we can expect to find noticeable curvature effects only at very great distances, and we cannot make reliable distance estimates for galaxies so far away. The only way we can judge their distance is by the faintness of their light. But we must also remember that we are looking far back in time. The intrinsic brightness of galaxies may change with time. Consequently we cannot be sure that a distant galaxy which is fainter than another is farther away; it may instead be at a different stage of evolution. Until we know more about evolutionary changes in galaxies, we shall not be able to reach any definite conclusions about the curvature of space from counts of the nebulae.

Models of the Universe

Relativistic cosmology went through several interesting stages. Due to an algebraic error in his calculations, Einstein concluded that the Universe must be static. (This was, of course, before the discovery of the red shift.) The only way to make such an idea work was to introduce some kind of repulsive force to counteract the gravitational one. This force, in contrast to any other known in physics, would have to be assumed to increase with distance. Einstein met this dilemma by introducing into his equations of general relativity the so-called "cosmological term," and that led to the famous spherical Universe — a finite cosmos closed on itself. But Einstein's static model failed to agree with astronomical observations: it was too small to represent the actual Universe.

Soon afterward the Dutch astronomer Willem de Sitter found another possible solution. His model of the Universe, however, turned out to be even less acceptable than Einstein's. It satisfied the equations only if one assumed that space was completely empty and there was no matter whatsoever!

Then in the early 1920s the Russian mathematician Alexander Friedmann noticed the error in Einstein's computation. He showed that with this correction one could get solutions of basic relativistic equations which yielded models of a Universe that changed with time. The matter was further developed by the Belgian cosmologist Georges Lemaître. Associating Friedmann's dynamic Universe with the new red-shift observations of Hubble and Humason, he formulated the theory of the expanding Universe in the form in which we know it now.

Einstein's original equations of a static Universe related its curvature to the mean density of matter in space and to an *ad hoc* cosmological constant. The present dynamic equations of the expanding Universe connect its curvature with two directly observable quantities: the mean density of matter and the rate of expansion. With the observed value of these two quantities one can calculate that the curvature of our Universe is negative, so that space is open and infinite. It bends in the way a western saddle does. The radius of curvature comes out as five billion light-years.

About five years ago an entirely new idea was introduced into theoretical cosmology by the British mathematicians Herman Bondi and Thomas Gold. They started from the assumption that if the Universe is homogeneous in space, it must also be homogeneous in time. This would mean that any region of the Universe must always have looked in the past, and will always look in the future, essentially the same as it looks now. The only way to reconcile this postulate with the well established movement of the galaxies away from one another was to assume that new galaxies are continuously being formed to compensate for the dispersal of the older ones. If new galaxies are being formed, then new matter must be continuously created throughout space. Bondi and Gold calculated that the creation of new matter must proceed at the rate of one hydrogen atom per hour per cubic mile in intergalactic space. This idea of Bondi and Gold was soon extended by the British astronomer Fred Hoyle, who modified the original Einstein equations of general relativity so that they would permit the continuous creation of matter in space.

Besides circumventing the philosophical question as to the "beginning" of the Universe, the Bondi–Gold–Hoyle theory claimed to dispose of the painful discrepancy in the estimates of the age of the Universe that was still troubling astronomers at the time. If new galaxies were continuously being created, the Universe must be populated with galaxies of all ages, from babies to oldsters living on borrowed time. Bondi, Gold and Hoyle assumed that the average age of the population was about one third of the figure of 1.8 billion years that Hubble had arrived at for the total age of the Universe, that is, 600 million years. According to this point of view, since our own galaxy is estimated to be several billion years old, we are living in a rather elderly member of the population.

The recent revision of distances that eliminated the age discrepancy and placed the age of the Universe at five billion years does not disprove the Bondi–Gold–Hoyle theory of a steady-state Universe; it merely raises the average age of galaxies to about 1.7 billion years and makes our own galaxy three times instead of nine times as old as the average. Nevertheless the elimination of the discrepancy does deprive the steady-state idea of its main support. As far as observations go, the weight of the evidence at present is definitely in favor of the idea of an evolving Universe rather than a steady-state one such as is envisioned by Bondi, Gold and Hoyle.

One of the most important recent pieces of evidence was a discovery made in 1948 by the U. S. astronomers Joel Stebbins and Albert E. Whitford. Using light filters of different colors, they measured the reddening of light from distant galaxies, and to their own and everyone else's great surprise they found the reddening to be about 50 per cent greater than could be accounted for by the red shift, or Doppler effect, due to the galaxies' movement away from us.

It is well known that light rays may be reddened by dust, which scatters and screens out the blue part of the light; the dust in the atmosphere is what makes the sun look red at sunrise and sunset. The excess reddening of the distant galaxies was therefore attributed at first to dust floating in intergalactic space. But when the investigators calculated how much dust would have to be present there to produce the observed reddening, they got an astounding result: the dust in intergalactic space would add up to 100 times as much matter as the total amount concentrated in the galaxies themselves! This finding not only contradicted all accepted views about the distribution of matter in the Universe but also played havoc with astronomers' distance scales and the theory of the curvature of space.

Fortunately further studies by Whitford extricated the astronomers from this impasse. To understand them we must look into the composition of galaxies. Baade has shown that there are two kinds of stellar populations: Population I consists predominantly of blue stars, with great clouds of dust and gas floating among them; Population II, mainly redder stars, has no dust or gas whatever. The spiral galaxies are made up largely of Population I, the elliptical ones of Population II. Since interstellar dust and gas afford material for forming new stars, one may assume that spiral galaxies are in a more or less steady state, with newborn stars replacing old ones that are slowly fading out. On the other hand, elliptical galaxies, lacking dust and gas, are producing no new stars to replace the dying population. The two types of communities may be likened respectively to the population of Cambridge, Mass., a dynamic community in which new births replace those who die, and to the Harvard University alumni of the class of 1925, a declining population.

Now Stebbins and Whitford had limited their original observations to elliptical galaxies. In his new studies Whitford included spiral galaxies, located in the same clusters. And he found that the light from the spirals showed no excess reddening! Thus the extra reddening of the light from the elliptical galaxies could not be due to any factor (such as dust) affecting it in its travel through space, since the elliptical and spiral galaxies observed lay side by side the same distance from us. The only possible conclusion was that the excessive redness of the distant elliptical galaxies is due to the fact that we see them now as they were in a distant past when they were intrinsically redder. This finding is one of the strongest evidences in favor of the idea that galaxies are evolving and against the theory of a steady-state Universe.

There are other arguments against that theory. For instance, if our own galaxy is older than the average, we should expect the stars in our system to be older and different from most of those in neighboring galaxies, but no such general difference has been observed. On the whole it appears that the steady-Universe theory, attractive as it may seem from certain philosophical points of view, is neither necessary nor correct.

The Evolving Universe

Returning now to Lemaître's theory of the expanding Universe, let us try to explain how the cosmos evolved from the original highly compressed, very hot gas to stars, galaxies and matter as we know it today. First of all we must consider the relation between matter (represented by particles such as protons, neutrons and electrons) and radiation (represented by light quanta). In classical physics it was customary to regard matter as ponderable and radiation as imponderable, but we know now that radiant energy has mass, which is calculated, according to Einstein's basic law, by dividing the quantity of energy by the square of the velocity of light. On the earth the weight of radiant energy is negligibly small compared to that of matter: the total mass of all the light quanta passing through the atmosphere on a bright, sunny day is less than a thousandth of a millionth of a millionth of a millionth of the weight of the air. Heat radiation is slightly heavier than light, but its weight amounts to only one microgram per 10 billion tons of air in the atmosphere!

In interstellar and intergalactic space the ratio is not so large: the mass of matter there is only about 1,000 times the mass of the stellar radiation. Still, in the Universe as we know it today matter is everywhere more massive than radiation. But it need not always have been so. During the early stages of the Universe's evolution the mass density of radiation must have exceeded that of ordinary matter. The reason for that conclusion, which the writer first suggested several years ago, lies in the different behavior of matter and radiation. Imagine two cylinders, one filled with a material gas, the other a vacuum containing only thermal radiation. Both cylinders are sealed and thermally insulated, and the one containing the radiation has its inner walls made of an ideal mirror which does not absorb radiation. The cylinders have movable pistons. Now we pull the pistons, increasing the volume of space in each cylinder. In the cylinder filled with material gas, the density of the gas will be reduced in direct proportion to the increase in volume. But in the other cylinder, the mass density of the radiation will fall off more sharply, because the energy (and consequently the mass) of each quantum of radiation will be reduced by reflection from the receding piston. The laws of physics tell us the radiation's mass density will decrease in the ratio of 4/3 to the increase in volume.

Applying similar considerations to the Universe as a whole, we arrive at the conclusion that once upon a time in the distant past radiant energy had the upper hand over ordinary matter; there must have been pounds and pounds of light quanta for every ounce of atoms.

A Universe filled almost entirely with thermal radiation presents a rather simple case in the relativistic theory of expanding space. One can show that, starting from the time of maximum compression, all distances will increase in proportion to the square root of the elapsed time, and that the temperature of the radiation will decrease in inverse proportion to the square root of the elapsed time. The temperature of the Universe at any date is equal to 15 billion degrees absolute (degrees Centigrade above absolute zero) divided by the square root of its age expressed in seconds. Thus we get a chronological picture of the "changing climate" of our Universe: at the age of five minutes its mean temperature was about one billion degrees absolute; at one day it was about 40 million degrees (comparable to the temperature at the center of the sun or of an atomic bomb); at 300,000 years it was 6,000 degrees (the temperature at the surface of the sun) and at 10 million years it was 300 degrees (about room temperature).

Computing the mass densities of radiation and of matter at various epochs, we can find the date of the great event when matter took over from radiation, i.e., surpassed it in mass density. The date was about the year 250,000,000 A.B. (After the Beginning). The temperature of space was then about 170 degrees absolute, and the density both of radiation and of matter was comparable with the present density of interstellar gas. The Universe, in short, was dark and cool.

The Genesis of Galaxies

The transition from the reign of thermal radiation to the reign of matter must have been characterized by a very important event: formation of giant gaseous clouds. From these "protogalaxies" the galaxies of today must have developed, somewhat later, by the condensation of gas into individual stars. During the period when matter had played only a secondary role in the infinite ocean of thermal radiation, it had had, so to speak, no will of its own; the particles of matter were "dissolved" in the thermal radiation, much as molecules of salt are dissolved in water. As soon as matter took the upper hand, however, the forces of gravity acting between the particles must have caused a growing inhomogeneity of the matter in space. The English astronomer James Jeans showed more than half a century ago that the size of the clouds into which a gas of particles will be collected by gravitational forces can be calculated from the density and temperature of the spread-out gas. Using Jeans's formula and the transition-period temperature and density values given above, we find that the primordial gas clouds must have been about 40,000 light-years across, and each cloud must have had a total mass about 200 million times that of our sun. These figures, derived purely from theory, are in quite reasonable agreement with the observed figures for the average dimensions and mass of the present galaxies. (The Milky Way and the Andromeda Nebula are considerably larger than the average galaxy.)

The protogalaxies were pulled apart by the general expansion process. Their material later condensed into billions of stars, presumably by repetition on a smaller scale of Jeans's accretion process. Planets were formed, and the Universe again became brightly illuminated, as a result of nuclear reactions taking place in the interiors of the stars. But these "secondary" processes are a topic in themselves, which we shall not discuss in detail here.

The Beginning

Let us now go back to the beginning — the earliest stages of expansion. According to our calculations, when our Universe was five minutes old its temperature was a billion degrees, and it must have been still higher before that. At such temperatures particles move with energies of millions of electron volts — energies comparable with those in modern atom-smashing accelerators. This means that nuclear reactions must have been going on at a high rate all through the matter of the Universe. It is natural to conclude that the chemical elements were formed, in the relative abundances that were to make up the Universe we know, during that early stage of evolution. This assumption is strengthened by the fact that the natural radioactive elements are calculated today, from the extent of decay, to be about five billion years old.

During the first few minutes of the Universe's existence matter must have consisted only of protons, neutrons and electrons, for any group of particles that combined momentarily into a composite nucleus would immediately have dissociated into its components at the extremely high temperature. One can call the mixture of particles *ylem* (pronounced eelem) — the name that Aristotle gave to primordial matter. As the Universe went on expanding and the temperature of ylem dropped, protons and neutrons began to stick together, forming deuterons (nuclei of heavy hydrogen), tritons (still heavier hydrogen), helium and heavier elements.

On the basis of what we know about the behavior of nuclear particles and of the assumptions about the rate of temperature and density changes in the expanding Universe, one can calculate the net result of all the possible nuclear reactions that must have taken place during those early minutes of the Universe' history. The time available for the formation of the elements must have been very short, for two reasons: (1) the free neutrons in the original ylem would have decayed rapidly, and (2) the temperature quickly dropped below the level at which nuclear reactions could take place. The mean life of a neutron is known to be only about 12 minutes; hence half an hour after the expansion had started there would have been practically no neutrons left if they had not been combined in atomic nuclei. Favorable temperature conditions lasted about the same length of time. Thus all the chemical elements must have been formed in that half-hour.

Many people would argue that it makes no physical sense to talk about half an hour which took place five billion years ago. To answer that criticism, let us consider a site, somewhere in Nevada where an atomic bomb was set off several years ago. The site is still "hot" with long-lived fission products. It took only about one microsecond for the nuclear explosion to produce all the fission products. And simple arithmetic will show that a period of several years stands in the same ratio to one microsecond as five billion years do to a half-hour!

Early Matter

Calculations of the rate at which elementary atomic nuclei would have been synthesized under the assumed conditions were carried out by the writer a number of years ago and were later extended by Enrico Fermi and Anthony L. Turkevich. The composite nuclei whose production was estimated were deuterium (a combination of a proton and a neutron), tritium (one proton and two neutrons) and two isotopes of helium. By the end of 30 minutes free neutrons would practically have disappeared, and after that there would be no further change in the relative abundances of these elementary nuclei. At that time the Universe, according to these calculations, would have consisted of roughly equal amounts of hydrogen and helium, and about 1 per cent of the original ylem would have been converted into rare isotopes of hydrogen and helium which could combine to form the nuclei of heavier elements.

Now the fact that the amounts of hydrogen and helium come out approximately equal in these calculations is highly gratifying, because this is just about the relative abundance of these two elements in the Universe today. The results of the calculations give good support to the expansion theory, for it can be shown that the Universe would have emerged from the ylem state consisting practically entirely of hydrogen or entirely of helium if conditions had been much different from those postulated.

Beyond these first two elements, however, the theory runs into a serious and as yet unresolved difficulty. The theory assumes that the light elements combined in successive steps to form the heavier ones. Helium consists of four nucleons (nuclear particles); that is, its atomic mass is four. The next nucleus should have the atomic mass five, but the fact is that no nucleus of mass five exists; at least, none of any appreciable length of life is known. For some reason five nucleons simply do not hold together. After helium 4 the next nucleus is an isotope of lithium of mass six. One must therefore assume that helium was built up to the next nucleus either by the simultaneous capture of two neutrons (an extremely unlikely event) or by fusion with a tritium nucleus. But the rate at which such fusions could have occurred under the given conditions is much too low to account for the amount of heavier elements that was actually produced. No likely reaction that bridges the gap at mass five has yet been found.

Beyond mass five there is little or no trouble; once that gap has been bridged, one can account quite satisfactorily for the relative abundances of the elements from lithium up through the periodic table to uranium, as has been shown by calculations carried out by the writer, Ralph A. Alpher and Robert C. Herman. If no way is found to bridge the gap, we may have to conclude that the main bulk of the heavier elements was formed not in the early stages of the Universe's expansion but some time later, perhaps in the interiors of fantastically hot stars.

The Explosion

A theory which suggests that our Universe started from an extremely compressed concentration of matter and radiation naturally raises the question: How did it get into that state, and what made it expand? In his original version of the expanding Universe Lemaître visualized the beginning as a giant "primordial atom" which exploded because of violent radioactive decay processes. But this conception is quite out of keeping with the picture of early evolution that we have arrived at. The young Universe must have consisted almost exclusively of high-temperature thermal radiation, and atoms, radioactive or not, could have played only a negligible role in its behavior.

A much more satisfactory answer can be obtained by considering the operation in reverse of those same relativistic formulae that we have used to describe the expansion process. The formulae tell us that various parts of the Universe are flying apart with an energy exceeding the forces of Newtonian attraction between them. Extrapolating these formulae to the period before the Universe reached the stage of maximum contraction, we find that the Universe must then have been collapsing, with just as great speed as it is now expanding!

Thus we conclude that our Universe has existed for an eternity of time, that until about five billion years ago it was collapsing uniformly from a state of infinite rarefaction; that five billion years ago it arrived at a state of maximum compression in which the density of all its matter may have been as great as that of the particles packed in the nucleus of an atom (*i.e.*, 100 million million times the density of water), and that the Universe is now on the rebound, dispersing irreversibly toward a state of infinite rarefaction.

Such motion is hyperbolic; it can be compared with the motion of a comet, which does not revolve around the sun as planets do but comes in from the infinity of space (in certain cases), sails around the sun in a bent path, developing a beautiful tail, and vanishes into infinity again without promise of return.

Before the Beginning

Any inquisitive person is bound to ask: "What was the Universe like while it was collapsing?" One might give a metaphysical answer in the words of Saint Augustine of Hippo, who wrote in his *Confessions*: "Some people say that before He made Heaven and Earth, God prepared Gehenna for those who have the hardihood to inquire into such high matters."

More recently a mathematical–physical answer was given by the Japanese physicist Chushiro Hayashi, and his idea has been elaborated by Alpher, Herman and James W. Follin of the Applied Physics Laboratory at The Johns Hopkins University. Considering the known facts about the behavior of fundamental particles, they came to the conclusion that the present chemical composition of the Universe is quite independent of its constitution before the state of maximum collapse. Transformations of particles must have occurred so rapidly during that state that the outcome was determined entirely by the conditions at the time rather than by what had gone on before.

Thus from the physical point of view we must forget entirely about the pre-collapse period and try to explain all things on the basis of facts which are no older than five billion years — plus or minus five per cent.

3

W. B. BONNOR*

Relativistic Theories of the Universe

UNTIL ABOUT THIRTY years ago it was possible to picture the universe as a static collection of stars and nebulae. There was no scientific reason to believe that it had ever undergone any significant change. The discovery that the universe was expanding meant that this simple view had to be given up, and the theories of cosmology which followed suggested that the past and future of the universe must be very different from the present.

The cosmological theories which have found widespread acceptance are those based on the general theory of relativity, and it is this view of the universe I shall discuss. Cosmology here tries to deal scientifically with some of the great issues which have in the past fallen in the domain of speculative philosophy — among them the origin of the universe. Some scientists have maintained that relativistic cosmology implies an act of creation in the finite past. This view I regard as mistaken, and I think it arises from defects in the theories which it is our duty to correct. There is one contemporary cosmology — the steady-state theory of Bondi, Gold, and Hoyle — in which, although creation occurs, it appears in a less unsatisfactory way. The final decision between this theory and those following from general relativity must await more precise observations.

Cosmology is built on two main observed phenomena. First, observations of the distant nebulae (or galaxies, as they are now often called)

*Reprinted from pp. 1–11 of *Rival Theories of Cosmology* by H. Bondi, W. B. Bonnor, R. A. Lyttleton, and G. J. Whitrow (1960), by permission of Oxford University Press.

show that the light we receive from them is redder than that from similar matter in our immediate neighbourhood. This we call the red-shift. The interpretation of this by ordinary physics — called the Doppler effect — is that the nebulae are receding from us at speeds proportional to the magnitudes of their red-shifts.

The second observation of fundamental importance is that the distribution of the nebulae seems to be, on a large scale, the same in all directions of space. This supports an assumption made, in one form or another, by all cosmological theories, and known as the Cosmological Principle. In the cosmology of general relativity, the principle asserts that, at a given time, observers like ourselves on other nebulae would see essentially the same picture of the universe as we do. In making this assumption we ignore local irregularities and think of the universe only on a grand scale.

The Cosmological Principle seems at first sight to conflict with our interpretation of the red-shift — that the nebulae are all receding from our own Milky Way. One might think that this recession implies that we are at the centre of the universe. One of the surprising results of cosmological theory is that there is no contradiction here. Every cosmic observer sees a similar recession of the nebulae, and we are no more at the centre of the universe than our counterparts on other nebulae. The recession of the nebulae is usually known as the expansion of the universe. In general relativity we prefer to think of space itself expanding and carrying the nebulae with it — like leaves in the wind — and not of nebulae moving away from each other through passive and indifferent emptiness. This is not merely a difference of words: the active role of space in dynamics is one of the main ideas which Einstein brought to physics when he created general relativity.

To tackle any physical problem in general relativity, such as the history of the universe, we have to find an appropriate solution of Einstein's field equations. For cosmology much of the basic work was done between 1917 and 1930 by de Sitter, Friedmann, Lemaître, and Eddington. The field equations do not give a unique answer to the cosmological problem, and there is a large number of solutions, all candidates to describe the actual universe. Each solution is called a model of the universe.

This plethora of world-models is something of an embarrassment to the relativistic theory, and it will be a great relief when a decision between them is reached by observation — as it almost certainly will be within the next decade or so. However, the abundance of relativistic models is not nearly as great as is sometimes thought, provided we rule out those which owe their existence to the notorious cosmological term inserted into the field equations by Einstein in 1917.

At that time nothing was known of the expansion of the universe, and Einstein added the cosmological term to obtain a static world-model.

Later it became clear that the original, unaltered field equations were quite capable of describing an expanding universe, and the cosmological term was no longer necessary. In fact, Einstein himself then abandoned it, and confined his attention to the much simpler models which arise as solutions of the original field equations. This is the best course on grounds of simplicity and economy of hypothesis, and the one which I think we should continue to adopt.

If we agree to abandon the cosmological constant, the more plausible models are of two types. The first type predicts that the expansion will continue for ever: the nebulae which we see will get fainter and fainter, and the average density of matter in the universe will continually diminish. According to the second type of model, the expansion is slowing down fairly rapidly, and will eventually change to a contraction. If this is correct, the distant nebulae will one day approach the Earth instead of receding from it, and to observers of that time the light from them will appear more violet than the corresponding terrestrial light, instead of redder. The prospect of this contraction need cause no anxiety, as it would not begin to happen for many thousands of millions of years.

According to the models of either type, the expansion started about 8,000 million years ago. We can, from the models, estimate the average density of matter in the universe at any given time. We find that this density becomes greater and greater as we go backwards in time towards the moment the expansion started. At that moment itself, the density is infinite. The models suggest no way in which this infinite density could have come about; they give no information about what the universe was like before the expansion started. The trail we have been following seems to come to a dead end.

It is for this reason that the start of the expansion is sometimes called the creation of the universe. The conclusion to be drawn from the failure of the models is, it is argued, that all matter, compressed to an enormous density, was created at this time. At the same moment some sort of explosion took place, and the expansion started.

This view I regard as highly misleading and unscientific. The difficulty to be faced is that at the start of the expansion certain quantities in our differential equations become infinite. This frequently happens with differential equations, and when it does the equation is said to contain a mathematical singularity. A singularity in the mathematics describing a physical problem is usually an indication of the breakdown of the theory, and the physicist's normal response is to try to get a better one.

This procedure has not generally been followed in cosmology, and some scientists have identified the singularity at the start of the expansion with God, and thought that at this moment he created the universe. It seems to me highly improper to introduce God to solve our

scientific problems. There is no place in science for miraculous inter-
ventions of this sort; and there is a danger, for those who believe in
God, in identifying him with singularities in differential equations, lest
the need for him disappear with improved mathematics.

To me the correct approach seems to be to admit that the present
cosmological models become unsatisfactory if one extrapolates them
back the 8,000 million years or so to the start of the expansion. This is
not to say that they are inadequate to describe the present, and the
immediate past and future; this they are probably capable of doing. But
they have to be altered so that they no longer become singular in the
distant past.

The first obvious difficulty here is that 8,000 million years is a very
long time, and anything we say about what the universe was like then is
bound to be tentative, to say the least of it. Cosmology here meets the
usual problems of any historical research concerned with the remote
past. Some physicists think that the extrapolations involved are so
enormous and the conclusions therefore so uncertain that the entire
activity is a waste of time. There is something to be said for this view,
but my argument against it is that to most people the past history of the
universe is such an exciting matter that it is worth speculating about.

Secondly, even if we suppose that the infinite density given by our
equations is a mathematical fiction with no physical meaning, it is
probable that there *was* a period of very high density and temperature
about 8,000 million years ago. This would be consistent with observed
facts, which suggest that the age of our own nebula is somewhere about
this figure. It is reasonable to suppose that after the period of intense
heat, the nebulae, including our own, formed as the universe cooled.
The effect of this period would be to obliterate evidence of what the
universe was like before the expansion started. Any relics of a previous
epoch would have been reduced to the uniformity of a gas, or even a
fluid of atomic particles. For this reason there is little hope of obtaining
by direct observations any information about the epochs before the
expansion. We have to proceed by more indirect inference. Here the
situation is more hopeful. I will describe some possible lines of attack,
with special reference to models of the second type. According to these
models the contraction, when it sets in, will eventually gather speed,
bringing the nebulae closer and closer together; and if we follow the
models to their end they reach a condition of infinite density — in fact,
a singular state like the one in which they began. If one is prepared to
regard the first singularity as the creation, the second presumably
represents the annihilation of the universe.

In my opinion it is more satisfactory to suppose that as the singular
state is approached some mechanism starts to operate which slows
down the contraction and ultimately reverses it. The universe is thus
launched on an expanding phase again, and starts a new cycle of exis-

tence. According to this picture, the history of the universe is an unending series of oscillations.

I want to explain two possible mechanisms for reversing the contraction. The first is suggested by a peculiar feature of the theory of relativity. According to Newton's theory the force of gravitation between two bodies is a function of their masses and their distance apart. In general relativity, however, the gravitational field of a body depends not only on its mass but also on the way it is stressed. A thrust or pressure augments the ordinary Newtonian gravitational force, but a tension reduces it. In fact, a body in a sufficiently high state of tension could exert a negative gravitational force — that is to say, a repulsion. A repulsion between particles of matter is just what is needed to reverse the final contraction of the universe. The difficulty is that matter in a gaseous form — such as one would expect to fill the universe at that time — can exert pressure but not tension. However, matter may show unexpected properties at the high temperature and density which must then prevail. We have little information about this at present, but further knowledge of the behaviour of matter in extreme conditions — such as those inside the stars — may help to decide whether this mechanism is feasible or not.

Another possible way in which the contraction might be reversed is revealed by some interesting recent work by Professor Heckmann of Hamburg. Heckmann supposes that the matter in the universe has a slight rotation. It then seems that the centrifugal force of this rotation is enough to reverse the contraction when the universe becomes very dense at the end of one of its oscillations. In cosmological theories until now it has always been supposed that there is no cosmic rotation, because none has been observed. However, Heckmann has shown that even a slight rotation, such as would be undetectable at present, would be sufficient to prevent the state of infinite density.

These suggestions are tentative, and it may be that neither is correct. Even if we can show definitely that some such mechanism would reverse the expansion, there are difficulties to be overcome. For example if the history of the universe is an infinite series of oscillations, we shall have to look carefully again at the Second Law of Thermodynamics; this law has often been thought to mean that the universe is gradually using up its mechanical energy and converting it irrevocably into heat. This would amount to a sort of running down of the universe, rather as a watch runs down as it uses up the mechanical energy stored in its spring. The idea of an unending series of equal expansions and contractions is evidently inconsistent with this view. However, it would be wrong to take this too seriously, because it has never been properly shown how the Second Law of Thermodynamics affects the universe as a whole.

There are undoubtedly many difficulties in explaining the start of the expansion. But what I want to emphasize is that this is a matter for scientific investigation, though by indirect and tentative methods. There is no reason whatever for downing tools and handing over to God 8,000 million years ago.

I have been describing cosmological theories founded on general relativity. The steady-state theory, which I referred to earlier, escapes the problem of the start of the expansion. This theory uses the basic ideas of relativity, but modifies Einstein's field equations. According to the steady-state model the universe, considered on a large scale, has always been much the same as it is now: in particular, the average density of matter does not change with the time. However, the observed recession of the nebulae implies a falling density, and this fact can be reconciled with an unchanging universe only if fresh matter appears to keep the density constant. The steady-state theory proposes that this fresh matter is being continually created out of nothing in empty space. The rate of creation is supposed to be very low, and below the limit of detection by present techniques of measurement.

Although the steady-state theory has no problem of singularities in the finite past, it suffers from one defect so serious that, in my opinion, it is hardly to be considered as an important rival to the relativistic theories. Since matter is a form of energy, the creation of matter out of nothing violates the principle of the conservation of energy. This principle has withstood all the revolutions in physics in the last sixty years, and most physicists would be prepared to give it up only if the most compelling reasons were presented. In fact, when the steady-state theory was originated, about ten years ago, the case for a drastic measure of this sort was rather strong. It then seemed that there was a discrepancy between the predictions of relativistic cosmology and observation. It has since turned out that the observations were wrong, and the relativistic theories are now in satisfactory agreement with the present empirical evidence.

The view I have been putting forward is that the universe has an unlimited past and future. This may seem in some ways as puzzling as if its history were finite. From the scientific aspect, however, this point is really one of methodology. Science should never voluntarily adopt hypotheses which restrict its scope. Sometimes restrictions are obligatory, as for example in the case of the Uncertainty Principle, which restricts the accuracy of certain physical measurements, but unless it is shown that such limitations apply to cosmology we should, I think, assume that our knowledge of the universe can stretch indefinitely into the past and into the future.

4

H. BONDI*

The Steady-State Theory of the Universe

IN COSMOLOGY, ONE is considering an extrapolation of physics as we know it here to a very much larger scale of phenomenon. What we have learnt in the laboratory is to be applied to the universe at large. Clearly, there are dangers and difficulties in making such an enormous extrapolation. Therefore, it may well be in place to discuss the underlying method — the method of scientific progress — on which all our work is based.

By far the most successful analysis of scientific method is due to Professor Karl Popper. In his view, which I regard as amply borne out by actual scientific procedure, hypotheses are formed in the minds of scientists in a way that is not wholly clear because undoubtedly a substantial element of imagination is involved. The purpose of a theory is to make forecasts that can be checked against observation and experiment. A scientific theory is one that it is in principle possible to disprove by empirical means. It is this supremacy of empirical disproof that distinguishes science from other human activities. We can never regard a theory as proved, because all we can say is that, so far, there have been no experiments contradicting it. A scientific theory, to be useful, must be testable and vulnerable. Cosmology, fortunately, must now be considered to be a science. It is a subject, like any other scientific subject, in which there are means of disproving theoretical forecasts by experiment and observation. It is true that most of these

*Reprinted from pp. 12–21 of *Rival Theories of Cosmology* by H. Bondi, W. B. Bonnor, R. A. Lyttleton, and G. J. Whitrow (1960), by permission of Oxford University Press.

are still rather difficult to make and require expensive equipment and great skill, but this is the way in which we shoot down cosmological theories.

If we now come back to the point I made first, about the enormous extrapolation required in order to apply laboratory physics to the universe at large, then we are immediately up against the question: can we really suppose that physical processes go on elsewhere as they do in our neighbourhood? Clearly, the answer to this question will depend on whether we are in a very special place in the universe or whether ours is a typical one. If our position in the universe in space and time is typical, then we can feel confident that our locally acquired knowledge is applicable elsewhere. If, on the other hand, the universe were very different elsewhere or at other times from what it is here and now, then we would need to know which aspects of our physical knowledge were truly permanent and which of them had just caught a mood of the moment of the universe. If we assume that all the physics we know is unchangeable, although the universe is changing, then we make a possible but quite arbitrary assumption.

Of course, it may be necessary to consider the very difficult problems of the variation of physics in a varying universe; but before we enter the enormous complication of this question, we first try to see whether our universe might not happen to be one that is the same everywhere and at all times when viewed on a sufficiently large scale. In examining this possibility, we by no means claim that this must be the case; but we do say that this is so straightforward a possibility that it should be disproved before we begin to consider more complicated situations.

We are thus led to consider a model of the universe which is uniform on a large scale, both in space and in time. This model is known as the steady-state model. It is a useful model because in it we can be sure that physics, as we know it here, applies everywhere else. Moreover, as I shall explain later in this talk, it is a model that makes many forecasts that can be checked by experiment and observation. Therefore, it is a testable and, accordingly, a useful scientific theory. It follows immediately from the assumptions of the steady-state theory that the universe must be expanding, for otherwise, as a simple argument shows, we would be drowned by a flood of light from the most distant regions. In order to be consistent with the assumption of uniformity the motion of expansion must be such that there is a velocity of recession proportional to distance. The effect of the recession will then prevent the flood of light. This indeed is the type of motion that is being observed.

Next, if we have such a motion, then it would seem at first sight that the mean density in the universe must be diminishing, because if the distances between the galaxies are increasing all the time, it follows that the same matter now fills a larger volume. However, this would be in flagrant contradiction with the postulate that the universe is the same at all times. The only way out of this difficulty is to suppose that there is a process of continual creation going on — a process by which, in the enormous spaces between the galaxies, new matter constantly appears. This new matter condenses and forms new galaxies to fill the increasing spaces between the older ones.

Furthermore, every star ages since it converts hydrogen into helium in order to supply the energy the star radiates into space. As each star in the galaxy goes through these changes, the galaxy itself ages. However, the *average* age of galaxies is kept down since new galaxies constantly form in the increasing spaces between the old ones. It is for this reason, in order to keep the average age constant, that we require the new matter to be laid down in the vast intergalactic spaces. Only in this way can new galaxies be formed so that the average distance between galaxies stays constant, although, because of the expansion of the universe, the distance between existing galaxies is all the time increasing. Old galaxies, as they move farther and farther away, become less and less observable.

The whole picture of the steady-state universe is, therefore, very much like a picture of a stationary human population. Each individual is born, grows up, grows old and dies, but the average age stays the same owing to the fact that, all the time, new individuals are being born. We have, in the steady-state theory, a very similar picture of the universe of galaxies. Old galaxies die by drifting into regions where they are harder and harder to observe, and new galaxies are formed all the time in the spaces between the old ones. In this way, we arrive at a universe that is on the large scale uniform and unchanging. Moreover, it is the only model of this type. Of course, it deviates from ordinary physics in assuming this phenomenon of continual creation of matter which is, indeed, a major infringement of present formulations of physics. Dr. Bonnor has argued that this process of continual creation violates the principle of conservation of energy which has withstood all the revolutions in physics in the last sixty years and which most physicists would be prepared to give up only if the most compelling reasons were presented; but this seems to me to be unsound. The principle of conservation of mass and energy, like all physical principles, is based on observation. These observations, like all experiments and observations, have a certain measure of inaccuracy in them. We do not know from the laboratory experiments that matter is absolutely conserved; we only know that it is conserved to within a very small margin. The simplest formulation of this experimental result seems to be to claim that matter must be absolutely conserved. But this is purely a mathematical abstraction from certain observational results that may contain, indeed are bound to contain, errors.

Now, in fact, the mean density in the universe is so low, and the time scale of the universe is so large, by comparison with terrestrial circumstances, that the process of continual creation required by the steady-state theory predicts the creation of only one hydrogen atom in a space the size of an ordinary living-room once every few million years. It is quite clear that this process, therefore, is in no way in conflict with the experiments on which the principle of the conservation of matter and energy is based. It is only in conflict with what was thought to be the simplest formulation of these experimental results, namely that matter and energy were precisely conserved. The steady-state theory has shown, however, that much simplicity can be gained in cosmology by the alternative formulation of a small amount of continual creation, with conservation beyond that. This may, therefore, be the formulation with the greatest overall simplicity. There is thus no reason whatever, on the basis of any available evidence, to put the steady-state theory out of court because it requires this process of continual creation. This would be indeed a prejudice, and not a scientific argument.

Finally, as I said at the beginning, we must see how testable this theory is. How many forecasts does it make that can be checked by observation and experiment? There is a whole class of observations based on a very simple consideration. When we see the most distant galaxies that we can observe, then we look at them, not as they are now, but as they were a long time ago, for the light that travelled from them to us took a long time to cover the distance between them and us.

In the case of the most distant galaxies visible in optical telescopes this time is probably around 5,000,000,000 years. If the universe as a whole is evolving in the way Bonnor suggested in the last talk, then, presumably, all the galaxies originated at more or less the same time. In particular, we can definitely say that in such a universe no galaxies originated very recently. According to relativistic theories, then, we see the distant galaxies at an earlier stage in their evolution than the near ones which we see as they are now, more or less. Therefore, one would expect some variations with distance in the appearance of the galaxy, or the colour of light that it sends out, or in the degree of clustering, or possibly in the likelihood that it is a strong emitter of radio waves observable by radio astronomy. Accordingly, if one looks out into space and compares the shapes of distant galaxies with those of near galaxies, or compares in the same manner any other of the characteristics I mentioned, then either one will or one will not find a variation with distance. On the basis of the steady-state theory, time does not matter. A long time ago the universe looked just the same as it does now. Accordingly, no such variation can occur in the picture of the steady-state theory. In the evolutionary pictures one would expect precisely such a variation. Therefore, if these observations are made and any variation is found, then the steady-state theory is stone dead. If no such variation is found, it does not necessarily mean that the evolutionary theories are wrong, because one can always say that the period of time into which we can look back is too short for any such changes to show themselves. Some such observations are within the range of existing equipment, or equipment now in process of being built. Indeed, from the point of view of the steady-state theory we have the very satisfactory situation that although two different observations of this type have been claimed to disprove the steady-state theory, in both cases it has since been shown that they involved far greater observational errors than had originally been believed. In one case the absence of any such variation has now been established, in the other no definite conclusions can be drawn at present. However, many of these tests may be practicable in the near future.

Next, I want to come to a point of great significance. Most physicists think that all elements were built up from hydrogen by some means or other. In the case of helium, it has been known for years that ordinary stars convert hydrogen into helium. But for a long time it was believed that, in order to make the elements heavier than helium, conditions of density and temperature were required such as could not be found anywhere in the universe as we know it now, not even in the centres of the stars. Dr. Bonnor, in his talk, referred to early stages of high density in the relativistic models. This led to the idea that the birthplace of the heavy elements was this primeval state of the universe. Naturally, we cannot have any such explanation in the steady-state theory. If there ever was a time when it was possible to synthesize heavy elements from hydrogen, then it must be possible to do so now. Everything that ever went on in the universe must, according to the steady-state theory, go on now. It therefore became a crucial question for the steady-state theory whether, in fact, the heavy elements were being synthesized now, contrary to the view held at one time. Inspired by the steady-state theory, such a search has indeed been going on, and has been entirely successful. We now know that, contrary to the earlier views, the heavy elements are synthesized at present in many reasonably common stars, and that these later burst, and so distribute the elements produced in their centres throughout space. In this way, a theory has been created that is remarkably accurate in accounting for the abundances of the elements. This theory is one of the great achievements of modern physics. Indeed, it is fair to say that, in the twelve years of its existence, the steady-state theory, by inspiring this work, has done more for physics than relativistic cosmology has done in thirty-five years. There are numerous other tests which I shall not describe now. Enough has happened in the twelve years that this theory has existed to show that it gives us a useful way of looking at the universe, a way that inspires new observations and is vulnerable to them.

5

MARTIN REES*

The 13,000,000,000 Year Bang

THE ACCELERATED ADVANCE of astronomy in the past 20 years has been due primarily to the exploitation of new parts of the electromagnetic spectrum—particularly the radio and X-ray bands. Our view of the cosmos is less biassed and incomplete than it was when one could study only the objects which shine in visible light, and has led to the concepts of pulsars, quasars, neutron stars, black holes and the "big bang". Perhaps the most extraordinary development of all has been the emergence of cosmology as a genuine observational science: there is now a general consensus that the Universe evolved from a primordial state of high density, and events that might have occurred within the first minutes of cosmic history are within the accepted framework of serious scientific discussion.

The expansion of the Universe was discovered in the 1920s, and by 1956 there was a large body of evidence that the galaxies were receding from each other at speeds proportional to their distance. It also seemed that, broadly speaking, the Universe was uniform and homogeneous, and that our Galaxy was not in any privileged position. The most straightforward inference is that the Universe was in some sense smaller at earlier epochs, and that about 10 billion (10^{10}) years ago all the galaxies were compressed together. But the advocates of the "steady state" theory contested this conclusion: they argued that the large scale structure of the Universe could be the same at all times,

*This article first appeared in *New Scientist*, London, the weekly review of science and technology: Vol. 72, No. 1029, 2 December 1976, pp. 512–515.

continuous creation of new material (and new galaxies) maintaining the Universe at the same mean density despite the overall expansion.

To discriminate decisively between an evolving and steady state Universe, one must observe objects so far away that their radiation has taken several billion years on its journey towards us; and the obvious difficulty is that ordinary galaxies at these distances are almost undetectably faint even with the use of a 200-inch telescope.

The importance of radio astronomy for cosmology first became evident in 1954, when Cygnus A — one of the most prominent features of the radio sky — was identified with a distant galaxy. This suggested that many detectable radio sources were so far away that their optical counterparts would be invisibly faint, and therefore that the radio astronomer could perhaps probe deeper into space (and so further back into the past) than his optical colleagues. It was claimed in the late 1950s and 1960s that the relative number of faint (and presumably distant) radio sources was too high to be consistent with a steady state cosmology but indicated that the Universe was evolving: the number of powerful radio sources was higher in the past when the galaxies were younger.

Later developments have vindicated this interpretation, but the radio data are sufficiently ambiguous that the controversy might well have continued to the present day if no other corroborating evidence had emerged. But the consensus really swung towards acceptance of a "big bang" cosmology after the discovery (in 1965) of the 2.7 K *microwave background* radiation. This radiation is generally interpreted as a relic of an early epoch when all the material in the Universe was as hot, dense and opaque as the interior of a star — the "primordial fireball". No plausible alternative theory seems able to account for the observed isotropy (independence of direction), energy content, and spectral distribution of this radiation (which has now been observed by more than 20 groups at a wide range of wavelengths).

This development was fully as important for cosmology as the discovery of the universal expansion. By the end of the 1960s, almost all cosmologists had come to accept the idea that the background radiation was a genuine survivor from the very early stages of an evolving big bang Universe. (The shift in opinion was rather similar to the changing attitude of geophysicists towards continental drift during the same decade.)

The microwave photons detected on Earth have been propagating uninterruptedly through space for 99.99 per cent of the time since the big bang — since long before galaxies could have existed in anything like their present form. The fact that the radiation apparently has the same temperature in all directions with a precision of one in a 1000 provides direct evidence that the Universe on a large scale is exceedingly homogeneous (it looks the same from all points) and isotropic (it looks the same in all directions from each point). This is a most remarkable circumstance — one might have thought that a chaotic early Universe would have more degrees of freedom open to it, and thus in some sense be more likely. Thus uniformity restricts the admissible description of the Universe to a very limited range of mathematically calculable models. Were this not so, progress in cosmology would be almost inconceivable.

If one assumed that the Universe were isotropic and almost homogeneous right back to the very early times, and assumed also that Einstein's general relativity is applicable, it would be possible to calculate the chemical composition of the material emerging from the big bang; and it is widely regarded as one of the triumphs of the theory that it enables us to predict that this material will be 25 per cent helium and 75 per cent hydrogen. The relevant nuclear reactions all occurred during the first 100 seconds or so of the explosion. This result is happily in accordance with present observations and solves a long-standing problem in theories of nucleogenesis: because, whereas the heavier elements can perhaps be adequately explained by nucleosynthetic processes associated with stellar evolution, it was for a long while a problem to explain the high abundance and relative uniformity of helium.

When Quasars Were Nearby

The discovery in 1963 of the first quasars was another key step, for it enabled astronomers to observe objects with redshifts larger than the faintest detectable galaxies. If these redshifts were indeed due to the universal expansion, this implied that quasars were much more luminous than ordinary galaxies, and raised the hope that optical astronomers could use them to discriminate more successfully between rival cosmologies. However, the intrinsic brightness of the quasars seemed to vary a great deal and even now — when several hundred are known — they still cannot provide anything beyond crude statistical evidence.

The most dramatic inference from these studies is that the Universe is by no means in a steady state, but that the density of quasars and powerful radio sources would have been thousands of times higher then than at the present time. At that epoch the Universe was less than a quarter of its present age. A hypothetical astronomer observing only two billion years after the big bang would perceive a vastly more active and dramatic environment: whereas our nearest bright quasar, 3C 273, is about 2000 million light years distant, he would be likely to find a similar object only 40 million light years away — 50 times closer — and appearing as bright as a fourth magnitude star. This evidence is crucially important to our understanding of how galaxies form and evolve.

When quasars were discovered, they were regarded as something qualitatively quite different from anything hitherto known. There was thus a general readiness to consider that they might involve some kind of "new physics", or that their redshifts might be due to something other than the universal expansion. This opinion has been repeatedly voiced by some astronomers, the controversy being fuelled by regular claims of peculiar effects and anomalies: systematic periodicities in the redshift distribution, physical association between quasars and nearby galaxies, and so on. Although the case for "anomalous redshifts" is still propounded, it cannot be said to have strengthened. Indeed the emphasis of the arguments seems to change year by year: the early anomalies or correlations are generally not borne out by analyses of newer and more extensive data (or even turn out to be mere artefacts); but new effects turn up to replace them. Nor do the various anomalies mesh together into any coherently-formulated alternative picture.

Probably even fewer astronomers would have accepted the idea that quasars were nearby if quasars had been discovered later than they were. We are now aware that many galactic nuclei contain non-stellar energy sources which seem to differ from quasars only in degree and not in kind. Such objects had not been investigated in 1963. Also, the discovery of neutron stars (in 1967) and, perhaps, of stellar-mass black holes has familiarised astrophysicists with the idea that a compact object can be powered by gravitational energy, which can be more efficient than nuclear energy in converting rest-mass into non-stellar radiant energy.

An increasingly plausible hypothesis is that radio galaxies, Seyfert galaxies, and probably quasars as well, are varied manifestations of the same general kind of violent activity in galactic nuclei. Among the suggested models proposed to explain this general phenomenon are that one is seeing a rapid succession of supernova-type explosions, resulting in the formation of a million Crab Nebulae almost in unison. Alternatively it has been speculated that a single magnetised supermassive spinning object may be involved, which accelerates particles rather like a giant pulsar. A third possibility is that a massive black hole lurks in the centre of these galaxies, which accretes gas from its surroundings rather like a scaled-up version of the X-ray source Cygnus X-1.

All these ideas invoke gravitation or gravitational contraction as the primary energy source. But it is still an entirely open question which of these three alternatives (if any) is more likely to be correct. Our best observational line of attack on this problem will involve detailed optical studies of quasars and the variable central regions of active galaxies; and investigations of the structure of compact radio sources by the technique of very long baseline interferometry.

Accepting that the Universe exploded from an initial "big bang", one might wonder whether it will go on expanding for ever. Or will the cosmic recession eventually halt? If it does, it will be succeeded by a phase in which the galaxies draw closer to each other (displaying blue shifts instead of redshifts), until they eventually collide and coalesce, their contents being finally engulfed in a universal fireball like the one from which they originally emerged.

In the simplest cosmological theories, where general relativity is assumed and the so-called "cosmical constant" is taken to be zero, the answer to this question just depends on the present average density of material in the Universe. If this exceeds a critical density of about 1 atom per cubic metre, then the deceleration is sufficient to cause eventual recollapse: if the density is lower, gravitational effects can never halt the expansion.

The masses of individual galaxies are rather uncertain. (There is, for instance, a lively current debate about whether the bulk of a galaxy's mass may actually be in an extensive "halo" too faint to show up on ordinary photographs.) However, even if we allow for this possibility, and also include enough "missing mass" in clusters of galaxies to make them gravitationally bound, one still falls short of the critical density by a factor of about 10. Nor, apparently, can intergalactic gas contribute the "critical" density without producing absorption, or X-ray background emission, in excess of that observed. There might, however, be a lot of stuff in intercluster space in some even more elusive form than diffuse gas (for example massive black holes or neutrinos): absence of evidence need not be evidence of absence!

Indirect evidence for a low-density (or "open") Universe — one which will expand for ever — comes from the recent discovery that deuterium (heavy hydrogen) exists in interstellar space. Ultraviolet observations have revealed it in atomic form, and radio astronomers have detected deuterated molecules in interstellar clouds. Deuterium, having a rather delicate nucleus, is destroyed (rather than synthesised) in ordinary stars. During the last few years, theorists have tried hard to think of ways of synthesising deuterium. It turns out that deuterium can be formed in the big bang. However the amount that survives is (unlike the amount of helium) sensitive to the density; and only a "low density" big bang produces enough. So far, nobody has thought of a plausible way of making deuterium by current astrophysical processes. This may mean that the theorists have not been ingenious enough. On the other hand, it may be a genuine argument in favour of an "open" Universe. (However there are, as in most cosmological arguments, some "escape clauses" which may appeal to those with an agoraphobic predilection for a closed Universe — for instance, the deuterium could be produced primordially to a "non-standard" closed model if the missing mass took the form of small black holes which already existed at the epoch of element formation.)

Helium and deuterium are the only important substances (other than hydrogen) that are believed to be relics of the "primordial fireball".

Other chemical elements are believed to have been synthesised in stars. All the carbon, oxygen, iron, and other elements on Earth may have been produced in stars, formed early in galactic history, which perhaps completed their lives by exploding as supernovae. The Solar System then condensed, several billion years after the Galaxy first formed, from material already contaminated by debris from such explosions.

Most of these ideas, and much of the relevant nuclear physics, had already been developed in the 1950s. The steady state theory actually provided a powerful impetus to these developments, because in this theory nucleosynthesis could not be relegated to a mysterious early epoch where conditions were different, but had to be going on in some present-day astrophysical environment. (Indeed, some people might regard the concept of stellar nucleosynthesis as the most constructive legacy of the steady state theory.)

How Galaxies Evolved

Another major problem has been galactic evolution. How and when did galaxies condense from primordial material? How is their gas content converted into stars? As a galaxy ages, how does it change its size and shape? What factors determine whether a protogalaxy becomes a spiral or an elliptical galaxy? Perhaps the major goal of optical and ultraviolet astronomy in the next decade will be to probe as deep as possible into space and accumulate data on all types of galaxies at various redshifts. By 1980 improved ground-based optical telescopes, the large space telescope, and X-ray telescopes should be contributing valuably to these studies by looking to greater distances and detecting emission from hot uncondensed gas in clusters of galaxies, and quasars at large redshifts.

Theorists hope that the physical principles governing the gross properties of galaxies will soon be understood to the same extent that we now understand the properties of individual stars. One would hope also to understand what makes the nuclei of galaxies (particularly young galaxies) undergo the violent activity which manifests itself in quasars, radio outbursts and the like.

The existence of galaxies implies that the early Universe cannot have been completely smooth, but must have contained some irregularities. Regions of slightly enhanced density, suffering an above-average deceleration, would eventually condense out from the expanding background. Many theorists have attacked this subject in recent years. Higher-precision observation of the microwave background radiation could reveal velocity perturbations at pregalactic epochs and thereby yield important clues. The goal of these studies is to understand the evolution from primordial fluctuations to galaxies like our own, without having to fall back too often to the statement "things are as they are because they were as they were".

It is now over 60 years since the general theory of relativity was enunciated, and the various "expanding Universe" solutions of Einstein's equations were already very familiar in the 1950s. But the prospects of discriminating between different cosmological theories were then dim; and Newtonian theory seemed almost entirely adequate for describing the dynamics and equilibrium of stars and galaxies. Relativity theory was then regarded as a rather stagnant topic — a glaring contrast with its present status as one of the liveliest frontiers of fundamental research.

There are several reasons for this renaissance in gravitational physics. It stems partly from the utilisation of new mathematical techniques, which would have revived interest in the theory even if there had been no hope of confrontation with observation. But it has also been stimulated by the accelerated progress of observational cosmology, and by the realisation that objects where relativistic effects are large — neutron stars and black holes — may actually exist.

In the short run, the most useful tests of gravitational theories may well come from high-precision experiments — radio interferometry, planetary radar, and so on — in the Solar System, even though there the relativistic effects are very small. Already these experiments are precise enough to exclude most of the rival theories; and to confirm general relativity, at least in the so-called post-Newtonian approximation, with a precision of a few per cent. But to study situations where gravity is overwhelmingly strong, one must look farther afield — to possible black holes, and to the big bang itself.

Nevertheless even now the astrophysical uncertainties are so great that one cannot, from observations of galaxies and quasars, decide whether or not the Universe is expanding in accordance with general relativity. However the primordial helium abundance is sensitive to the expansion rate of the early Universe which in turn depends on the assumed theory of gravity. In some alternative theories the helium abundance at least lends some support to a general relativistic Universe.

If one takes the big bang seriously, there is no reason for stopping our backward extrapolation at the time of helium formation, when the "age of the Universe" was about 100 seconds. The primordial material would have attained nuclear densities about 10 millionths of a second after the big bang. Before this time the densities and pressures are so extreme that the behaviour of matter is sensitive to current uncertainties in elementary particle physics. But if, as perhaps we should, we envisage time on a logarithmic scale, to ignore the first 10^{-5} seconds would seem a severe omission indeed!

The early stages of the big bang are in many sense analogous to the

time-reversal of gravitational collapse into a black hole (and to the fate
that will overtake everything if the Universe is destined to recollapse),
and relativity theory predicts that the densities and space curvatures
should become arbitrarily high as we approach close to the initial
instant $t = 0$. When the space curvature becomes sufficiently great (the
first 10^{-23} seconds) it is believed that particle pairs can be created out
of the gravitational fields in an analogous manner to the creation of
electron–positron pairs in strong electromagnetic fields. When the
curvatures reach even more extreme values (10^{-43} seconds) it is accepted that Einstein's theory cannot be an adequate description and
that a full-blown theory of quantum gravity is required.

When a stellar mass object collapses to become a black hole the
regions of such extreme space curvature are deep inside the horizon at
the Schwarzschild radius, shrouded from view. But this is not so for the
big bang, where there is, in principle, a causal chain extending right
back to the "singularity." Many relativists believe that the global isotropy and homogeneity of the Universe, a much more puzzling feature
than the existence of the small amplitude fluctuations which develop
into galaxies, is imposed by quantum gravitational effects at the very
earliest times. This is one of the motivations for the current interest in
quantum effects and pair creation in curved space–time: an important
and hopeful step towards a full theory of quantum gravity.

We also know that the big bang was "hot"—which means more
precisely that the photons comprising the primordial radiation out-
numbered the ordinary particles (protons, neutrons, and so on) by a
factor of about one hundred million. There is still no satisfactory explanation of this number (or, equivalently, for the high entropy of the
Universe), and it would be a great step forward if its value could be
understood.

Some physicists have been attracted to the idea that the Universe as a
whole may be symmetric between matter and antimatter. In the very
hot initial instants of the big bang, protons, antiprotons, and so on
would exist in profusion. But they would tend to annihilate as the
Universe cooled down, and the problem with this idea is to explain why
any particles survive, and why the Universe is not now almost pure
radiation.

Twenty Years On

In the past 20 years, new observational techniques have revealed a
greater range and richness of cosmic phenomena than had hitherto
been suspected. The discoveries have often been made by people who
would not call themselves astronomers in the traditional sense, using
techniques developed primarily for other practical goals. Indeed, the
constricting artificiality of the traditional subdisciplinary boundaries

within astronomy and space science is now generally recognised. More and more observational programmes now involve coordinated studies in different wavebands. Also, the remarkable interdependence of cosmic processes is now appreciated. For instance, the abundance and distribution of chemical elements within the Solar System was partly determined by processes occurring throughout the early evolution of the whole Galaxy. And, on more fundamental levels, some theorists suspect that the properties of elementary particles — and indeed many key features of the everyday world — are somehow determined by what happened in the initial instants of the "big bang".

Most physicists now recognise the importance of exploiting the "cosmic laboratory" to study the properties of matter under conditions too extreme to be simulated terrestrially: the densities in neutron stars and the big bang; the magnetic field strengths of pulsars; the energies of particles in cosmic rays; and the properties of the plasma in radio galaxies. Astrophysicists attempting to interpret cosmic phenomena find themselves faced with problems whose solution demands the combined efforts of physicists spanning an increasingly broad range of expertise.

One would like to be able to predict what astronomical advances will be achieved in the next 20 years. But experience warns us against doing this, because the main payoff and vindication of past projects — ground-based and space research alike — has usually lain in the entirely unforeseen new phenomena that they have revealed. It may be that the next few years will see fewer complete surprises: after all, we have now had at least a glimpse of the sky over essentially the whole electromagnetic spectrum. The initial exploratory phase may then be succeeded by a period of consolidation, detailed studies, and model building, in which the more leisured pace of novel discoveries allows theorists to catch up! However the newer techniques, particularly the infrared, and those utilising space techniques, are still in the pioneering stages when order-of-magnitude improvements are feasible within a decade. (And the optimists may hope soon to exploit non-electromagnetic channels of information such as neutrinos and gravitational waves.)

6

JAYANT NARLIKAR*

Was There a Big Bang?

Ten years ago Geoffrey Burbidge wrote an article in *Nature* entitled "Was there really a big bang?" I cannot improve upon his remarks on cosmology in the early-1970s. "To the outsider and even to many inside, it looks, at first sight, as though considerable progress has been made in recent years, so that the outline of the way in which the Universe has evolved is understood and only the details need to be explained . . . Those who have read widely in the earlier and more recent cosmological literature . . . are aware that views of cosmology at any epoch are largely determined by the ideas of a few strong individuals, rather than by an objective appraisal of the information available . . ."

These remarks apply even more forcefully to the state of cosmological research today. If popular and to a large extent serious scientific literature is anything to go by, the big-bang model of the Universe is as firmly established in cosmology as the periodic table is in chemistry and DNA is in molecular biology. Yet, some cosmologists, albeit a minority, do sometimes wonder whether the confidence so often claimed in the big bang picture is justified by our observational knowledge of the Universe. In this article I will air a few of these misgivings.

First, what is the big bang model? In its simplest form the model is based on the theoretical work of A. Friedmann in 1922. Friedmann solved the equations of general relativity and came up with models of

*This article first appeared in *New Scientist*, London, the weekly review of science and technology: Vol. 91, No. 1260, 2 July 1981, pp. 19–21.

an expanding universe. In an expanding universe the basic constituent units, the galaxies, move apart from one another. Thus a typical cosmic triangle obtained by joining the positions of any three galaxies G_1, G_2, G_3 expands in size.

The expansion may be characterised by a scale factor which we may denote by S. A mathematical equation tells us how S changes with time. There is not just one Friedmann model; there are many. But all of them share one common feature. In every model there was an epoch in the past when the scale factor S was zero. This is the epoch now commonly identified with the epoch of the "big bang".

Towards the end of the 1920s, the expanding-universe models received observational support from the data compiled by Edwin Hubble and Milton Humason working with the 254-cm (100-inch) telescope at Mount Wilson in southern California. The data showed systematic increases in the wavelengths of spectra of nearby galaxies. The fractional increase in wavelength is called "red shift" and it is usually denoted by the letter z. A naive interpretation of red shift is through the doppler effect. If the galaxies are all moving away from us we should see just such an increase in wavelengths in their spectra.

Hubble and Humason also found that the red shifts of galaxies increased with faintness; that is, the fainter the galaxy seemed on the photographic plate the larger was its red shift. Assuming that the galaxies look increasingly faint as their distances (D) from us increase, Hubble was able to deduce a linear law of the following type: $cz = HD$, where c = speed of light and H = a constant, now known as Hubble's constant.

In the expanding-universe picture, the red shift can be explained quite simply. Suppose light left galaxy G_1 at the epoch t_1 and reached the galaxy G_2 at the later epoch t_2. Then to G_2 the light from G_1 appears red-shifted by the fraction by which the scale factor increased between the two epochs. Notice that light leaving G_2 at the epoch t_1 will arrive at G_1 at the epoch t_2 with the same red shift. Thus there is nothing special about us observing red shifts from all other galaxies: observations made from any other galaxy would lead to the same Hubble law. This is one of the symmetries of an expanding universe.

Weaknesses of Big Bang Cosmology

Symmetries like the one described above are among the many attractive features of the Friedmann models. The models are simple solutions of the otherwise very complicated equations of general relativity. Moreover, they provided a ready interpretation of Hubble's law. It was not surprising, therefore, that cosmologists took these models as the starting point of their investigations. What *is* surprising is that they are now being considered as the last word in cosmology. As papers are regularly published which take the above fact for granted, I will play here the role of a devil's advocate and look at the weaknesses of the big-bang cosmology.

I begin with a philosophical point, although I will soon move on to hard facts. What is the physical implication of $S = 0$? At this epoch, which is denoted by $t = 0$ on the cosmic time axis, the separation between any two galaxies was zero. The entire Universe was therefore confined to zero volume. In fact it is argued that the entire Universe burst out at time zero in a tremendous explosion (hence the "big bang") and the present apparent recession of the galaxies is an indication of the early violent activity. But how did this explosion occur? Why did it occur when it did? And what preceded it? Did matter exist prior to $t = 0$, or was it created in the explosion? If the latter version is correct, how was matter created in apparent violation of the law of conservation of matter and energy? Questions like these are either conveniently relegated to "domain outside physics" or dismissed as philosophical nonsense.

There might have been some justification in ignoring the $t = 0$ epoch as too remote if it were indeed too far back in the past. Unfortunately, as astronomical time scales go, this is not the case. Defining the time elapsed since the big bang up to the present epoch as the "age" of the Universe it is possible to compute it in any Friedmann model. While the answer varies from model to model there is an upper limit to the age; and this is given by the reciprocal of H, the Hubble constant. I will denote this upper limit by T.

There are many uncertainties in the determination of Hubble's constant and hence in the value of T. The present estimate of T lies in the range of 9 to 18 billion (1 billion $= 10^9$) years. Although in the 1970s the upper end of the above range was favoured it is now believed that T may be closer to 13 billion years (*New Scientist*, vol. 85, p. 844). If this value is correct it spells trouble for the big-bang models. For this value is the *upper limit* given by such models, and it is attained only in the idealised model of an empty universe. The presence of matter tends to slow down the expansion of the model universe and to reduce its age. If there is enough matter in the real Universe to slow down its expansion to a momentary standstill followed by contraction then its present age cannot exceed two-thirds of T, that is about 9 billion years. Astronomers are uncertain as to how much matter is actually present in the Universe. Although visible matter in the form of galaxies is only a few per cent of the above critical requirement, there are indications that there may also be substantial amounts of non-luminous matter. If it turns out that the Universe contains matter close to the critical value its age may be closer to 9 rather than 13 billion years (*New Scientist*, vol. 88, p. 582).

These time scales may appear large to a non-astronomer. Certainly the age of the Universe as estimated above is larger than the age of the Earth and the Solar System (around 4.6 billion years). However, astronomers know of older objects in the Universe; for example, some of the globular star clusters are estimated to be at least 10 to 15 billion years old. And there is no guarantee that these are the oldest objects in the Universe. So unless the age determinations are wrong or the value of T is much higher than thought likely at present we are faced with the conclusion that the big-bang Universe is simply not old enough to accommodate all the objects found in it!

Looking into the Past

As we look at remote objects we see them as they were a long time ago. This is because our means of observation is light (electromagnetic radiation) travelling with a finite speed. A light year, the distance covered by light in one year, is approximately 10 million million kilometres. Thus if we look at a galaxy a billion light years away, we see it as it was a billion years ago. So in principle, the further we probe the Universe the further back in time we see it. How far have atronomers observed to date? How close to the big bang have they probed the Universe?

One measure of this probe is the red shift. As we saw earlier, the larger the red shift, the smaller was the scale factor at the time light left the source. The big-bang epoch has infinite red shift. What are the z-values of the most remote galaxies seen to date? These values do not exceed 1. The rest is extrapolation all the way to $z = \infty$. Of course extrapolations *per se* are a common feature of science and often serve to push back the frontiers of knowledge. But we must not confuse speculative extrapolations with direct evidence.

At this stage one may ask: "What about quasars?" Quasars were discovered in 1963, and are a class of astronomical objects with large red shifts ranging up to $z = 3.53$. Thus quasars do extend our domain of observation closer to the big-bang epoch, *provided* we can be certain that their red shifts do arise from the expansion of the Universe! Contrary to the impression prevalent within the astronomical community or outside it, this interpretation is open to doubts.

It would take too much space to give here all aspects of the controversy about quasars. I illustrate one aspect with the help of two triplets of quasars discovered by Cyril Hazard, of Cambridge University, and Chip Arp of the California Institute of Technology, in 1979. The perfect linear alignment of each trio suggests that the quasars in each set are physically associated with one another. Yet, their red shifts are markedly different. Thus if the quasars X, Y, Z owe their red shifts to the expansion of the Universe, then by Hubble's law they must be at different distances from us, the quasar X being the one farthest away.

Their apparent alignment must therefore be attributed to pure accident. The presence of not one but two such cases on the same photographic plate makes it even more remarkable. How probable is such a
situation on the basis of pure chance? If the probability comes out very
low then we must suspect the cosmological interpretation of these red
shifts and argue that the quasars must indeed be physically associated
(*New Scientist*, vol. 88, p. 157, and vol. 90, p. 163).

It is still too early to say what the outcome of the quasar controversy
is going to be — so the quasars cannot yet be confidently considered as
probes of the remote and the past Universe. Even if they are so considered, their red shifts do not take us anywhere near the big-bang epoch.

In addition we must distinguish between evidence for evolution and
the evidence for the big bang. In 1948 Hermann Bondi, Thomas Gold
and Fred Hoyle proposed the concept of the steady-state universe. As
its name implies, the large-scale properties of this model do not change
with time. Such a universe is therefore without a beginning and without
an end and does not have a big-bang epoch. In the first two decades
following its inception considerable observational effort was spent in
ascertaining whether the real Universe is changing with time or is
steady. In his article in *Nature* in 1971, Burbidge reviewed such evidence as was then available and concluded that contrary to claims made
for an evolving (changing) universe by the observers from time to time,
an objective appraisal of the data left the issue open. A more recent
study (to appear in *Astrophysics and Space Science*) comes to a similar
conclusion.

But even if the evidence is that the Universe is evolving, that does not
tell us whether there was a big bang. This evidence uses observations of
galaxies, radio sources and quasars and is therefore limited to epochs
more recent than that given by $z = 3.53$. Any conclusion with regard to
the big bang depends on the *extrapolation* of this data by the theorist
and therefore depends on the model he chooses.

So what direct evidence do we have that the Universe had a big
bang? The strongest and the most direct evidence claimed for the big
bang so far is the microwave background radiation first observed by
Arno Penzias and Robert Wilson of Bell Laboratories in 1965. If the
Universe originated in a *hot* big bang its temperature just after creation
was very high and it began to drop as the Universe continued to
expand. For example, the temperature one second after the big bang
was about ten billion degrees absolute. What should the temperature
be now?

According to the calculations the relic radiation from the hot era of a
big bang universe of the early Universe should have the spectrum of
black-body radiation first calculated by Max Planck in the early days of
quantum theory. When, therefore, successive measurements of the
microwave background at different wavelengths began to show similar-

ity with the black-body spectrum, the evidence was considered conclusively in favour of the big bang. In 1979, however, measurements by D. P. Woody and P. L. Richards at the University of California, Berkeley, showed deviations from the Planckian spectrum that are considered statistically significant. If future experiments continue to show these deviations, that should worry the supporters of the big bang.

But the actual measured temperature of 3K is itself something of a mystery. Translated into the language of particle physics it implies that there are about ten billion photons for every baryon (sub-atomic particles such as the proton and neutron) in the Universe. According to the big-bang cosmology this ratio has remained unchanged since the early epochs. Why this ratio and no other? Particle physicists are trying to see the answer to this riddle through a unified theory of basic interactions of physics (*New Scientist*, vol. 87, p. 869).

To astrophysicists, however, the observed energy density of the microwave background radiation suggests other coincidences. This energy density is not too different to the energy densities observed in other astrophysical phenomena in the Universe, such as starlight, cosmic rays, galactic magnetic fields and so on. Does this mean that the microwave background also is of astrophysical origin and is not a relic of the big bang? This suggestion does not now evoke a vehement negative response from the pro-big-bang cosmologists as it did in the 1960s.

What of the theoretical foundations on which the big bang is based? This cosmology is based on Albert Einstein's general theory of relativity. How far has this theory been tested? To what extent is this theory to be trusted in our extrapolations all the way to the big-bang epoch?

How Universal Is Relativity Theory?

Several experimental tests in the Solar System have confirmed the predictions of general relativity. Certainly, in comparison with Isaac Newton's law of gravitation or any other competing theories of gravity, relativity has come out triumphant. However, these tests were conducted under conditions where the effects of gravity are relatively weak. In cosmology, close to the big bang, the gravitational effects are strong and we are therefore using the theory in conditions very different from those under which it has been tested. This aspect is often forgotten when categorical statements are made about the early Universe.

As an example of the above point I mention the hypothesis that the gravitational constant is slowly changing with time. This constant, denoted by G, was introduced by Newton to quantify the strength of gravitational attraction. According to general relativity, G is strictly a constant. Is it?

Paul Wesson has recently reviewed the observational checks that can be made on the above hypothesis (*Physics Today*, vol. 33, p. 32). A slow variation of *G* will not be seen in the experimental tests of relativity referred to above. It will, however, affect the Moon's motion round the Earth, the motion of planets round the Sun, the internal structure of the Earth, the evolution of the Sun and other stars, etc. There is some positive evidence in favour of the hypothesis, the most recent being based on an assessment Thomas Van Flandern, of the US Naval Observatory, has made of the data on the Moon's motion. *G* may be decreasing by a few parts in a billion per century! Small though this rate is, if confirmed, it is sufficient to rule out general relativity in its present form (*New Scientist*, vol. 81, p. 856).

Another theoretical consideration relates to quantum theory. Most physicists today would agree that classical physics is at best an approximation to quantum physics. When we get down to very small scales of space and time classical physics has to give way to quantum physics. For example, the classical equations of electromagnetic theory formulated by James Maxwell tell us that an electron circling round a proton would in a short time spiral inwards and fall on the proton. Quantum electrodynamics on the other hand gives stable electron orbits with energy levels in agreement with those observed for the hydrogen atom. In the same way, what is the quantum version of general relativity? Does it also lead us to the same conclusion as the classical theory that the Universe did have a big bang? These questions have not yet been resolved.

These arguments should indicate to the uncommitted that the big-bang picture is not as soundly established, either theoretically or observationally, as it is usually claimed to be. This is not to say that the picture is wrong and should be abandoned: I simply mean that the cosmological problem is still wide open and alternatives to the standard big-bang picture should be seriously investigated.

Are there any alternatives? While writing a review article with A. K. Kembhais on "Non-standard cosmologies" (*Fundamentals of Cosmic Physics*, vol. 6, p. 1) I came across several alternatives to standard cosmology which could serve as useful starting points. The reason that alternatives like these are not so well known or not well enough investigated is partly because of the prevalent view that the big-bang picture correctly describes the Universe. Personally I think that closing one's options at this stage is harmful to the development of the subject as a branch of science.

In the beginning of this century most astronomers believed that the Universe extended as far as our Galaxy only. This view was demolished in the 1920s by improved observational techniques. In 1948 Fred Hoyle was criticised by particle physicists for proposing baryon creation in the steady-state model. Today some of the best brains in particle physics are busy devising theories in which the number of baryons in the Universe is not conserved.

Looking towards the future I find the launching of the Space Telescope in the mid-1980s as one of the significant developments of new technology. By enabling the astronomers to observe objects up to 50 times fainter than hitherto possible with ground-based instruments this telescope is expected to improve and enlarge our understanding of the extragalactic world. Astrophysicists of today who hold the view that "the ultimate cosmological problem" has been more or less solved may well be in for a few surprises before this century runs out.

7

ADOLF GRÜNBAUM*

The Pseudo-Problem of Creation in Physical Cosmology

1. Introduction

VARIOUS WRITERS CONFUSE the genuine question "Does the physical universe have a temporal *origin*, and — if so — what does physical cosmology tell us about it?" with the quite different pseudo-problem "Was there a *creation* of the universe, and — if so — what light can science throw on it, if any?" Thus, the cosmologist Hermann Bondi (1961, pp. 140 and 152) tells us that in "theories of creation in the past only," such as the big bang cosmogony, "the problem of the origin of the universe, that is [sic], the problem of creation is . . . being handed over to metaphysics" (p. 143). As Bondi sees it, the steady-state theory propounded by himself and Thomas Gold in 1948 brings "the problem of creation . . . within the scope of physical inquiry" (p. 140), if only because it postulates *continual* "creation" such that "no events in the past are required that have no counterpart now" (p. 152). Therefore, Bondi claimed heuristic scientific superiority for the steady-state theory vis-à-vis its big bang rival:

> the hypothesis of continual creation is more fertile in that it answers more questions [about the origin of matter] and yields more . . . results that are, at least in principle, observable. To push the entire question of creation into the past is to restrict science to a discussion of what happened after creation while forbidding it to examine creation itself. (p. 152)

*Copyright © 1989 by Adolf Grünbaum. All rights reserved. This article appeared in *Philosophy of Science*, Vol. 56, No. 3, Sept. 1989, pp. 373–394, and is reprinted by permission of its editor.

In diametrical opposition to Bondi, the physicist Herbert Dingle rejects as perpetually miraculous the violation of matter-conservation by the "continual creation" of new hydrogen atoms in the steady-state theory. And he sees that violation as overtaxing our credulity even more than does biblical creation out of nothing: "It [the Bondi and Gold theory] exempts us from having to postulate a single initial miracle on condition that we admit a continuous series of miracles" (quoted by Loren Eiseley in *Scientific American* 189, July 1953, p. 81). But, as against Dingle, the physicist Philip Morrison opines that it is the big bang theory, rather than its steady-state rival, which purportedly requires a greater reliance on supernatural miracles (Letter, *Scientific American*, September 1953, p. 14).

The physical cosmologist Jayant Narlikar (1977) is instructively articulate in his confusion of the question of the origin of the universe with the pseudo-problem of its creation. And having conflated these two different questions, he feels entitled to complain that "most cosmologists turn a blind eye" to the latter:

> The most fundamental question in cosmology is, 'Where did the matter we see around us originate in the first place?' This point has never been dealt with in the big bang cosmologies in which, at $t = 0$, there occurs a sudden and fantastic violation of the law of conservation of matter and energy. After $t = 0$ there is no such violation. By ignoring the primary creation event most cosmologists turn a blind eye to the above question. (pp. 136–137)

Narlikar had set the stage for this formulation of his question as follows:

> So we have the following description of a big bang Universe. At an epoch, which we may denote by $t = 0$, the Universe explodes into existence. . . . The epoch $t = 0$ is taken as the event of 'creation'. Prior to this there existed no Universe, no observers, no physical laws. Everything suddenly appeared at $t = 0$. The 'age' of the Universe is defined as the cosmic time which has elapsed since this event . . .
>
> Although scientists are not in the habit of discussing the creation event or the situation prior to it, a lot of research has gone into the discussion of what the Universe was like immediately after its creation. (p. 125)

During the past three decades, the astronomer Bernard Lovell (1961, 1986) has given an explicitly theological twist to the most fundamental cosmological questions by making two major claims: (1) There is an inescapable problem of creation in both the steady-state and big bang cosmologies, but neither of them is capable of offering a scientific solution to it; and (2) a satisfactory explanatory solution "must eventually move over into metaphysics for reasons which are inherent in modern scientific theory" (1961, p. 125) by postulating *divine* creation. As Lovell sees it, "the major issue" between the competing steady-state and big bang models of the universe is "whether creation is occurring now and throughout all time in the past and in the future, or whether the fundamental material of the universe was created in its entirety some billions of years ago" (pp. 118–119). As for the big bang theory, he declares explanatory bankruptcy. Having assumed that in the classical, pre-quantum versions of this theory, one can meaningfully speak of "the time before the [big bang]" (p. 99), he feels entitled to reason that "One must still inquire . . . how the primeval gas [of the big bang] originated. Science has nothing to say on this issue" (pp. 98–99). And why does he think that science is thus silent? Because the purported creation of matter at the "definite moment" of the big bang is "beyond human investigation" (p. 117). Yet, in his view, the supposed problem of creation "can tear the [human] individual's mind asunder" (p. 125) by its gnawing, inescapable intellectual challenge. Therefore, Lovell repeatedly chides those whom he calls "materialists" for indifference, neglect or evasion of the problem (pp. 112, 122, and 125).

But what of the steady-state theory? Though Lovell (1961) endorses Bondi's investigative tribute to it vis-à-vis its big bang rival, he contends that nonetheless it too "has no solution to the problem of the creation of matter" (p. 117), because it provides no "information about the nature of the energy input which gave rise to the created [hydrogen] atom" (p. 124). Yet Bondi explicitly denies that there is any "energy input" in the sense of the principle of energy-*conservation*, which is denied by the steady-state theory. As he put it (1961: p. 144): "It should be clearly understood that the creation here discussed is the formation of matter not out of radiation but out of nothing." And, as will emerge in Section 3.A, the crucial point will turn out to be that, in the steady-state theory, such *non*-conservative matter accretion is claimed to transpire *without any kind of external cause*, bcause it is held to be cosmically the spontaneous, natural, unperturbed behavior of the physical world!

I shall argue that the genuine problem of the origin of the universe or of the matter in it has been illicitly transmuted into the pseudo-problem of the "creation" of the universe or of its matter by an external cause.

At present, the big bang theory is in vogue, whereas the Bondi and Gold steady-state theory is largely defunct on empirical grounds. Indeed, as will be noted in Section 4, the so-called "inflationary" early expansion, grand unified theories, and quantum cosmology have modified these earlier twentieth century cosmologies. Yet it will be instructive philosophically to examine Lovell's argument for divine creation in the context of the earlier two rival theories despite their replacement by the current models. As it will turn out, the philosophical issues have remained essentially the same, although the technical details have changed considerably. Thus, my thesis will be two-fold: If the big bang theory — as modified by quantum theoretical considerations governing two "vacuum" states close to the big bang phase (Hawking, 1988, Chap. 8)—is true, it provides no support at all for Augustine's old philosophical doctrine of divine creation out of nothing (*"ex nihilo"*). And if, alternatively, the steady-state theory had been true, it would have provided no support for the claim that the *non*-conservative matter accretion asserted by it requires an *external cause* such that God is busy creating hydrogen atoms around the clock through all past and future eternity. By the same token, if there were non-conservative energy formation in an "inflationary" universe, while the energy-*density* remains constant, no *external*, let alone supernatural, cause would be warranted. In the case of the big bang theory, the creationist reading of it is, of course, not just that the big bang itself followed upon a state of so-called nothing. Instead, this transition could not have occurred quite naturally but required an *external cause* supplied only by God. On that view, ever since then, God has been thus unemployed, as it were, for about 12 billion years, because the big bang model of the general theory of relativity features the conservation-law for matter—energy, which obviously precludes any non-conservative formation of physical entities.

Most recently, however, the plasma cosmology originally developed by Hannes Alfven, which assigns a critical cosmic role to hot, electrically charged gases, has posed a major challenge to the gravity-dominated big bang cosmology (*The New York Times*, February 28, 1989, p. C1). By featuring a universe that has *existed forever*, without any beginning, plasma cosmology altogether obviates even the temptation to invoke divine creation ex nihilo. Such preclusion of creation will become important, if plasma cosmology turns out to supplant the big bang theory in response to recent observational findings that presumably contradict some of the latter's evolutionary tenets.

As I shall endeavor to show in detail, the question of creation is just as ill-posed in the context of the recent rival physical cosmologies as was the following sort of problem, which agitated philosophers until the middle of the 18th century: Why do ordinary material objects (e.g., tables) not simply vanish into nothingness? As Philip Quinn has remarked, there were thinkers until at least the 18th century (e.g., Jonathan Edwards) who took this question very seriously. Thus, in René Descartes' "Meditation III," he simply assumed, at least tacitly, that when a physical system is closed, it will simply *not* obey matter-conservation spontaneously and quite naturally *without* external intervention. Having made that assumption, he was driven to suppose that an *external cause* supplied by God's activity was required at every instant of time to prevent matter from *lapsing into nothingness*. Ironically, whereas Lovell calls God to the rescue as the cause of the continual non-conservative hydrogen production in the steady-state universe, Descartes (1967) assigns that same indispensable causal role to the deity just to keep contingently existing material objects from vanishing into thin air:

> It is as a matter of fact perfectly clear and evident to all who consider with attention the nature of time, that, in order to be conserved in each moment in which it endures, a substance has need of the same power and action as would be necessary to produce and create it anew, supposing it did not yet exist, so that the light of nature shows us clearly that the distinction between creation and conservation is solely a [conceptual] distinction of the reason [rather than of ontological causation]. (p. 168)

Bernard Lovell's recent paper "Reason and Faith in Cosmology" (1986) is a technically up-dated concise version of the philosophical argument that he had developed in more detail in his earlier book (1961), which was based on his 1958 lectures over the BBC entitled "The Individual and the Universe."

Just what are the (tacit) assumptions that inspire Lovell's and Narlikar's particular questions? And are these assumptions warranted in the contexts of the theories to which they address their questions? I shall contend that they are *not*! And if not, then there is no basis for Lovell's claim that, since neither the big bang nor the steady-state theory answer his creation questions, they are unsatisfactory without divine creation. Indeed, as we shall see, his questions rest, in each case, on assumptions that are *denied* by precisely the theories to which he is addressing them. And instead of justifying his presupposed assumptions against these denials, he simply takes them for granted without argument. In this way, he assumes rather than shows that good theories need to answer the questions he addresses to them.

After all, a question cannot be regarded as a well-posed challenge, merely because the questioner finds it psychologically insistent, experiences a strong feeling of puzzlement, and desires an answer to it. This fact is completely obvious in the case of asking a man when he last beat his wife. If, in fact, he does not beat his wife, then it is not a well-posed question to ask him whether or when he stopped beating her. And if the question is nonetheless put to him, and he denies beating her at all, it is illegitimate to accuse him of *evading* the question or of indifference to it. It would be legitimate to challenge the man's denial of wife-beating by offering evidence that he does beat her after all. Such evidence would legitimate the question. Thus, the debate on whether the man has answered the question is pointless, until the underlying assumption of wife-beating is validated. Similarly, if—as we first learned from the chemist Lavoisier—there is indeed matter-conservation (or matter–energy conservation) in a closed finite system on a macroscopic scale *qua spontaneous, natural, unperturbed behavior of the system*, then Descartes was *empirically* wrong to have assumed that such conservation requires the intervention of an *external cause*. And, if he is thus wrong, then his claim that external divine intervention in particular is needed to keep the table from disappearing into nothingness is based on a false presupposition. More generally, if the presupposition of a philosophical or scientific question is false, then the question is at best misleading and at least ill-posed or pointless.

Thus, I hope to show by an analysis of the particular assumptions which inspire Lovell's major questions that they are ill-posed *in just this way*. It will then be seen how he used these misguided questions to give an altogether unwarranted *theological* twist to the rivalry between the steady-state and big bang theories of cosmogony. In particular, as we shall see, Lovell's aforecited statement of "the major issue" between them as one of the *timing* of creation is *not at all* a philosophical refinement or deepening of the question whether the big bang or the steady-state cosmology is true.

2. The Traditional Creation Argument

In order to deal with the recent creation issue in physics, I must first offer an analysis of an old argument for divine creation or so-called first cause that all of us have encountered in the history of philosophy quite independently of sophisticated astronomical theories. It is a version of the "cosmological argument" for the existence of God that is both familiar and most germane to our concerns. There are, however, various other versions [Rowe (1975); Craig (1979)]. And I do *not* claim that my charge of pseudo-problem applies necessarily to all of the questions addressed by these other versions. Thus, I am disregarding the view of *timeless* causation set forth by Augustine in Book XI of his *Confessions*, which was accepted by subsequent medieval theists, but which I find either unintelligible or incoherent.

The relevant creation argument proceeds from the premise that there is a question as to where everything came from, or of *"how"* the world came into being, or as to who or what caused everything. Thus the question more or less tacitly assumes some sort of temporal beginning for the physical universe, preceded *temporally* by a supposed state of nothingness. And the aim of the argument is to show that we cannot understand the supposed beginning or origin of the world without the assumption that there was a creation out of nothing by a creator. More specifically, the argument claims to establish the necessity for postulating creation by starting out with the premise that things have "causes" in the senses granted by common sense or ordinary science, or even by the sceptical common sense of a hard-headed engineer. Thus, the starting point is the following premise:

"Everything has a cause" to the extent to which causes are acknowledged in explanations of ordinary experience or of scientifically explained phenomena.

From the premise that everything has a cause, the following conclusions are then claimed to follow:

The physical universe *as a whole* had a beginning a finite time ago as a result of an act of creation out of nothing by a single, conscious external CAUSE or agent. And that external cause or creator is then claimed to be the personal God of the biblical theistic tradition.

Let me now comment on the basic premise of the argument. Fortunately, our purposes do not require the ambitious attempt of giving an adequate analysis of the concept or concepts of cause as used in the explanations of ordinary or natural experiences. Instead, our examination of the argument from creation requires only that we attend to certain relevant aspects of that concept of cause.

Note first that there are a vast number of cases of causation by physical forces and, more generally, of causally connected natural events *in which no human or other conscious agents are involved.* Earthquakes and the melting of snow on uninhabited mountain tops in the spring are causal chains of events, but no conscious agents are involved. Similarly for the freezing of a lake, for example. But there are *other* cases such as the production of statues, cakes, and dresses, in which conscious fashioners like sculptors, bakers, homekeepers, and seamstresses *are* causally involved as agents. What will be important for the argument, however, is that in many instances of causation, there simply is no involvement of conscious agents.

Secondly, consider cases of causation which do involve the intervention of conscious fashioners or agents, such as the baking of a cake by a person. In such a case, the materials composing the cake owe their particular state of being in cake-form partly to acts of intervention by a conscious agent. But clearly, the very existence of the atoms or molecules composing the cake cannot be attributed to the causal role played by the activity of the agent. Thus, even if we were to assume that agent-causation does differ interestingly from event-causation, we must recognize that ordinary agent-causation is still only a *transformation* of matter (energy).

Let me now point out a whole series of fallacies, divided into groups, which the defender of the old creation hypothesis commits in deriving his conclusions from his stated premise. I am going to discuss a whole series not in order to employ "overkill" on the argument, but because I regard all of these fallacies to be quite instructive for our purposes in their own right.

Group 1. Even for those cases of causation which involve conscious agents or fashioners, the premise does not assert that they ever create anything *out of nothing;* instead, conscious fashioners merely TRANSFORM PREVIOUSLY EXISTING MATERIALS FROM ONE STATE TO ANOTHER; the baker creates a cake out of flour, milk, butter, etc., and the parents who produce an offspring do so from a sperm, an ovum, and from the food supplied by the mother's body, which in turn comes from the soil, solar energy, etc. Similarly, when a person dies, he or she ceases to exist *as a person*. But the dead body does not lapse into nothingness, since the materials of the body continue in other forms of matter or energy. In other words, all sorts of organized wholes (e.g., biological organisms) do cease to exist only *as such* when they disintegrate and their parts are scattered. But their parts continue in some form.

Since the concept of *cause* used in the conclusion of the argument involves creation *out of nothing*, we see that it is plainly different from the concept of cause in the premise. And for this reason alone, the conclusion does not follow from the premise deductively. Nor is it even supported by it inductively. Indeed, *if* the principle of conservation of energy or mass – energy were to have unrestricted validity, there could *not* have been any temporal process of creation *out of nothing*, since there could then not have been any *time* at which the amount of matter – energy was less than now. But let us note that even an unrestricted conservation principle does not rule out a cosmological model featuring a first moment of time, i.e., a model featuring *an instant that has no temporal predecessor*. Why not? Because the conservation of matter or energy requires only that *at all existing times*, the amount of matter – energy has to be the same. Such conservation does *not* require that every instant have a temporal predecessor. Indeed, one of the big bang models does feature a first instant along with energy conservation, *if* one can include the so-called singularity in its space-time.[1]

Furthermore, we saw that only some cases of causation involve conscious agents. Hence it again simply does not follow from the premise, nor is it supported by the premise, that prior to the evolution of conscious organisms on earth or elsewhere, a supposed first state or any other state of the total physical universe should be attributed to the intervention of a conscious agent.

Worse yet, even if some conscious agency or other were needed in every individual case of causation in daily life and science — which it is not! — it would hardly follow that there is some *one* single conscious agency which was required causally for the occurrence of the supposed

---

[1]Hawking and Ellis (1973, p. 3) give a brief, non-technical characterization of the concept of singularity as follows: "One can think of a singularity as a place where our present laws of physics break down [because important physical quantities are ill-defined or infinite there]. Alternatively, one can think of it as representing part of the edge of space – time, but a part which is at a finite distance instead of at infinity." Thus, at this "edge," the world-lines representing the space – time careers of mass-points, photons, and other elementary physical entities originate or come close together. For a more technical account, see Hawking and Ellis (1973, Chap. 8), and Torretti (1983, Section 6.4). But, when we discuss big bang models below, we shall emphasize Torretti's important *caveat* regarding the inclusion of a first event in the space – time.

first state of the *total* physical universe. This inference commits the elementary fallacy of "composition" and is just as invalid as the following argument, which derives a false conclusion from a true premise: Since every human has a mother, there is some one woman who was everyone's mother. (Formally speaking, this inference fallaciously commutes a universal quantifier with an existential one.)

Group 2. As we know, the big bang theory of cosmogony, which I shall discuss in Section 3.B, relies on specific observational evidence to justify its postulation of a finite cosmic past of the order of 12 billion years, such that there simply did not exist any instant of time *before* then. For now, I need to emphasize, however, that there is nothing at all in the concept of causality as such which warrants the claim that all causal chains must ultimately originate in the finite past from a cause that is *itself uncaused.* The gratuitous assertion that causality as such requires such an uncaused cause induces the conclusion that the universe *must* have had a first instant of time, rather than featuring a past in which *every* instant had a temporal predecessor. But causality as such is fully compatible logically with *physical* causal chains which extend infinitely into the past (both ordinally and metrically), instead of having a common temporal origin in a bounded finite past.[2]

The belief that the existence of causes for physical events requires a bounded past can originate fallaciously in several ways. Let us consider some of the most likely sources of this error. One such source is the *psychological* experience of time on which people draw, when they are presented with the following hypothesis: For any physical state whatever, there is at least one earlier physical state that is its (partial or total) cause. When a person thinks of the ever earlier causal antecedents *one-by-one*, that person soon experiences thought-fatigue. People just tire of thinking about ever earlier events. As we know, since each act of thought requires a minimum positive amount of time, it is impossible to review the members of an infinite set in thought one-by-one in a finite time [Grünbaum (1968), pp. 52, 67–68]. In this way, thought-fatigue may fallaciously induce the conclusion that physical causal chains cannot possibly extend into an unbounded past, and that physical causation occurred only over a bounded past, so that there had to be a first moment of time. This fallacy gains added plausibility from an unconscious appeal to our memory, which contains only finitely many bits. But scientific understanding can do much better than such intuitive, *experiential* picturing of the past.

---

[2]A past that is devoid of any first instant of time is *ordinally infinite*, because every instant of it has a temporal predecessor. But such a past need *not* be of infinite *duration*, since it could be *metrically* finite in years or other units of time. In a metrically infinite past, the number of units of time is infinite.

Another way in which people are tempted to insist on a bounded past involves the commission of a fallacy similar to the one illustrated by my earlier trivial example of motherhood. The reasoning starts out from the claim that such macroscopic objects as the earth, trees, people, mountains, and individual stars are first fully formed as such by causal processes from earlier, more primitive states. Thus such macro-objects *each* have their own respective beginnings in time in at least the following sense: For each of them, there is a time such that it did *not* exist in its final form before then, but did exist as of then or since. Incidentally, without additional theory, the correctness of this claim of temporal origin is by no means obvious in regard to all elementary particles, for example, *some* of which might conceivably have existed in their present form throughout all past time. But let us grant the claim for macro-objects. Since there may well be infinitely many of them, it then still does not follow that there must have been a *single time* such that all such objects whatever in the universe originated at or since that time.

This conclusion of a bounded past *would* follow, if the number of macro-objects in the universe were *only finite*, because a finite number of them must have originated at only finitely many times. But the defender of the inference has offered no reason for assuming that there are only finitely many macro-objects in the world! And even if there were, this would not preclude that these finitely many objects could have originated in their usual form as a result of an infinitude of prior transformations, from matter or energy existing earlier in other forms *during an unbounded past!* For example, in the case of the so-called "pair creation" of a particle and its anti-particle, such as a positron and an electron, their rest-mass formation *as such* occurs by conversion of other forms of energy such as a gamma ray into them.

Besides, if literally *everything* — including the universe as a whole — has a cause to which it owes either its state-of-being or even its very existence, it becomes imperative to ask for the *cause* of God's state-of-being or even existence. Why should He be an uncaused cause? As Schopenhauer has observed, those who try to exempt God from their universal causal assertion treat causation like a hired carriage that is dismissed upon reaching its desired destination.

Group 3. At this point, the argument is sometimes abandoned in favor of claiming that creation out of nothing *"passes all understanding"* and that scientific theories of cosmogony leave much to be desired in the way of providing answers to well-conceived questions. To this I say: If the creation hypothesis is indeed beyond human understanding, then it cannot even be meaningfully *taken on faith* without evidence, and it becomes completely hopeless to try to give a causal argument for it. After all, if the hypothesis itself is beyond human understanding, then even the person who is willing to believe it on faith admits that he or she does not know what is to be believed. Our human species may well be limited by intrinsic intellectual horizons of some sort, just as theoretical physics, for example, cannot be understood by dogs. Yet the fact remains that one can meaningfully believe only a claim whose *content* one understands, even if one is willing to believe without evidence on sheer faith. If the belief-content is incomprehensible, what is it that is being believed?

Therefore, if creation out of nothing (*ex nihilo*) is beyond human understanding, then the hypothesis that it occurred *cannot explain anything*. Even less can it then be required to fill explanatory gaps that exist in scientific theories of cosmogony. Indeed, it seems to me that if something literally passes all understanding, then nothing at all can be said or thought about it by humans. As Wittgenstein said: Whereof one cannot speak, thereof one must be silent. Dogs, for example, do not bark about relativity theory. Thus, any supposed hypothesis that literally passes *all* understanding is simply meaningless to us, and it certainly should not inspire a feeling of awe. To stand in awe before an admittedly incomprehensible hypothesis is to exhibit a totally misplaced sense of intellectual humility! It is useless to reply to this conclusion by saying that the creation hypothesis may be intelligible to "higher beings" than ourselves, if there are such. After all, it is being offered to *us* as a causal explanation!

So much for the reasons which lead me to regard the *traditional* first cause version of the "cosmological" argument for divine creation as multiply unsound. We are now ready to examine Lovell's attempt to base a new creation argument on the two most influential physical cosmologies of the twentieth century: the steady-state theory, on the one hand, and the "big bang" cosmogony, on the other.

3. The New Creation Argument

A. The Alleged Philosophical Defects of the Steady-State Theory

First, I need to comment on the unfortunately misleading uses of the words "creation" and "annihilation," which are carried over from theology into the contemporary literature of physics and philosophy of science. The semantic *caveat* I shall issue will apply to both of the received rival twentieth-century cosmologies, though not to the new rival plasma cosmology.

The word "creation" suggests a creating *agency* as well as a *process* in which something new is being produced. And the traditional theological assertion of divine creation out of nothing makes two further claims: (1) Before the created objects existed, the *only* entity that existed was God. In short, there was nothing besides God. (2) God was the agency responsible for the change from the so-called state of "nothing" to the state in which other sorts of entities existed. These notions are conveyed by the theological overtones of the term "creation." In English at least, this term is also used in other contexts in which it conveys the formation of something new, but need not suggest that the new object came from "nothing." But especially in the description of processes that conform to energy-*conservation* laws, the use of the terms "creation" and "annihilation" can be very misleading.

Take, for example, the phrases "pair creation" and "pair annihilation," which are familiar from the theory of particle reactions. In that theory, these phrases are employed to describe energy-conserving processes featuring the *inter-transformation* between radiation and a particle-pair consisting of one kind of particle and its anti-particle. Thus, when an electron and a positron collide, their rest-mass is *converted* into two photons of gamma radiation, which do carry energy. While the rest-mass of these photons may well be zero, this gamma radiation is obviously much more than just "nothing." Nevertheless, even the distinguished philosopher of physics Hans Reichenbach wrote (1956, p. 265) that the particle and its anti-particle disappear "into nothing." Evidently, the phrase "pair annihilation" obscures the fact that the energy of the original positive rest-mass of the particles reappears in the resulting gamma radiation, although the term "annihilation-*radiation*" is not similarly misleading. Corresponding remarks apply to the transformation of gamma radiation into an electron–positron pair: Such pair-production is certainly not a case of pair-"creation" *out of nothing*.

This energy-conservation in the theory of particle reactions contrasts sharply with the explicit postulation of its *violation* in the now abandoned steady-state cosmology of Bondi and Gold. Unfortunately, as we recall, Bondi himself (1961, p. 144) uses the term "creation" misleadingly to describe this denial of energy-conservation in that cosmology: "It should be clearly understood that the creation here discussed [in the context of the steady-state theory] is the formation of matter not out of radiation but out of nothing." Alas, the term "creation" suggests misleadingly that Bondi was postulating the operation of a creator or creating *agency*. But, more fortunately, he goes on to use the much better term "formation." In the Bondi and Gold theory, the formation of new matter cannot be conservative, because they assume that the *density* of matter is constant over time even as the universe is *expanding*; i.e., their theory features the conservation of density but *not* of matter. But I urge that this violation of matter–energy conservation be described by means of such words as "matter-increase," and "accession or accretion of matter," rather than by the term "creation."

As indicated in the Introduction, the current observational credentials of the steady-state cosmology are generally held to be poor. Yet, the steady-state theory has the merit of making many daring predictions which can be and, to some extent, have been tested. For example, it demands that the thermonuclear reactions in ordinary stars should be able to produce the heavy elements such as uranium out of what was originally hydrogen. And, indeed, this demanding prediction was very fruitful for the development of the theoretical understanding of nuclear reactions in stars. As another example, the theory predicts that the age distribution of the galaxies should be *uniform* for distant galaxies no less than for near ones. There seems to be an emerging consensus among astrophysicists that the theory is not viable for reasons of the following sort: (i) If the red shift from quasars is indeed a bona fide Doppler shift, then the presumed known distribution of quasars is actually contrary to the theory, and hence counts as refuting evidence against it. (ii) There is the evidence of the 3 K microwave background radiation which, though not necessarily contrary to every version of the theory, is fairly hard to accommodate in it [Peebles (1971), p. 24; Weinberg (1972), pp. 617–618]. Yet that radiation was predicted by Gamow's version of the big bang cosmogony. Thus, given the availability of a rival *evolutionary* cosmogony, the number of adherents of the steady-state theory is dwindling rapidly to the point that now "only few will still defend it" [Rindler (1977), p. 202]. But earlier a somewhat less pessimistic note was sounded by Weinberg (1972, pp. 464, 617–619). And, as John Leslie has pointed out to me, most recently Narlikar (1988, pp. 219–225) has claimed that the currently popular so-called "inflationary" model of the universe is an up-dated form of Fred Hoyle's version of the steady-state theory, as distinct from the Bondi and Gold original with which we have been concerned. The affinity between the new inflationary and old steady-state theories derives from the fact that the new theory features the conservation of *energy density* as the universe inflates very rapidly. This feature is the counterpart of the conservation of *matter density* in the old steady-state versions.

To gain perspective on Lovell's (1961, p. 117) philosophical complaint that the "steady-state theory has no solution to the problem of the creation of [new] matter," let us first look at the lesson that can be learned from the history of science in regard to the evidential warrant for postulating *external causes* for the behavior of physical and biological systems [Grünbaum (1973), pp. 406–407].

According to Aristotle, an external force is needed as the cause of a sublunar body's non-vertical motion. In his physics, the demand for such a disturbing external cause to explain such motion arises from the following assumption: When a sublunar body is not acted on by an external force, its *natural*, spontaneous unperturbed behavior is to be at rest at its "proper place," or — if it is not already there — to move vertically toward it. Yet, as we know, Galileo's analysis of the motions of spheres on inclined planes led him to conclude that the empirical evidence speaks against just this Aristotelian assumption. As Newton's First Law of Motion tells us, uniform motion never requires any external force as its cause; only accelerated motion does. Any of us who sat helplessly in a car while it was gliding along with essentially constant velocity on a wet road while hydroplaning can appreciate that Galileo and Newton were right. But, if so, then the Aristotelian demand for an *explanation* of any non-vertical sublunar motion *by reference to an EXTERNAL, perturbing force* begs the explanatory question by means of a false underlying assumption, rather than asks a well-posed legitimate question as to the "why" of non-vertical sublunar motion. By the same token, Galileo and Newton could only shrug their shoulders or throw up their hands in despair, if an Aristotelian told them that he has a solution to the "problem" of the *external* cause of such uniform motion, whereas they do not. It would, of course, be legitimate for the Aristotelian to *try* to offer empirical evidence that Newton's First Law is false despite Galileo's observations on an inclined plane. But begging the question hardly constitutes such evidence.

I claim that an Aristotelian who would reason *like Lovell* could just as well say the following: If a sublunar body moves non-vertically while *not* being subjected to an external physical force, then we must explain this motion — even if it is uniform — as the result of external *supernatural* divine intervention. Let me justify this claim.

Just as Galileo and Newton rejected, on empirical grounds, the Aristotelian idea of rest or vertical motion as the naturally inevitable, unperturbed state of sublunar bodies, so also Bondi and Gold rejected matter-conservation on the huge cosmological scale as the inevitable natural career of externally undisturbed physical systems. Instead, as we recall, they postulated *density*-conservation in an expanding universe, which requires non-conservative matter accretion. And just as it is a matter of *empirical* fact whether uniform motion requires a force as its external cause, so also is the question whether the natural, spontaneous, unperturbed behavior of physical systems conserves the quantity of matter *or* rather its density. After all, our scientific conceptions as to which state of affairs is the spontaneous, natural and unperturbed one are no better than the scope of their supporting evidence. And, as the history of science shows all too clearly, as our evidence grows, so also these conceptions need to be changed by stretching our intellectual horizons.

If matter-conservation is indeed the natural, unperturbed course of things, even on a cosmological scale, then the steady-state theory is physically false. On the other hand, if large-scale *density*-conservation is the spontaneous, *unperturbed*, natural state, as a matter of empirical fact, then Lovell is not entitled to his stubborn dogmatic insistence that, *in every theory, matter*-conservation *must* be held to be the natural state! Yet just that insistence is the basis for his demand for an external supernatural cause to explain the matter-*increase* required by density-conservation in an expanding universe. Thus, as we saw in Section 1, he complains (1961, p. 124) that the steady-state theory makes no provision for "the energy *input* which gave rise to the created [hydrogen] atom" (my italics). No wonder, therefore, that, in his view, the *non-conservative* matter-production postulated by Bondi and Gold poses a "problem of creation" so acute that it "can tear the individual's mind asunder." To prevent such mental disintegration, he urges that "we move over into metaphysics" (p. 125) and characterize the matter-increase causally as a miracle by saying that "the creation process is a divine act which is proceeding continuously" (p. 117). Thus, in that sense, Lovell is prepared to accept the steady-state cosmology if observation were to confirm it empirically. Ironically, he overlooked that Descartes had claimed divine intervention to explain matter-*conservation*, after assuming a state of nothingness to be the unperturbed natural state of the world. In a steady-state world containing humanoids who live long enough to observe its matter-accretion many, many times, it would seem quite natural to them.

We see that the hypothesized matter-increase in a steady-state universe is turned into a divine miracle only by the gratuitous, dogmatic insistence on matter-conservation as *cosmically* the natural state, *no matter what the empirical evidence*. Those who share Lovell's view of miraculousness cannot justify a criterion of "naturalness" that would turn the continual accretion of new matter into something "outside the natural order" instead of just being itself a part of that very order. I therefore conclude that Herbert Dingle's rejection of matter accretion as miraculous was ill-founded.[3] Thus, Lovell, the theist, and Dingle, the atheist, made identically the same mistake of thinking that the matter-increase would be miraculous, although they made opposite uses of that mistake in their attitude toward the steady-state theory. Philosophically, they are brothers under the skin in this context. Thus, both Dingle and Lovell overlook the following key point: *Just as a theory postulating matter-conservation does not require God to prevent the conserved matter from being annihilated, so also the steady-state theory has no need at all for a divine agency to cause its new hydrogen to come into being!*

The argument that I have developed on the basis of the history of physics from Aristotle to Bondi and Gold could likewise be based on the history of inquiry into the natural possibility of the spontaneous, unperturbed generation of living substances from inorganic materials. After Pasteur's work led to the denial of that possibility in an oxidizing atmosphere, Oparin and Urey asserted it for a reducing atmosphere *over much longer time periods* [Grünbaum (1973), pp. 571–574].

---

[3] I pointed out the pitfalls of the miracle concept in this context in a letter in *Scientific American*, December, 1953. In a private communication to me (dated December 11, 1953), Professor Bondi wrote that, in his view, my point in the letter "was in great need of being stated." And he added: "Naturally I found it particularly enjoyable that you discussed the matter with reference to an unsound criticism of our [Bondi and Gold] theory."

B. The Big Bang Theory

Let us now turn first to the alleged problem of "creation" posed by the pre-quantum version of the big bang theory, as treated by Lovell, Narlikar, and even Bondi. When that theory is being contrasted with its steady-state rival, it is often called "evolutionary." And it tells us that, before the chemical elements were formed, an explosion of primeval matter resulted in the present expansion of the universe. That explosion is called "the big bang." It may perhaps still be an open question whether the big bang might be somehow accommodated in a mathematically meaningful fashion in an Einsteinian universe such that the big bang is *not* a singular boundary of space–time. In one such sketchily envisioned model, the big bang would have been preceded by an infinite sequence of prior contractions and expansions, like those of a musical accordion. But quite apart from current technical doubts about the eternally oscillating model of the universe, it does not even provide a *point of departure* for the argument from creation *ex nihilo*. Therefore, I shall now consider just the particular models which at first glance *seem* to warrant the sort of questions asked by Narlikar and Lovell.

These models have been claimed to allow two cases: Let me discuss them separately. But I must note at once the *caveat* issued by Torretti (1979, pp. 328–329; 1983, pp. 210–219; 1984, p. 197) that only the *second* of these cases is a bona fide one of general relativity, whereas the first one is not. I nonetheless deal with the latter as well, because Narlikar and others have invoked it to claim, as we saw, that $t = 0$ is a bona fide instant at which "the primary creation event" actually occurred (Narlikar 1977, pp. 136–137).

Case (i) features a cosmic time interval that is *closed* at the big bang instant $t = 0$, and furthermore, *this instant had no temporal predecessor*. In this case, $t = 0$ was a singular, temporally first event of the physical space–time to which all of the worldlines of the universe converge. This means that *there simply did not exist any instants of time before $t = 0$!* But it would be (potentially) misleading to describe this state of affairs by saying that "time began" at $t = 0$. This description makes it sound as if time began in the same sense in which, say, a musical concert began. And that is misleading, precisely because the concert was actually preceded by actual instants of time, when it had *not yet* begun. But, in the big bang model under consideration, there were no such earlier instants before $t = 0$ and hence no instants when the big bang had not yet occurred. Lovell (1961, p. 106) is quite unaware of these facts when he speaks mistakenly of a "metaphysical scheme before the beginning of time and space." Similarly, there is no basis for Narlikar's (1977, p. 125) lament that "scientists are not in the habit of discussing . . . the situation prior to it [the big bang]."

To suggest or to assume tacitly that such prior instants existed after all is simply incompatible with the physical correctness of this model and thus implicitly denies its soundness. Since Aristotle believed that a first instant of time is *inconceivable* (*Physics*, Book VIII, 251b), he implicitly denied even the logical possibility of the model, and therefore also its physical possibility. It is now clear that the physical correctness of this model is also implicitly denied by anyone who asks any of the following questions: "What happened *before* $t = 0$?", "what *prior* events CAUSED matter to come *into* existence at $t = 0$?", or "what *caused* the big bang to occur at $t = 0$?" In just this vein, Lovell (1961, pp. 98–99) asks "how the primeval gas originated" and then complains that "Science has nothing to say on this issue." But each of these questions presupposes that $t = 0$ was preceded by other existing moments of time. Yet just this assumption is denied by the very model to which these questions are being addressed!

Therefore, we can now draw the following major conclusions: If Narlikar and Lovell take the given big bang model to be physically true, then the questions they have addressed to it are illegitimate, because then these questions are based on a false presupposition. Of course, they are indeed entitled to reject the model by giving cogent reasons for postulating the existence of times *before* $t = 0$. But, failing that, it is altogether wrong-headed for them to complain that — even when taken to be physically adequate — this model fails to answer questions based on assumptions which it denies as false. As we saw, Newton's laws of motion cannot be expected to answer a question calling for the specification of an external cause (force) of uniform motion. And a man who never beats his wife cannot be expected to answer the question: "When did you start or stop beating her?"

This question-begging presupposition of instants before $t = 0$ is also made in another form by asking in the context of the *pre*-quantum models: "How did the matter existing *at* $t = 0$ come *into* being?" The model to which this is addressed features the *conservation* of matter–energy. Thus, it asserts that, at all existing instants of time, the total matter–energy content of the universe was the same. To ask how this matter came *into* existence in the first place is to presuppose not only earlier moments of time, but also the *non*-existence of any matter at those supposed earlier times. Yet precisely these presuppositions are denied by the matter-conservation asserted by the model. Therefore, Narlikar (1977, pp. 136–137) was simply dead wrong when he wrote: "in big bang cosmologies . . . at $t = 0$, there occurs a sudden and fantastic violation of the law of conservation of matter and energy." Even the term "sudden" tacitly trades on times prior to $t = 0$. And these illegitimate ways of begging the question generate the so-called "problem of creation"! By the same token, it was wrong for the physicist Orear (1963, p. 243) to say that the big bang model features "sudden creation."

Besides Narlikar and Lovell, even Bondi (1961, pp. 74 and 140) thought that there is a problem of creation in the big bang model of general relativity, though not in his own steady-state model. But the big bang model simply denies that any matter at all comes *into* existence *non*-conservatively. It appears, therefore, that, with respect to the big bang theory, Bondi fell into the same error as Lovell and Narlikar. But so did the atheistic British astrophysicist Bonnor (1964, pp. 111–112), who rejects the model of Case (i) partly because he mistakenly believes that it supports a theological interpretation of cosmogony.

Recall that the oscillating "accordion" universe mentioned at the start of this Section B is irrelevant to our concerns, since it does not even provide a point of departure for the creation *ex nihilo* argument.

I should emphasize that if, as in the version of quantum cosmology outlined in Section 4 below, the "big bang" is no longer held to comprise *all* early past time ($t \geq 0$) but to start later, then *it may well no longer be misguided* to ask "what caused the big bang?", as in Davies (1984, Chap. 12). But, in that quantum version, general relativity turns out to tell us *why* there is an "inflationary" expansion, thereby obviating any explanatory resort to an external divine cause!

Case (ii). This subclass of big bang models differs from those in Case (i) by excluding the mathematical singularity at $t = 0$ as not being an actual moment of time. Thus, their cosmic time interval is *open* in the past by lacking the instant $t = 0$, although the duration of that past interval in years is finite, say 12 billion years or so. But just as in Case (i), no instants of time exist *before* $t = 0$ in Case (ii). And despite the equality of finite duration of the time intervals in the two models, the crucial difference between Case (ii) and Case (i) is the following: In Case (ii), *there is no first instant of time at all*, just as there is no leftmost point on an infinite Euclidean line that extends in both directions. And in both Case (i) and Case (ii), the non-existence of time *before* $t = 0$ allows that matter has *always* existed, although the age of the universe is finite in either case. And this assertion is true because, in this context, the term "always" refers to all actual past instants of time.

Nevertheless, even in Case (ii), the finite age of the universe has tempted some people to make the tacit false assumption that there were moments of time after all *before* the big bang, an assumption incompatible with both models. And once this question-begging assumption is made, the door is open for all the same illegitimate, ill-posed creation questions that I undermined à propos of Case (i).

We are now ready to see that despite the replacement of the classical big bang theory by quantum cosmology, the philosophical issues with which we have been concerned, as well as their resolution, remain essentially the same.

4. Quantum Cosmology

In a very recent paper, Weisskopf (1989) gives an account of quantum cosmogony that links up with the above classical story of the big bang expansion of the universe. Relying on that account, we note first that there are two sorts of vacuum (p. 36): The "true" and "false" ones respectively. The former features empty space and "energy fluctuations," though it is said to be devoid of matter and energy proper. The false vacuum, on the other hand, contains energy *without* matter. Referring to the initial true vacuum state, Weisskopf (p. 36) recalls the biblical statement "The world was without form and void, and darkness was upon the face of the deep." But, as we shall see, the clear affinity between that vague biblical statement and the assertion of an initial true vacuum in the technical sense of particle physics turns out to be *altogether unavailing to the proponent of divine creation out of nothing!*

The initial true vacuum state does not last. There is a transition from it to the false vacuum: "Everything, including the true vacuum, is subject to fluctuations — in particular to energy fluctuations. The field that provides energy to the false vacuum is absent in the true vacuum, but not completely. There must be fluctuations in the field. Thus, at one moment a small region somewhere in space may have fluctuated into a false vacuum" (p. 36). In a follow-up letter (*New York Review of Books*, March 16, 1989), Weisskopf asks:

> How can energy fluctuations occur in a true vacuum that is supposed to be free of energy and matter? (p. 43)

And he replies:

> No doubt the statement I made, if applied to the true vacuum, contradicts the idea of total emptiness. *In this sense the common concept of a vacuum is not valid.* The recognition of fundamental fluctuations in empty space is one of the great achievements of quantum mechanics. In some special cases the existence of such fluctuations has been established by experiment. And that is the basis of the idea that indeed something can come out of nothing. (p.43: my italics)

Thus, according to quantum theory, this sort of emergence of energy, which is *ex nihilo* only in a rather Pickwickian sense, proceeds in accord with pertinent physical principles, rather than as a matter of inscrutable external divine causation.

As is known from Einstein's general theory of relativity, a false vacuum "is bound to expand suddenly and explosively, filling more and more space with false vacuum." Just this "inflationary" expansion, which is far more rapid than the rates familiar from the classical conceptions of the expanding universe, "is supposed to be the Big Bang!" (p. 37).

When a specified large size is attained, the inflationary explosion stops, and a true vacuum emerges but, by one microsecond thereafter, the energy contained in the false vacuum shows up as light as well as in the form of various particles and anti-particles. In this sense, a "mechanism" for matter-formation is envisioned by this current theory. Thereafter, our universe goes into the previously familiar, relatively "slow" expansion. Some 300,000 years later, atoms are formed when protons and helium nuclei capture electrons. In due course, stars are born from the hot hydrogen and helium gases, and so, subsequently, are galaxies.

For precisely the reasons I developed à propos of the classical big bang at $t = 0$, there is no warrant at all for invoking an external cause — let alone a divine one — for the initial true vacuum. Hawking (1988) reaches the conclusion that there is no problem of creation, because at that stage, the very distinction between space and time becomes mushy, as does the notion of an initial singular instant of time. A *fortiori*, there is no warrant for seeking an external cause of any sort for effecting the various successive transitions from the true vacuum to the false one, then to the "inflationary expansion", and finally to the more familiar slow expansion that features the formations outlined above. After all, all these transitions are matters of natural physical laws.

Besides, such physicists as Hartle and Hawking (1983, pp. 2961–2962) and Vilenkin (1983, p. 2851) speak misleadingly of certain primordial physical states as "nothing," even though these states are avowedly only "a realm of unrestrained quantum gravity," which is "a state with no classical space-time" [Vilenkin (1983), p. 2851]. And if the very notion of physical time becomes problematic in fundamental physics, as urged by John Wheeler, then even the *temptation* to misinvoke divine creation *ex nihilo* is altogether undercut!

In his 1986 paper, Lovell referred to an updated big bang model that features an initial quantum vacuum state, followed by the expansion. And he said in effect: If we call $t = 0$ a state of "nothing," then this model provides a scientific justification of Augustine's theory of creation out of nothing. But in the discussion after his oral delivery of the paper at a 1986 Locarno congress, I offered my arguments above against his reasoning: Why, I asked, should the transition from the vacuum state to the expansion require any *external cause* at all, let alone a divine one? I was delighted that, in Lovell's reply, he then expressed agreement with me [Lovell (1986), p. 109].

More generally, I conclude that neither the big bang cosmogony nor the steady-state cosmology validates the traditional cosmological argument for divine creation. But, as we see, that argument dies hard.

ACKNOWLEDGMENTS

I thank P. Davies, R. Gale, A. Janis, J. Leslie, P. L. Quinn, R. Torretti, and J. Wheeler for reading earlier versions of this essay and making helpful suggestions.

REFERENCES

Bondi, H. (1961). *Cosmology*. 2nd ed. New York: Cambridge University Press.
Bonnor, W. (1964). *The Mystery of the Expanding Universe*. New York: Macmillan.
Craig, W. L. (1979). *The Kalam Cosmological Argument*. New York: Harper & Row.
Davies, P. C. W. (1984). *Superforce*. New York: Simon & Schuster.
Descartes, R. (1967). *Meditation III*, in *Philosophical Work by Descartes*, Vol. 1, edited by E. S. Haldane and G. R. Ross. New York: Cambridge University Press.
Grünbaum, A. (1968). *Modern Science and Zeno's Paradoxes*. 2nd ed. London: Allen & Unwin.
Grünbaum, A. (1973). *Philosophical Problems of Space and Time*. 2nd ed. Dordrecht & Boston: Reidel.
Hartle, J. B., and Hawking, S. W. (1983). Wave function of the universe. *Physical Review D*, 28: 2960–2975.
Hawking, S. W. (1988). *A Brief History of Time: From the Big-Bang to Black Holes*. New York: Bantam Books.
Hawking S. W., and Ellis, G. F. R. (1973). *The Large-Scale Structure of Space–Time*. New York: Cambridge University Press.
Lovell, A. C. B. (1961). *The Individual and the Universe*. New York: New American Library (Mentor Book MD330).
Lovell, A. C. B. (1986). Reason and faith in cosmology. Italian translation: "Ragione e Fede in Cosmologia." *Nuova Civilta Delle Macchine* 4 [Nos. 3/4 and 15/16], 101–108.
Narlikar, J. (1977). *The Structure of the Universe*. Oxford: Oxford University Press.
Narlikar, J. (1988). *The Primeval Universe*. Oxford: Oxford University Press.
Orear, J. (1963). *Fundamental Physics*. New York: Wiley.
Peebles, P. J. E. (1971). *Physical Cosmology*. Princeton: Princeton University Press.
Reichenbach, H. (1956). *The Direction of Time*. Berkeley: University of California Press.
Rindler, W. (1977). *Essential Relativity*. 2nd ed. New York: Springer.
Rowe, W. L. (1975). *The Cosmological Argument*. Princeton: Princeton University Press.
Torretti, R. (1979). Mathematical Theories and Philosophical Insights in Cosmology, in *Einstein Symposium Berlin*, edited by H. Nelkowski, et al. New York: Springer, pp. 320–335.
Torretti, R. (1983). *Relativity and Geometry*. New York: Pergamon Press.
Torretti, R. (1984). "Kosmologie als Zweig der Physik," in *Moderne Naturphilosophie*, edited by B. Kanitscheider. Würzburg: Königshausen and Neumann, pp. 183–201.
Vilenkin, A. (1983). Birth of inflationary universes. *Physical Review D*, 27: 2848–2855.
Weinberg, S. (1972). *Gravitation and Cosmology*. New York: Wiley.
Weisskopf, V. (1989). The origin of the universe. *Bulletin of the American Academy of Arts & Sciences* 42: 22–39. Reprinted in *The New York Review of Books*, 36, No. 2, pp. 10–14.

8

G. F. R. ELLIS*

Cosmology and Verifiability

The Cosmological Problem

RELATIVISTIC COSMOLOGY AIMS to determine the structure of the universe from a fusion of the results of astronomical observations with knowledge derived from local physical experiments. The problem of determining this structure[1] is centred on the fact that there is only one universe to be observed, and that we effectively can only observe it from one space–time point. Because it is a unique object, we cannot infer its probable nature by comparing it with similar objects; and (on the scale we are considering) we are unable to choose the time or position from which we view it. Our predicament is analogous to that of a premaritime man living on a small island in an ocean, who observes around him a host of other small islands apparently scattered at random on a seemingly limitless sea. Unable to move from his island, his theory of the world in which he lives can only be based on this partial view.

Unverifiable Assumptions

Given this situation, *we are unable to obtain a model of the universe without some specifically cosmological assumptions which are com-*

*Reprinted from *Quarterly Journal of the Royal Astronomical Society*, Vol. 16, No. 3, 1975, by permission of the Society's Treasurer and of Blackwell Scientific Publications Ltd. The selection represents pp. 245–252 of a paper which continues, much more technically, to p. 264.

pletely unverifiable. Because we wish to talk about regions we cannot directly influence or experiment on, our theory is at the mercy of the assumptions we make. To illustrate this, consider the possibility that our friend on the island might be of a theological disposition; and might have decided that there was in fact only one island in the world, surrounded by an ocean which ended at a beautifully painted diorama constructed by an artistic and kindly God, giving him the illusion of a limitless sea covered by islands. In an exactly analogous way, a modern cosmologist who was also a theologian with strict fundamentalist views could construct a universe model which began 6000 years ago in time and whose edge was at a distance of 6000 light years from the solar system. A benevolent God could easily arrange the creation of this universe not only so that suitable fossils would be present in the Earth (having been created, together with the rest of the universe, 6000 years ago) to imply a long geological history, but also so that suitable radiation was travelling towards us from the edge of the universe to give the illusion of a vastly older and larger expanding universe. It would be impossible for any other scientist on the Earth to refute this world picture experimentally or observationally; all that he could do would be to disagree with the author's cosmological premises.

What has been violated here is the expectation that the ordinary laws of everyday physics, carefully and correctly applied, will lead to correct inferences about what exists; for such application of these laws leads (in these unusual universes) to expectations different from what would actually be there. To exclude this possibility, we invoke the first of our unverifiable assumptions about the universe: *whenever normal physical laws can be applied, they correctly predict the structure of the universe.* I shall call this the *local predictability assumption.* There are two facets to this requirement: firstly, that the normal physical laws we determine in our space–time vicinity are applicable at all other space–time points. This demand for uniformity in Nature is necessary for reasonable predictions to be made about distant parts of the universe; for otherwise there is too much arbitrariness in what we can suppose. Without this guide, we have no suitable set of rules to tell us what to expect. In any case we have a set of physical laws which are locally valid, and the established scientific policy—based on the "Occam's razor" or "minimal assumption" attitude—is to continue extrapolating, applying these laws in larger domains and to more distant points, unless something makes it clear that this is the wrong procedure. Note that this does not exclude, for example, theories in which the gravitational constant varies; all this amounts to (assuming we know the law which determines how this "constant" varies) is that local physical laws are rather more complex than we might originally have supposed. The second aspect of this statement is the implication that we keep on applying these laws as long as this is possible; and the resulting expectations are fulfilled. It is this aspect (expressed mathematically in the requirement that space–time be inextendible)[2] which prevents our universe model beginning or ending at an edge such as the one described above.

Having adopted this principle, one might hope it would not be necessary to make further unverifiable assumptions in order to obtain a reasonably unique cosmological model from our observations. However, the nature of the observations we are able to make prevents fulfilment of this hope. Two facts lead to this conclusion. First, we are unable to examine directly space–time itself, or the distribution of matter in it; rather we observe particular objects—stars, galaxies, quasistellar objects, dust, and so on—in space–time, and only when we have somehow determined their intrinsic properties can we deduce their distribution and the properties of the intervening space–time.[3] Second, we simply do not have the astrophysical information needed to determine their nature sufficiently accurately. This is partly because there is a wide variation in the properties of individual objects in each class; partly because we simply do not understand the nature of some of the classes of objects we are observing; and to a very large extent because the light we receive from the more distant objects was emitted a long time ago. Thus we need to have a satisfactory theory of their time-evolution in order to determine their intrinsic properties at the time they emit the light by which we observe them. We do not have such a theory. So, for example, having obtained measurements of the radio brightness of a radio source, we are unable to determine directly from our measurements whether we are receiving radiation emitted from a bright source a long time ago, or from a weaker source which is relatively nearby, or from a weak source which is very far away but appears anomalously bright because of the curvature of the intervening space–time. The situation is similar to that of the isolated man on the island if he is able to measure accurately the apparent sizes of the other islands, but does not know their intrinsic sizes. Any particular island he sees might be a small one nearby, or a much larger one a long way off. A new principle is needed to order the observations.

As presented thus far, the argument may sound rather weak; it may seem that introduction of a new principle is a counsel of expediency rather than necessity. Might it not be that given suffieicnt time for increased understanding of the astrophysics involved, the problem would eventually simply go away; for then we would have sufficient information to use the observed objects as "standard candles" which could be reliably used to chart the universe? This is most unlikely to be the case, not only because of the nature of the difficulties encountered in astrophysics, but because of one fundamental aspect of our present knowledge of the universe which has not been mentioned so far.

This crucial feature is that the universe appears to be *isotropic about us* to an extraordinary accuracy. In particular the number counts of distant radio sources show that their average distribution is the same in all directions; the X-ray background radiation is isotropic to better than 5 per cent; and the microwave background radiation is isotropic to better than 0.2 per cent.[4] No matter what direction we choose in order to obtain information about the large-scale structure of the universe, we obtain the same answer as for any other direction. Thus there seem (on a cosmological scale) to be no preferred directions about us; we are unable to point in a certain direction and say "the centre of the universe lies over there"; in fact we are unable to say that any direction is particularly different from any other.

To consider the consequences of this, suppose our astonished friend on his island found that his observations lead to the same conclusion. He would then be able to use this fact to construct for himself models of his world, even though he did not know the distances of the islands he observed. He would, after a while, discover there were two possible situations. Either the islands could be scattered uniformly over a uniform ocean in such a way that all islands were roughly the same distance from the island nearest to them, and so that the world looked very much the same to any observer on any island; or they could be distributed in some other way, for example with all the islands that looked smaller a much smaller distance from their nearest neighbours than all the islands that looked larger. The common feature of all these other ways of arranging the islands would be that they were all centred on his own island; by measuring the positions of all the islands in the sea one would with complete certainty deduce that his own island was at the centre of the visible part of the world. Although he himself would not be able to point out any direction as the direction to the centre of the world, an intelligent observer on any of the other islands he could see would indeed be able to do so; and all such observers would point at his own island!

The situation in relativistic cosmology is precisely similar. We can construct all space–times which would give exactly isotropic observations about one particular galaxy; and they are either exactly spatially homogeneous and isotropic space–times, which are isotropic about every galaxy — in this case, all galaxies are equivalent — or they are centred on that one galaxy. This galaxy is then at the centre of the universe.[5] The actual universe, which is not exactly isotropic about us, may then be expected to be very similar to one or other of these idealized possibilities.

In ages gone by, the assumption that the Earth was at the centre of the universe was taken for granted. As we know, the pendulum has now swung to the opposite extreme; this is a concept that is anathema to almost all thinking men. This is partly because we now believe that our Galaxy is no different from millions of others; more fundamentally, it is due to the Copernican–Darwinian revolution in our understanding of the nature of man and his position in the universe. He has been dethroned from the exalted position he was once considered to hold.

It would certainly be consistent with the present observations that we were at the centre of the universe, and that, for example, radio sources were distributed spherically symmetrically about us in shells characterized by increasing source density and brightness as their distance from us increased.[6] Although mathematical models for such Earth-centered cosmologies have occasionally been investigated, they have not been taken seriously; in fact, the most striking feature of the radio source counts is how this obvious possibility has been completely discounted. The assumption of spatial homogeneity has inevitably been made, and has led to the conclusion that the population of radio sources evolves extremely rapidly.[7] What has therefore happened is that an unproven cosmological assumption has been completely accepted and used to obtain rather unexpected information about astrophysical processes.

It seems likely that reasonable theories will continue to be based on this assumption. One may adopt this view simply because our own Galaxy seems a rather undistinguished place to be the centre of the universe, or because of deeper philosophic reasons. In any case, we shall accept the implied attitude, and turn to consider the different ways it can be formalized. Important differences in our concept of the universe arise if we formalize it in different ways.

Uniformity Principles

The traditional way of codifying the view that we occupy an average, rather than a highly special, position in the universe is to adopt the *Cosmological Principle*[8]: that is, the assumption that *the universe is spatially homogeneous*. This principle implies the existence of a cosmic time, and states that all measurable properties are the same at the same cosmic time. In particular, our observations of the isotropy of the universe would mean that all other observers viewing the universe at the same time would find their observations equally isotropic. Hence one obtains as idealized universe models the exactly spatially homogeneous and isotropic (or *Robertson–Walker*) space–times.[9] These are supposed to represent the smoothed-out structure of the universe: a more realistic universe model can be obtained by superimposing small perturbations on this completely smooth substratum.

The Cosmological Principle is a positive statement with far-reaching consequences. An alternative way of proceeding is to make a negative statement. Thus we might make the assumption: *we are not at the centre of the universe*. (I shall refer to this as the *Copernican Principle*.) As has been indicated above, this principle together with the observed isotropy of the universe about us again leads us to perturbed Robertson–Walker space–times as models of the observed universe.

To illustrate the differences between these two approaches, consider once again our marooned natural philosopher. Having formulated for himself a "Cosmological Principle"—that every part of the world is identical with every other part—he triumphantly announces his homogeneous and isotropic world model: the world is a completely smooth ball. Not only are all points equivalent to each other, but for every point, observations made in any direction are equivalent to observations made in any other direction. His lady-friend—who has been around all the time, but engaged on other enterprises—now correctly but somewhat unkindly points out that the world does not look very uniform to her. This necessitates him explaining that the world model was not meant to be an exact model of the world, but only an approximate one showing its basic, overall structure; a more adequate model would be obtained by thinking of a lot of islands scattered all over the idealized smooth ball. The homogeneity is meant to be understood in some unspecified statistical sense.

As his friend's reaction is not completely positive, he broods overnight and the next day formulates his "Copernican Principle"—that their own island is not at the centre of the world. He then easily convinces her that this principle—not being stated as an exact requirement of uniformity—is readily amenable to a statistical discussion; and that (because of the isotropy of the world about their island) it leads to the conclusion that the world they see is approximately a smooth ball with islands scattered over it in a uniform way. He is delighted to find she accepts the principle as compelling, and the resulting world-model as an obvious consequence. The new formulation has the advantage that unlike the Cosmological Principle which only applies to highly idealized models of the world, the Copernican Principle can be applied to realistic world models; and so is a more satisfactory way of formalizing the assumption.

Nevertheless, in practice these principles may be interpreted so as to lead to the same ideas about the observed universe. The problem lies elsewhere, as our friend realizes with a sinking feeling when his companion asks him "Gee, does that mean there are islands just like ours in all the parts of the world we can't see?" This question puts him in a quandary. His Cosmological Principle made a definite prediction about all the unobservable areas over his horizon, namely that conditions there are the same as conditions near him. But he has no observational information whatever about these regions, nor will he ever obtain such information in the foreseeable future; so this conclusion is a direct result of his completely unverifiable assumption about the world. If he merely assumes the Copernican Principle, this orders his world the same way in the observable region, because he knows that in this region the world is nearly isotropic about him. But he does not have any such information about the unobservable regions, and accordingly the Copernican Principle (as formulated here) makes no particular prediction about these hidden regions. Indeed, according to the available evidence they could be totally different from the areas near him. Thus there could be many more islands, or many fewer, or no islands, or perhaps a continent in some part or other; or perhaps his whole concept of the world as a roughly uniform ball might be wrong, for while it might have that form near him, it could be, for example, that the region he saw was just the top of a mountain based on some landform of completely unknown shape.

The situation in cosmology is essentially the same. The Cosmological Principle determines a complete universe model; the Copernican Principle only a model of the observed part of the universe. The first model is satisfying because it is complete, but unsatisfying because it makes predictions about parts of the universe which are beyond observation; one has only one's faith in the integrity of this principle to validate these predictions. The second model is satisfying in that it only attempts to state conditions in the observable parts of the universe, but is therefore also unsatisfying, as there are further regions of the universe which it does not attempt to describe.

NOTES

1. An informative discussion of the theoretical basis of cosmology is given in H. Bondi, *Cosmology* (Cambridge University Press, 1960). A useful discussion of the history of the subject is in J. D. North, *The Measure of the Universe* (Oxford University Press, 1965).
2. I shall, as discussed later, assume that General Relativity is the correct theory describing space–time and gravitation.
3. The way this can be done locally has been carefully described by Kristian and Sachs, *Astrophys. J.*, **143**, 379 (1966).
4. A very readable discussion of recent observations and their interpretation is in D. W. Sciama, *Modern Cosmology* (Cambridge University Press, 1971). A more detailed discussion of the physics involved is in S. Weinberg, *Gravitation and Cosmology* (Wiley and Sons, 1972); a detailed review of recent observational data has been given by Longair, *Rept. Progr. Phys.*, **34**, 1125 (1971).
5. In certain such universes, there could be *two* centres. The argument then proceeds unchanged; there are two galaxies whose situation is completely different from that of all other galaxies in the universe. In an expanding universe, isotropy of the *world picture* (the universe as *seen* by the observer) implies either anthropocentricity, or homogeneity and isotropy of the *world map* (the instantaneous map of the universe he constructs, utilizing his knowledge that light travels at a finite speed).
6. Systematic redshifts could be observed in such an Earth-centered universe even if it were static.
7. See Reference (4) above.
8. The various principles are discussed in detail by Bondi and North (1). Many

other reviews of cosmology discuss them, but in less detail, see e.g. the reviews in (4); for a recent reappraisal, see Harrison's articles in *Comm. Astrophys. Space Phys.*, 6, 23; 29 (1974). We have not here elaborated on the *Perfect Cosmological Principle* (the assumption that the universe is homogeneous in space *and* time) as experimental evidence seems to be against it.

9. See the references in notes 1 and 4, or the review articles in *General Relativity and Gravitation*, Ed. R. K. Sachs (Academic Press, 1971) (Proceedings of the 47th International School of Physics "Enrico Fermi"); or in *Cargese Lectures in Physics, Volume 6*, Ed. E. Schatzmann (Gordon and Breach, 1973).

9

R. H. DICKE*

Dirac's Cosmology and Mach's Principle

THE DIMENSIONLESS GRAVITATIONAL coupling constant

$$\frac{Gm_p^{\,2}}{\hbar c} \sim 5 \times 10^{-39} \tag{1}$$

with m_p the mass of some elementary particle, for definiteness taken as the proton, is such a small number that its significance has long been questioned. Thus Eddington[1] considered that all the dimensionless physical constants, including this one, could be evaluated as simple mathematical expressions. Dirac[2] considered that such an odd number must be related to other numbers of similar size, characterizing the structure of the universe. However, most physicists seem to believe that a dimensionless constant, such as (1), is provided by Nature, cannot be calculated, and is not in any way related to other numbers.

Dirac noted that most physical and astrophysical dimensionless constants are of the order of magnitude of integral powers (positive and negative) of the number 10^{40}, where such numbers as $m_p/m_e \sim 1,800$ and $\hbar c/e^2 \sim 137$ are said to be of the order of unity, the zero power of 10^{40}. He considered unlikely the accidental correspondence of the apparently unrelated, enormous numbers, and he suggested some unknown causal connexion.

*Reprinted by permission from *Nature*, Vol. 192, No. 4801, November 4 1961, pp. 440–441. Copyright © 1961, Macmillan Magazines Ltd.

One of these large numbers is:

$$T \frac{m_p c}{\hbar} \sim 10^{42} \tag{2}$$

with T the Hubble age of the universe. For an evolutionary universe, T varies with time. This suggested to Dirac that all the large numbers vary with time, with numbers of the order of $(10^{40})^n$ varying as T^n. Dirac[2] constructed a cosmology based on this idea, and Jordan[3] produced a proper relativistic theory of Dirac's cosmology.

The three principal large numbers are given by equations 1 and 2, and by the mass of the universe to its visible limits, expressed as:

$$\frac{M}{m_p} \sim 10^{80} = (10^{40})^2 \tag{3}$$

According to Dirac's hypothesis, these three numbers should vary as the −1, 1, and 2 power of the time respectively.

It should be noted that it is necessary to assume more than a connexion between the three numbers (1), (2), and (3) to justify Dirac's hypothesis. In addition, one must assume that the apparent interconnexion between the three numbers is independent of time. This assumption could be supported by a statistical argument. If the present value of T were to be considered conceptually as a random choice from a wide range of possible values of T, the present "choice" would have had a small a priori probability, and an accidental correspondence of the type exhibited by the three numbers would have been unlikely. In view of the inexactness of the interrelation between the three numbers, a very wide range of possible values of T and a small a priori probability must be assumed if Dirac's hypothesis is to receive support from this type of argument.

It will be shown that, with the assumption of an evolutionary universe, T is not permitted to take one of an enormous range of values, but is somewhat limited by the biological requirements to be met during the epoch of man.

The first of these requirements is that the universe, hence galaxy, shall have aged sufficiently for there to exist elements other than hydrogen. It is well known that carbon is required to make physicists.

It is known that the galaxy was formed initially from hydrogen only. Hence, the minimum time for the start of the epoch of man is set by the age of the shortest-lived stars, for elements, other than hydrogen, are formed in the interior, and distributed at the death, of the star.

An upper limit for the epoch of man is set by the requirement that he has a hospitable home in the form of a planet circling a luminous star. This time is set by the maximum age of a star capable of producing energy by nuclear reactions. For stars less massive, gravitational contraction is halted by the onset of electron degeneracy pressure, before central temperatures rise high enough for the onset of nuclear reactions. The mass of the longest-lived stars can be computed assuming that electron degeneracy occurs at the nuclear reaction temperature. This gives for the lower bound on M_s, the mass of the star:

$$\frac{M_s}{m_p} \sim 10^{-3} \left(\frac{\hbar c}{G m_p^2} \right)^{3/2} \tag{4}$$

where m_p is again the proton mass. According to the above definition of order of magnitude, 10^{-3} is to be regarded as equivalent to unity and this number is of the order of magnitude of $(10^{40})^{3/2}$.

The life-span of a star of this mass can be calculated, assuming that the emission and opacity are determined by free-free transitions (the bremsstrahlung radiation and absorption process). This lifetime is:

$$T_{max} \sim \left(\frac{m_p}{m} \right)^{5/2} \left(\frac{e^2}{\hbar c} \right)^3 \left(\frac{G m_p^2}{\hbar c} \right)^{-1} \frac{\hbar}{m_p c^2} \tag{5}$$

after dropping numerical factors, where m is the electron mass. Dropping the "unity factors", this becomes:

$$\frac{m_p c^2}{\hbar} T_{max} \sim \left(\frac{G m_p^2}{\hbar c} \right)^{-1} \tag{6}$$

in agreement with equations (1) and (2). In similar fashion, T_{min}, as determined by requirements for stellar stability, is of the same order of magnitude. Thus, contrary to our original supposition, T is not a "random choice" from a wide range of possible choices, but is limited by the criteria for the existence of physicists.

Two problems remain. Why is the gravitational coupling constant so small? Why does the square root of the number given by equation (3) agree with the reciprocal of (1)? Both of these questions are answered by introducing Mach's Principle. According to the interpretation of Mach's Principle sometimes made[4-6], the gravitational coupling constant is not fixed but is determined by the mass distribution of the universe in such a way that:

$$\frac{GM}{c^3 T} \sim 1 \tag{7}$$

Combining equations (7) and (6) gives the expression obtained by combining equations (1) and (3).

The reason for the smallness of the gravitational coupling constant is the enormous amount of matter in the universe. This may not be a very satisfactory answer, and it cannot be completely satisfactory until the problem of mass creation is understood.

The statistical support for Dirac's cosmology is found to be missing. However, the existence of physicists now and the assumption of the validity of Mach's Principle are sufficient to demand that the order-of-magnitude relations between the three numbers, given by equations (1), (2) and (3), be satisfied.

NOTES

1. Eddington, A. S., *Theory of Protons and Electrons* (Cambridge Univ. Press, 1936).
2. Dirac, P. A. M., *Proc. Roy. Soc., A,* **165**, 199 (1938).
3. Jordan, P., *Schwerkraft und Weltall* (Braunschweig, 1955).
4. Sciama, D. W., *Mon. Not. Roy. Astro. Soc.,* **113**, 34 (1953).
5. Dicke, R. H., *Amer. Scientist,* **47**, 25 (1959).
6. Brans, C., and Dicke, R. H., *Phys. Rev.,* **124**, No. 3 (1961).

10

BRANDON CARTER*

Large Number Coincidences and the Anthropic Principle in Cosmology

1. Introduction

PROF. WHEELER HAS asked me to say something for the record about some ideas that I once suggested (at the Clifford Memorial meeting in Princeton in 1970) and to which Hawking and Collins have referred (*Astrophys. J.* **180,** 317, 1973). This concerns a line of thought which I believe to be potentially fertile, but which I did not write up at the time because I felt (as I still feel) that it needs further development. However, it is not inappropriate that this matter should have cropped up again on the present occasion, since it consists basically of a reaction against exaggerated subservience to the "Copernican principle."

Copernicus taught us the very sound lesson that we must not assume gratuitously that we occupy a privileged *central* position in the Universe. Unfortunately there has been a strong (not always subconscious) tendency to extend this to a most questionable dogma to the effect that our situation cannot be privileged in any sense. This dogma (which in its most extreme form led to the "perfect cosmological principle" on which the steady state theory was based) is clearly untenable, as was pointed out by Dicke (*Nature* **192**, 440, 1961), if one accepts (a) that specially favourable conditions (of temperature, chemical environ-

*By courtesy of the International Astronomical Union, reprinted from M. S. Longair (ed.), *Confrontation of Cosmological Theories with Observational Data*, pp. 291–298. All rights reserved. Copyright © 1974 by the IAU.

ment, etc.) are prerequisite for our existence, and (b) that the Universe evolves and is by no means spatially homogeneous on a local scale.

My own interest in this matter arose from reading Bondi's (1959) book *Cosmology* in which certain widely known "large number coincidences" are listed as evidence justifying the introduction of various exotic theories (e.g. involving departures from normally accepted physical conservation laws) of which early examples were the "varying G" theories of Dirac and Jordan. I am now convinced of the opposite thesis: i.e. that far from being evidence in favour of exotic theories these coincidences should rather be considered as confirming "conventional" (General Relativistic Big Bang) physics and cosmology which could in principle have been used to predict them all in advance of their observation. However these predictions do require the use of what may be termed the *anthropic principle* to the effect that what we can expect to observe must be restricted by the conditions necessary for our presence as observers. (Although our situation is not necessarily *central*, it is inevitably privileged to some extent.)

The three independent coincidences listed by Bondi provide convenient illustrations of three classes of theoretical prediction:

(1) the traditional kind—without use of the anthropic principle;

(2) those which only require the use of a "weak" anthropic principle; and

(3) those which require the invocation of an extended (and hence rather more questionable) "strong" anthropic principle. In describing these examples I shall express all quantities in terms of dimensionless units in which Newton's constant G, the speed of light c, the Dirac–Planck constant h and Boltzman's constant k, are all set equal to unity.

2. Prediction of the Traditional Kind

The first "large number coincidence" on Bondi's list consists of the observation that although stars come with widely varying sizes and colours—from red giants to white dwarfs (and more recently neutron stars)—they always have a mass M equal in order of magnitude (i.e. within one or two powers of ten) to the *inverse* of the gravitational coupling constant, $m_p^2 \sim 10^{-40}$, where m_p is the proton mass. In terms of the total baryon number $N \sim M/m_p$ this may be expressed as

$$N \sim m_p^{-3}, \tag{1}$$

where both sides are of the order of 10^{60}. Although Jordan (1947) considered that this coincidence required a revolutionary cosmological explanation, it is now widely known that it is predicted by the conventional theory of stellar formation by condensation from diffuse gas clouds. The basic idea is that protostars will be unstable to fragmentation or continuous mass loss until they have separated out into units small enough to be supported at least to a significant extent by non-relativistic gas pressure, which first occurs when condition (1) is satisfied. Beyond this point the star will be stable so no further subdivision occurs. (I have given a very brief resumé of the well-known steps leading to the derivation of the stability limit (1) in a recent article in *J. Phys.* **34**, c7–39, 1973.)

3. Prediction Based on the Weak Anthropic Principle

The second "large number coincidence" is the observed fact that the Hubble fractional expansion rate H of the Universe is equal to within a few powers of ten to the reciprocal of the same large number, i.e.

$$H \sim m_p^3. \tag{2}$$

Dicke (*Nature* **192**, 440, 1961) pointed out that this too could have been predicted, provided we accept that the present age t of the Universe is *not* determined purely at random but is most likely to have the order of magnitude of a typical main-sequence stellar lifetime. This is plausible because at times much later than this the Galaxy will contain relatively few (and mainly very weak) energy producing stars, whereas at times much shorter than this the heavy elements (whose presence seems necessary for life) could not have been formed. For a typical star somewhat larger than the Sun, in which the opacity is dominated by Thomson scattering, the luminosity may be estimated crudely as

$$L \sim e^{-4} m_e^2 m_p^{-1},$$

where m_e is the electron mass, given by $m_e/m_p \sim 1/1830$, and where $e^2 \sim 1/137$ is the fine structure constant. If all the mass energy were available, the lifetime would be given by M/L where $M \sim m_p^{-2}$. The actual available energy fraction $\sim 10^{-2}$ roughly cancels the order of unity factor $e^4(m_p/m_e)^2$ so one obtains for the hydrogen burning lifetime of a typical main sequence star, and hence also for the present age of the Universe, the very rough estimate

$$t \sim m_p^{-3}. \tag{3}$$

This prediction provides a good illustration of the use of the *"weak" anthropic principle* to the effect that we must be prepared to take account of the fact that our location in the universe is *necessarily* privileged to the extent of being compatible with our existence as observers. In an open universe, or in a closed universe whose present age t is small compared with its predicted total lifetime τ, "conventional" cosmology gives

$$H \sim t^{-1}. \tag{4}$$

Hence the prediction (3) (which is confirmed *directly* by local estimates of the age of the Galaxy) leads on naturally to the prediction of the cosmological relation (2).

4. Prediction Based on the Strong Anthropic Principle

In his 1961 discussion Dicke did not mention the alternative that is also possible a priori, namely that if the Universe is closed its present age t might be already comparable with its total lifetime τ. Quite generally, given (3), we must obviously have

$$\tau \gtrsim m_p^{-3}. \tag{5}$$

In the latter case, i.e. if this held as an order of magnitude *equality*, (4) would no longer hold and instead of (2) one would have the alternative coincidence $\tau \sim m_p^{-3}$. Quite apart from the fact that it is not observationally confirmed (even if it is finite, τ appears unlikely to be as small as the value given by (5)), this last possibility may be considered intrinsically less likely than the alternative (2) because it implies a fairly severe restriction not merely on *our location* within the Universe but on one of the fundamental parameters of the *Universe itself* (in this case its lifetime τ).

However even the inescapable weak prediction (5) places a significant restriction on the fundamental cosmological parameters. In the simple hot big bang model it is convenient to work with two basic cosmological constants, η and κ, defined in terms of the black body temperature T, the (root mean square) baryon number n, and the scalar curvature K of the homogeneous space sections, by

$$\eta = \frac{n}{T^3}; \qquad \kappa = \frac{K}{T^2}. \tag{6}$$

Assuming the Universe is not radiation dominated all its life, (i.e. assuming that the matter contribution $\sim nm_pT^3$ to the mean mass density ρ becomes greater at some stage than the radiation contribution $\sim T^4$) then the total lifetime τ will be given by

$$\tau \sim \eta m_p \kappa^{-3/2} \tag{7}$$

(in consequence of the Friedmann equation $12\,H^2 + \kappa = 16\pi\rho$), unless κ is negative, in which case the lifetime is infinite. Hence (5) gives

$$\kappa \lesssim \left(\frac{\eta^2}{m_p}\right)^{1/3} m_p^3. \tag{8}$$

[This situation holds necessarily if $\eta^2 \gtrsim m_p$. However if $\eta^2 \lesssim m_p$ one could conceive the possibility of a permanently radiation dominated universe, for which the criterion is $\kappa \gtrsim \eta^2 m_p^2$, giving $\tau \sim \kappa^{-1}$ instead of (7). In this case one would have to replace (8) by $\kappa \lesssim m_p^3$.]

Condition (8) is a good example of a prediction based on what may be termed the *"strong"* anthropic principle stating that the Universe (and hence the fundamental parameters on which it depends) must be such as to admit the creation of observers within it at some stage. To paraphrase Descartes, "Cogito ergo mundus talis est".

By further use of this principle one can also place an a priori *lower* limit on κ, provided one accepts the conventional hypothesis that galaxies (whose existence is presumably necessary for the formation of stars and hence of life) are formed by condensation, starting as relatively small density fluctuations in an otherwise homogeneous background. Since the pioneer work of Lifshitz (*J. Phys.* **10**, 116, 1946) many studies have confirmed (1) that density irregularities could not grow before the matter density has become dominant and the temperature T has dropped several powers of ten below the Rydberg ionisation energy $\frac{1}{2}e^4 m_e$ so as to allow decoupling of the matter from the radiation pressure. (2) fluctuations could not have developed even then if K at that epoch was negative, unless its magnitude was very small compared with that of ρ, since otherwise the fluctuations would have had almost as much excess kinetic energy (represented by the H^2 term in the Friedmann equation) as the Universe as a whole, and hence would have gone on expanding in spatial extent without ever reaching a stage of recontraction. This gives the *a priori* limit

$$(-\kappa) \ll (e^4 m_e)\,(\eta m_p), \tag{9}$$

where the strength of the inequality depends on the assumed magnitude of the initial fluctuations.

Taken in combination the two limits (8) and (9) provide the derivation (to which Hawking and Collins referred) of the third of the "large number coincidences" listed by Bondi, namely the observation that at the present time

$$\rho \sim H^2, \tag{10}$$

which is equivalent, by (2), to Eddington's famous relation

$$nH^{-3} \sim m_p^{-3} \tag{11}$$

stating that the "number of particles in the visible universe" is the inverse square of the gravitational coupling constant. By the Friedmann equations (10) and (11) are also equivalent to the much less striking condition that at the present epoch

$$|K| \lesssim \rho, \tag{12}$$

which in turn (since it gives $\rho \sim \eta m_p T^3 \sim m_p^6$ by (2)) is equivalent to the epoch invariant relation

$$|\kappa| \lesssim \left(\frac{\eta^2}{m_p}\right)^{1/3} m_p^3. \tag{13}$$

However this follows immediately (thus completing the derivation of (10) and (11)) from the a priori conditions (8) and (9) *provided* that the factor $(e^4 m_e/m_p) (\eta/m_p)$ is not extremely large compared with $(\eta^2/m_p)^{1/3}$. Given the values of the e^2, m_e and m_p this is roughly equivalent to the requirement that the ubiquitous factor $(\eta^2/m_p)^{1/3}$ be not extremely large compared with unity. This condition is in fact comfortably satisfied, since (by a coincidence that from the present point of view is much more striking and fundamental than (10) and (11)) the factor $(\eta^2/m_p)^{1/3}$ turns out to be remarkably close to unity, i.e.

$$\eta \sim m_p^{1/2} \tag{14}$$

(the exact value being subject to the uncertainty in the amount of "missing" matter).

To sum up, only if η had been extremely large compared with its actual value given by (14) would it have been conceivable on the basis of conventional theory for (10) and (11) to have turned out otherwise. It follows that the confirmation of (10) and (11) cannot fairly be considered as positive evidence favouring the introduction of highly non-conventional theories such as those of Dirac and Eddington.

It remains true however that whereas a prediction based only on the *weak* anthropic principle (as used by Dicke) can amount to a complete physical explanation, on the other hand even an entirely rigorous prediction based on the *strong* principle will not be completely satisfying from a physicist's point of view since the possibility will remain of finding a deeper underlying theory explaining the relationships that have been predicted. Thus the anthropical prediction of (13) does not rule out the possibility (or desirability) of constructing, e.g. a Machian framework that would require $\kappa = 0$, underlying ordinary gravitational theory (cf. Sciama: 1953, *Monthly Notices Roy. Astron. Soc.* **113**, 34).

5. World Ensembles and the Gravitational Constant

It is of course always philosophically possible — as a last resort, when no stronger physical argument is available — to promote a *prediction* based on the strong anthropic principle to the status of an *explanation* by thinking in terms of a "world ensemble". By this I mean an ensemble of universes characterised by all conceivable combinations of initial conditions and fundamental constants (the distinction between these concepts, which is not clear cut, being that the former refer essentially to local and the latter to global features). The existence of any organism describable as an observer will only be possible for certain restricted combinations of the parameters, which distinguish within the world-ensemble an exceptional *cognizable* subset. A prediction based on the strong anthropic principle may be regarded as a demonstration that the feature under consideration is common to all members of the cognizable subset. Subject to the further condition that it is possible to define some sort of fundamental a priori probability measure on the ensemble, it would be possible to make an even more general kind of prediction based on the demonstration that a feature under consideration occurred in "most" members of the cognizable subset.

One of the features of the Universe that one might attempt to explain in this way (although I see no reason to despair of the possibility of a more conventional kind of explanation) is the weakness of the gravitational coupling constant. A possible clue to such an explanation comes from the fact that whereas most of the gross features of various kinds of star scale up or down without qualitative change as m_p^2 is varied (see diagram in *J. Phys.* **34**, c7–39, 1973) a significant exception is the division of main sequence stars into the qualitatively different blue giants (in which energy gets out mainly by radiative transfer) and red dwarfs (in which energy gets out mainly by convection) which depends rather critically on the actual value of the gravitational coupling constant m_p^2 in relation to the values of the electromagnetic coupling constant e^2 and the mass ratio m_e/m_p.

The reason why the lower mass main sequence stars are convective is essentially that the radiative transfer rate is not sufficient to raise the surface temperature T_e above the *critical* value — a power of ten or so lower than the Rydberg energy $\frac{1}{2}e^4 m_e$ — below which ionisation and dissociation reactions lower the adiabatic index so as to produce local instabilities; by a process whose importance was first recognised by Hayashi, this gives rise to convection which will usually be sufficient to stop the temperature dropping much below the critical value. For a not too small (radiation pressure dominated) star, with mass given roughly by (1), the Thomson scattering formula already referred to in the derivation of (3) leads to the rough estimate

$$T_e^4 \sim 10^{-2} e^{-4} m_e^2 m_p T^2$$

for the surface flux T_e^4, where T is the central temperature, which will be given roughly by

$$T \sim 10^{-2} e^4 m_p$$

(calculated from the temperature required for Coulomb barrier penetration for hydrogen burning). Clearly to avoid having T_e small compared with the ionisation energy we need

$$m_p \gtrsim e^{12} \left(\frac{m_e}{m_p} \right)^2. \tag{15}$$

This condition is satisfied, but — by a remarkable coincidence — *only just*. As a result the more massive (radiation pressure dominated) main sequence stars are indeed convective, but the smaller main sequence stars (in which the opacity is increased above the Thomson value by free-free and bound-free transitions) are predominantly convective. If the gravitational coupling constant were weakened significantly below the critical value given by (15) (or if the fine structure constant were increased by only a very small amount, the other parameters remaining fixed) then the main sequence would consist entirely of convective red stars. Conversely if the gravitational constant were rather stronger than it is (or if the fine structure constant were very slightly reduced) then the main sequence would consist entirely of radiative blue stars.

This suggests a conceivable world ensemble explanation of the weakness of the gravitational constant. It may well be that the formation of planets is dependent on the existence of a highly convective Hayashi track phase on the approach to the main sequence. (Such an idea is of course highly speculative, since planetary formation theory is not yet on a sound footing, but it may be correlated with the empirical fact that the larger stars — which leave the Hayashi track well before arriving at the main sequence — retain much more of their angular momentum than those which remain convective.) If this is correct, then a stronger gravitational constant would be incompatible with the formation of planets and hence, presumably, of observers. If the a priori probability measure on the world ensemble is such as to favour values of the coupling constants relatively close to unity, then the actual order of magnitude of the gravitational constant would be explained completely.

Similar but even stronger arguments can be made placing *a priori* restrictions on the fundamental parameters of nuclear physics. For example it is well known that the "strong" coupling constant is only marginally strong enough to bind nucleons into nuclei: if it were rather weaker hydrogen would be the only element, and this too would presumably be incompatible with the existence of life.

The acceptability of predictions of this kind as explanations depends on one's attitude to the world ensemble concept. Although the idea that there may exist many universes, of which only one can be known to us, may at first sight seem philosophically undesirable, it does not really go very much further than the Everett doctrine (see B. S. De Witt: 1967, *Phys. Rev.* **160**, 113) to which one is virtually forced by the internal logic of quantum theory. According to the Everett doctrine the Universe, or more precisely the state vector of the Universe, has many branches of which only one can be known to any well defined observer (although all are equally "real"). This doctrine would fit very naturally with the world ensemble philosophy that I have tried to describe.

Even though I would personally be happier with explanations of the values of the fundamental coupling constants etc. based on a deeper mathematical structure (in which they would no longer be fundamental but would be derived), I think it is worthwhile in the meanwhile to make a systematic exploration of the a priori limits that can be placed on these parameters (so long as they remain fundamental) by the strong anthropic principle. *If* it were to turn out that strict limits could always be obtained in this way, while attempts to derive them from more fundamental mathematical structures failed, this would be able to be construed as evidence that the world ensemble philosophy should be taken seriously—even if one did not like it.

11

B. J. CARR*

On the Origin, Evolution and Purpose of the Physical Universe

1. Introduction

THE PURPOSE OF this talk is three-fold. Firstly, I wish to review the picture for the origin and evolution of the physical universe currently favoured by cosmologists. In this task I will be speaking strictly in my capacity as a physicist but I will try to emphasize those features of the favoured picture which seem to me to have potential theological significance. Not being a theologian myself, I will not aspire to state what that significance is but what I say may at least stimulate others to do so. Secondly, I wish to emphasize the various ways in which the standard picture, while remarkably successful in its concordance with observation, poses various enigmas which are as yet unexplained by conventional physics. Most of these enigmas reduce to the fact that our universe seems to be very special in its large-scale structure: compared to the most general cosmological models allowed by relativity theory, it appears to be remarkably simple. I will argue that this simplicity may in some sense be necessary for our existence, although it is also possible that it is a consequence of presently unknown physics. This will lead me, in the third part of my talk, to discuss what has become known as the Anthropic Principle. This involves the notion that certain features of the universe — such as the values of various physical constants — are

*This article first appeared as pp. 237–253 of *The Irish Astronomical Journal*, Vol. 15, No. 3, March 1982, an issue devoted to "Cosmos and Creation." Copyright © *The Irish Astronomical Journal*, 1982.

determined by the requirement that life should arise. The evidence for the Anthropic Principle lies in a large number of unexplained "coincidences" involving the physical constants. I will discuss these coincidences and, veering for a while outside my professional domain, consider to what extent they might be interpreted as indicating that the universe has a purpose.

2. The Structure and Evolution of the Universe

At first sight, the most striking feature of the night sky is its constancy. Besides its rotation due to the Earth's spin and the motion of the planets, the configuration of stars never seems to change. We now know that this constancy is an illusion. Our Sun is just one of 10^{11} stars which form our galaxy, the Milky Way, and all these stars rush around with speeds of order 10^2 km s^{-1}. Their apparent lack of motion is merely due to their enormous distances, the most distant ones being about 10^5 light-years away. Moving even faster and even further away are other galaxies. The nearest galaxy is 10^6 light-years away and the furthest ones — visible only through the most powerful telescopes — are at distances of 10^{10} light-years. Of particular significance is the way in which these galaxies move: as Hubble discovered in the 1920's, all galaxies seem to be moving away from us with a speed proportional to their distance. Their speed is inferred from the Doppler shift in the frequency of their radiation and their distance is deduced from their apparent brightness. Hubble's name is given to the constant which measures how much the recession speed increases with distance; it is of order 30 km s^{-1} per million light-years.

The Copernican Principle, which says that we are not in a privileged position in the universe, requires that every other galaxy sees its neighbours receding in exactly the same way. In this case one may interpret Hubble's law as indicating that the whole universe is expanding. One can understand this by visualizing galaxies as dots on a sheet of elastic which is being stretched in every direction. This analogy illustrates two points: firstly, no galaxy is entitled to regard itself as the centre of the expansion and, secondly, the galaxies' recession is caused, not by their expanding into a pre-existing static space, but by space itself expanding. This dynamic aspect of space is generated by the matter it contains in a way described by General Relativity theory. Indeed Einstein could have predicted the cosmological expansion before it was discovered. Unfortunately, he was so affected by the popular misconception of the time, that the universe was static and unchanging, that he modified his theory so that the universe need not expand: he added a so-called "cosmological repulsion term" which was just sufficient to balance the gravity of the matter. In so doing, he failed to make the most important prediction of his career. Indeed he later referred to the cosmological constant as "the greatest mistake of my life".

An obvious implication of the expansion of the universe would seem to be that it is *evolving*, that is to say, it should look different at different times. This does not, in fact, follow as a logical necessity. For example, the Steady State theory proposed that matter is continuously created in such a way that, despite its expansion, the universe would always look the same. Nowadays, however, the Steady State theory is virtually discarded since we have ample evidence that the universe has not looked the same at all epochs (for example, from the increase in the number of quasars and radio sources at earlier times and from other observations to be described below). Nearly all cosmologists therefore now subscribe to the view that the universe is changing, in the sense that it must have been more compressed in the past. Thus, when the universe was about a tenth of its current size, its present structure would have disappeared because galaxies would have merged, and if one extrapolates the expansion back as far as possible, one would expect the whole universe to be compressed into a point of infinite density at a time in the past of order the inverse of the Hubble constant. This gives rise to the now popular "Big Bang" theory in which the universe started off with a huge explosion some 10 billion years ago, under the impetus of which the galaxies (or, more accurately, space itself) are still rushing outwards. We cannot pretend to understand the moment of the Big Bang itself since all known physics breaks down at infinite densities. For this reason the Big Bang is sometimes referred to as a "singularity". Even our ideas of space and time break down then, the usual space–time topology being destroyed by little-understood quantum gravity effects. Within the context of known physics it is therefore meaningless to ask what happened *before* the Big Bang because time itself began then. This is not to say that we will never have a theory of what happened at the initial moment but, if we ever do, it will have to be a theory which transcends the usual space–time description of General Relativity.

The notion that the physical universe had a finite beginning — something which the writers of Genesis seem to have appreciated — clearly has potential theological significance, so one might ask whether there is any way, apart from invoking the Steady State theory, in which this conclusion can be circumvented. One way to avoid an initial singularity would be to suppose that the galaxies are accelerating in their recession. In this case, the universe would have been expanding more slowly at earlier times and it need not necessarily have passed through a state of infinite density. Indeed it may have been originally collapsing, with a turn-around occurring at a relatively low density. Unfortunately, this possibility is not consistent with relativity theory since this predicts that the cosmological expansion rate must *decrease* with time as a result of the galaxies' mutual gravitational attraction. In this case, unless one invokes a cosmological constant, the occurrence of an initial singularity would seem to be inevitable. The assertion that the initial singularity must have been a single *point* is less straightforward since this depends on the universe's being very symmetrical. If the expansion rate varied slightly with direction, one might expect the universe to tend to a "pancake" or "cigar" type configuration as one goes back in time. However, even in this case, powerful theorems predict that there must be a singularity (i.e. a breakdown of physics) somewhere in the past, although not all the matter in the universe necessarily encounters it. In this sense General Relativity might be said to predict its own failure! Two other observations would seem to support the notion that the universe had a finite beginning. Firstly, the age of the universe inferred from the cosmological expansion is very close to the age of the Earth and the age of stars as deduced by independent methods. Secondly, the most straightforward way to avoid Olbers' paradox (the expectation that the night sky should be as bright as the surface of a typical star, which it clearly is not) is to assume that the universe has been expanding for a finite time.

The same deceleration which necessitates the occurrence of a singularity in the past may also cause the cosmological expansion to stop at some time in the future. In this case the universe could recollapse to the same sort of singularity from which it started. However, relativity predicts that this can happen only if the matter in the universe has sufficient density. The critical density required is specified uniquely by the Hubble constant and is about 10^{-29} g cm^{-3} (or 10^{-5} atoms cm^{-3} if the matter were uniformly distributed and all in the form of ordinary atoms). It is presently uncertain whether or not the density of the universe exceeds this critical value but, if it does, the universe may one day return to the same sort of state from which it arose. What would happen after the recollapse is unclear. Conceivably, the universe could bounce into a new expansion phase, like a phoenix born out of the ashes of its predecessor, although physics cannot yet explain what could cause this bounce. If it does occur, one might envisage a "cyclic" universe which continues to expand, collapse and bounce indefinitely. Such a cyclic behaviour has aesthetic appeal to some people, perhaps because of the pervasiveness of other cyclic processes in Nature. For example, even around 500 B.C. an Indian cosmologist announced: "One thousand mahayugas — 4,320,000,000 years of human reckoning — constitute a single day of Brahma. I have known the dreadful dissolution of the universe. I have seen all perish, again and again, at every cycle. At that terrible time every single atom decays into the primal, pure waters of eternity, whence all originally arose". This knowledge was allegedly procured through clairvoyance. Although cosmologists nowadays place more faith in their telescopes than their psychic faculties, it is amusing that the first recorded estimate of Hubble's constant —predating Hubble by 2500 years—was actually correct to an order of magnitude.

If the density of the universe is *less* than critical, it will continue to expand forever. In this case, the Milky Way will get progressively isolated. Eventually its constituent stars will burn out, leaving black hole or neutron star or white dwarf remnants, and by about 10^{25} years most of it will have collapsed into a single black hole. By about 10^{31} years all the protons in the universe may have decayed (for reasons discussed later) and eventually even the black holes will have disappeared by evaporating into radiation. Thus one would end up with a universe devoid of the usual sort of matter. The prospects of life continuing in such a universe may seem bleak. However, Dyson has pointed out that, by undergoing progressively long periods of "hibernation", life could in principle organize its energy resources in such a way as to persist indefinitely. Whether one regards the recollapsing or ever-expanding universe as having more aesthetic appeal is clearly a matter of individual taste!

The question of the ultimate fate of the universe is also, in theory, related to the question of its size. If the universe has less than the critical density, space should extend for ever, that is to say, there should be an infinite number of galaxies. On the other hand, if it has more than the critical density, space is finite in extent. This is best envisaged by comparing space to the surface of a spherical balloon: the surface area of the balloon is finite and, if one travels far enough in a particular direction, one eventually returns to one's starting point. If one imagines that the balloon is being inflated and then deflated, one also introduces the idea that space is expanding and recollapsing. Of course, this is only an analogy since space is 3-dimensional and the surface of the balloon is 2-dimensional. However, the analogy does illustrate what we believe to be genuine features of a universe which is destined to recollapse: namely, that such a universe would only contain a finite number of galaxies and that an astronaut travelling in a straight line would eventually return to his starting point. These peculiar features arise because in General Relativity matter curves space and, if there is enough matter, it will curve space so much that it closes up on itself. The greater the density, the smaller the volume of the space and the sooner it recollapses. If the universe has slightly more than the critical density, it contains about 10^{12} galaxies and will recollapse in about 20 billion years.

The idea that space is curved raises a curious metaphysical question. For if space is curved and perhaps closed (like the surface of a balloon), what is the significance of the higher dimensional space in which it is embedded? What exists beyond the "surface" of the physical universe? As far as General Relativity is concerned, this question is meaningless.

The geometry of space can be determined entirely intrinsically (i.e. from measurements which can be made within the surface) and the picture of an embedding space is invoked only for the purpose of visualization. One need not therefore attribute to the embedding space any literal existence. On the other hand, one cannot logically exclude its literal existence. This possibility presumably has metaphysical implications, but I will resist the temptation to pursue them here.

Another crucial feature of the universe is that it seems to be bathed in a sea of radiation. This radiation exhibits two vital properties: its intensity as a function of wavelength exhibits a so-called "black-body" spectrum; and it looks the same in every direction. The first feature indicates that the radiation is a residue from a much earlier period in the history of the universe. This is because radiation can only have a black-body spectrum if it has interacted with matter sufficiently to be thermalized. At present the matter in the universe is too diffuse for thermalization to occur. However, in the past its density would have been much larger. Thermalization could have occurred provided the length-scale of the universe was once a thousandth of its present size and this would have been the case when the age of the Universe was about 10^6 y. The black-body spectrum of the background radiation is thus good evidence that the Big Bang picture applies at least back until then. Incidentally, 10^6 y is well before the formation of galaxies, which occurred at around 10^9 y. The significance of the radiation looking the same in every direction will be discussed later.

The temperature of the background radiation today is very low, only about 3 K, and its energy density is about 10^4 times smaller than that of the matter. Nevertheless the photons are so numerous (around 10^3 cm^{-3}, or about 10^8 times as numerous as the atoms) that they contain most of the heat content of the universe. Furthermore, as one goes back in time, the radiation would have got hotter. In particular, when the age of the universe was 10^6 y, the temperature would have been 4000 K, hot enough to ionise the matter, and it is precisely this ionization which permitted the matter and radiation to interact enough to establish a black-body radiation spectrum then. Before 10^6 y, the universe would have consisted of a plasma of electrons and nuclei, both thermally coupled to and therefore evolving with the same temperature as the background radiation. Note that, as one goes back in time, the radiation density grows faster than the plasma density because of its temperature increase and, before about 10^4 y, it would actually dominate the density of the universe. The period before 10^4 y is therefore called the "radiation era". One might say the universe was mainly light then, something which is clearly reminiscent of Genesis' "Let there be light".

In describing the history of the universe before 10^4 y, it is best to go backwards rather than forwards in time since our knowledge of physics, and hence our confidence in the standard picture, decreases at earlier times. Our motto might therefore be that of the Oxford University Edwardian Society: "Forward into the past". With this point of view, the "next" significant event in the history of the universe occurs in the period $1 - 10^2$ seconds after the Big Bang. This is the period of cosmological nucleosynthesis, when elements heavier than hydrogen are formed. Before 1 s the only nuclei are protons and neutrons, with a neutron/proton ratio determined by the weak interactions. This ratio freezes out with a value of about $\frac{1}{8}$ when the weak interaction rate becomes slower than the cosmological expansion rate at around 1 s. The protons and neutrons have a tendency to fuse together due to strong interactions. However, this tendency is counteracted by the background photons, which can smash any nuclei heavier than hydrogen apart until the temperature falls below 10^9 K at around 10^2 s. Thereafter, the protons and neutrons are free to combine, first forming deuterium nuclei (one proton plus one neutron) and then helium nuclei (two protons plus two neutrons). After 10^2 s one expects roughly 25% of the universe's mass to be in helium with a tiny residue (about 10^{-5} by mass) in deuterium. The fact that these abundances coincide almost exactly with observation is evidence that the Big Bang picture may be correct all the way back to 1 s; one might regard the helium and deuterium as "fossils" of the state of the universe then. Elements heavier than helium can only have been produced by stars in the period long after cosmological nucleosynthesis.

At 1 s the temperature of the universe is 10^{10} K, hot enough for pairs of electrons and positrons to be created. (A photon can pair-produce a particle and an antiparticle providing its energy exceeds the rest masses of the particles involved.) Before 1 s, therefore, the number of electrons and positrons should be roughly equal to the number of photons. When the temperature goes above 10^{13} K at 10^{-5} s, the background photons become energetic enough to produce pairs of hadrons; thus the number density of, for example, protons and antiprotons should also become comparable to that of the photons. This means that, before 10^{-5} s, the present photon-to-proton ratio of 10^8 should be manifested as a slight excess of protons over antiprotons, viz. one extra proton for every 10^8 proton–antiproton pairs. Only after 10^{-5} s do all the protons and antiprotons which can do so annihilate, leaving just those protons without partners. The tiny asymmetry between matter and antimatter at 10^{-5} s is crucial for our existence, because all the matter which we observe in the universe today derives from it. If there was no asymmetry, all the matter and antimatter would have annihilated at 10^{-5} s to produce a universe of pure light.

The state of the universe before 10^{-5} s, during the so-called hadron era, depends on details of strong interaction physics which are presently uncertain. Probably the nucleons are dissociated into their constituent quarks at some point, leaving the universe as a sort of "quark soup". Even though protons and anitprotons do not exist in this phase, the asymmetry between matter and antimatter can still be maintained as an asymmetry between the number of quarks and antiquarks. It might seem pretentious to claim to know how matter behaves in such extreme conditions; after all, the density before 10^{-5} s exceeds nuclear density. Nevertheless, in principle, laboratory experiments tell us how matter behaves up to temperatures as high as 10^{16} K, so we have some basis for speculating about the state of the Universe all the way back to 10^{-12} s.

Physicists even have *theories* of how matter behaves at temperatures above 10^{16} K. Although these theories have not been tested experimentally, they make the remarkable prediction that at around 10^{-35} s after the Big Bang, when the temperature is about 10^{28} K, all the known forces of nature except gravity should be "unified" into a single force (i.e. the strength of all the interactions should become comparable). Only after this time would this unified force break down into the strong, weak and electromagnetic forces with which we are familiar today. The particles which transmit this unified force, in the same way that photons transmit the electromagnetic force, would be some 10^{15} times as heavy as the proton, but at temperatures above 10^{28} K they would be as numerous as all the other particle species. These massive particles have the property that they can interact in a way which allows the relative amounts of matter and antimatter to be modified. Indeed, according to the "Grand Unified Theories" which predict the existence of these particles, the generation of a tiny asymmetry between the amount of matter and antimatter is inevitable and it could well be sufficient to explain the excess of protons over antiprotons needed at 10^{-5} s. In this case, the matter which now exists could be a fossil from a time when the universe we see today had the size of a pea! We do not yet have definitive evidence that Grand Unified Theories are correct. However, they may soon be tested because one of their other predictions is that protons should decay. Their decay time would have to be at least 10^{31} y (an effect alluded to earlier), which is much longer than the present age of the universe, but the decays could still be detected by scrutinizing a sufficiently large quantity of matter. Indeed such decays may already have been detected. It is ironic that the same laws which allow matter to exist now may also require that it eventually disappears.

In our journey backwards in time, the earliest epoch we can meaningfully discuss occurs 10^{-43} s after the Big Bang, when the temperature is 10^{32} K and the density is 10^{94} g cm^{-3}. In such extreme conditions little understood quantum gravity effects become important and the usual space–time structure breaks down into a sort of space–time "foam". From the point of view of classical physics, 10^{-43} s *is* the beginning of the Universe. Since we do not yet have a complete theory of quantum gravity, we cannot speculate about what happens then; but, clearly, cracking the code of quantum gravity may give important insight into the nature of the initial Big Bang singularity.

This completes our description of the standard picture for the evolution of the physical universe. Of course, it might seem absurd to speculate about the nature of the universe at the sort of unimaginably early times discussed above, so one might justifiably ask how seriously it should be taken. The first point to emphasize is that one should not dismiss speculation about what happened in the first second of the universe just because this is such a short time in comparison to its present age. After all, cosmologists usually think in terms of logarithmic time and, with this perspective, the period 10^{-43} s to 1 s is *more* extended than the period 1 s to 10^{17} s. Indeed, as the above discussion indicates, some of the most important features of the universe may derive from processes which occurred then. Nevertheless, it would be naive to assume that the standard view of what happens at very early times is necessarily correct. Personally, I would be reluctant to take the standard picture *too* seriously before 1 s and, as indicated earlier, the uncertainties become progressively large as one goes further back. For example, the most glaring worry of the standard picture, and one which will be highlighted in the next section, is its assumption that the early universe is the same everywhere (i.e. perfectly uniform) even though there is no obvious reason why this should be. Despite this, we can certainly claim to have some ideas of what physics may pertain at very high temperatures and the remarkable point is that, if one is prepared to combine these ideas with the assumption that the universe is uniform, one can make definite predictions. Indeed part of the reason for our interest in the early universe is that it provides a "laboratory" in which to test theories which could not be tested elsewhere.

3. Enigmas in the Standard Picture

One might get the impression from the preceding discussion that our understanding of the structure and evolution of the universe is almost complete. However, such an impression would be illusory since underlying the standard picture are a number of enigmas. It is upon these enigmas which I wish to dwell in this section.

One problem concerns the question of whether the universe has enough matter in it to recollapse. In principle one can determine this by examining how fast the universe is decelerating, that is, by studying the deviations from linearity in the relationship between redshift and distance at large distances. In practice this has proved impossible because one determines the distance of a galaxy by its apparent brightness. Since one is looking further into the past as one looks at greater distances, there might be an intrinsic evolution in the brightness of galaxies which could mask any cosmological deceleration effects. However, other methods do give some indication of how much mass is in the universe and these lead to a very surprising conclusion. For example, one can tell how much mass is associated with clusters of galaxies by measuring how fast the individual galaxies move around in the gravitational field of the cluster. Such observations indicate that large clusters contain 10 to 100 times as much mass as the visible galaxies themselves. One can also deduce the mass of an individual galaxy by measuring the speed with which stars and gas move around its centre. From this one infers that some galaxies, including our own Milky Way, have an invisible halo which extends much further than the visible stars and which contains at least 10 times as much mass. (From a theological point of view, the term "halo" is a misnomer since a halo is usually associated with light and it is precisely the light which is missing in the galactic context!) It is probable that the material which makes up the dark mass in clusters of galaxies and galactic halos is the same, but it is still very uncertain what this material is: it could be black holes or very low mass stars or even massive neutrinos. In any case, it is a remarkable feature of the universe that at least 90% of its matter content is invisible.

Even though there is definitely a "missing mass" problem, it is still not clear whether there is enough mass to make the universe recollapse since this would require that about 99% of the universe be invisible and the actual fraction may only be 90%. However, it should be stressed that the really surprising point is that the density of the universe is so close to critical at all. This is because the ratio of the actual density to the critical density gets progressively close to 1 as one goes into the past, and the fact that the density is within a factor of 10 of the critical value now implies that its deviation from the critical value must have been even smaller at earlier times. For example, the deviation would only have been one part in 10^{16} at 1 s and one part in 10^{60} at 10^{-43} s. There is no known physical reason why the initial expansion rate should have been so finely tuned, so one is bound to speculate why this should be. One suggestion is that we could not be here if things were otherwise: for if the expansion rate were slightly too low, the universe would recollapse before life had time to arise (indeed the most likely universe would be one which recollapsed in 10^{-43} s); on the other hand, if the expansion rate were slightly too high, life could not arise either because galaxies could not have formed amid the general expansion.

Another surprising feature of the universe is its remarkable isotropy (i.e. the fact that it looks the same in every direction, at least on scales larger than clusters of galaxies). This is hinted at even by galaxy counts, but it is emphasized most dramatically by observations of the 3 K background radiation. Studies show that, apart from a tiny Doppler effect due to our peculiar velocity, the temperature of this radiation is the same to one part in 10^3 on all angular separations greater than 1 arcmin. Since the radiation was last scattered 10^6 y after the Big Bang, this implies that the cosmological expansion rate was the same in every direction to one part in 10^3 then. This is an enigma because, in the simple Big Bang picture, at any time in the history of the universe there can have been no causal interaction on scales larger than the distance travelled by light (roughly the speed of light times the age of the universe). But at 10^6 y this distance corresponds to an angular scale of a few degrees, so how can the background radiation temperature be correlated on angular scales much larger than this? What mechanism can have synchronized the expansion rate in parts of the universe which were causally disconnected? There is indirect evidence that the cosmological expansion must have been isotropic even 1 s after the Big Bang because, otherwise, the results of cosmological nucleosynthesis would no longer accord with observation. It is interesting that the isotropy issue may be related to the question of why the universe's density is so close to critical; for it can be shown that the universe is stable to the growth of anisotropies only if its density is exactly critical. Thus any explanation for the first enigma may also shed light on the second.

Another surprising feature of the universe, and one which we implicitly assumed throughout our discussion of its evolution, is its remarkable large-scale homogeneity: on scales larger than clusters of galaxies it is assumed to look the same everywhere. It must be stressed that this does not, in fact, imply its isotropy since one could have a universe which looked anisotropic in the same way everywhere. On the other hand, the existence of structure in the universe implies that there must have been *some* inhomogeneities at early times. We believe galaxies and clusters of galaxies formed from small density fluctuations: overdense regions would then expand more slowly than the background, eventually stop expanding (if the local density exceeds the critical density) and finally collapse to form bound systems. Understanding the origin of these density fluctuations is itself an enigma but, in the present context, the mystery lies in the fact that the *amplitude* of the inhomogeneities, like the background expansion rate, must have been very finely tuned. If it was too small, galaxies could never have arisen; but, if it was too large, the whole universe would have collapsed into black holes at early times, again precluding the existence of galaxies.

Both the isotropy and homogeneity problems are best solved by postulating that the universe started off very smooth. Of course, why this should be the case is itself an enigma because *a priori* one might think that the universe would be more likely to start off chaotic, with large inhomogeneities and anisotropies on all scales. Indeed some cosmologists have suggested that the universe did start off chaotic, but that it got smoothed out as a result of various dissipative effects at early times. This now seems unlikely, partly because one would expect much more heat to be generated in such a situation than is presently contained in the background photons, and partly because it is difficult to understand how known dissipative processes could eradicate arbitrarily high chaos anyway. It is conceivable that quantum gravity effects could smooth the universe at 10^{-43} s, but then this *is* essentially the beginning of the universe. Most cosmologists threfore prefer the notion that the universe *began* very smooth, with either very small fluctuations or none at all; in the latter case the fluctuations required for galaxies must arise spontaneously at some later epoch. But why should the universe have started so smooth? Among all possible cosmological solutions to Einstein's equations, the set of solutions which are as simple as our universe is tiny. Thus, unless God created the universe with the limited computational ability of physicists in mind, its simplicity would seem to be very unlikely.

A related problem concerns the Second Law of Thermodynamics; this says that the entropy or lack of order in the universe must increase with time (at least globally — there may be local pockets of order as evidenced by the existence of life). This law therefore defines an "arrow of time" with respect to which we may say that the universe is "running down". The reason for this law has always posed something of a problem and the resolution usually given is that the universe started off with very special, highly ordered, initial conditions. In other words, the universe is running down because it started off "wound up". But how was it wound up? Boltzmann suggested that our universe is just part of a much larger one in which a freak fluctuation (a statistical deviation from the Second Law) happened to produce a state of low entropy. However, since the probability of this is one in 10 to the power 10^{80}, much less than the probability of a chimpanzee writing a Beethoven symphony by chance, this suggestion does not seem very plausible. A theologian would obviously be tempted to speculate that God wound up the universe. A physicist might prefer to invoke quantum gravity but, in any case, both are equally mysterious!

We may summarize this section by saying that, in several respects, the universe is very special in its qualitative structure; it is far more simple than one might have expected through chance alone. There are hints that this simplicity may in some sense be necessary for our existence, in which case one might wish to attribute it to the foresight of a Creator. Such an inference may, however, be premature because it is possible that some of the fore-mentioned enigmas may be solved by conventional physics. For example, there are already suggestions that the Grand Unified Theories may be able to shed light on the isotropy and near critical-density problems. This is because some of these theories predict a phase transition at about 10^{-35} s, in which "bubbles" of the universe could expand exponentially fast for a while due to the generation of the sort of cosmological constant which Einstein invoked to make the universe static. The material within these bubbles would automatically evolve towards isotropy and a critical density, so it is conceivable that the whole visible universe was once contained in such a bubble. In this light, the sort of cosmological specialness discussed so far is not very compelling evidence that the universe was created with the purpose of producing life. However, in the next section, I wish to discuss other features of the universe which provide considerably stronger evidence for this point of view.

4. The Anthropic Principle

It is clear that physics has played a decisive role in shaping man's view of the world in which he lives; it has provided him with a model of reality on all scales from the microscopic world of subatomic particles to the cosmos itself. Yet one feature which is noticeably absent from this model is its creator, man himself. That physics has little to say about the place of man in the universe is perhaps not surprising when one considers the fact that most physicists probably regard man, and more generally consciousness, as being entirely irrelevant to the functioning of the universe. He is seen as no more than a passive observer, with the laws of Nature, which he assiduously attempts to unravel, operating everywhere and for all time, independent of whether or not man witnesses them.

A few physicists, however, have reacted to this impersonal view by suggesting that some of the features of the physical world may depend crucially on our being here. For example, let us ask the obvious question: Why is the universe as big as it is? Most cosmologists would respond with the following mechanistic sort of answer: "The universe began with a Big Bang and is expanding. At any particular time, the size of the observable universe is the distance travelled by light since the Big Bang. Since the universe's present age is about ten billion years, its present diameter is about ten billion light years". Inherent in this straightforward answer is the belief that there is no compelling reason the universe has a diameter of ten billion light years; it just happens that the universe is ten billion years old.

There is, however, another answer to this question, one which Dicke first gave nearly 20 years ago. "The Universe", he said, "must have aged sufficiently for there to exist elements other than hydrogen, since it is well known that carbon is required to make physicists". The carbon of which Dicke speaks, as well as many other elements, is produced by cooking inside stars. This process takes several billion years. Only after this time can the star explode as a supernova, scattering the newly-baked elements throughout space, where they may eventually become part of life-evolving planets. So we see that, to produce life, the universe must be at least several billion years old. Furthermore, the universe cannot be much older than this, else all the material would have been processed into stellar remnants. Why then is the universe as big as it is? Because if it were much smaller or larger, we would not be here to observe it. This startling conclusion turns the mechanistic answer on its head. The very hugeness of the universe which seems at first to point to man's insignificance is actually determined by his existence! This is not to say that the universe *itself* could not exist with a different size, only that we could not be aware of it when its size was different.

By this argument, at least one feature of the universe, its size, is very dependent on the awareness of man. The conjecture that certain features of the world are determined by man's existence in this way has become known as the *"Anthropic Principle"*. Admittedly, if the above argument were the only one in favour of the Anthropic Principle, it would not be very compelling. After all, it could just be a coincidence that the age of the universe happens to be about the time required to produce intelligent life. However, we will see that many other features of the world can be accounted for by invoking the Anthropic Principle, features which would otherwise have to be regarded as purely fortuitous. Indeed the evidence for the Anthropic Principle rests almost entirely on the large number of numerical "coincidences" in physics which seem to be prerequisites for the emergence of life.

In order to make clear exactly what the Anthropic Principle claims to explain, it is necessary to present a brief outline of the physicist's worldview. To do this we must go somewhat beyond our earlier cosmological considerations. Physics claims that the structure of the world is determined by various fundamental constants: for example, the speed of light (c), Planck's constant (h), the gravitational constant (G), the charge of the electron (e), and the masses of various elementary particles like the proton (m_p) and the electron (m_e). Certain combinations of these constants have a special physical significance. Thus $h/2\pi m_p c$, which is about 10^{-13} cm, specifies the size of the proton; and $h^2/4\pi^2 m_e e^2$, which is about 10^{-8} cm, specifies the size of the atom. By making other combinations we can form "pure numbers", that is, combinations in which all the units of mass, length and time have cancelled out. For example, the so-called "fine structure" constant, $\alpha = 2\pi e^2/hc$, is about 10^{-2}. This determines the strength of the electromagnetic interaction and it plays a crucial role in any situation in which electromagnetism is important. Another important dimensionless number is the gravitational fine structure constant, $\alpha_G = 2\pi G m_p^2/hc$, which is about 10^{-38}. This determines the strength of the gravitational interaction and it plays an important role in determining the structure of very large objects (like stars). The fact that α_G is so much smaller than α reflects the fact that the gravitational force between two protons is so much smaller than the electromagnetic force between them. Gravity dominates the structure of large bodies only because large bodies tend to be electrically neutral so that the electric forces cancel out.

What is remarkable is that straightforward physics shows that, to an order of magnitude, α and α_G determine the mass and size of nearly every naturally occurring object in the universe. For example, one can show that all stars will have a mass of roughly $\alpha_G^{-3/2}$ times the proton mass; the largest planets (like Jupiter) will have a mass which is smaller than this by a factor $\alpha^{3/2}$; the mass of a typical galaxy will be roughly $\alpha^4 \alpha_G^{-2}$ times the proton mass; and the mass of a man — if we assume that he must live on a planet with a suitable temperature and a life-supporting atmosphere and that he must not shatter whenever he falls down — will be of order $(\alpha/\alpha_G)^{3/4}$ times the proton mass. One can also express the *size* of these objects in terms of α, α_G and the size of the atom.

These dependences allow one to predict amusing relationships between the different scales of structure in the universe. For example, the mass of a man is the geometric mean of the mass of a planet and the mass of a proton. It should be stressed, however, that such relationships, as well as the dependences on α and α_G from which they derive, should not be regarded as coincidences. Nor do they depend on the Anthropic Principle (except in so far as we have invoked various life-supporting conditions in determining the scale of man). They are merely necessary and logical outcomes of conventional physics.

Let us now return to Dicke's assertion that the age of the universe must be roughly the nuclear-burning time of a star. We can make this argument more specific because physics predicts that the lifetime of a star is roughly α_G^{-1} times the microphysical timescale associated with the proton $h/2\pi m_p c^2$ (the time light takes to traverse the size of a proton, about 10^{-23} s). One can infer that the ratio of the size of the universe to the size of an atom must be of order α/α_G, the ratio of the electromagnetic and gravitational forces between two protons. Thus the Anthropic Principle explains why these two ratios must have the same huge value of 10^{36}. The fact that these ratios are so close has been appreciated for some time, but without resort to the Anthropic Principle it just has to be regarded as a coincidence. Knowing that the age of the universe is α_G^{-1} times the proton timescale allows one to infer that the number of protons in it must be of order α_G^{-2}, thus explaining another well-known coincidence.

Dicke's statement of the Anthropic Principle might be termed the "weak" version. It says nothing about either the laws of physics themselves or the actual values of the fundamental constants. It accepts the laws and the observed values as given and then attempts to explain various features of the universe. We are now going to examine the deeper question of whether anthropic arguments can pin down the values of the natural constants themselves. The notion that this may be possible is sometimes referred to as the "*Strong Anthropic Principle*". The strong principle is so called because, if true, it would obviously have much more predictive power and philosophical significance than the weak principle invoked by Dicke.

That the weak principle may not be the whole story is also suggested by the fact that all the scales discussed above are relative. If the fine structure constants differed from what we observe them to be, all the scales would change but the basic relationships between them would be the same. For example, if G (and hence α_G) were a million times larger, planetary and stellar masses, which go like $\alpha_G^{-3/2}$, would be a billion times smaller; but there would still be stars, albeit with a nuclear burning time reduced by a factor of a million. Moreover, Dicke's argument would still apply, though an observer in such a universe would exist only when its age was around 10,000 years and he would see a universe whose mass was 10^{12} times smaller than our own. If one fixed α_G but allowed α to change, the effects would be less extreme, but still very noticeable. But could life arise in such a speeded-up universe? Neither conventional physics nor the Weak Anthropic Principle has anything to say about the matter; nothing determines the actual values of α and α_G. But the strong principle is much more definitive. It says that life can *only* exist if the fundamental constants have their observed values, or at least satisfy certain observed relationships.

The first example of an argument which appeals to the Strong Anthropic Principle was given by Carter and relates to the existence of what are called "convective" stars. We say a star is convective if the heat generated in its core by nuclear reactions is transported to the surface primarily by way of large-scale motions of the stellar material itself. This tends to be the case for small enough stars (red dwarfs). By contrast, larger stars (blue giants) tend to be "radiative" in the sense that the heat gets out primarily via the flow of radiation. The dividing line between the two types is some critical mass which depends on α and α_G. This critical mass happens to lie in the mass range in which stars actually exist, that is around $\alpha_G^{-3/2}$ times the proton mass, only because of the remarkable coincidence that α_G is of order the *twentieth* power of α. If α_G were slightly larger, all stars would be radiative. If it were slightly smaller, all stars would be convective. Now there are arguments which suggest that planets can only form around convective stars. If we believe that life can only exist on planets, this means that α_G could not be much larger than α^{20}. On the other hand, if α_G were much smaller than α^{20}, all stars would be chemically well-mixed as a result of convection. Such stars would probably not form supernovae and hence could not scatter the heavy elements needed for life into space. Thus the Anthropic Principle already gives us one approximate relationship between α and α_G. In particular, it explains why α_G is so much smaller than α.

The fact that α_G is much smaller than α has another anthropic interpretation. Since the mass of the universe is $\alpha_G^{-2}m_p$ and the mass of a star is $\alpha_G^{-3/2} m_p$, the number of stars in the universe is about $\alpha_G^{-1/2}$. If one assumes that the origin of life depends on chance processes which have a low *a priori* probability, one evidently wants the number of potential sites for life (i.e. the number of stars) to be very large. This requires α_G to be very small, although the argument does not say how small.

The convective condition does not pin down the actual values of α and α_G, it only specifies a scaling law between them. If we had one more such relationship, we could predict a unique value for each. Another relationship does in fact exist. It does not come from an anthropic argument, but from an argument in quantum field theory. While the details are too complicated to go into here, the conclusion is that a self-consistent quantum field theory is possible only if α^{-1} is of order the natural logarithm of α_G^{-1}. This relation, together with the convective star condition, implies that α must be about 10^{-2} and α_G must be about 10^{-40}, as observed. In view of the simple dependences on α and α_G of the different scales of structure in the universe, this suggests that the appearance of our universe is determined, not merely in part, but to a very large degree by our existence.

So far we have talked about things larger than atoms. We now divert our attention to objects smaller than atoms. On this scale, two more fundamental forces of nature come into play: the strong force (which holds the nucleus of an atom together and binds the quarks within a nucleon) and the weak force (which governs radioactive decay). Like gravity and electromagnetism, the strength of these forces can be described by dimensionless fine structure constants: the strong force constant is denoted by α_S and has a value of order 10; the weak force constant is denoted by α_W and has a value of order 10^{-10}. Although the strong and weak forces are many orders of magnitude stronger than the gravitational force, they are both very short range; they become negligible at distances of 10^{-13} cm and 10^{-15} cm, respectively. For this reason the strong and weak forces do not play an important role in determining the structure of objects larger than atoms.

The numbers α_S and α_W are also involved in several coincidences, some of which involve the masses of various elementary particles. For example, the ratio of the strong fine structure constant to the electric fine structure constant is close to the ratio of the proton mass to the electron mass; and the difference between the mass of the neutron and the mass of the proton is very nearly twice the electron mass. The striking thing is that these and other nuclear coincidences seem necessary for life because, were things otherwise, there could not exist the variety of chemical elements necessary for our existence. Indeed, given that α is anthropically determined, the nuclear anthropic conditions are sufficient to determine, not only α_S, but also most of the elementary particle masses.

The weak force does not at first sight play a very important role in everyday life. Yet the weak fine structure constant α_w is also involved in an interesting anthropic relationship: α_w is roughly the quarter power of the gravitational fine structure constant and this relationship is just what is required to produce an interesting amount of helium through cosmological nucleosynthesis. We recall that the cosmological helium production is determined by the time at which the weak inter-actions become slower than the cosmological expansion rate, and this depends sensitively on the relationship between α_G and α_w. If α_w were slightly smaller, the entire universe would have burned to helium and there would never be any water, another possible prerequisite for life. If α_w were slightly larger, there would have been *no* helium produc-tion. Although a universe lacking in helium might not be incompatible with life, the same relationship between α_w and α_G is associated with another condition which limits the size of α_w in both directions. It turns out that the fact that α_G is of order $\alpha_w{}^4$ explains why the flux of neutrinos from the core of a star can blow off its envelope during its supernova phase. As we have seen, supernovae play a crucial role in producing the elements necessary for life. So, if we accept that α_G must be $\alpha_w{}^4$ for life to arise, and if we believe α_G is determined anthropi-cally, we must also accept that α_w is so determined.

To summarize these arguments is simple: nearly all the constants of nature may be determined by the Anthropic Principle. But what are we to make of all this? Are we to be impressed with the Anthropic Princi-ple's explanation of the aforementioned coincidences, or are we to discard it as a metaphysical curiosity? Let us start by listing the objec-tions. Firstly, all evidence is after the fact. It would be much more impressive if the Anthropic Principle could be used to *predict* a coinci-dence, but so far this has not been done. Secondly, we may have been unduly anthropocentric in our view of the prerequisites for life. We have assumed the necessity of elements heavier than hydrogen and special types of stars and planets, but we have not taken into account the possibility of more exotic life-forms such as might exist in interstel-lar space. In order for such an exotic life form to be consistent with our anthropic arguments, we would have to show that its chemistry and environment required the same values of the fundamental constants as deduced above. Finally, the Anthropic Principle does not give *exact* values for the constants, but only their orders of magnitude. The situa-tion would be more satisfactory if their values could be pinned down more precisely.

Nonetheless, it cannot be denied that there are a number of remark-able coincidences in nature and these do warrant some sort of explana-tion. The point is, not that there are coincidences, but that these coincidences are just what is required for life. It is this deeper level of coincidence which makes the Anthropic Principle so striking. Of course, where arguments are based on the existence of coincidences, the weight of evidence rests very strongly on the *number* of them. Thus the future status of the Anthropic Principle as an explanation for certain features of the universe will depend on the number of further anthropic relations which are discovered or, better still, predicted and then discovered.

There remains the interpretation of the Anthropic Principle. To begin with, we should stress that we have not stated that the universe does not exist if we are not here to observe it; we have only stated that, if we are here to observe it, the universe must be the way it is. Wheeler has suggested a more radical interpretation in which the universe does not even come into being in a well-defined way until an observer is produced who can perceive it. In this case, the very *existence* of the universe depends upon life. However, many people find Wheeler's viewpoint unpalatable in view of its rather mystical overtones.

There is another framework for the Anthropic Principle which might seem more plausible. This is the "Many Worlds" interpretation of quantum mechanics, proposed nearly 20 years ago by Everett. One of the underlying features of quantum theory is that a system is not in a well-defined state until one makes a measurement or observation of it. Prior to the measurement, the system—which might in principle be the entire universe—is in an undefined superposition of states and it takes an act of measurement or observation to force the system into a particular one. Quantum mechanics allows one to predict the *probability* that the measurement will have a specific outcome, but it does not determine the result with certainty. This concept is very strange, especially when applied to situations where the quantum uncertainty on a microscopic level can manifest itself on a macroscopic level. The most dramatic example of this is the "Schrödinger Cat Paradox", where the uncertainty in whether a single radioactive atom has decayed results in a superposition of a dead cat and a live cat until someone peeps to see what has happened! Everett resolves these problems by saying that the universe splits into parallel branches whenever an observation is made, each branch corresponding to a possible outcome of the observation. Thus in one universe, Schrödinger's cat lives; in another, it dies. It is only a slight extrapolation of this scheme to imagine an ensemble of "parallel" universes, each of which differs in the values of its fundamental constants. In some universes α is big, in others α is small, but only in a tiny fraction of these many worlds will the values be such that life can evolve.

Another framework for the Anthropic Principle could be envisaged if the universe is closed and undergoes cycles of expansion and collapse. Some people speculate that, in this situation, the values of the fundamental constants could be changed at each bounce. However low the probability of their having values conducive to life, with an infinite number of cycles, life is bound to arise sometimes. During the favourable cycles intelligence can flower and the universe can become aware of itself. Men may even develop an Anthropic Principle to explain their existence. During the other cycles, life will never evolve and the questions will never be asked.

Both the "Many Worlds" and "Many Cycles" explanations for the Anthropic Principle are rather bizarre and I would not recommend that either be taken too seriously. My reason for mentioning them is to emphasize that it is conceivable the Anthropic Principle may one day be given a physical basis. But what if it transpires that there is no satisfactory physical explanation? In this case, one would have to conclude either that the features of the universe invoked in support of the Anthropic Principle are *only* coincidences or that the universe was indeed tailor-made for life. I will leave it to the theologians to ascertain the identity of the tailor!

12

RICHARD SWINBURNE*

Argument from the Fine-Tuning
of the Universe

I

IN THIS PAPER I seek to examine the force of an argument to the existence of God from the widely discussed fact that the boundary conditions of our Universe and the laws of its evolution are of a very special kind which alone could lead to the evolution of intelligent life. A full-length account of the recent scientific work relevant to such an argument has been given by J. D. Barrow and F. J. Tipler in their book *The Anthropic Cosomological Principle*[1]; and I shall assume that the detailed scientific facts are as they state them. My concern is to assess the evidential force of the work which they describe. In doing so I take further and more rigorously the argument of some recent philosophical papers by John Leslie.[2]

Why is intelligent life in special need of explanation? Why is there anything more to be explained if a Universe contains intelligent life than if it does not? Because, intelligent life is something which a creator God would have the power and abundant reason for bringing about, and so a phenomenon which, if he exists, would be quite likely to occur. If it is also (as the argument from fine-tuning claims) something not in the least likely to occur except as a result of God's agency, then its occurrence is evidence for God's existence. This, as I argued in my

*This work is being published for the first time. Copyright © 1989 by Richard Swinburne. All rights reserved.

I am most grateful to Dr. W. E. Parry for advice on points of physics discussed herein.

160

book *The Existence of God*,[3] is the structure of all worthwhile arguments for the existence of God; and indeed the kind of structure exemplified by all inductive arguments for anything at all. Where e is our evidence and h our hypothesis and k our background knowledge, e confirms h (in the sense of "raises the probability of h above what it would be on mere background knowledge"), $P(h/e \cdot k) > P(h/k)$, if and only if $P(e/h \cdot k) > P(e/k)$.[4] This follows from a theorem of the calculus of probability known as Bayes' Theorem; and is, I have argued, a crucial principle at work for assessing hypotheses in science, history and all other areas of inquiry. With e as the phenomenon of intelligent life, k a background of the existence of a Universe governed by natural laws but not necessarily ones such as to yield intelligent life, and h as the hypothesis of theism; e, I shall argue, confirms h.

II

God by definition is omnipotent and so has the power to bring about a Universe organized to produce intelligent life; but what reason does he have for doing so? The supremely valuable thing about intelligent life is that it is a mental life. Humans have a mental life of sensation, thought, purpose, desire, and belief. Sensations, thoughts and purposes are conscious events; desires and beliefs are mental states to which the subject may (if he chooses) have access in consciousness, but which may also continue while he is unaware of them. The higher animals have a much less full mental life than men, and plants and the lower animals have none. A full-blown human mental life is something of great value. Humans have beliefs, and beliefs about the world which are responsive to how the world is; they alter their beliefs in the light of experience and argument; and these beliefs are often so well justified that they amount to knowledge. Knowledge is in itself a supreme good. It is good that there should be beings who understand this cosmic process and who reflect upon it. It is good that there be beings who can make a difference to things through their choice; they have purposes. It is especially good if their purposes are formed through conscious reflection on the worth of the ends to be pursued, and to some extent independently of causes impinging on them, viz., if they have indeterministic free will.[5] Such beings are mini-creators. It is good too that such beings have a character and be able to form that character in part for themselves; this involves their having inbuilt inclinations to do certain kinds of action. These inclinations are desires; and human desires are alterable through training over time. The satisfaction of desire is happiness, and without desire to be satisfied there cannot be happiness. And it is good, finally, that there be beings with sensations — with colors to admire, smells to relish, and tingles to enjoy. So a God, who is by definition good, has abundant reason for bringing about human beings and other beings who have some kind of mental life. It is good that among the differences which organisms can make to the world is the formation, nurture, and education of other organisms. A God who gives to creatures children gives them a supreme responsibility.

But human beings are not characterized by a mental life alone. They are embodied in the sense that it is through stimuli landing on their bodies that they are caused to have sensations and acquire beliefs, and it is through their bodies that they execute their purposes. Through my eyes and ears I learn about the world, and through my legs and arms I make a difference to it. What reason has a God to make creatures with a mental life who are embodied? Why not creatures who know about the world without needing eyes to see with, or ones who can move the furniture without needing to do so by means of arms and legs?

The answer is that embodiment allows us to learn (or to choose not to learn) to control our mental life and to grow in power over and knowledge of the world. The natural world is a world governed by simple natural laws. If our sensations are caused by events in that world we can observe which events cause which sensations, and then put ourselves into positions where (because of the predictable conformity of events to scientific laws) causes will bring about those events which are the immediate cause of those sensations we want to occur and not those we don't. If I find that fire causes my hand to burn and the latter causes acute pain, then, knowing the predictable behavior of fire, I can avoid this source of pain in the future by not allowing my hand to go near the fire in the future. We can learn also to improve the quality and quantity of our justified beliefs. If our beliefs are caused by stimuli impinging on our bodies, we can find out (by cross-checking with other beliefs) when these stimuli are misleading and then discount beliefs acquired in a certain kind of way. And we can find out which stimuli are reliable indicators of things new or small or distant, and thus extend the range of our justified beliefs. We can learn the principles of optics and apply them to constructing telescopes, looking through which will allow us to have perceptions and so beliefs about remote events. And finally, learning what causes what, we can extend the range of our control. Learning the laws of mechanics, we can apply them to send space rockets to the moon. One of the ways in which we can grow in knowledge and control is by acquiring knowledge of how to communicate with others (learning to use foreign languages, the telephone, and radio) and thereby learning how to exercise control which results from cooperative effort. Embodiment in a world of simple natural laws puts us in a framework where causes and effects operate independently of us, and thus allows us to grow in knowledge by seeing how effects are signs of causes, and in control by using causes to bring about effects. But we cannot choose to grow unless there are procedures of knowledge acquisition and control which we can acquire; and there cannot be procedures unless there is an independent realm of simple (and so understandable and reliable) scientific laws. Enmeshed in such a world we have the power to choose what sort of beings to be; to grow or to neglect to grow. And among the knowledge we will acquire is knowledge of the beauty of a marvellous world. A God has good reason for making not merely conscious agents, but embodied conscious agents, agents with bodies through which they acquire sensations are beliefs and through which they make a difference to things, bodies which are constituents of a world conforming to simple scientific laws.

Now I think that, for reasons which I cannot give adequately here, but have argued elsewhere,[6] there cannot be a scientific explanation for the occurrence of consciousness. Sensations and thoughts are such different things from the kinds of events with which the rest of science deals that there cannot be a super-science which deals both with the mental and physical. Science cannot explain why the organisms which evolution produced were conscious beings rather than unconscious robots; and I have argued elsewhere that that fact provides a further argument for the existence of God. My concern in this paper is not, however, with the evolution of consciousness, but with the fact that there are human and animal bodies suited for the embodiment of conscious beings. For the rest of this paper, I shall understand my datum that there exist intelligent organisms, more precisely than I have understood it hitherto, as the datum that there exist bodies which are suitable vehicles for the embodiment of conscious beings. For the reasons which I have given, a God would both be able and have reason to produce intelligent organisms.

If this production of intelligent organisms is to have value, the world has to be governed, as we have seen, by simple scientific laws (which the conscious beings could come to understand and manipulate). God has another and quite different reason for making an orderly Universe —order is beautiful, total chaos is ugly. Even if God alone perceives the Universe, he has reason for making it beautiful. But he has the power and abundant reason for putting in such a universe intelligent organisms. He could do so either directly (as most, but not all thinkers before Darwin supposed that he had done); or indirectly, making the world with boundary conditions and scientific laws such as to give rise to intelligent organisms. All the evidence accumulated by scientists over the past 200 years shows overwhelmingly that present-day intelligent organisms (i.e., human and animal bodies) evolved gradually from inanimate matter in accord with scientific laws over thousands of millions of years. So God did not produce intelligent organisms directly. But if all the evidence is that the occurrence of boundary conditions and laws such as to permit the evolution of intelligent organisms are *a priori* (that is, unless there is a God) very unlikely, then (by the argument developed earlier) that is evidence that God brought them about; and thereby indirectly brought about the existence of intelligent organisms. He made an intelligent-organism-producing Universe.

III

Now what features does a body have to have to be a vehicle of the kind described for the expression of consciousness? It needs to turn the incoming stimuli (light, sound, touch, etc.) into sensations and into true-belief-correlates, that is, brain states which are correlates of true beliefs about features of the stimulus source; and to turn purpose-correlates, that is, brain states which vary with the purposes which agents seek to execute into limb movements which will effect those purposes. The kind of complexity needed depends on the kind of belief and purpose which the agent has. For complex beliefs and purposes of the kind described in the previous section, a complex brain is needed. To acquire quickly many true beliefs of varying kinds useful for the execution of their purposes, organisms need limbs to give them mobility. For learning and ratiocination to be possible, memory is crucial; and substantial, embodied memory involves brain states stable over long periods as the correlates of memory beliefs. To be effective over a continuing period and changing environment, the organism needs to have a mechanism of self-repair. And, unless inorganic material had the power spontaneously to give rise to more life, organisms need—in order to have responsibility for children—to have the power of self-reproduction.

So intelligent organisms need a large, stable body, with sense organs (sensitive to a diversity of stimuli), an information processor, a memory bank, an energy processor; and limbs giving mobility. A life based on carbon, in combination with certain other elements, especially hydrogen, oxygen, and nitrogen, has just these features. With a valence of 4, carbon can enter into many different chemical combinations. Carbon compounds are stable over long periods of time; but are also metastable in that they can easily be induced to interact further. Hence "more information can be stored in carbon compounds than in those of any other element."[7] Together with hydrogen, nitrogen and oxygen, carbon can form long, complex chain molecules; and, together with calcium giving skeletal rigidity, such an information-processing system can be made a continuing independent component of the Universe. For reproduction we need self-replicating molecules transmitting organism-forming instructions by a genetic code; the nucleic acids formed of the crucial molecules of carbon, hydrogen, nitrogen and oxygen have these properties.[8] Carbon-based life requires for its stability a moderate range of temperature and pressure; and, for its purposes to have much effect, a solid planet on which to live.

Given the present constituents of the Universe (energy and fundamental particles) and the laws of their behavior, it is highly doubtful whether there could be any other kind of intelligent life. It has sometimes been suggested that silicon could replace carbon in its central role; but this seems doubtful in that silicon compounds do not have the stability of carbon compounds.[9] Another recent suggestion has been that intelligent systems of particles relying on the "strong" interaction for their organization might exist inside neutron stars; but it seems doubtful whether they could have nearly as much information-processing capacity as does carbon-based life on Earth.[10] So let us suppose, plausibly enough, that carbon-based life is the only possible kind of life (given the present constituents of the Universe and the laws of their behavior). If silicon-based life is possible, the argument below would not need much alteration (for the conditions necessary for its evolution are very similar to those necessary for the evolution of carbon-based life); and neutron-star life is too speculative a suggestion to be taken into account at this stage.

IV

Laws of nature determine which states of the Universe give rise to which succeeding states. The present consensus of evidence is that certain *a priori* very unlikely features of laws are necessary for the occurrence of carbon-based life.

This section may not be fully comprehensible to those without adequate scientific background. I suggest, nevertheless, that such readers read through these pages; they will get the main message, that laws of nature need to have very special features indeed if carbon-based life is to occur.

Given the four fundamental forces and the basic array of fundamental particles (photons; leptons, including electrons; mesons; and baryons, including protons and neutrons), the strengths of forces and masses of particles have to have to each other ratios within certain narrow bands if the larger chemical elements, including carbon, are to occur at all; and the Pauli exclusion principle has to hold. This principle (applying to all fermions, e.g., electrons and protons) says that in one system (e.g., one atom) only one particle of the same kind can be in a given quantum state. In consequence there are only a small number of possible energy states for the electrons of an atom, and only a small number of electrons can be in each state. While the basic laws of quantum theory ensure the stability of the atom — electrons do not collapse onto the nucleus — the Pauli principle leads to the electrons being arranged in "shells." Hence atoms of a finite number of different kinds can be formed, by different numbers of electrons surrounding the nucleus; and molecules can be formed by bonds between the electrons of different atoms. No exclusion principle, no chemistry. But not much chemistry unless there is plenty of possibility for different structures to be built up, to be relatively stable, to interact, and to form new structures. For that we need atoms to be large structures with plenty of empty space between well-defined central nuclei and electrons. For that we need both of two crucial dimensionless numbers to be small: α, the fine structure constant, $e/\hbar c \sim (137)^{-1}$, and β, the electron-to-proton mass ratio, $m_e/m_n \sim (1836)^{-1}$. Their small value makes possible the long chains of molecules, such as DNA, which make life possible.[11] But α and β too small would not give stable enough atoms. Another dimensionless number is crucial for the existence of the right kind of nuclei to form atoms of many different elements — α_s ($\equiv g_s^2/4\pi \sim 0.2$), a crucial constant in the nuclear force. There are three possible systems (nuclei or components of nuclei) with two nucleons — the deuteron (proton + neutron), the diproton (proton + proton), and the dineutron (neutron + neutron). But with the present value of α_s, neither the dineutron nor the diproton is a stable state. An increase in α_s of 0.3% would bind the dineutron (i.e., allow the formation of a stable dineutron) and one of 3.4% would bind the diproton. If the diproton were bound, all the hydrogen would have been burned to helium in the early stages of the big bang, and so no hydrogen compounds or long-lived stable stars could be formed. A decrease in α_s of 9% would unbind the deuteron, and this would prevent the formation of elements heavier than hydrogen.[12] Either variation would have the consequence that the larger elements, including carbon, could not exist. A slight increase in electromagnetic force (and so in α) would have the same effect.[13] Other constants are possibly also crucial, such as the value of Δm, the neutron–proton mass difference which approximately equals m_e, the mass of the electron; if this value were much different, protons would decay before they could form stable nuclei.[14] And so on.

Further, given the actual laws of nature or laws at all similar thereto, boundary conditions will have to lie within a narrow range of the present conditions if intelligent life is to evolve (or else they will have to lie well outside that range; this point will be discussed later). If the Universe had a beginning, the boundary conditions are the arrangements and properties of the stuff of the Universe at that time — the way the Universe started off. Present evidence suggests an initial singularity, the formation of the Universe by explosion from a "big bang" some fifteen thousand million years ago. For the formation of intelligent life in a universe expanding from an initial singularity, conditions at the time of the big bang have to be (within narrow ranges) just right (or, more precisely, as going backward we approach the time of the big bang asymptotically, conditions must asymptotically approach values within certain narrow ranges). The initial rate of expansion is critical. If (for the actual value of the gravitational and other constants) the initial velocity of expansion were slightly greater than the actual initial velocity, stars and so the heavier elements would not form; if it were slightly less, the Universe would collapse before it was cool enough for the elements to form.[15] It has been calculated that (barring a possible qualification from "inflation theory" to which we will come shortly) a reduction in the rate of expansion of one part in a million million would lead to premature collapse; and an increase by one part in a million would have prevented the evolution of stars and heavier elements.[16] Some initial inhomogeneity in the distribution of radiation is needed if galaxies, and so stars, are to be produced. Too much would lead to black holes being formed before stars could form.[17] In the beginning there was a very slight excess of baryons over anti-baryons; all but the excess baryons became radiation. If the excess number were even slighter, there would not be enough matter for galaxies or stars to form. If it were greater, there would be too much radiation for planets to form.[18] And so on. The Universe has to start with the right density and amount of inhomogeneity of radiation and velocity of expansion, and that means (within a very narrow range) the actual amount.

V

So, for both laws and boundary conditions crucial variables must lie within a narrow range. Such is what the current physics seems to show. But this branch of physics is highly unstable; new theories are produced each year. Changes are possible which would have the consequence that variables can vary within a much wider range and yet life still evolve. One possible change, though in my amateur judgment an unlikely one, is that it be discovered that the boundary conditions are significantly different from what has been supposed; e.g., that the Universe did not evolve from an initial singularity, but from a very dense state resulting, perhaps, from a prior collapse, or perhaps from a quantum mechanical fluctuation of the "vacuum".[19] Such a change, probably going with the adoption of the view that the Universe was infinitely old, would have the consequence that a far wider range of boundary conditions would give rise to life.

The role of "boundary conditions" in a backwardly eternal (i.e., infinitely old) Universe may need clarification. Imagine a billiard table sealed under a glass cover in which the balls move in a vacuum (and that any energy transfer to or from the outside can be discounted). The laws of collision govern the interaction of the balls which bounce off each other and off the walls for the indefinite future. It could have been that this process was started off by someone arranging the balls and giving them an initial push before the table was sealed. In that case the boundary conditions would be the initial conditions (arrangement and velocity of balls), and they together with the laws of collision would determine all the subsequent behavior of the balls. The possible positions of the balls would be determined by the initial conditions. Some initial conditions would allow the balls to arrange themselves in all the (logically) possible arrangements during the course of a subsequent infinite time. Yet some initial conditions (e.g., the balls moving initially with velocities parallel to each other and to the walls) will ensure that the balls occupy only a few of the possible arrangements even in the course of infinite time. Suppose on the other hand that the process has been going on for ever (i.e., is not merely forwardly but backwardly eternal). Then the set-up may still have certain features at a given time which ensure that only a narrow set of possible arrangements either ever have been or ever will be occupied (e.g., again, if at one time the balls are moving parallel to each other and to the walls), or, much more likely, features which ensure that in the course of infinite time backward and forward, all possible arrangements of those balls occur. However, the sealing of the table still ensures that the only possible arrangements are arrangements of those balls—there cannot be more or less balls in the past or future. The "boundary conditions" of an infinite Universe are those features of its conditions at any one time (e.g., in a Newtonian universe, the quantity of energy) which determine the possible future and past states.

Now, if the Universe is backwardly eternal, its present state may be such that we can infer that it must pass through such and such a range of states in the course of infinite time. These might include all the logically possible states of matter–energy; but that is not very likely, for some kind of principle of conservation of energy (within quantum limits) will ensure that past (and future) states are limited to rearrangements of the existing amount of energy. However, although all of this would have to be worked out, it is highly plausible to suppose that (for given scientific laws), life is much more likely to evolve at some time in the course of the history of our Universe if it has an infinite past than if it has a finite past. There is more time for more possible arrangements of the constituents of the Universe. Nevertheless, the present evidence suggests a finite age of some 15 billion years.

The alternative change in physics might be discovery that the laws are other than previously supposed; in particular that the laws are such as to bring forth intelligent life out of a much wider range of boundary conditions than had hitherto been supposed. "Inflation theory" suggests just that. Inflation theory tells us that regions of the Universe with certain features may be subject, soon after the big bang, to a random, vast faster-than-light expansion leading to a cooler homogeneous and isotropic region.[20] So features such as homogeneity and isotropy for which a narrow range of initial conditions were thought vital are now said to be expected, given certain laws, to arise from a wider range of initial conditions. However, it seems difficult to get a satisfactory version of inflation theory which is not highly complex, and so ill justified by data; and it is doubtful whether the range of critical conditions necessary for intelligent life would be significantly widened by such a theory.[21] What is most unlikely is that physicists will change their views about the values of the constants of those laws which have to operate for the very existence of life (as opposed to those which have to operate if it is to evolve from certain boundary conditions); e.g., the values of α and β.

Our judgments as to just how narrow are the ranges within which crucial variables of boundary conditions and some of the constants of scientific laws have to lie in order to permit the evolution of intelligent life must be very tentative. However, the significant balance of evidence, as, following Barrow and Tipler, I have assessed it, is that, given boundary conditions and physical laws of the kind which in fact operate in our Universe, these variables have to lie within very narrow ranges —for instance, given the four forces and the kind of formula which governs their operation (e.g., approximately an inverse square law of gravitational attraction), the constants which appear in those laws have to lie within very narrow ranges; and given an initial singularity, the initial velocity of recession has to lie within a very narrow range.

Now certainly if we vary a number of different constants of laws, or even change the laws entirely, and alter the boundary conditions in a large way (e.g., suppose no initial singularity), then no doubt intelligent life could evolve as a result of a quite different mechanism. There is no logical necessity tying its evolution to the particular laws and boundary conditions which we have. But the crucial point is that any *slight* variation in these would make life impossible. John Leslie compares the situation to a dart transfixing a cherry hanging on a wall, surrounded by a cherry-less region, which would be no less impressive even if there were plenty of cherries in distant regions.[22]

One must go on to add that even if the necessary conditions for intelligent life are satisfied, it is still, in Barrow and Tipler's estimate, only likely to occur very rarely. In their estimate, hominoid life (i.e., life with the kind of intelligence possessed by man) is likely to occur on planets immensely many light-years apart, and so on at most three or four planets within the visible universe. Intelligent life of the kind which I have analyzed will occur somewhat, though not very much, more frequently. They reach their estimate by pointing out that, given the occurrence of heavy elements on a planet at the right temperature, ten crucial steps were needed for the evolution of man[23]: the origin of the genetic code, of aerobic respiration, of glucose fermentation, of photosynthesis, of mitochondria, of the precursors of neurons, of an eye precursor, of the endoskeleton, of the chordates, and finally of the intelligence characteristic of *Homo sapiens*. They suggest that each of these steps is crucial and that the probabilities of their occurrence during the length of time a biosphere can continue (i.e., the length of time that the stars continue on main sequence) are each so low as to yield the above estimate of the probability of the occurrence of hominoid life.[24] If the Universe is spatially infinite, there will no doubt (given the crucial range of laws and initial conditions) be an infinite number of occurrences of hominoid life. Dependent on the exact form of laws and boundary conditions, the same may hold if the Universe is an oscillating universe — in the course of infinite time, hominoid life may evolve an infinite number of times. The infrequency of hominoid life or of intelligent life generally is, however, irrelevant to the argument. The argument appeals only to the fact that certain conditions are necessary for intelligent life at all.

Any moderately precise estimate of what proportion of logically possible laws and boundary conditions would allow life seems impossible. There is no obvious way of setting about counting here. All that is clear is that within the kind of region of laws and boundary conditions for which we can get some feeling of proportions, the range allowing life is probably very small indeed. In these circumstances, the best policy for assessing the worth of the argument from fine-tuning would seem to be initially to suppose background knowledge (k), that the Universe began from an initial singularity and that laws have the form of our four-force laws, and then consider the force of the further evidence (e) that the initial conditions and constants of laws had just those values which allowed life to evolve. A priori this is very unlikely, but, for the reasons given earlier, much to be expected if there is a God (h). Hence, since $P(e/h \cdot k) >> P(e/k)$; $P(h/e \cdot k) >> P(h/k)$. That evidence has significant confirming value for the hypothesis that there is a God. If anyone supposes that we can have some idea of the relative proportion of set-ups among all logically possible laws and boundary conditions which would yield life, then they can transfer the information treated above as background knowledge into e and simply take as the background knowledge the conformity of nature to scientific laws. My guess is that the proportion might be somewhat higher without the restriction to an initial singularity (for the reason that any arrangement of matter is more likely to occur given an infinite time than given only a finite time), but somewhat lower among laws of quite different forms. (For example, it is well known that orbits of bodies traveling around a center of force are not stable if the attractive force varies with an inverse power of 3 or greater.) But in the absence of more definite theory, while allowing for some overestimate (arising from the restriction to an initial singularity), we must go on the evidence and theory we have available, and what that shows is that to the extent to which we can have some reasonable assessment of the force of the evidence, the peculiar values of the constants of laws and variables of initial conditions are substantial evidence for the existence of God, which alone can give a plausible explanation of why they are as they are.

VI

How can the conclusion that such life provides substantial evidence for the existence of God be avoided? There seem to be two "ways out" considered in the current literature.

The first is by a certain kind of interpretation of the "anthropic principle." An anthropic principle says, roughly, that laws and boundary conditions must be such that life evolves, for otherwise no one would be observing it. Precise statements of the "weak anthropic principle" and "strong anthropic principle" vary somewhat, and the variation often turns a trivial truth into an obvious falsity or vice versa. As interpreted by Barrow and Tipler,[25] the weak anthropic principle says simply that the obvious datum that there are observers now at the present region of space and time (distinguished by the general character of Earth and solar system, present distribution and density and evolved state of galaxies, etc.) tells us that all theories with laws and boundary conditions such that they have the consequence that there will not be observers in such a region of space and time are false. So interpreted, the principle is a trivial truth; to be true, a theory must be compatible with evidently true data of observation. However, Barrow and Tipler easily slide into careless expositions of the principle, carrying interpretations which would render it obviously false — e.g., "Many observations of the natural world, although remarkable *a priori*, can be seen in this light as inevitable consequences of our own existence."[26] The suggestion might seem to be that our existence is in some sense the *cause* of the laws of nature and boundary conditions being the way they are (because if they were not that way we wouldn't be able to observe them). That suggestion is nonsense. The laws of nature and boundary conditions cause our existence; we do not cause theirs.

On a certain occasion the firing squad aim their rifles at the prisoner to be executed. There are twelve expert marksmen in the firing squad, and they fire twelve rounds each. However, on this occasion all 144 shots miss. The prisoner laughs and comments that the event is not something requiring any explanation because if the marksmen had not missed, he would not be here to observe them having done so. But of course the prisoner's comment is absurd; the marksmen all having missed is indeed something requiring explanation; and so too is what goes with it — the prisoner being alive to observe it. And the explanation will be either that it was an accident (a most unusual chance event) or that it was planned (e.g., all the marksmen had been bribed to miss). Any interpretation of an anthropic principle which suggests that the evolution of observers is something which requires no explanation in terms of boundary conditions and laws being a certain way (either inexplicably or through choice) is false.

Other interpretations of anthropic principles turn them into interesting and probably false contingent scientific claims. Thus, for Barrow and Tipler, the "strong anthropic principle" originally expressed, ambiguously, as: "The Universe must have those properties which allow life to develop within it at some stage in its history" is then supposed to have the implication that "The constants and laws of Nature must be such that life can exist."[27] This I understand as claiming that the laws are such that, whatever the boundary conditions, life will evolve at some time. That seems very dubious. As I claimed earlier, science suggests that the laws are such that if the Universe had begun with an even bigger "big bang", life would never have evolved.

Anthropic principles serve only to obfuscate.

VII

A marginally more plausible way to avoid the theistic conclusion is by postulating many worlds or universes. Suppose that our universe is one of many, some of which have different laws and some of which have different boundary conditions from ours. Many of these are such that intelligent life will not evolve in them; but ours of course is such that it will. Ours is a universe within a super-universe of universes of different kinds. If there are millions of executions, it is to be expected, given that even good marksmen miss sometimes, that just occasionally all the marksmen will miss with all their shots. A hundred tosses of heads in a row is by itself an event which leads to suspicion of cheating; but if it is but one series of tosses among at least 2^{100} such series generated by the same process, the suspicion is perhaps unwarranted—the unusual sometimes happens in a large enough collection of events.

Now if we have reason to believe that there are such other universes, it will form part of our background knowledge by which to assess the worth of the argument that our universe is life-evolving. Let k_2 be the background knowledge that there are a trillion orderly universes with different laws and boundary conditions from each other, and k_1 be the background knowledge that there is at least one such; e be the evidence that there is a universe which is life-evolving, and h the hypothesis that there is a God. Then $P(e/k_2)$ will be quite high, not significantly different from $P(e/k_2 \cdot h)$, and so e will certainly be no significant evidence for h. Whereas $P(e/k_1)$ looks very low and so much lower than $P(e/k_1 \cdot h)$, and so e is evidence for h. If we have the background knowledge incorporated in k_2, the argument to h won't work. But do we?

What is meant by a "universe"? Sometimes cosmologists understand by "our universe" the physical objects (galaxies, dust, energy, etc.) currently observable by us, or (which on some physical theories is wider) those which are or will be at some future time observable from Earth, or which were at some time observable from Earth; and there are variants of these kinds, distinguishing universes by the physical objects which lie within some "horizon"[28] of the Earth. Then other "universes" are other regions of space (of similar size) lying spatially beyond our universe in one of these ways. Reasonable inductive principles certainly suggest that there are such universes. If we cut up our universe into many regions, varying in their distance and direction from Earth, evidence of observation shows that at the same instant of cosmic time, equally dense matter is to be found in each, and so, that beyond each equally dense region lies another one.[29] That is good reason for supposing that the same holds when we pass beyond the horizon. But the same evidence which shows that there are in this sense other universes, shows also that they have the same general character as our own — both in respect of boundary conditions and in respect of laws.

That the laws of nature are the same in distant regions as in our own is indeed an assumption which could not in general be shown false. For to learn the character of those regions we suppose that laws of nature which hold in our region hold in the intervening space, and that enables us to interpret certain data in our region (e.g., marks on our telescopes' photographic plates) as caused by certain events in those regions. Supposing that light travels in straight lines with the same velocity as in our region, we infer from the marks on our telescopes' photographs the density of galaxies in those regions. Without the assumption that in general the same laws held, we could have no knowledge of how matter — energy did behave in distant regions. True, the assumption that most of the laws were the same in the distant region might allow us to make inferences about the behavior of matter in that region which showed that one or two laws were different. But I know of no such evidence. And we could have no evidence for a general difference of laws. By "laws" I mean "fundamental laws"; that is, laws not derivable from more basic laws. We could have evidence that in our region matter behaved in certain ways because of some peculiar feature of this region (e.g., the density of matter here). And that evidence would show us that matter would behave in different ways in a region which had a different character. But we could only reach that conclusion because we had the evidence of how the behavior of matter varied with that feature of the region; that is, because we had evidence of a place-independent law showing how the behavior of matter varied with variation in that feature.

We could, however, in principle obtain evidence that the current arrangement of matter – energy (e.g., the number and kind of galaxies, their density and velocity) was very different in some distant region. But the evidence is abundant that that is not so; the universe in different regions is everywhere approximately the same in the arrangement of its matter – energy at the same cosmic instant. The most striking evidence of this comes from the observable isotropy of the universe;

distant regions seen from telescopes in the southern sky look just the same as distant regions seen from telescopes in the northern sky.

So, even if we treat spatially distant regions as different universes, we have good reason to suppose that they are like our own in boundary conditions and laws, and, like our own, life-evolving. The same applies, and for similar reasons, if we treat temporally distant parts of our spatial region as different "universes." If we have reason to believe that there was such a universe (viz., that there was matter – energy here) billions of years ago, that can only be because it is the simplest explanation of many present data that they were caused by states of that universe billions of years ago. Since that "universe" belongs to and is causally continuous with our universe, it has by definition the same boundary conditions. The ultimate constituents of our "universe" are the same. We extrapolate backward by assuming certain laws to hold then and during the intervening period. But the only laws which we are justified in supposing to hold are those which form part of a set giving the simplest explanation of present data. True, the extrapolation backward of most such laws might allow us to infer with justification a state of affairs in which some one or two laws which now hold did not hold. But there could be no evidence that in general the laws of nature were different, and again I know of no evidence for supposing that even one law differed in its operation in the past. Again, in talking about laws, I am talking about fundamental laws. We could have evidence for supposing that there are certain regularities of behavior characteristic of our temporal era, deriving from some general feature thereof, such as the density of matter, which would not hold in the past "universe"; but that evidence would be evidence that there is a time-invariant law showing how these regularities depend on that general feature; we would have evidence of the latter fundamental law because it provided the simplest explanation of a vast range of present data, including those regularities. But we could not have any evidence of any general, random, non-law-dependent, change in the patterns of the behavior of matter as we go backward in time. We could not, for example, have any evidence that certain "constants" of nature change over time in a non-law-dependent way.[30] The only past "universes" of which we have evidence are those with the same boundary conditions and laws as our own; and so they will be, eventually (either during their existence or during that of their successor "universe"), life-evolving. What goes for past universes, goes for future "universes" too, by a similar pattern of argument; so they too, or their predecessor universe, must be life-evolving. That any past and future "universes" for the existence of which we have evidence have in general the same laws and boundary conditions as our own is, I have been arguing, a necessary truth (the necessity of which follows from the very criteria we use of what is evidence for what). That the same is so of spatially distant "universes" is a contingent truth but one very well evidenced by data (including, above all, the observable isotropy of the universe). The difference between the two cases arises from the fact that the boundary conditions of past and future universes in our spatial region are (by definition) the same as our own. The similarity of the boundary conditions of spatially distant universes to those of our own is a contingent truth. Similar conclusions with respect to the similarity of laws and boundary conditions follow by extrapolation to "universes" distant in both space and time from our own; we extrapolate to a spatially distant universe and thence to an earlier or later universe in that spatial region, and reach the conclusion that there too boundary conditions and laws are quantitatively the same. So the evidence is that in all regions of space and time spatially related to (i.e., at some distance in some direction from) and temporally related to (i.e., earlier than or later than) our own, laws and boundary conditions are quantitatively the same; and thus, at some time, life-evolving. If we insist on calling these regions different "universes," in the crucial respects they are the same as our own. It is, I think, less misleading to talk of them as regions of one universe (the whole consisting of all the physical objects spatiotemporally related to ourselves).

What of the possibility of other "universes" not spatially related to ourselves? We can only have knowledge of them if at some time they have interacted with our own (either causing effects in our world; or as effects of a common cause which had effects in our world). The only such worlds seriously discussed in the scientific literature are the many worlds of Everett's "Many Worlds Interpretation" (MWI) of Quantum Theory.[31] The ψ-function of quantum theory describes the deterministic evolution of a system; however, when a measurement is made on the system, there is a "collapse of the wave packet"—the ψ-function yields for observation only one of a number of possible values; which one is not entailed by a description of the function. The quantum cosmologist seeks a ψ-function for the evolution of the whole Universe, and interprets the notion of the "measurement"of this function as the occurrence of any processes external to the development of the function, such as the occurrence of a non-gravitational field which would define a scale length,[32] which give values to variables of the system. MWI then seeks to save the determinism of quantum theory by saying that every measurement splits the Universe into a number of different universes, each realizing one of the possible values of the ψ-function. We are only in one of those universes and so only observe the value realized in our universe. Measurement, MWI holds, does not indeterministically select only one of the possible evolutions of the function. (Barrow and Tipler claim that often only the measuring instrument is split, not the whole Universe; the only difference between the two universes after a measurement with two possible outcomes is that one contains an instrument having one record, and the other contains an instrument having a different record. But although this may be the only qualitative difference it remains the case that, on MWI, there exist two numerically different universes, although the qualitative differences between them concern only a small part of the two universes. For the other parts of one universe are such that observers there can be affected only by one value of the measurement; and the other parts of the other universe are such that observers there can be affected only by the other value. Everything has been split.)

Now this understanding of quantum theory does indeed involve postulating many worlds, infinitely many worlds. Barrow and Tipler claim[33] that MWI suggests a preference for certain forms of quantum theory over others (e.g., certain constraints on cosmological boundary conditions), and those forms have observable consequences, and that is one of its advantages. The other suggested advantage is an advantage common to all "many-worlds" theories, that we do not need to postulate that its boundary conditions lie within a very narrow range in order to explain why our universe has various features rather than others. We avoid that need if we say that all possible universes exist (each starting from a different development in early stages); ours is just one of infinitely many.

I cannot, however, see that MWI could ever be a justified interpretation of any form of quantum theory, whatever form is best supported by observation. For its basic idea is to postulate an infinity of worlds, the states of which will never produce *any* observable effects in our world. And the reason for doing this is to save the determinism of the ψ-function and to avoid the need for very detailed boundary conditions. But MWI would have to postulate so many worlds! To start with, it has to say that "measurements," and so world-splittings, are very frequent. Further, since some outcomes of measurement are more probable than others, this can only be interpreted by MWI by saying that for each outcome there are more possible worlds in which there is that outcome than worlds in which there is the other outcome. So, although there may be only a finite number of possible outcomes of each measurement, for each outcome (varying with the outcome) there are a considerable number of possible worlds. And among the things which the measurement duplicates are the observers; every time a measurement is made by a human observer, he is split into two.[34]

It should now be apparent that if postulating infinitely many worlds were necessary to save the determinism of quantum theory and to avoid having to postulate that the boundary conditions lie within a very narrow range, it would be best instead to interpret the ψ-function indeterministically, as a probability wave describing the physical probabilities of the behavior of the real constituents of the Universe, and to postulate that the boundary conditions do lie within the narrow range. It is a crucial tenet of the scientific method that entities are not to be postulated beyond necessity. We are right to postulate unobservable entities of a few kinds and simple patterns of behavior, if their behavior would explain many complex or coincidental observations. And if a logical consequence of postulating, for these reasons, some entities, is that there are other entities which will not causally affect our observations, that is acceptable, so long as our theory does not get too top-heavy. But to postulate infinitely many worlds in order to save a preferred interpretation of a formula, which is in no way obviously simpler than the alternative explanation, and to avoid having to postulate a very narrow range of boundary conditions (which have to lie within a certain range anyway), seems crazy. MWI is like an enormous inverted pyramid of theory resting on a vertex of observation.

We can only have knowledge of worlds not spatially related to our own if our own is different from what it would be if there were no such worlds. MWI does not provide that evidence. It is the main scientific contender to do so on grounds other than the fact that our universe is life-evolving. That is, we do not have independent background knowledge of the type k_2. As far as our background knowledge is concerned, we have no reason for supposing that there are worlds other than our own with significantly different laws and boundary conditions.

What, finally, of the suggestion that, although we do not have any other reason (background knowledge) for supposing the existence of "many worlds," the fact that our world is productive of intelligent life is reason for supposing that there are, more or as much reason as for supposing that there is a God. The supposition (h_2) would be that an infinity of worlds with varying laws and boundary conditions exists, not caused by anything else, our intelligent-life-producing world (e) being but one of them. With h_1 as the existence of God, the suggestion is that (with k as tautological, i.e., zero, background knowledge) $P(h_2/e \cdot k) \geq P(h_1/e \cdot k)$.

This suggestion does not deny that e confirms (that is, raises the probability of) h_1. It suggests only that e confirms h_2 equally well. Given that, roughly speaking, both h_1 and h_2 lead us to expect e equally well $[P(e/h_1 \cdot k) = P(e/h_2 \cdot k)]$, whether e makes h_1 or h_2 more probable depends on whether, apart from e, h_1 or h_2 is more probable anyway. That depends on whether h_1 or h_2 is the simpler theory—the one postulating fewer new entities, mathematically simpler modes of behavior, less arbitrary coincidences, etc. Such factors determine the theory's prior probability on zero background knowledge k. In symbols, the prior probability of h_1 is represented by $P(h_1/k)$, of h_2 by $P(h_2/k)$. By Bayes' theorem, if $P(e/h_1 \cdot k) = P(e/h_2 \cdot k)$, $P(h_1/e \cdot k) > P(h_2/e \cdot k)$ if and only if $P(h_1/k) > P(h_2/k)$. Scientists can always construct an infinite number of theories (some of them highly complex) able to predict any finite set of data. If they are ever to be justified in saying that one of these theories is more probably true than any other (or that its predictions are more probably true than those of any other such theory), it can only be on the basis of factors such as those I stated, determining simplicity. On any reasonable understanding of simplicity,

I suggest, $P(h_2/k)$ will be absurdly low compared to $P(h_1/k)$. The postulation of God is the postulation of *one* entity of a simple kind (the simplest kind of person there could be, having no limits to his knowledge, power and freedom).[35] The postulation of the actual existence of an infinite number of worlds, between them exhausting all the logical possibilities, many of them consisting of an infinite quantity of matter – energy behaving in accord with simple laws over infinite time, which are not caused by anything else, which do not causally affect each other, but which between them exhaust the logical space without any one being qualitatively identical to any other, is to postulate complexity and non-prearranged coincidence of infinite dimensions beyond rational belief. Hence, $P(h_2/e \cdot k) << P(h_1/e \cdot k)$. The existence of God is much more likely on the evidence of our life-producing world than the existence of "many worlds."

There are no good grounds for adopting any form of "many-worlds" hypothesis, except ones which postulate "universes" belonging to the same spatio-temporal realm as our own, which have the same intelligent-life-producing properties. The existence of our world with its power to produce intelligent life (and of other such worlds if they exist) is therefore confirming evidence of the existence of God. Together with other evidence not discussed here it does, I believe (as I have argued elsewhere[36] with respect to the other evidence alone) render the existence of God significantly more probable than not.

NOTES

1. Clarendon Press, 1986.
2. He has argued from the fine-tuning of the Universe in a series of articles: Anthropic principle, world ensemble, design, *American Philosophical Quarterly* 19:141–151, 1982; Cosmology, probability, and the need to explain life, in N. Rescher, (ed.), *Scientific Explanation and Understanding*, University Press of America, 1983, pp. 53–81; Observership in cosmology: The anthropic principle, *Mind* 92:573–79, 1983; Modern cosmology and the creation of life, in E. McMullin (ed.), *Evolution and Creation*, pp. 91–120, University of Notre Dame Press, 1985; The scientific weight of anthropic and teleological principles, in N. Rescher, (ed.), *Current Issues in Teleology*, pp. 111–119, University Press of America, Lanham, Maryland, 1985, and The prerequisites of life in our universe, in *Newton and the New Direction in Science*, pp. 229–258, G. V. Coyne, M. Heller, and J. Zycinski, (eds.), Vatican Observatory, Vatican City State, 1988. For his account of explanation by the action of God as explanation by "ethical requiredness," see his *Value and Existence*, Blackwell, Oxford, 1979. I shall not discuss here the latter aspect of his views, but rely instead on the positive reasons which I shall articulate to see the fine-tuning of the Universe as providing evidence for a God of the traditional kind.
3. Clarendon Press, 1979.
4. For all fillings of p and q, "$P(p/q)$" represents the probability of p, given evidence q. "$\cdot$" represents "and," "$>$" represents "greater than," "$>>$" represents "very much greater than," "$<$" represents "less than," "$<<$"

represents "very much less than," "≥" represents "greater than or equal to."

5. For argument that humans do have indeterministic free will, see my *The Evolution of the Soul*, Clarendon Press, 1986, chap. 13. See this book generally for amplification of the points about the mental life which distinguishes humans and animals from inanimate things.

6. See *The Evolution of the Soul*, chap. 10.

7. Barrow and Tipler, p. 547.

8. On self-reproduction and self-repair, see Barrow and Tipler, *op. cit.*, pp. 510–523.

9. Barrow and Tipler, *op. cit.*, pp. 545ff.

10. *Op. cit.*, pp. 343–6.

11. Barrow and Tipler, pp. 295–305.

12. *Op. cit.*, pp. 321ff.

13. *Op. cit.*, p. 326.

14. *Op. cit.*, p. 400.

15. *Op. cit.*, pp. 410ff.

16. Papers by S. W. Hawking and by R. H. Dicke and P. J. E. Peebles cited in John Leslie, Anthropic principle, world ensemble, design, p. 141.

17. Barrow and Tipler, pp. 414–419.

18. *Op. cit.*, pp. 401–408.

19. *Op. cit.*, pp. 440ff.

20. *Op. cit.*, pp. 430–440.

21. *Op. cit.*, pp. 438ff. and p. 502. See also John Leslie, The prerequisites of life in our universe.

22. "Anthropic Principle, World Ensemble, Design", p. 143.

23. Barrow and Tipler, pp. 556–570.

24. The infrequency of life in the Universe led to my feeling (*The Existence of God*, p. 136) that its occurrence was a relatively random event, and so not evidence of a Creator. I did not take seriously the fact that laws and boundary conditions had to lie within a certain range if there was to be life at all, and for that reason I underestimated the strength of an argument of this kind.

25. *Op. cit.*, p. 16.

26. *Op. cit.*, p. 219.

27. *Op. cit.*, p. 21.

28. See (e.g.) my *Space and Time*, 2nd. ed., Macmillan and Co., 1981, chap. 12.

29. The approximate homogeneity and isotropy of the Universe within the region observable by telescope after making allowance for the fact that we observe more distant regions as they were at periods of time longer ago, is well evidenced by observation. See Barrow and Tipler, pp. 414–430.

30. P.A.M. Dirac postulated that the gravitational "constant" varied with time in a law-dependent way. See Barrow and Tipler, pp. 20ff. Even this hypothesis did not prove well-justified.

31. Barrow and Tipler, pp. 472–496.

32. *Op. cit.*, pp. 499ff.

33. *Op. cit.*, pp. 493–496.

34. I have noted elsewhere that there are considerable philosophical difficulties in supposing that persons can be split. See (e.g.) *The Evolution of the Soul*, pp. 149ff.

35. For argument on this, see *The Existence of God*, chap. 5. See note 4 of the present paper for the meaning of the symbols used in this paragraph.

36. *The Existence of God*.

13

HEINZ R. PAGELS*

A Cozy Cosmology

THE UNIVERSE, IT seems, has been finely tuned for our comfort; its properties appear to be precisely conducive to intelligent life. The force of gravity, for example, could hardly be set at a more ideal level. If it were somehow adjusted upward by just a bit, the stars would consume their hydrogen fuel much more rapidly than they now do. Our sun might burn itself out in less than a billion years (instead of ten billion years), hardly enough time for life as complex as the human species to evolve. If, on the other hand, gravity were nudged downward a notch, the prospects for the evolution of intelligent life would be no less bleak. The sun, now burning more slowly, would cool down and become much too chilly to sustain life as we know it.

The ratio of photons (particles of light) to nuclear particles (protons and neutrons) also falls within a most convenient range. In Einstein's gravity equations, which describe the laws that govern the evolution of the universe, this ratio plays a critical role in determining the rate at which the cosmos expands. If the ratio were forty billion to one instead of four hundred million to one, the universe would expand so rapidly that stars and galaxies might not have formed, in which case there would be nowhere for life to live.

Yet another quite convenient characteristic of the universe has to do with the relative masses of protons and neutrons. The neutron is ever so slightly the more massive of the two, and so free neutrons — neutrons

*Reprinted from *The Sciences*, Vol. 25, No. 2, March/April 1985, pp. 35–38. Copyright © The New York Academy of Sciences, 1985.

180

not confined in atomic nuclei—can, and do, decay into protons. If we could alter the masses of these subatomic particles by a small fraction of 1 percent, we could make the proton the heavier. Hydrogen atoms, in this imaginary universe, would then be unstable, since the protons that constitute their nuclei would spontaneously decay into neutrons. Hydrogen (which comprises about 74 percent of the observed matter in the universe) could not exist—and thus, presumably, neither would the stars that consume it nor the life that basks in the resulting glow.

Similar examples abound. Again and again, scientists have been struck by the observation that if a given characteristic of the universe were only slightly different, then life would be impossible. Some physicists have come up with an explanation for these many instances of good fortune. It is possible, they argue, that any number of the many alternative universes we can imagine—places with stronger gravity, or weightier protons, than our universe—actually exist. But, because they are not conducive to life, there are no physicists or philosophers in these universes to contemplate them. Thus, the physical properties we observe are the properties of a specially selected stretch of time and space—one that spawned life; so, the compatibility of these properties with life is hardly surprising. As the physicist John D. Barrow has put the proposition: "The observations of cosmological parameters made by astronomers are the victims of an all-embracing selection effect—our own existence." This line of argument has been given a name: the anthropic principle.

To judge from the present flow of books and magazine articles, one would think that the anthropic principle is sweeping through science like wildfire. Barrow and the astrophysicist Joseph Silk give it serious consideration in their recent book, *The Left Hand of Creation*, and *The Anthropic Cosmological Principle*, coauthored by Barrow and the physicist Frank J. Tipler, is scheduled for publication soon. *Stephen Hawking's Universe*, a book published in 1984, devotes a chapter to the repeated use of the anthropic principle by Hawking, the British cosmologist who has done so much to bring the current theory of the cosmos into being. Paul Davies, another British cosmologist and a quantum field theorist, wrote about the principle seven years ago in *The Sciences* and, more recently, discussed it in the English popular magazine *New Scientist*. And only last year, a novel application of the principle was the subject of a generally favorable editorial in the esteemed British journal *Nature*.

My own view is that this is all much ado about nothing. The anthropic principle is deeply flawed and has no place in physics or cosmology. Although billed by its proponents as a major principle, it in fact makes no progress toward solving the great mysteries of the universe. Indeed, it confronts us with a new mystery: How can such a sterile idea reproduce itself so prolifically?

The anthropic line of reasoning can be traced back at least as far as 1955, when the mathematician G. J. Whitrow, of Imperial College, London, published an article, in *The British Journal for the Philosophy of Science,* in which he contended that the reason we find the universe to be three-dimensional is that life could not exist in other dimensions. The Princeton physicist Robert Dicke, however, was the first to articulate the anthropic principle clearly. In a 1957 article in *Reviews of Modern Physics,* he suggested that the fundamental physical constants, such as the gravitational constant and the charge on the electron, are "not random but conditioned by biological factors," central among them the fact that organisms must exist in order for these constants to be measured.

In the nearly three decades since Dicke's paper was published, a number of scientists have invoked the anthropic principle in their writings. But it is often not clear how strongly they believe in it, and whether they aren't simply using it (with some success, admittedly) as a kind of intellectual tease. More often than not, the principle is described in forceful and intriguing terms but either not endorsed or given only the faintest embrace.

A noteworthy exception is the position of Brandon Carter, an English cosmologist. Since 1974, when he coined the term "anthropic principle," he has been one of the principle's strongest advocates. He sees it as providing a middle ground between the pre-Copernican view, which saw the universe as being centered on humanity, and the post-Copernican view, which denies humanity *any* special cosmological status. "Although our situation is not necessarily central," Carter has written, "it is privileged to some extent." The anthropic principle, he believes, has at last put our position in the universe in proper perspective.

In some respects, though, Carter's worldview is the product of an anthropocentricism as profound as that which underlay the pre-Copernican view of the universe; the anthropic principle is born of a most provincial outlook on what life is. Its adherents assume that all life must resemble, in broad form at least, life on this planet.

The annals of science fiction suggest how mistaken this assumption could turn out to be. The English astronomer Fred Hoyle (who, ironically, was among the first to cite the anthropic principle) has written a story in which intelligent life exists as a cloud of gas. The sun itself, according to another piece of science fiction, may be intelligent, but so slow in its thought processes that no mental gyrations are apparent to us. By exercising this much imagination, we can see how a universe with stronger or weaker gravity, or a different ratio between photons and nuclear particles, could produce forms of intelligence that bore no resemblance to life as we know it. If the scientists among such beings applied anthropic reasoning, they would probably conclude that a universe like ours could not give rise to life because its fundamental constants do not agree with theirs.

Whether applied by extraterrestrial (or extrauniversal) beings to rule out our existence or by us to rule out theirs, the anthropic principle is an unscientific idea; it uses the unknown (life and the forms it *might* take) to explain the known (the observed properties of the universe) rather than the other way around. As such, the anthropic principle never *predicts* anything—not the appearance of a comet, nor the outcome of a laboratory experiment; it is, as the astrophysicists Bernard J. Carr and Martin J. Rees, both then of Cambridge University, noted in *Nature* several years ago, "entirely *post hoc.*" What's more, unlike other principles of physics, the anthropic principle is not testable. It is all well and good to imagine universes with various gravitational constants and estimate the prevailing physical properties, but there is no way we can actually go to an imaginary universe and check for life. We are stuck with our universe, and powerless to alter its fundamental constants. So long as this is the case, the anthropic principle will be immune to experimental falsification—a sure sign that it is not a scientific principle.

A glance at recent scientific history demonstrates how utterly the anthropic principle fails to shed light on the nature of the universe. In 1973, Hawking and Barry Collins, both of Cambridge University, published a paper addressing the isotropy of the universe—the fact that it looks much the same in all directions. The galaxies, for example, are evenly distributed over the entire sky, not lumped into one place, and the microwave background radiation (the heat left over from the primordial big bang) is also equably spread across the universe. Hawking and Collins argued that out of all the possible initial conditions of the universe, only a small set could produce such isotropy. To explain this seemingly improbable circumstance, they invoked the anthropic principle. Since in highly anisotropic universes matter would never form into galaxies, stars, and planets, life (at least as we know it) would have no place to reside. So, we should not be surprised to peer out and find that our universe is isotropic. If it were not, there would be no one to do the peering. There is nothing wrong with this reasoning. But is it necessary? Aren't there better ways for scientists to spend their time?

As it turns out, there are. Scientists who devoted their energies to finding a more conventionally scientific explanation have arrived at a theory that many cosmologists now subscribe to; the big bang, they believe, was preceded by something called the inflationary epoch, which can be well represented by the image of a balloon being blown up. Initially, the balloon may be wrinkled and twisted. But, upon inflation (an exceedingly rapid inflation, in the case of the nascent universe), its many inhomogeneities get "stretched away." The result, we believe, was a uniform space for the universe and a uniform distribution of the matter in it. If this idea is correct, then Hawking and Collins's application of the anthropic principle was simply unnecessary.

In this application, the anthropic principle assumed the milder of its two forms; it was used to account for an observed property of the universe, but not for the fundamental constants—the force of gravity, the neutron–proton mass ratio, and other precisely defined quantities that figure critically in the mathematical foundation of physics. Stronger versions of the principle—attempts to explain the fundamental constants themselves—have been no more fruitful. Take, for example, the ratio of photons to nuclear particles, which partly determines the rate at which the universe expands. Over the last several years, this ratio has been explained by both the inflationary universe hypothesis and the new unified field theories (theories that account, within a single framework, for three of the four basic forces, such as electromagnetism and the "weak" and "strong" interactions of subatomic particles). So, this constant is more profitably viewed as a consequence of the laws of nature than as the legacy of some selective principle.

Such constants are often called "arbitrary"—not because they lack a precise numerical value (that can be determined by experiment) but because physicists have not yet devised a theory to explain them. We know of no reason, for example, why the gravitational constant couldn't have another value. This arbitrariness is distasteful to theoretical physicists because it highlights their failure, as yet, to provide an exhaustive explanation for the physical structure of the world. They would like to believe what Einstein said: "There are no *arbitrary* constants. . . . Nature is so constituted that it is possible logically to lay down such strongly determined laws that within these laws only . . . completely determined constants occur."

Although the master theory that would reduce the number of arbitrary constants to zero continues to elude physicists, they are making progress toward it. Only two decades ago, the equations of particle physics included dozens of unexplained parameters, but the electroweak unified field theory of the early 1970s showed that virtually all of them follow from the laws of physics. Today, there are only about nineteen arbitrary constants in the physical laws that describe nature at the microscopic level. If science continues to dispel our ignorance at the present rate, the anthropic principle will soon be relegated to its proper role: as a museum piece in the history of science, gathering dust.

A few years ago, at a dinner honoring the physicist Eugene Wigner, I encountered Robert Dicke, who was a teacher of mine during the late 1950s, about the time he first endorsed the anthropic principle. After all these years, I asked, what was his view of the idea he helped put on the map? Dicke said he now thought that unless there was an element of arbitrariness in the origin of the universe, the anthropic principle was without content. His point was this: if the physical laws prevailing at the birth of the universe fixed the fundamental constants in cement, then anthropic reasoning is unnecessary; the universe is completely determined, and the question of whether life can evolve was answered from the beginning; even if there were billions of distinct and separate universes, they would all be basically the same, assuming that the same set of laws governed the origin of each. But if there is some randomness in the way the fundamental constants are set, then there could be universes that, though created in accordance with the laws that reign in our universe, differ from it fundamentally. In that event, Dicke believes, then indeed the anthropic principle is worthy of consideration.

Dicke's remark echoes Einstein's comment that he worked on physics to find out "if God had any choice in creating the universe the way He did." Physicists still do not know whether such "choice" existed, but some believe that the theory of quantum mechanics leaves room for it. The origin of the universe, they argue, involved quantum processes, which determine the probability of individual events but not the events themselves — just as the probability of the outcome of a given throw of the dice is determined by reliable statistical laws but no single outcome can be confidently predicted.

If these physicists are right — and, further, if there are many such universes, all created in accordance with laws that leave room for randomness in the fundamental constants — then the anthropic principle makes *some* sense; the fundamental constants may differ from one universe to the next, and some universes, unfit for habitation, may represent lethal throws of the quantum dice.

But how likely is such a scenario, and how will we ever know for sure if it is correct? Moreover, even if we accept the notion that random processes played an important role in the creation of the universe, it does not follow that the fundamental constants in any other universe differ from ours. The differences may be more superficial — a slight variation, for example, in the distribution of galaxies and stars. My own view is that although we have not yet discovered the most basic physical laws, if we do, the possibility of life in a universe governed by those laws will in some sense be written into them. The existence of life is not a selective principle acting on those laws; rather, it is a consequence of them. Whether or not I am right, it is simply premature to invoke the anthropic principle until the origin of the universe is much better understood.

Why, in the meantime, do some scientists continue to honor the anthropic principle with their attention? At least part of the answer is beyond the reach of scientific analysis, and lies somewhere in the realm of personal taste and individual psychology. Still, we can speculate. Perhaps the frustration and exasperation intrinsic to searching for a complete account of the cosmic parameters have gotten the better of some physicists and cosmologists. And, certainly, the anthropic principle's simplicity accounts for some of its appeal, particularly to the growing number of scientists who write for a popular audience. It is easier to convey a simple redundancy — that we can only see what we can see — than to grapple with the abstract mathematical arguments following from the unified field theories. In many respects, the anthropic principle is the lazy man's approach to science.

In fairness, it should be noted that those who appeal to the anthropic principle are not seeking in it a *causal* explanation of universal properties; they do not contend that the existence of life causes the constants to have their observed values. As Paul Davies has put the argument: "[Anthropic] reasoning so far, while compelling, does not really *explain* the large-scale features of the universe so much as *constrain* them. It is only possible to say that if they differed markedly from what we observe we would not be here to wonder about it."

Do Davies's words punch a hole in my argument? If the anthropic principle is not explanatory after all, then it is, strictly speaking, not competing with the conventional program of scientific explanation. True enough. But the fact remains that the anthropic principle is an alternative approach to thinking about the mysteries of the universe, and in that respect detracts from real science. Physicists who dwell on it are, in effect, giving up on the attempt to find a truly fundamental explanation for the nature of things. The anthropic principle is needless clutter in the conceptual repertoire of science.

There does exist a line of thinking that *is* in direct competition with the anthropic principle. Edward Harrison, in his textbook *Cosmology*, advises his readers early on: "We shall occasionally refer to the anthropic principle, and the reader may, if it is preferred, substitute the alternative theistic principle." The theistic principle is quite straightforward: the reason the universe seems tailor-made for our existence is that it *was* tailor-made for our existence; some supreme being created it as a home for intelligent life. Of course, some scientists, believing science and religion mutually exclusive, find this idea unattractive. Faced with questions that do not neatly fit into the framework of science, they are loath to resort to religious explanation; yet their curiosity will not let them leave matters unaddressed. Hence, the anthropic principle. It is the closest that some atheists can get to God.

14

STEPHEN JAY GOULD*

Mind and Supermind

HARRY HOUDINI USED his consummate skill as a conjurer to unmask legions of lesser magicians who masqueraded as psychics with direct access to an independent world of pure spirit. His two books, *Miracle Mongers and Their Methods* (1920) and *A Magician Among the Spirits* (1924), might have helped Arthur Conan Doyle had this uncritical devotee of spiritualism been as inclined to skepticism and dedicated to rationalism as his literary creation Sherlock Holmes. But Houdini campaigned a generation too late to aid the trusting intellectuals who had succumbed to a previous wave of late Victorian spiritualism — a distinguished crew, including the philosopher Henry Sidgwick and Alfred Russel Wallace, Charles Darwin's partner in the discovery of natural selection.

Wallace (1823–1913) never lost his interest in natural history, but he devoted most of his later life to a series of causes that seem cranky (or at least idiosyncratic) today, although in his own mind they formed a curious pattern of common thread — campaigns against vaccination, for spiritualism, and an impassioned attempt to prove that, even though mind pervades the cosmos, our own earth houses the universe's only experiment in physical objects with consciousness. We are truly alone in body, however united in mind, proclaimed this first prominent exobiologist among evolutionists (see Wallace's book *Man's Place in the*

*From *The Flamingo's Smile, Reflections in Natural History*, by Stephen Jay Gould, pp. 392–402, with the permission of W. W. Norton & Company, Inc., and of Penguin Books Ltd. Copyright © 1985 by Stephen Jay Gould.

Universe: A Study of the Results of Scientific Research in Relation to the Unity or Plurality of Worlds, 1903).

Wallace's basic argument for a universe pervaded by mind is simple. I also regard it as both patently ill-founded and quaint in its failure to avoid that age-old pitfall of Western intellectual life — the representation of raw hope gussied up as rationalized reality. In short (the details come later) Wallace examined the physical structure of the earth, solar system, and universe and concluded that if any part had been built ever so slightly differently, conscious life could not have arisen. Therefore, intelligence must have designed the universe, at least in part that it might generate life. Wallace concluded:

> In order to produce a world that should be precisely adapted in every detail for the orderly development of organic life culminating in man, such a vast and complex universe as that which we know exists around us, may have been absolutely required.

How could a man doubt that his favorite medium might contact the spirit of dear departed Uncle George when evidence of disembodied mind lay in the structure of the universe itself?

Wallace's argument had its peculiarities, but one aspect of his story strikes me as even more odd. During the last decade, like the cats and bad pennies of our proverbs, Wallace's argument has returned in new dress. Some physicists have touted it as something fresh and new — an escape from the somber mechanism of conventional science and a reassertion of ancient truths and suspicions about spiritual force and its rightful place in our universe. To me it is the same bad argument, only this time shorn of Wallace's subtlety and recognition of alternative interpretations.

Others have called it the "anthropic principle," the idea that intelligent life lies foreshadowed in the laws of nature and the structure of the universe. Borrowing the term from an opponent who used it for scorn, physicist Freeman Dyson proudly labels it "animism," not because the idea is lively or organic but from the Latin *anima*, or "soul." (Dyson's essay, "The Argument from Design," in his fine autobiography, *Disturbing the Universe*, provides a good statement of the argument.)

Dyson begins with the usual profession of hope:

> I do not feel like an alien in this universe. The more I examine the universe and study the details of its architecture, the more evidence I find that the universe in some sense must have known that we were coming.

His defense is little more than a list of physical laws that would preclude intelligent life, were their constants just a bit different, and physical conditions that would destroy or debar us if they changed even slightly. These are, he writes, the "numerical accidents that seem to conspire to make the universe habitable."

Consider, he states, the force that holds atomic nuclei together. It is just strong enough to overcome the electrical repulsion among positive charges (protons), thus keeping the nucleus intact. But this force, were it just a bit stronger, would bring pairs of hydrogen nuclei (protons) together into bound systems that would be called "diprotons" if they existed. "The evolution of life," Dyson reminds us, probably "requires a star like the sun, supplying energy at a constant rate for billions of years." If nuclear forces were weaker, hydrogen would not burn at all, and no heavy elements would exist. If they were strong enough to form diprotons, then nearly all potential hydrogen would exist in this form, leaving too little to form stars that could endure for billions of years by slowly burning hydrogen in their cores. Since planetary life as we know it requires a central sun that can burn steadily for billions of years, "then the strength of nuclear forces had to lie within a rather narrow range to make life possible."

Dyson then moves to another example, this time from the state of the material universe, rather than the nature of its physical laws. Our universe is built on a scale that provides, in typical galaxies like our Milky Way, an average distance between stars of some 20 million million miles. Suppose, Dyson argues, the average distance were ten times less. At this reduced density, it becomes overwhelmingly probable that at least once during life's 3.5-billion-year tenure on earth, another star would have passed sufficiently close to our sun to pull the earth from its orbit, thus destroying all life.

Dyson then draws the invalid conclusion that forms the basis for animism, or the anthropic principle:

> The peculiar harmony between the structure of the universe and the needs of life and intelligence is a manifestation of the importance of mind in the scheme of things.

The central fallacy of this newly touted but historically moth-eaten argument lies in the nature of history itself. Any complex historical outcome — intelligent life on earth, for example — represents a summation of improbabilities and becomes thereby absurdly unlikely. But something has to happen, even if any particular "something" must stun us by its improbability. We could look at any outcome and say, "Ain't it amazing. If the laws of nature had been set up just a tad differently, we wouldn't have this kind of universe at all."

Does this kind of improbability permit us to conclude anything at all about that mystery of mysteries, the ultimate origin of things? Suppose the universe were made of little more than diprotons? Would that be bad, irrational, or unworthy of spirit that moves in many ways its wonders to perform? Could we conclude that some kind of God looked like or merely loved bounded hydrogen nuclei or that no God or mentality existed at all? Likewise, does the existence of intelligent life in our universe demand some preexisting mind just because another cosmos would have yielded a different outcome? If disembodied mind does exist (and I'll be damned if I know any source of scientific evidence for or against such an idea), must it prefer a universe that will generate our earth's style of life, rather than a cosmos filled with diprotons? What can we say against diprotons as markers of preexisting intelligence except that such a universe would lack any chroniclers among its physical objects? Must all conceivable intelligence possess an uncontrollable desire to incarnate itself eventually in the universe of its choice?

If we return now to Wallace's earlier formulation of the anthropic principle, we can understand even better why its roots lie in hope, not impelling reason. First, we must mention the one outstanding difference between Dyson's and Wallace's visions. Dyson has no objection to the prospect of intelligence on numerous worlds of a vast universe. Wallace upheld human uniqueness and therefore advocated a limited universe contained within the Milky Way galaxy and an earth impeccably designed, through a series of events sufficiently numerous and complex to preclude repetition elsewhere, for supporting the evolution of intelligent life. I do not know the deeper roots of Wallace's belief, and I have little sympathy for psychobiography, but the following passage from his conclusion to *Man's Place in the Universe* surely records a personal necessity surpassing simple inference from scientific fact. The preexisting, transcendent mind of the universe, Wallace writes, would allow only one incarnation of intelligence, for a plurality

> . . . would introduce monotony into a universe whose grand character and teaching is endless diversity. It would imply that to produce the living soul in the marvellous and glorious body of man — man with his faculties, his aspirations, his powers for good and evil — that this was an easy matter which could be brought about anywhere, in any world. It would imply that man is an animal and nothing more, is of no importance in the universe, needed no great preparations for his advent, only, perhaps, a second-rate demon, and a third or fourth-rate earth.

This major difference in opinion about the frequency of intelligent life should not mask the underlying identity of the primary argument advanced by Wallace and by modern supporters of the anthropic principle: intelligent life, be it rare or common, could not have evolved in a physical universe constructed even a tiny bit differently; therefore, preexisting intelligence must have designed the cosmos. Wallace's description of his supporters could well include Dyson: "They hold that the marvellous complexity of forces which appear to control matter, if not actually to constitute it, are and must be mind-products."

Yet the universe used by Wallace to uphold the anthropic principle could not be more radically different from Dyson's. If the same argument can be applied to such different arrangements of matter, may we not legitimately suspect that emotional appeal, rather than a supposed basis in fact or logic, explains its curious persistence? Dyson's universe is the one now familiar to us all—awesome in extent and populated by galaxies as numerous as sand grains on a sweeping beach. Wallace's cosmos was a transient product of what his contemporaries proudly labeled the "New Astronomy," the first, and ultimately faulty, inferences made from a spectrographic examination of stars.

In Wallace's limited universe, the Milky Way galaxy spans some 3,600 light-years in a cosmos that, by Lord Kelvin's calculation, could not be more than twice as large in total diameter (space beyond the Milky Way would be populated by few, if any, stars). A small "solar cluster" of stars sits in the center of the universe; our own sun lies at or near its outer limit. A nearly empty region extends beyond the solar cluster, followed, at a radius of some 300 light-years from the center, by an inner ring of stars and other cosmic objects. Another and much larger region of thinly populated space lies beyond the inner ring, followed by a much larger, densely filled outer ring, the Milky Way proper, with a span of 600 light-years, and lying 1,200 to 1,800 light-years from the center.

Wallace's version of the anthropic principle holds that life requires each part of this intricate physical universe, and that life could only arise around a sun situated where ours resides by good fortune, at the outer edge of the central solar cluster. All these rings, clusters, and empty spaces must therefore reflect the plan of preexisting intelligence.

Wallace's argument requires that distant stars have a direct and sustaining influence upon our earth's capacity to support life. He flirts with the idea that stellar rays may be good for plants as he desperately tries to argue around a contemporary calculation that the bright star Vega affords the earth about one 200-millionth the heat of an ordinary candle one meter distant. He even advances the dubious argument that since stars can impress their light upon a photographic plate, plants may also require the same light to carry out their nighttime activities —quite a nimble leap of illogic from the fact that film can *record* to the inference that living matter *needs*.

But Wallace didn't press this feeble, speculative argument. Instead, he emphasized that life depends upon the detailed physical structure of the universe for the same reason that Dyson cites in his two major examples: the evolution of complex, intelligent life requires a central sun that can burn steadily for untold ages, and such stable suns develop only within a delicate and narrow range of physical laws and conditions. Dyson emphasizes stellar density and diprotons; Wallace argued that appropriate suns could only exist in a universe structured like ours and only at the edge of a central cluster in such a universe.

In Wallace's universe, stars are concentrated in three regions; the outer ring (or Milky Way proper), the inner ring surrounding the central cluster, and the central cluster itself. The outer ring of the Milky Way is too dense and active a region for stable suns. Stars move so rapidly and lie so close to each other that collisions and near approaches will inevitably disrupt any planetary system before intelligent life evolves.

Wallace then claims that solar stability cannot (as we believe today) arise as a product of a star's own fuel supply (he knew little of radioactivity and nuclear fusion). Stars can burn steadily only if they are constantly supplied with new matter flowing from elsewhere. This matter moves, by gravitation, from outer regions of the universe (particularly from the ring of the Milky Way) toward the center, where our sun resides. The inner ring cannot harbor stable suns, since too much extraneous matter bombards it. The center of the solar cluster won't do, because it receives too little nurturing material. Only at the outer edge of the solar cluster, where (and surely by design) our sun resides, can a star obtain the proper balance of material to burn steadily for enough time to foster the evolution of intelligence.

Every detail of cosmic design conspires to permit life on a planet circling such a fortunately situated sun. We need the Milky Way to supply external fuel. We need the inner ring as a filter, allowing just the right amount of fuel to pass through. We need a central cluster where stars move slowly and do not interfere with each other. Could all this have happened without some directing intelligence? Eighty years after Wallace's book, our universe could not be more radically different, yet human hope continues to impose the same invalid argument upon it.

A final, important difference separates Wallace from Dyson and most modern supporters of the anthropic principle. Our contemporary advocates develop their arguments and then present their conclusion — that mind designed the universe, in part so that intelligent life might evolve within it — as a necessary and logical inference. Wallace was far too good a *historical* scientist to indulge in such fatuous certainty; he understood only too well that ordered and complex outcomes can arise from accumulated improbabilities. He therefore recognized and presented forthrightly the alternative interpretation:

> One considerable body, including probably the majority of men of science, will admit that the evidence does apparently lead to this conclusion, but will explain it as due to a fortunate coincidence. There might have been a hundred or a thousand life-bearing planets, had the course of evolution of the universe been a little different, or there might have been none at all.

This fine scientist, wearied by age and by so many lonely battles for idiosyncratic causes, but still incisively self-critical, then presented his favored interpretation, honestly recognizing its basis in a comforting view of life that could not be proved:

> The other body, and probably much the larger, would be represented by those who, holding that mind is essentially superior to matter and distinct from it, cannot believe that life, consciousness, mind, are products of matter. They hold that the marvellous complexity of forces which appear to control matter, if not actually to constitute it, are and must be mind-products.

I cannot deny that this second view, the anthropic principle, is a *possible* interpretation of the evidence, although I favor the first explanation myself. (Always be suspicious of conclusions that reinforce uncritical hope and follow comforting traditions of Western thought.) I do not object to its presentation and discussion, so long as its status as a possible interpretation, not a logical inference, receives proper identification — as Wallace did eighty years ago, and Dyson did not in our own time. I, for one, will seek my hope elsewhere. I would also be surprised, but not in the slightest displeased, if, *mirabile dictu*, Wallace and Dyson were right after all.

Postscript

Several readers informed me (as I should have remembered) that Mark Twain's famous essay, "The damned human race," was written as an explicit response to Wallace's version of the anthropic principle. Part 1 of this series, entitled "Was the world made for man?," carries as its epigraphic quote: "Alfred Russell [sic for Russel] Wallace's revival of the theory that this earth is at the centre of the stellar universe, and is the only habitable globe, has aroused great interest in the world." Twain, in his inimitable manner, then retells the history of life in five pages, assuring us that all the rich and unpatterned diversity could only represent a long pageant of preparation for that geological final second of human habitation! — so much for Wallace's assertion that the universe must have been designed with us in mind.

I was fascinated to read how many other themes of these essays lie embedded in Twain's succinct satire. For example, he explicitly cites Kelvin as his authority for the earth's *great* age — an affirmation of my argument that Kelvin's work, in his own day and contrary to the common myth portraying him as an arrogant villain against empirical science, was interpreted as proof of the earth's comfortable antiquity, not as a constraint upon the immensity of time: "According to these [Kelvin's] figures, it took 99,968,000 years to prepare the world for man, impatient as the Creator doubtless was to see him and admire him. But a large enterprise like this has to be conducted warily, painstakingly, logically."

Mark Twain's ending presents a wonderful metaphor (literature and popular science contain so many) for the earth's great age relative to the length of human habitation. (I view it as a kind of literary ancestor to John McPhee's image in *Basin and Range* — that if we envision geological time as the old English yard, the distance from the King's nose to the tip of his outstretched arm, one stroke of a file applied to the nail of his middle finger would erase all of human history.)

> Such is the history of it. Man has been here 32,000 years. That it took a hundred million years to prepare the world for him is proof that that is what it was done for. I suppose it is. I dunno. If the Eiffel Tower were now representing the world's age, the skin of paint on the pinnacle-knob at its summit would represent man's share of that age; and anybody would perceive that that skin was what the tower was built for. I reckon they would, I dunno.

15

GEORGE GALE*

Cosmological Fecundity: Theories of Multiple Universes

1. General Introduction

SPECULATING ABOUT UNIVERSES other than our own is an ancient and honorable activity. Philosophers and scientists of the ancient world were no less imaginative in this respect than are those of modern and even contemporary times. When the total record of these speculations is examined, an incredible range of styles, reasons, arguments, and consequences is found. Clearly, if any understanding of contemporary thinking about multiple universes is to be had, it will only be against the background of its age-old genesis.

Fortunately, for all their incredible diversity, multiple universes fall into only three broad groups. This is true not only for today's specimens, but for ancestor examples as well. Moreover, since the earlier examples are also easier to understand, it is possible to introduce the subject in a reasonably orderly fashion via a brief examination of cases from the past.

Following this historical introduction to the basic forms of multiple-universe models, contemporary proposals will be described. At this point, a further issue will be raised. Recent speculations about multiple universes have a wide variety of motivating reasons. As will become clear, understanding the reasons that contemporary cosmologists have for speculating about multiple universes is crucial to our wider understanding of present theories about the universe in general. Because of this, each particular model will be set into the context of the reasons for its existence.

2. Types of Multiple Universes

Multiple-universe models may be classified according to the means by which each model's universes are separated from one another: space, time, or some other dimension. Since it is perhaps the simplest type to see clearly, let us look first at spatially multiple universes.

2.1. Spatially Multiple Universes

> So, naturalists observe, a flea
> Hath smaller fleas that on him prey;
> And these have smaller still to bite 'em,
> And so proceed *ad infinitum*.
>
> Swift

Two main ingredients are involved in the generation of ideas of spatially multiple universes. The first, infinite divisibility of space, might perhaps be linked to mathematical developments, most especially those seen in the limit-taking operations of the differential calculus. But in addition to these conceptual developments concerning the spatial "container," of perhaps even greater significance were observational developments in the "contents." Swift's mention of naturalists in the doggerel above is no accident. Early microscopic investigations, particularly the discovery of micro-organisms, attracted the immediate and enthusiastic attention of all informed persons. The existence of living beings in a world within our world captured the imagination quite fiercely. As Capek notes, following P. M. Schuhl, human "imagination seems to be dominated by the 'theme of Gulliver,' in which we envisage world within world — an infinite series, in Whitehead's words, 'like the Chinese toy with a nest of boxes, one within the other'."[1]

The completeness of these worlds must be emphasized. It is not just that our world contained these beings as a part. Rather, these beings lived in another world, different from our own, which was their own, and complete in and of itself. Pascal tells the story more eloquently than anyone. Beginning with a mite, Pascal divides and subdivides until his listener thinks no further division be conceivable:

> Perhaps he will think that here is the smallest point in nature. I will let him see therein a new abyss. I will paint for him not only the invisible universe, but all that he can conceive of nature's immensity in the womb of this abridged atom. Let him see therein the infinity of the universes, each of which has its firmament, its planets, its earth, in the same proportion as in the visibile world; in each earth animals, and in the last mites, in which he will find again all that the first had, finding still in these others the same thing without end and without cessation.[2]

Here Pascal imagines an infinite series of universes, each within the other, each complete, even to the presence of the mite — not to mention Swift's flea! One fascinating point to note is that all of these conceptions presume the existence of life in each of the universes. Most likely this simply reflects the genesis of spatially multiple universe notions in the microscopic investigations current at the time.

Yet the idea of life within the whole series of universes did not wane as the microscope became more familiar. It continued even unto the present day. Fournier d'Albe claimed that the atoms of our universe are the suns of the next smaller universe, while the electrons are its planets, and so on forever. And, as Capek notes, "in the true spirit of Pascal he even spoke about the 'chemistry and biology of the infraworld'." Of course, d'Albe, in concert with nearly everyone else, does not limit his speculations to the microworld: relative to, e.g., the galaxies, we play the micro-role for their macro-super-organisms.

To conclude this section, let us allow a more modern thinker, A. N. Whitehead, to sum up the central notion of spatially multiple universes:

> From what science has discovered about the infinitely small and the infinitely vast, the size of our bodies is almost totally irrelevant. In this little mahogany stand may be civilizations as complex and diversified in scale as our own; and up there, the heavens, with all their vastness, may be only a minute strand of tissue in the body of a being in the scale of which all our universes are as a trifle.[3]

As we shall see below, contemporary cosmologists retain in their own speculations most of the essential properties seen here: differences of scale, completeness and self-containedness of universes, and possible infinite extension in both directions of scale. One *prima facie* difference, however, is that in modern versions of the spatially separated universes model life is not presumed. Rather, life is allowed to emerge only as a highly improbable consequence of statistical variations among the members of the infinite set of worlds. But before we examine this, we must first briefly introduce the two remaining categories of multiple-universe model, the temporally multiple and the other-dimensionally multiple models.

2.2. TEMPORALLY MULTIPLE UNIVERSES

> The universe is thus shown to be a circular movement which has already repeated itself an infinite number of times, and which plays its game for all eternity.
>
> Nietzsche

Intrinsic to temporally multiple universes is the notion of return to zero time via a cycle of some sort. The return to zero allows a new beginning, from which anything (and everything, given infinite duration) may/will happen. Accomplishing the cycle requires some sort of mechanism, usually a cosmologic one. According to the classical Greek models, the parts of the great wheel of the sky — the stars and planets —would return to their original positions after some vast series of revolutions. Time would reset, and begin again.

Modern versions also require cosmological machinery, these mechanical elements bolstered by reference to statistical–probabilistic functions. Nietzsche is typical in this regard:

> If the universe may be conceived as a definite quantity of energy, as a definite number of centers of energy — and every other concept remains indefinite and therefore useless — it follows therefore that the universe must go through a calculable number of combinations in the great game of chance which constitutes its existence. In infinity, at some moment or other, every possible combination must once have been realized; not only this, but it must have been realized an infinite number of times.[4]

In his *The Direction of Time*, H. Reichenbach also relies upon statistical models:

> but if we shuffle long enough, we must by pure chance eventually come back to the original state, because the probability of arriving at such an arrangement is larger than zero.[5]

But the major problem was a physical one: even given statistics, what could possibly be a *physical* mechanism embodying the principle of the "shuffle of cards"? Spencer, Croll, and Ritter imagined cosmic collisions; Arrhenius relied upon radiation pressure; and, curiously enough, Rankine developed an idea of the "reflecting walls of the universe" — an initial version of a closed system view of the world.[6]

We must ask, however, to what effect the universe runs through its infinitude of cycles. The answer is not long in coming. Corresponding to its role in spatially multiple universes, life occupies a central place in temporally multiple universes as well. Spencer says it clearly:

> And thus there is suggested the conception of a past, during which there have been successive Evolutions analogous to that which is now going on; and a future during which successive other such Evolutions may go on — ever the same in principle but never the same in concrete results.[7]

Contemporary versions of temporally multiple-universe theory are relevantly similar to these historical examples. In particular, they use some mechanism or other (usually an expanding–collapsing–expanding–collapsing, etc., "breathing" universe scheme) to run the universe through an infinite sequence of cycles. Statistical concepts are then called in to authorize scrambling the features of each individual cycle, the hope being that life, no matter how highly improbable in general, will come up a winner in at least one oscillation of the universe.

2.3. OTHER-DIMENSIONAL MULTIPLE UNIVERSES

Although the term "other-dimensional" is of necessity vague, it still retains some essential kernels of meaning. In the first place, whatever the "other dimension" is, it always acts like an analog of space, rather than time. This means that the multiple universes exist simultaneously, and not successively. Second, the universes' type of existence is related in some way to the concept of "possibility." This is a bit tricky to understand, but not impossible. Think of the following situation. You are trying to plan what to do this evening. You could go to a dance, see a movie, read a book, sleep, watch a video, and so on. It is fair to say that each of these possibilities *exists* for you, since, indeed, each is a real, actual, genuine possibility. Note further that the set of possibilities exists simultaneously. That is, it is simultaneously possible that tonight you could go to a dance, see a movie, read a text, etc.

Because of the space-like simultaneously possible existence of the multiple worlds in this sort of scheme, it has been popular to refer to it as a "parallel worlds" model. Parallel-world plots are much beloved of science fiction writers, who use the scheme to ask questions about worlds like our own, except that particular possibilities turned out differently; for example, the South won the Civil War, or Caesar didn't cross the Rubicon, or just about any other imaginable variation of past occurrences.

The original version of this whole scheme was proposed by the German physicist–mathematician–philosopher Gottfried Wilhelm Leibniz in 1686. Leibniz realized that if there were any sense to Christianity's claim that God freely chose this world to create, then it must be the case that God had other worlds in mind that he could — but didn't — choose to create. Thus was born the concept of the infinite set of logically possible worlds.

As Leibniz notes, since all possible varieties must assume all possible values, each world may differ from its nearest neighbor by only the slightest amount. Thus, for example, there is a world in which Peter did not betray Christ, and one in which Caesar did not cross the Rubicon. Moreover, although he himself did not mention it, there obviously must be worlds in which life exists, but not as we know it, and others in which life does not exist in any form at all. God's task on this theory, then, is to find the Best of All Possible Worlds, and choose to create it.

Contemporary other-dimensional multiple-world theories preserve all the main features of Leibniz' original design. In particular, they use the simultaneous existence feature of spatial relations, and they involve the general idea of possible existence, although rather than Leibniz' logical possibility, most of today's entries in this category of multiple-world theory rely on the idea of causal probability central to quantum physics. The result is that they postulate many worlds which have actually been created, instead of just being really possible. But these worlds are like Leibniz' possible worlds in an important respect; namely, that there are infinitely many of them, each differing in a just noticeable way from its nearest neighbor.

This completes our historical introduction to the types of multiple-world theories. We are now prepared to examine the contemporary cosmological scene.

3. Contemporary Multiple Universes

Contemporary multiple-universe theories (or as they are most commonly known, multiple-world theories) came into existence in a rich variety of ways. Some were created on purpose; others simply emerged as sometimes unforeseen consequences of theories directed toward an unrelated set of phenomena. In all cases, however, the ultimate result is a growing realization that our world might not be alone in the Universe. MacRobert put this point quite nicely: he notes that "after 50 years, the Big Bang universe of galaxies already seems a little constricted, naggingly inadequate," a conclusion quite in line with the idea that "whatever else is in the character of nature . . . we find that it does not economize on its size and richness."[8]

Contemporary multiple-world theorizing originated with Carter's 1974 proposal that a World Ensemble—an infinite set of different (coexisting) worlds—could fulfill a useful cosmological function by logically grounding the so-called "Anthropic Coincidences."[9] The term "coincidence" here reflects the fact that cosmological conditions necessary to support human (anthropic from the Greek) life require simultaneous satisfaction of a large number of apparently unrelated, highly improbable—thus highly coincidental—variables.[10] Carter's point was that if a World Ensemble did exist, then a world which contained human life would not be so improbable as it is if there is only one universe.

Although some recent authors have claimed that all contemporary Multi-World Theory (MWT) proposals have their origins, as did Carter's, in the need to explain the anthropic coincidences, this is certainly not the case.[11] Carter's World Ensemble is an other-dimensional MWT, since it exists in the infinite collection of quantum theoretical world lines (more on this later). Given this categorization of Carter's World Ensemble, it follows that non-Carter-type MWTs, especially spatial and temporal ones, are not necessarily linked to the anthropic coincidences, either in origin or function. Obviously, however, there is nothing to prevent MWTs, once created, from such linkage. My point here is simply to highlight the fact that MWTs and Anthropic Principle arguments are logically distinct from one another. With this in mind. let me now examine contemporary MWTs.

3.1. Spatial MWTs

Today's versions of spatial MWTs differ widely in the mechanism that they use to actually create the many different worlds. However, each alike depends upon the common notion that if space (or superspace, or whatever — it makes little real conceptual difference) is large enough, preferably infinite in extent, then there will be plenty of places where independent worlds might develop. And, following the well-known quantum theoretical dictum that "whatever can happen, will,"[12] cosmological ecology will ensure that each and every one of these niches is filled with *some* world or another. Let us now examine these spatial MWT cases in some detail.

The simplest spatial MWT is developed in a series of papers by G. F. R. Ellis and various colleagues. In these articles Ellis has defended the idea that the observational evidence suggests that we live in a low-density, homogeneous, open and infinite universe.[13] In the most recent article, he and Brundrit consider the possibilities of life in such a universe.[14] On the assumption that we take seriously the conditions specified, especially homogeneity and infinity, then "we can obtain non-zero probabilities for occurrences of conditions within any *specified* finite neighborhood of [=with any specified degree of similarity to] those on earth."[15] Indeed, the similarity collapses to identity, since "it is highly probable that there exist infinitely many worlds on which there are 'duplicate' populations to that on our own world."[16]

As the authors note in contrast to a Carter World Ensemble, a universe such as they propose has "no need to postulate some hypothetical statistical ensemble — it exists in the infinite universe!"[17] One of their major conclusions is that "we do believe this argument shows that the consequences of unbounded space-like sections in cosmology need more thought than has hitherto been given to them."[18]

It must be noted that Ellis and Brundrit's proposal makes explicit and heavy reliance on the principle that finite probability exercised in infinite space equals infinite variation in the frequencies of the values of the variables involved. Indeed, as they note, one way to evade their argument would be "to deny that life comes into existence on the basis of scientific probability."[19]

Questions of universe creation or evolution, or of the mechanics of life creation, are not touched by Ellis's considerations. Rather, he and his colleagues seem interested only in tracing out the many consequences of a low-density cosmological model of the Friedmann–Robertson–Walker type, which is the standard type assumed by contemporary cosmologists.

In contrast to Ellis's position, one line of MWT development came into being specifically as an attempt to describe the cosmogonical moment — the moment of the creation of the universe. This line of thought was instituted by E. P. Tryon's 1973 speculations about vacuum fluctuation. Initially Tryon's thought was not directed toward cosmogenesis. Rather, he had become fascinated by the apparent fact that the "universe's total mass–energy seems equal to its total gravitational potential."[20] If this were true, then the two values would cancel out, leaving the universe with a zero net energy.[21] And this is important, since it implies that the universe, in one important sense — amount of net energy (and hence mass) — is equal to "nothing", a pure vacuum.

Enter quantum theory. In a quantum field, particles are constantly being created from the vacuum, living for a brief period, then dying. An event such as this completely "spontaneous, temporary emergence of particles from a vacuum is called a vacuum fluctuation, and is utterly commonplace in quantum field theory".[22] As long as a particle does not violate the laws of mass–energy conservation, its creation is unproblematic. Accordingly, if the universe could be conceived to be akin to a particle, and given that its zero net energy doesn't conflict with the conservation law, then the universe could be conceived to have been created as a vacuum fluctuation event.

Although Tryon's model seemed highly speculative and, indeed, a highly implausible case of getting something (the universe) from nothing (the vacuum), it had one saving grace: it explained cosmogenesis in such a way that Tryon was "encouraged to believe that the origin and properties of the universe may be explicable within the framework of conventional science".[23]

In this original article, Tryon refers to MWT apparently only coincidentally. After noting that vacuum fluctuations were utterly commonplace, which strictly implies the probable existence of many worlds, Tryon continues on to say that "our Universe is simply one of those things which happen from time to time".[24] Then, in response to the question of life in a universe, he explicitly invokes the two elements of an anthropic coincidence explanation. First comes the probability-based Carter-like World Ensemble. Reasoning exactly as Ellis would six years later, Tryon states that "I do not claim that universes like ours occur frequently, merely that the expected frequency is non-zero" and, in quantum theory "every phenomenon that could happen in principle actually does happen occasionally in practice".[25]

At this point an Anthropic Principle is asserted: "The second part of my answer lies in the principle of biological selection, which states that any Universe in which sentient beings find themselves is necessarily hospitable to sentient beings".[26]

Tryon's theory had some obvious problems. For one thing, it predicted a closed universe. Second, it contained equal amounts of matter and antimatter. The former point lacked support from a sizable number of physicists, while the latter essentially lacked any support at all. Yet, for all its problems, Tryon's theory had such a creative spark about it, that its influence expanded into a veritable research program, with many workers and many, very different model lines.

A bit of history helps here. The present situation in spatial MWTs combines elements from two separate lines of investigation. The first line involves Tryon's work, which as we just saw, concerned the instant of creation itself and, especially, focused upon the possible mechanism(s) at work in cosmogenesis. At roughly the same time, a second and separate line of work developed to theorize about the instant or so immediately *following* creation. This line of work was an outgrowth of the long-standing search for a "unified field theory." It focused on the first 10^{-30} seconds of the universe's existence because only during this incredibly brief interval, or so the researchers thought, could the total unification of the four basic fields/forces—if such unification indeed existed—be found. During this investigation, the first genuinely cooperative venture between cosmologists and particle theorists, was created a synthesis between elements of Grand Unified Theories (GUTs) and cosmology.[27] This synthesis, known as "The Inflationary Universe," is principally associated with the work of Alan Guth.

Guth's model envisages a sudden, accelerating expansion of the universe shortly after its creation. This inflationary period is designed to eliminate two drastic problems of the standard big bang model. To put the case quite crudely, it aims to account, on the one hand, for the seemingly paradoxical distributions of matter required for today's observable astronomical homogeneities (equal distribution of matter producing uniform background radiation) and, on the other, for today's observable astronomical inhomogeneities (unequal distribution of matter producing both galaxies and empty space).

Although Guth's original version has needed considerable help, today's standard model of post-creation universe evolution is essentially a development of his inflationary big bang.[28] Nicely enough, the inflationary model had a feature, probably unnoticed at the time, which turned out to be of relevance for MWT: the inflating universe constituted a domain within a larger space, a space in which places were available for other domains to be. Although this MWT possibility was not specifically noted by Guth, some of his intellectual descendants—especially J. Richard Gott—found direction inspiration here, as I will note in a moment.

Meanwhile, Tryon's cosmogonical line of work was being developed as well. Tryon's original proposal had been (somewhat independently) developed by Brout, Englert, and Gunzig[29] into a two-stage model that produced an open, homogeneous, and isotropic Universe. And although Brout et al.'s development of the Tryon-type model made no explicit addition to MWT, they did conclude with a tantalizing query: "What is the criterion that selects *this* Universe? . . . is there some finite probability that there is some other universe which has been created elsewhere?"[30]

The line of development originated by Tryon culminated in an influential paper by Atkatz and Pagels.[31] Following discussion of the advances made by Tryon, Brout et al., and others, Atkatz and Pagels note that the problem still remained to characterize specifically the nature of the cosmological vacuum fluctuation. Their choice was to investigate a series of universes having properties susceptible of generation by a quantum tunneling event modeled on radioactive decay. Their finding was that indeed such a mechanism could successfully create a universe out of a flat vacuum. Unfortunately, as they note, "we find a finite tunneling amplitude exists *only* for those spaces with finite three-volume on the Euclidean section"; in other words, compact universes were the only possible results of their analyses of the tunneling mechanism.[32]

Cosmology, cosmogony, and MWT finally came together in the work of J. Richard Gott.[33] Gott's work connects a Tryon-style quantum field cosmogony to a cosmological model featuring a Brout et al. universe evolution, but one which has been adapted to include Guth-style inflation.[34] In other words, Gott's work produces a complete universe theory, from creation time, through the important early stages of evolution and development, right on through until the end. More importantly for our purposes, Gott's investigation of Guth's inflationary domains (here referred to as "bubbles") eventuates in a distinct and comprehensible MWT. "Guth," he says, "wanted the bubbles to coalesce and fill space so as to eventually lead to a single Friedmann cosmology." But it couldn't be done. In the end, Gott embraces MWT:

> In contrast, I propose that each bubble produces a $k = -1$ cosmology [with a spacetime similar to our own] . . . Guth cosmologies with $k = +1$, 0, -1 can each produce in principle an infinite number of disjoint $k = -1$ (bubble) cosmologies.[35]

At roughly the same time, other theorists were also seriously investigating MWTs within the inflationary universe scenario. Sato et al.[36] showed the possibilities for formation of an infinite number of "daughter universes" from inflationary expanding bubbles of false vacuum trapped within the domain(s) of true vacuums. As they note, "a false vacuum region surrounded by true vacuum bubbles becomes eventually a black hole or a wormhole".[37] Separate daughter universes are formed as wormholes and ultimately evaporate. The process will most likely continue as well within nucleated regions of the daughter universes, thus bringing about "granddaughter, great-granddaughter, great-great-granddaughter," and so on, ad infinitum. Indeed, the process of making many worlds seems inevitable, given the vacuum fluctuation + inflation model:

> . . . although the Creator might have made a unitary universe, the universe itself is also capable of bearing child universes, which are again capable of bearing universes, and so on.[38]

In general, the inflationary universe scenario appears to have provided a comfortable home for MWTs and their development. This is particularly evident in Linde's extensive review of cosmogonical + cosmological models.[39] As Linde notes, "after the phase transition [inflationary expansion] the universe becomes divided into infinitely many mini-universes" of different particle symmetries. This has definite implications for life. A comfortable particle symmetry [$SU(3) \times U(1)$, mirroring that of our own world] "should exist inside infinitely many mini-universes, and all other 'desert islands' (in which other kinds of life may exist) are of no importance to us".[40]

Linde's comments here are to be directly associated with an ensemble of worlds. Referring to Guth's comment[41] that the inflationary scenario provides the only example of a "free lunch" (since all matter is created from nothing), Linde compares the ensemble of worlds to that free lunch's menu: "Now we can add that the inflationary universe is the only lunch at which all possible dishes are available."[42]

Review of the above cases shows MWTs alive and well in cosmological space. They are by now an accepted element in complete cosmological theories, and, contrary to the skepticism they earlier aroused, spatial MWTs are now "utterly commonplace," to adopt Tryon's description in another context.

3.2. CONTEMPORARY TEMPORAL MWTS

All temporal MWTs are versions of the basic oscillating universe model. According to this scheme, the universe contains enough matter to be closed. Thus, if the universe is an expanding one, there will be some time when the expansion ceases and contraction begins. Just after the instant of minimum contracted size, the universe "bounces" and, big bang style, begins another phase of expansion. There are obvious metaphysical and aesthetic reasons in favor of this model. As MacRobert justly remarks:

> The idea of an oscillating universe, in which the Big Bang resulted from the recollapse of a previous phase of the universe, gained currency merely because it avoided the issue of creation—not because there was the slightest evidence in favor of it.[43]

The first quantitative work on the oscillating universe was carried out by Tolman in 1934.[44] Landsberg and Park generalized the model in 1975.[45] One result of these works has posed an enormous problem for oscillating universe MWT strategies. If their analyses are correct, then each phase of oscillation would terminate with the contracted universe in a higher state of entropy than the preceding one. This implies in practice that the succeeding phase would be both spatially larger and temporally longer than its ancestors. Using present observational values, Silk has calculated that probably no more than 100 cycles have preceded our own.[46] Such a number of cycles is far too small to justify MWTs. Consequently, recent efforts have focused on ways to avoid the increasing entropy problem.

Wheeler initiated the present series of responses. His picture considers the laws of physics to be valid far beyond the scale of time of a single cycle of the universe, and envisages the universe to be "reprocessed" each time it passes from one cycle to the next.[47]

There are some difficulties with this picture. For one thing, Wheeler has not hypothesized any particular scheme for reprocessing: What is the mechanism? *What* gets reprocessed? etc. Certainly, he holds the laws of physics valid across the "Big Crunch". But what, then, can/does change? Possibly certain constants; certainly initial conditions. However, it just isn't clear on this view how different each cycle might be from its predecessors.

Two other ingenious schemes advance the model further than does Wheeler. These are due to Markov, and to Linde, some of whose work was discussed earlier.

Markov's idea is that, during the contracting phase, "daughter universes" may be formed in some particularly dense inhomogeneities.[48] As Markov notes, large pockets of entropy would be enclosed in the daughter cells. Any such cell "differs from its mother universe only in the smallness of its dimensions," particle matter, etc., and "correspondingly by small-ness of the global entropy."[49] Of course, during subsequent oscillations, "small-ness" will vanish "due to entropy increase" and "in this sense our Universe, if closed, may be regarded as a daughter universe which has split from its mother universe".[50] Since each closed daughter effectively hides its entropy from the mother, the process of splitting is in principle extensible ad infinitum. Indeed, "generally speaking, in a daughter universe there may exist its own closed universe, etc.," leading to a "peculiar hierarchic structure of the universe as a whole."[51]

Clearly, Markov's idea provides a genuine MWT, and, as he implies directly, there certainly will be universes specific to those who belong in them:

> The idea that daughter universes can be formed does not contradict the law of entropy increase, but entropy increase in oscillating does not contradict the finite dimensions and the lifetime of *our* Universe.[52]

Since there is "*our* Universe," it makes no sense to deny that there could be "*their* Universe" as well.

In contrast to the loophole that Markov found in the principle of entropy increase, Linde flatly denies that the principle can apply across the "Big Crunch".[53] His mechanism is an ingenious (albeit speculative) extension of the general form of quantum theories. Two general features need to be understood for Linde's move to make sense.

The first feature concerns quantum interactions. Quantum theories have been developed for three of the four forces and their particles: strong, weak, and electromagnetic. Only gravity still resists statement in quantum form. Not all of the particles respond to all the forces. Thus, neither weak nor electromagnetic particles respond to the strong force. Yet all particles feel the gravitational force.[54]

Second, in a quantum confinement phase, such as the strong force's quark confinement phase, the particles in question are each always in a bound state; that is, no free particles exist. Indeed, it would take infinite energy to free up a single particle. Now, consider the fact that "in the gravitational confinement phase (if such a phase can exist) *any* particle would have infinite energy."[55] Such a phase would be expected to occur during the final instants of gravitational collapse of the universe. Once it happens "no real particle excitations can exist and the entropy of the universe vanishes".[56]

Although this might seem to be a conjurer's trick, it is, on the contrary, founded precisely and explicitly upon the thermodynamic relation between entropy and order. As Linde notes, his mechanism "does not contradict the second law of thermodynamics, since any thermodynamical description of the gravitational confinement phase is impossible because of the absence of particles and of any possibility of disorder in matter."[57]

Moreover, each phase of the universe is different from the others, which is of some importance to some versions of MWT. Perhaps this, Linde's model, at last provides a good interpretation of Wheeler's "reprocessing": "In our case all the entropy and all inhomogeneities of the contracting universe disappear in the purgatory of the de Sitter stage, and then are generated anew in each cycle."[58] It would seem that, given the robust models presented by Linde and Markov, there is plenty of life left in the oscillating universe model. This strongly disputes Smith's claim to the contrary that "at present the evidence favors the conclusion that there is no WE [World Ensemble] composed of oscillating worlds."[59]

3.3. OTHER-DIMENSIONAL MWTs

Our basic theory of the matter of the universe is quantum theory. Quantum theory is inherently probabilistic. That is, if one uses the theory to predict where an emitted particle will collide with a target, the answer is given in a wave equation which lists a continuous series of positions and the probabilities of the impact's being there. No way exists mathematically to pare the series down to just one member. Yet when a measurement is made, the particle is of course found in only one position, and with a probability equal precisely to 1. Interpretation of the clash between continuous, multipoint equation, and discrete, indeed singular, measurement, has fostered a 50-year philosophical discussion. The majority of physicists believe the Copenhagen interpretation, which holds that the probability wave is true, until the measurement is made, at which time the measurement is true. In between the last instant of probability and the first instant of measurement, the probability wave with infinite quickness "collapses."

The major problem here is that the probability wave function genuinely describes a genuine wave phenomenon, each part of which is (and must be) equally real. Moreover, the situation described is one of "superposition," simultaneous existence, replete with interference effects and everything else. What happens to all these really existing elements during the infinitely quick collapse of the wave function? The Copenhagen interpretation, which is the majority view among physicists, quite self-consciously doesn't touch this issue. Some physicists have recoiled from the obvious difficulties of the Copenhagen view.

First Hugh Everett, and then he along with B. S. DeWitt, developed an alternative theory to account for this issue.[60] Basically, the theory takes the wave function literally as being true about each and every one of the different probable states it describes. From this it follows that measurement does not "collapse" the probability function into a unitary value; rather, it simply moves the observer[61] along his or her own world's own worldline among the infinitely many possible ones. All of the probable states exist together, "parallel" (in some sense) to one another in the quantum phase–space dimension.

Carter's original invoking of the World Ensemble MWT relied on Everett's quantum "multi-verse" as an interpretive model. According to this, each probability state corresponds to a real state in a real world, no two of the worlds being identical.[62] All possible probable values of all possible measurements will of necessity be included.

Smith has noted one restriction which apparently applies to an Everett-type model: "Everett implicitly presumed that values of the constants are preserved in each branching."[63] This would appear to seriously limit the values assumable by all phase-state variables. That is, although there could indeed be many worlds (indeed, an infinity), they might differ even only by one atom's quantization; for example by the direction of the atom's spin. Recent work by Mukhanov, however, tends to cast some doubt on the force of this restriction.[64] Mukhanov starts from the point of view of the early universe and quantum theory. In an extremely strong and detailed criticism of the standard Copenhagen interpretation, he notes, among other things, that Copenhagen quantization of the entire universe is not "meaningful":

> Hence, quantization of the Universe is also meaningless because *outside* the universe there are no observers and apparatus that could make measurements.[65]

Using an extreme realist approach to Everett's theory, Mukhanov not only links each superposition term to a different universe, he asserts that superposition interference is caused by the existence of other universes: "The existence of other universes is just what accounts for interference effects."[66]

In the end, Mukhanov ties the Everett MWT and quantum theory into an inextricable causal tangle: "Using this approach, one can interpret quantum mechanics as a theory the very *existence* of which is due to the existence of many worlds."[67] One major question, of course, is what benefits Mukhanov's heroic realism gains here. Some benefits accrue simply in terms of quantum theory interpretation. For example, "the $|\psi>$-vector is in one-to-one correspondence with the states of objects from an ensemble of systems and is meaningful irrespective of experiments," and hence *every* term in the expansion has a concrete referent.[68] Other benefits are more cosmological in nature. Thus, all possible values of observable quantities are realized in different universes:

> This means that all the conceivable processes, if the probability of their realization is not exactly equal to zero, take place in reality. In particular, the events of small probability (for example, heat overflow from a cold body to a hot one) are also realized.[69]

It would appear that Mukhanov bypasses Smith's objection that Everett "implicitly preserved" the constancy of the laws of physics across worlds. He does so by adopting a statistical interpretation of the laws of physics and associating them only with those worlds which are probabilistically "typical."[70]

Such a move is not unique to Mukhanov. Nielsen, in a series of investigations using stochastic gauge theory, has shown that the laws of physics, which are derived from the fundamental Lagrangian for the universe, show up in a Gaussian distribution.[71] Again, as in Mukhanov, physical laws may be linked to the set of "typical" universes, with extremal universes having wildly divergent and idiosyncratic "laws" of their own.

Barrow and Tipler put a realist interpretation on these statistical interpretations. That is, they take the existence of a frequency value for each law as an indication of the existence of a universe in which that law is instituted: "If the laws of Nature manifested at low energy are statistical in origin, then again, a *real* ensemble of different possible universes actually does exist."[72]

These realistic statistical interpretations certainly provide for a wide variation among possible universes. Indeed, Nielsen's ensemble would allow a massive photon, certainly a change in a constant.

It would appear that recent work on other-dimensional MWTs indicates a genuine viability in this method of theorizing about other worlds. Moreover, so long as the philosophical perplexities remain endemic in quantum measurement theory, Everett ensembles remain viable regardless of their possible roles in cosmological service as MWTs.

NOTES

1. M. Capek, *Philosophical Impact of Contemporary Physics* (Princeton: D. Van Nostrand, 1961), pp. 21–22.
2. B. Pascal, *Pensées*, W. F. Trotter (trans.), (New York: Dutton, 1931), p. 17.
3. A. N. Whitehead, *Dialogues*, L. Price (ed.) (Boston: Little, Brown, 1954), pp. 367–368.
4. F. Nietzsche, *Complete Works*, Vol. IX (Edinburgh: Foulis, 1913), p. 430.
5. H. Reichenbach, *The Direction of Time* (Berkeley: Univ. of California Press, 1956), p. 111.
6. Capek, *op. cit.*, p. 129.
7. H. Spencer, *First Principles*, 4th ed. (New York: Appleton, 1896), p. 550.
8. A. MacRobert, *Sky and Telescope*, March 1983, p. 213.
9. B. Carter, Large number coincidences and the anthropic principle in cosmology, in M. S. Longair, *Confrontation of Cosmological Theories with Observational Data* (Boston: Reidel, 1974), p. 291ff.
10. G. Gale, *Scientific American*, December 1981, p. 154.
11. Q. Smith, *Pacific Philosophical Quarterly*, **67**; 73, 1986.
12. E. P. Tryon, Is the universe a vacuum fluctuation? *Nature* Vol **246**: [(14) Dec] 387, 1973.
13. G. F. R. Ellis, *Quarterly Journal of the Royal Astronomical Society* 16;245, 1975; G. F. R. Ellis, *Journal of General Relativity and Gravitation* 9; 87, 1978; G. F. R. Ellis, R. Maartens, and S. D. Nel, *Monthly Notices of the Royal Astronomical Society* **184**; 439, 1978; G. F. R. Ellis and G. B. Brundrit, *Quarterly Journal of the Royal Astronomical Society* **20**; 37, 1979.
14. Ellis and Brundrit, *ibid.*
15. Ibid., p. 39.
16. *Ibid.*, p. 37.
17. *Ibid.*, p. 38.
18. *Ibid.*, p. 39.
19. *Ibid.*
20. E. P. Tryon, *loc. cit.*
21. MacRobert, *op. cit.*, p. 211.
22. Tryon, *op. cit.*, p. 397.
23. *Ibid.*
24. *Ibid.*
25. *Ibid.*, pp. 396–397.
26. *Ibid.* One wonders about the obvious coincidences here. Carter didn't publish his first World Ensemble + Anthropic Principle discussion until 1974 (Carter, *op. cit.*). Yet here, in 1973, Tryon has it all. One possibility: Carter had presented the World Ensemble idea in a Cambridge preprint in 1968, and at the Clifford Memorial Meeting at Princeton in 1970. Perhaps there was some first- or second-order interaction between the two men via one of these routes.

27. A. H. Guth, The Inflationary Universe: a possible solution to the horizon and flatness problems. *Physical Review* **D23**: 347, 1981; A. H. Guth, *10^{-35} seconds after the Big Bang*, MIT preprint CTP 991, 1982.
28. A. H. Guth and P. J. Steinhardt, The Inflationary Universe. *Scientific American,* **250**; 116, 1984.
29. R. Brout, F. Englert, and E. Gunzig, The creation of the universe as a quantum phenomenon. *Annals of Physics* **115**: 78, 1978.
30. *Ibid.,* p. 98.
31. D. Atkatz and H. Pagels, Origin of the universe as a quantum tunneling event. *Physical Review* **D25**; 2065, 1982.
32. *Ibid.,* p. 2066.
33. J. R. Gott, Creation of open universes from de Sitter space. *Nature,* **295**; 304, 1982.
34. R. Brout, F. Englert, and P. Spindel, *Physical Review Letters* **43**; 417, 1979.
35. *Ibid.,* p. 305.
36. K. Sato, H. Kodama, M. Sasaki, and K. Maeda, Multi-production of universes by first-order phase transitions of a vacuum. *Physics Letters* **108B**; 103, 1982.
37. *Ibid.*
38. *Ibid.,* p. 106.
39. A. D. Linde in G. W. Gibbons, S. W. Hawking, and S. T. C. Siklos (eds.), *The Very Early Universe* (Cambridge: University Press, 1982), p. 205.
40. *Ibid.*
41. Guth, 1982, *op. cit.*
42. Linde, *op. cit.*
43. MacRobert, *op. cit.,* p. 211.
44. R. C. Tolman, *Relativity, Thermodynamics and Cosmology* (Oxford: Clarendon Press, 1934), p. 340 ff.
45. P. T. Landsberg and D. Park, Entropy in an oscillating universe. *Proceedings of the Royal Society, London* **A346**; 485, 1975. This paper and Tolman's work are discussed in some detail in Smith, *op. cit.,* pp. 78–81.
46. Cited in Smith, *ibid.*
47. C. M. Patton and J. A. Wheeler, Is physics legislated by cosmogony?, in C. J. Isham, R. Penrose, and D. W. Sciama (eds.), *Quantum Gravity* (Oxford: Clarendon Press, 1975), p. 557.
48. M. A. Markov, Entropy in an oscillating universe in the assumption of universe 'splitting' into numerous smaller 'daughter universes.' In M. A. Markov, V. A. Berezin, and V. P. Frolov, *Proceedings of the Third Seminar on Quantum Gravity* (Moscow: World Scientific, 1985), p. 3.
49. *Ibid.,* p. 6.
50. *Ibid.*
51. *Ibid.*
52. *Ibid.,* p. 7.
53. Linde, *loc. cit.*
54. Linde, *ibid.:* ". . . all particles are colored with respect to gravitational interaction."
55. *Ibid.*
56. *Ibid.*
57. *Ibid.*
58. *Ibid.*
59. Smith, *op. cit.,* p. 80. Although Linde's work was published in 1982, and Markov's in 1985, Smith (1986) mentions them not.
60. In B. S. DeWitt and N. Graham (eds.), *The Many-Worlds Interpretation of Quantum Mechanics* (Princeton: Princeton University Press, 1973).

61. Smith misses this point (Smith, *op. cit.*, p. 76). Rather than, as Smith claims, the world's state splitting, it is the *observer's* state which "splits," moving him/her along the measured trajectory through the multi-phase probability space. This significant point is made quite strongly by J. D. Barrow and Frank J. Tipler in *The Anthropic Cosmological Principle* (Oxford: Clarendon Press, 1986), p. 495.

62. Carter, *op. cit.*

63. Smith, *op. cit.*, p. 77.

64. V. F. Mukhanov, On the many worlds interpretation of quantum theory, in Markov *et al.*, *op. cit.*

65. Mukhanov, *op. cit.*, p. 22.

66. *Ibid.*

67. *Ibid.*

68. *Ibid.*

69. *Ibid.*, p. 28.

70. *Ibid.*

71. Nielsen, in one marvelous work, asks, "Did God have to fine-tune the Universe in order to get a massless photon?": see H. B. Nielsen, in J. Andric, I. Dadic, and N. Zovko (eds.), *Particle Physics 1980* (Dordrecht: North Holland). Nielsen's answer: "No."

72. Barrow and Tipler, *op. cit.*, p. 257.

16

JOHN ARCHIBALD WHEELER*

Beyond the End of Time

*Gravitational Collapse as the Greatest
Crisis in Physics of All Time*

THE UNIVERSE STARTS with a big bang, expands to a maximum dimension, then recontracts and collapses: no more awe-inspiring prediction was ever made. It is preposterous. Einstein himself could not believe his own prediction. It took Hubble's observations to force him and the scientific community to abandon the concept of a universe that endures from everlasting to everlasting.

Later work of Tolman (1934), Avez (1960), Geroch (1967), and Hawking and Penrose (1969) generalizes the conclusion. A model universe that is closed, that obeys Einstein's geometrodynamic law, and that contains a nowhere negative density of mass–energy, inevitably develops a singularity. No one sees any escape from the density of mass–energy rising without limit. A computing machine calculating ahead step by step the dynamical evolution of the geometry comes to the point where it can not go on. Smoke, figuratively speaking, starts to pour out of the computer. Yet physics surely continues to go on if for no other reason than this: Physics is by definition that which does go on its eternal way despite all the shadowy changes in the surface appearance of reality.

*From *Gravitation* by Charles W. Misner *et al.* Copyright © 1970, 1971. Reprinted with the permission of W. H. Freeman and Company. (The material is extracted from Chapter 44.)

Some day a door will surely open and expose the glittering central mechanism of the world in its beauty and simplicity. Toward the arrival of that day, no development holds out more hope than the paradox of gravitational collapse. Why paradox? Because Einstein's equation says "this is the end" and physics says "there is no end." Why hope? Because among all paradigms for probing a puzzle, physics proffers none with more promise than a paradox.

No previous period of physics brought a greater paradox than 1911. Rutherford had just been forced to conclude that matter is made up of localized positive and negative charges. Matter as so constituted should undergo electric collapse in $\sim 10^{-17}$ sec, according to theory. Observation equally clearly proclaimed that matter is stable. No one took the paradox more seriously than Bohr. No one worked around and around the central mystery with more energy wherever work was possible. No one brought to bear a more judicious combination of daring and conservativeness, nor a deeper feel for the harmony of physics. The direct opposite of harmony, cacophony, is the impression that comes from sampling the literature of the 'teens on the structure of the atom. (1) Change the Coulomb law of force between electric charges? (2) Give up the principle that an accelerated charge must radiate? There was little inhibition against this and still wilder abandonings of the well-established. In contrast, Bohr held fast to these two principles. At the same time he insisted on the importance of a third principle, firmly established by Planck in quite another domain of physics, the quantum principle. With that key he opened the door to the world of the atom.

Great as was the crisis of 1911, today gravitational collapse confronts physics with its greatest crisis ever. At issue is the fate, not of matter alone, but of the universe itself. The dynamics of collapse, or rather of its reverse, expansion, is evidenced not by theory alone, but also by observation; and not by one observation, but by observations many in number and carried out by astronomers of unsurpassed ability and integrity. Collapse, moreover, is not unique to the large-scale dynamics of the universe. A white dwarf star or a neutron star of more than critical mass is predicted to undergo gravitational collapse to a black hole. Sufficiently many stars falling sufficiently close together at the center of the nucleus of a galaxy are expected to collapse to a black hole many powers of ten more massive than the sun. An active search is under way for evidence for a black hole in this Galaxy. The process that makes a black hole is predicted to provide an experimental model for the gravitational collapse of the universe itself, with one difference. For collapse to a black hole, the observer has his choice whether (1) to observe from a safe distance, in which case his observations will reveal nothing of what goes on inside the horizon; or (2) to follow the falling matter on in, in which case he sees the final stages of the collapse, not only of the matter itself, but of the geometry surrounding the matter, to indefinitely high compaction, but only at the cost of his own early demise. For the gravitational collapse of a closed model universe, no such choice is available to the observer. His fate is sealed. So too is the fate of matter and elementary particles, driven up to indefinitely high densities. The stakes in the crisis of collapse are hard to match: the dynamics of the largest object, space, and the smallest object, an elementary particle—and how both began.

The Black Box: The Reprocessing of the Universe

No amount of searching has ever disclosed a "cheap way" out of gravitational collapse, any more than earlier it revealed a cheap way out of the collapse of the atom. Physicists in that earlier crisis found themselves in the end confronted with a revolutionary pistol, "Understand nothing—or accept the quantum principle." Today's crisis can hardly force a lesser revolution. One sees no alternative except to say that geometry fails and pregeometry has to take its place to ferry physics through the final stages of gravitational collapse and on into what happens next. No guide is evident on this uncharted way except the principle of simplicity, applied to drastic lengths.

Whether the whole universe is squeezed down to the Planck dimension, or more or less, before reexpansion can begin and dynamics can return to normal, may be irrelevant for some of the questions one wants to consider. Physics has long used the "black box" to symbolize situations where one wishes to concentrate on what goes in and what goes out, disregarding what takes place in between.

At the beginning of the crisis of electric collapse one conceived of the electron as headed on a deterministic path toward a point-center of attraction, and unhappily destined to arrive at a condition of infinite kinetic energy in a finite time. After the advent of quantum mechanics, one learned to summarize the interaction between center of attraction and electron in a "black box:" fire in a wave-train of electrons traveling in one direction, and get electrons coming out in this, that, and the other direction with this, that, and the other well-determined probability amplitude. Moreover, to predict these probability amplitudes quantitatively and correctly, it was enough to translate the Hamiltonian of classical theory into the language of wave mechanics and solve the resulting wave equation, the key to the "black box."

A similar "black box" view of gravitational collapse leads one to expect a "probability distribution of outcomes." Here, however, one outcome is distinguished from another, one must anticipate, not by a single parameter, such as the angle of scattering of the electron, but by many. They govern, one foresees, such quantities as the size of the system at its maximum of expansion, the time from the start of this new cycle to the moment it ends in collapse, the number of particles present, and a thousand other features. The "probabilities" of these outcomes will be governed by a dynamic law, analogous to (1) the Schrödinger wave equation for the electron, or, to cite another black box problem, (2) the Maxwell equations that couple together, at a wave-guide junction, electromagnetic waves running in otherwise separate wave guides. However, it is hardly reasonable to expect the necessary dynamic law to spring forth as soon as one translates the Hamilton–Jacobi equation of general relativity into a Schrödinger equation, simply because geometrodynamics, in both its classical and its quantum version, is built on standard differential geometry. That standard geometry leaves no room for any of those quantum fluctuations in connectivity that seem inescapable at small distances and therefore also inescapable in the final stages of gravitational collapse. Not geometry, but pregeometry, must fill the black box of gravitational collapse.

Little as one knows the internal machinery of the black box, one sees no escape from this picture of what goes on: the universe transforms, or transmutes, or transits, or is *reprocessed* probabilistically from one cycle of history to another in the era of collapse.

However straightforwardly and inescapably this picture of the reprocessing of the universe would seem to follow from the leading features of general relativity and the quantum principle, the two overarching principles of twentieth-century physics, it is nevertheless fantastic to contemplate. How can the dynamics of a system so incredibly gigantic be switched, and switched at the whim of probability, from one cycle that has lasted 10^{11} years to one that will last only 10^6 years? At first, only the circumstance that the system gets squeezed down in the course of this dynamics to incredibly small distances reconciles one to a transformation otherwise so unbelievable. Then one looks at the upended strata of a mountain slope, or a bird not seen before, and marvels that the whole universe is incredible:

> mutation of a species,
> metamorphosis of a rock,
> chemical transformation,
> spontaneous transformation of a nucleus,
> radioactive decay of a particle,
> reprocessing of the universe itself.

If it cast a new light on geology to know that rocks can be raised and lowered thousands of meters and hundreds of degrees, what does it mean for physics to think of the universe as being from time to time "squeezed through a knothole," drastically "reprocessed," and started out on a fresh dynamic cycle? Three considerations above all press themselves on one's attention, prefigured in these compressed phrases:

destruction of all constants of motion in collapse;
particles, and the physical "constants" themselves, as the
"frozen-in part of the meteorology of collapse;"
"the biological selection of physical constants."

The gravitational collapse of a star, or a collection of stars, to a black hole extinguishes all details of the system except mass and charge and angular momentum. Whether made of matter or antimatter or radiation, whether endowed with much entropy or little entropy, whether in smooth motion or chaotic turbulence, the collapsing system ends up as seen from outside, according to all indications, in the same standard state. The laws of conservation of baryon number and lepton number are transcended [Wheeler (1971)]. No known means whatsoever will distinguish between black holes of the most different provenance if only they have the same mass, charge, and angular momentum. But for a closed universe, even these constants vanish from the scene. Total charge is automatically zero because lines of force have nowhere to end except upon charge. Total mass and total angular momentum have absolutely no definable meaning whatsoever for a closed universe. This conclusion follows not least because there is no asymptotically flat space outside where one can put a test particle into Keplerian orbit to determine period and precession.

Of all principles of physics, the laws of conservation of charge, lepton number, baryon number, mass, and angular momentum are among the most firmly established. Yet with gravitational collapse the content of these conservation laws also collapses. The established is disestablished. No determinant of motion does one see left that could continue unchanged in value from cycle to cycle of the universe. Moreover, if particles are dynamic in construction, and if the spectrum of particle masses is therefore dynamic in origin, no option would seem left except to conclude that the mass spectrum is itself reprocessed at the time when "the universe is squeezed through a knot hole." A molecule in this piece of paper is a "fossil" from photochemical synthesis in a tree a few years ago. A nucleus of the oxygen in this air is a fossil from thermonuclear combustion at a much higher temperature in a star a few 10^9 years ago. What else can a particle be but a fossil from the most violent event of all, gravitational collapse?

That one geological stratum has one many-miles long slope, with marvelous linearity of structure, and another stratum has another slope, is either an everyday triteness, taken as for granted by every passerby, or a miracle, until one understands the mechanism. That an electron here has the same mass as an electron there is also a triviality or a miracle. It is a triviality in quantum electrodynamics because it is assumed rather than derived. However, it is a miracle on any view that regards the universe as being from time to time "reprocessed." How can electrons at different times and places in the present cycle of the universe have the same mass if the spectrum of particle masses differs between one cycle of the universe and another?

Inspect the interior of a particle of one type, and magnify it up enormously, and in that interior see one view of the whole universe [compare the concept of monad of Leibniz (1714), "The monads have no window through which anything can enter or depart"]; and do likewise for another particle of the same type. Are particles of the same pattern identical in any one cycle of the universe because they give identically patterned views of the same universe? No acceptable explanation for the miraculous identity of particles of the same type has ever been put forward. That identity must be regarded, not as a triviality, but as a central mystery of physics.

Not the spectrum of particle masses alone, but the physical "constants" themselves, would seem most reasonably regarded as reprocessed from one cycle to another. Reprocessed relative to what? Relative, for example, to the Planck system of units,

$$L^* = (\hbar G/c^3)^{1/2} = 1.6 \times 10^{-33} \text{cm},$$
$$T^* = (\hbar G/c^5)^{1/2} = 5.4 \times 10^{-44} \text{ sec},$$
$$M^* = (\hbar c/G)^{1/2} = 2.2 \times 10^{-5} \text{ g},$$

the only system of units, Planck (1899) pointed out, free, like black-body radiation itself, of all complications of solid-state physics, molecular binding, atomic constitution, and elementary particle structure, and drawing for its background only on the simplest and most universal principles of physics, the laws of gravitation and black-body radiation. Relative to the Planck units, every constant in every other part of physics is expressed as a pure number.

No pure numbers in physics are more impressive than $\hbar c/e^2 = 137.0360$ and the so-called "big numbers" [Eddington (1931, 1936, 1946); Dirac (1937, 1938); Jordan (1955, 1959); Dicke (1959, 1961, 1964); Hayakawa (1965a,b); Carter (1968)]:

$\sim 10^{80}$ particles in the universe,

$$\sim 10^{40} \sim \frac{10^{28} \text{ cm}}{10^{-12} \text{ cm}} \sim \frac{\text{(Radius of universe at maximum expansion)}}{\text{("Size" of an elementary particle)}},$$

$$\sim 10^{40} \sim \frac{e^2}{GmM} \sim \frac{\text{(Electric forces)}}{\text{(Gravitational forces)}},$$

$$\sim 10^{20} \sim \frac{e^2/mc^2}{(\hbar G/c^3)^{1/2}} \sim \frac{\text{("Size" of an elementary particle)}}{\text{(Planck length)}},$$

$$\sim 10^{10} \sim \frac{\text{(Number of photons in universe)}}{\text{(Number of baryons in universe)}}.$$

Some understanding of the relationships between these numbers has been won [Carter (1986)]. Never has any explanation appeared for their enormous magnitude, nor will there ever, if the view is correct that reprocessing the universe reprocesses also the physical constants. These constants on that view are not part of the laws of physics. They are part of the initial-value data. Such numbers are freshly given for each fresh cycle of expansion of the universe. To look for a physical explanation for the "big numbers" would thus seem to be looking for the right answer to the wrong question.

In the week between one storm and the next, most features of the weather are ever-changing, but some special patterns of the wind last the week. If the term "frozen features of the meteorology" is appropriate for them, much more so would it seem appropriate for the big numbers, the physical constants and the spectrum of particle masses in the cycle between one reprocessing of the universe and another.

A per cent or so change one way in one of the "constants," $\hbar c/e^2$, will cause all stars to be red stars; and a comparable change the other way will make all stars be blue stars, according to Carter (1968). In neither case will any star like the sun be possible. He raises the question whether life could have developed if the determinants of the physical constants had differed substantially from those that characterize this cycle of the universe.

Dicke (1961) has pointed out that the right order of ideas may not be, here is the universe, so what must man be; but here is man, so what must the universe be? In other words: (1) What good is a universe without awareness of that universe? But: (2) Awareness demands life. (3) Life demands the presence of elements heavier than hydrogen. (4) The production of heavy elements demands thermonuclear combustion. (5) Thermonuclear combustion normally requires several 10^9 years of cooking time in a star. (6) Several 10^9 years of time will not and cannot be available in a closed universe, according to general relativity, unless the radius-at-maximum-expansion of that universe is several 10^9 light years or more. So why on this view is the universe as big as it is? Because only so can man be here!

In brief, the considerations of Carter and Dicke would seem to raise the idea of the "biological selection of physical constants." However, to "select" is impossible unless there are options to select between. Exactly such options would seem for the first time to be held out by the only over-all picture of the gravitational collapse of the universe that one sees how to put forward today, the *pregeometry black-box model of the reprocessing of the universe.*

Proceeding with all caution into uncharted territory, one must nevertheless be aware that the conclusions one is reaching and the questions one is asking at a given stage of the analysis may be only stepping stones on the way to still more penetrating questions and an even more remarkable picture. To speak of "reprocessing and selection" may only be a halfway point on the road toward thinking of the universe as Leibniz did, as a world of relationships, not a world of machinery. Far from being brought into its present condition by "reprocessing" from earlier cycles, may the universe in some strange sense be "brought into being" by the participation of those who participate? On this view the concept of "cycles" would even seem to be altogether wrong. Instead the vital act is the act of participation. "Participator" is the incontrovertible new concept given by quantum mechanics; it strikes down the term "observer" of classical theory, the man who stands safely behind the thick glass wall and watches what goes on without taking part. It can't be done, quantum mechanics says. Even with the lowly electron one must participate before one can give any meaning whatsoever to its position or its momentum. Is this firmly established result the tiny tip of a giant iceberg? Does the universe also derive its meaning from "participation"? Are we destined to return to the great concept of Leibniz, of "preestablished harmony" ("Leibniz logic loop"), before we can make the next great advance?

Rich prospects stand open for investigation in gravitation physics, from neutron stars to cosmology and from post-Newtonian celestial mechanics to gravitational waves. Einstein's geometrodynamics exposes itself to destruction on a dozen fronts and by a thousand predictions. No predictions subject to early test are more entrancing than those on the formation and properties of a black hole, "laboratory model" for some of what is predicted for the universe itself. No field is more pregnant with the future than gravitational collapse. No more revolutionary views of man and the universe has one ever been driven to consider seriously than those that come out of pondering the paradox of collapse, the greatest crisis of physics of all time.

NOTES

Avez, A., 1960, "Propriétés globales des espace-temps périodiques clos," *Acad. des Sci., Paris, Comptes Rend.* 250, 3583–3587.

Carter, B., 1968, "Large numbers in astrophysics and cosmology," unpublished preprint, Institute of Theoretical Astronomy, Cambridge, England.

Dicke, R. H., 1959, "New research on old gravitation," *Science 129,* 621–624.

Dicke, R. H., 1961, "Dirac's cosmology and Mach's principle," *Nature 192,* 440–441.

Dicke, R. H., 1964, *The Theoretical Significance of Experimental Relativity,* Gordon and Breach, New York.

Dirac, P. A. M., 1937, "The cosmological constants," *Nature 139,* 323.

Dirac, P. A. M., 1938, "New basis for cosmology," *Proc. R. Soc. London A 165,* 119–208.

Eddington, A. S., 1931, "Preliminary note on the masses of the electron, the proton, and the universe," *Proc. Cambridge Phil. Soc.* 27, 15–19.

Eddington, A. S., 1936, *Relativity Theory of Protons and Electrons*, Cambridge Univ. Press, Cambridge, England.

Eddington, A. S., 1946, *Fundamental Theory*, Cambridge Univ. Press, Cambridge, England.

Geroch, R. P., 1967, *Singularities in the Spacetime of General Relativity: Their Definition, Existence, and Local Characterization*, doctoral dissertation, Princeton University.

Hawking, S. W., and R. Penrose, 1969, "The singularities of gravitational collapse and cosmology," *Proc. R. Soc. London A 314*, 529–548.

Hayakawa, S., 1965a, "Cosmological interpretation of the weak forces," *Prog. Theor. Phys.* 33, 538–539.

Hayakawa, S., 1965b, "Atomism and cosmology," *Prog. Theor. Phys. Supp.*, special number, Yukawa thirtieth anniversary issue, 532–541.

Jordan, P., 1955, *Schwerkraft and Weltall*, Vieweg und Sohn, Braunschweig.

Jordan, P., 1959, "Zum gegenwärtigen Stand der Diracschen kosmologischen Hypothesen," *Z. Phys.* 157, 112–121.

Leibniz, G. W., 1714, *La Monadologie*. English translation available in several books; parts included in P. P. Wiener, ed., *Leibniz Selections*, Scribners, New York, 1951.

Planck, M., 1899, "Über irreversible Strahlungsvorgänge," *Sitzungsber. Deut. Akad. Wiss. Berlin, Kl. Math. — Phys. Tech.*, 440–480.

Tolman, R. C., 1934, *Relativity, Thermodynamics, and Cosmology*, Clarendon Press, Oxford.

Wheeler, J. A., 1971, "Transcending the law of conservation of leptons," in *Atti del Convegno Internazionale sul Tema: The Astrophysical Aspects of the Weak Interactions; Quaderno N. 157*, Accademia Nazionale dei Lincei, Roma, pp. 133–164.

17

EDWARD P. TRYON*

Is the Universe a Vacuum Fluctuation?

RECENT OBSERVATIONS CONFIRM that the 2.7 K background radiation does indeed have a blackbody spectrum (see refs. 1 and 2), which establishes beyond reasonable doubt that some version of the big bang theory is correct. Here I propose a specific big bang model which I believe to be the simplest and most appealing imaginable—namely, that our Universe is a fluctuation of the vacuum, where "vacuum fluctuation" is to be understood in the sense of quantum field theory.

Creation

In any big bang model, one must deal with the problem of "creation". This problem has two aspects. One is that the conservation laws of physics forbid the creation of something from nothing. The other is that even if the conservation laws were inapplicable at the moment of creation, there is no apparent reason for such an event to occur.

The prevailing attitude towards creation is that our Universe is probably undergoing merely one in an infinite sequence of expansions (with intervening contractions). According to this view the Universe has always existed, so its origin lies in the infinite past where it is hopefully not a problem for science.

The preceding viewpoint may indeed be correct, but it leaves unan-

*Reprinted by permission from *Nature*, Vol. 246, No. 5433, December 14 1973, pages 396–397. Copyright © 1973 Macmillan Magazines Ltd.

swered two important questions. First, by what mechanism does the Universe "bounce back" from each contraction? No satisfactory mechanism has ever been proposed. Second, why does the Universe have its particular values for energy, electric charge, baryon and lepton number and so on?

In my model, I assume that our Universe did indeed appear from nowhere about 10^{10} yr ago. Contrary to widespread belief, such an event need not have violated any of the conventional laws of physics. The laws of physics merely imply that a Universe which appears from nowhere must have certain specific properties. In particular, such a Universe must have a zero net value for all conserved quantities.

Conservation

The conserved quantities of physics fall into two categories— discrete and continuous. The discrete quantities are those which characterise elementary particles: electric charge, baryon and lepton number, strangeness and so on. All these quantities have equal magnitude but opposite sign for particles and anti-particles. Hence the discrete conservation laws simply imply that a universe which appears from nowhere must consist equally of matter and anti-matter. Such a possibility is consistent with the properties which have so far been established for our own Universe. (The possibility that our Universe consists equally of matter and anti-matter has been studied by many authors; for a recent review see ref. 3.)

Of the remaining conservation laws, the most important for cosmology is that concerning energy: although matter and energy can be converted into each other, the net energy remains constant if an intrinsic energy of mc^2 is assigned to each piece of matter.

The Universe has an enormous amount of mass energy, and this might be thought to preclude a creation of the cosmos from nothing. There is, however, another form of energy which is important for cosmology, namely gravitational potential energy. The gravitational energy of a mass m due to its interaction with the rest of the Universe is given roughly by

$$E_g \approx -GmM/R$$

where G is the gravitational constant and M denotes the net mass of the Universe contained within the Hubble radius $R = c/H$, where H is Hubble's constant.

The density of matter which has so far been observed is somewhat less than the critical value ρ_c required for the Universe to be closed:

$$\rho_c = 3H^2/8\pi G$$

Sandage's recent determination[4] of the cosmic deceleration parameter indicates, however, that our Universe probably is closed, in which case the true ρ exceeds ρ_c. If I assume the critical density in my estimate of E_g, I obtain

$$E_g \approx -mc^2/2$$

Hence within a factor of order unity, the negative gravitational energy of any piece of matter is sufficient to cancel the positive mass energy of mc^2. This naive argument indicates that the net energy of our Universe may indeed be zero.

P. Bergmann has presented a more sophisticated argument which indicates that any closed universe has zero energy. In its simplest form, the argument proceeds as follows (J. M. Cohen, private communication).

Suppose the Universe were closed. Then it would be topologically impossible for any gravitational flux lines to escape. If the Universe were viewed from the outside, by a viewer in some larger space in which the Universe were imbedded, the absence of gravitational flux would imply that the system had zero energy. Hence any closed universe has zero energy.

The preceding remarks indicate that our Universe may have zero net values for all conserved quantities. If this be the case, then our Universe could have appeared from nowhere without violating any conservation laws.

Quantum Field Theory

To indicate how such a creation might have come about, I refer to quantum field theory, in which every phenomenon that could happen in principle actually does happen occasionally in practice, on a statistically random basis. For example, quantum electrodynamics reveals that an electron, positron and photon occasionally emerge spontaneously from a perfect vacuum. When this happens, the three particles exist for a brief time, and then annihilate each other, leaving no trace behind. (Energy conservation is violated, but only for the brief particle lifetime Δt permitted by the uncertainty relation $\Delta E \, \Delta t \sim h$, where ΔE is the net energy of the particles and h is Planck's constant.) The spontaneous, temporary emergence of particles from a vacuum is called a vacuum fluctuation, and is utterly commonplace in quantum field theory.

If it is true that our Universe has a zero net value for all conserved quantities, then it may simply be a fluctuation of the vacuum, the vacuum of some larger space in which our Universe is imbedded. In answer to the question of why it happened, I offer the modest proposal that our Universe is simply one of those things which happen from time to time.

One might wonder how a vacuum fluctuation could occur on such a grand scale. My answer is in two parts. The first is that the laws of physics place no limit on the scale of vacuum fluctuations. The duration is of course subject to the restriction $\Delta E \, \Delta t \sim h$, but this merely implies that our Universe has zero energy, which has already been made plausible.

The second part of my answer lies in the principle of biological selection, which states that any Universe in which sentient beings find themselves is necessarily hospitable to sentient beings. I do not claim that universes like ours occur frequently, merely that the expected frequency is non-zero. Vacuum fluctuations on the scale of our Universe are probably quite rare. The logic of the situation dictates, however, that observers always find themselves in universes capable of generating life, and such universes are impressively large. (We could not have seen this universe if its expansion-contraction time had been less than the 10^{10} yr required for *Homo sapiens* to evolve.)

In summary, observations imply that a big bang occurred about 10^{10} yr ago. One might suppose that the Universe has always existed, undergoing periodic expansions and contractions. There is, however, no known mechanism by which the Universe might bounce back from a contraction. Furthermore, to assume the Universe is infinitely old is to evade, rather than illuminate, the issues of its origin and quantum numbers.

I assume The Universe to be undergoing its initial expansion, evidently having appeared as a fluctuation of the vacuum. The conservation laws of physics then imply that our Universe has the quantum numbers of the vacuum, including zero energy. Hence our Universe must be homogeneous, isotropic and closed, and must consist equally of matter and anti-matter. All these predictions are supported by, or consistent with, present observations.

My model is admittedly speculative, and is still in an early stage of development. Quantum theory does, however, imply that the vacuum should be unstable against large scale fluctuations in the presence of a long range, negative energy, universal interaction. Gravitation is precisely such an interaction, so I am encouraged to believe that the origin and properties of our Universe may be explicable within the framework of conventional science, along the lines indicated here.

NOTES

1. Muehlner, D., and Weiss, R., *Phys. Rev.*, **D7**, 326 (1973).
2. Hegyi, D. J., Traub, W. A., and Carleton, N. P., *Phys. Rev. Lett.*, **28**, 1541 (1972).
3. Omnès, R., *Phys. Rep.*, **3C** 1 (1972).
4. Sandage, A. R., *Phys. Today*, **23**, 34 (1970).

18

PAUL DAVIES*

What Caused the Big Bang?

The Genesis Paradox

WHENEVER I GIVE a lecture on cosmology one question never fails to be asked: What caused the big bang? A few years ago I had no real answer. Today, I believe we know what caused the big bang.

The question is actually two rolled into one. We should like to know why the universe began with a bang, what triggered this explosive outburst in the first place. But behind this physical enigma lies a deeper metaphysical mystery. If the big bang represents the origin of physical existence, including that of space and time, in what sense can anything be said to have *caused* this event?

On a purely physical level, the abrupt appearance of the universe in a huge explosion is something of a paradox. Of the four forces of nature which control the world, only gravity acts systematically on a cosmic scale, and in all our experience gravity is attractive. It is a pulling force. But the explosion which marked the creation of the universe would seem to require a pushing force of unimaginable power to blast the cosmos asunder and set it on a path of expansion which continues to this day.

People are often puzzled in the belief that if the universe is dominated by the force of gravity it ought to be contracting, not expanding. As a pulling force, gravity causes objects to implode rather than ex-

*From Chapter 12 of *Superforce* by Paul Davies. Copyright © 1984 by Glenister Gavin Ltd. Reprinted by permission of Simon & Schuster, Inc., New York, and of the author.

plode. For example, a highly compact star will be unable to support its own weight, and may collapse to form a neutron star or a black hole. In the very early universe, the compression of material exceeded that of even the densest star, and this fact often prompts the question of why the primeval cosmos did not itself turn into a black hole at the outset.

The traditional response leaves something of a credibility gap. It is argued that the primeval explosion must simply be accepted as an initial condition. Certainly, under the influence of gravity, the rate of cosmic expansion has continually slowed since the first moment, but at the instant of its creation the universe was expanding infinitely rapidly. No force caused it to explode in this way, it simply started with an initial expansion. Had the explosive vigour been less extreme, then gravity would very soon have overwhelmed the dispersing material, reversing the expansion and engulfing the entire cosmos in a cata-strophic implosion, producing something rather like a black hole. As it happened, the bang was big enough to enable the universe either to escape its own gravity and go on expanding for ever under the impetus of the initial explosion, or at least to survive for many thousands of millions of years before succumbing to implosion and annihilation.

The trouble with this traditional picture is that it is in no sense an explanation for the big bang. Once again, a fundamental feature of the universe is merely attributed to an *ad hoc* initial condition. The big bang "just happened." We are left uncomprehending as to why the force of the explosion had the strength that it did. Why did the universe not explode more violently still, in which case it would be expanding much faster today? Alternatively, why is it not expanding much slower, or even contracting by now? Of course, had the cosmos *failed* to explode with sufficient violence, and rapid collapse overtaken it, we should not be here to ask such questions; but that is hardly an explanation.

Closer investigation shows that the genesis paradox is actually deeper than this. Careful measurement puts the rate of expansion very close to a critical value at which the universe will just escape its own gravity and expand for ever. A little slower, and the cosmos would collapse, a little faster and the cosmic material would have long ago completely dispersed. It is interesting to ask precisely how delicately the rate of expansion has been "fine-tuned" to fall on this narrow dividing line between two catastrophes. If at time 1 s (by which time the pattern of expansion was already firmly established) the expansion rate had dif-fered from its actual value by more than 10^{-18}, it would have been sufficient to throw the delicate balance out. The explosive vigour of the universe is thus matched with almost unbelievable accuracy to its gra-vitating power. The big bang was not, evidently, any old bang, but an explosion of exquisitely arranged magnitude. In the traditional version of the big bang theory we are asked to accept not only that the explosion just happened, but that it happened in an exceedingly contrived fashion. The initial conditions had to be very special indeed.

The rate of expansion is only one of several apparent cosmic "miracles." Another concerns the pattern of expansion. As we observe it today, the universe is extraordinarily uniform on the large scale, in the way that matter and energy are distributed. From the viewpoint of a distant galaxy, the overall structure of the cosmos would appear almost identical to its aspect from Earth. The galaxies are scattered throughout space with a constant average density, and at every point the universe would look the same at all orientations. The primeval heat radiation which bathes the universe arrives at Earth with a uniform temperature in every direction accurate to one part in ten thousand. This radiation has travelled to us across thousands of millions of light years of space, and would carry the imprint of any departures from uniformity encountered on the way.

The large-scale uniformity of the universe continues to be preserved with time as the universe expands. It follows that the expansion itself must be uniform to a very high degree. Not only is the rate of expansion the same in all directions, it is the same from region to region within the cosmos. If the universe were to expand faster in one direction than the others, it would depress the temperature of the background heat radiation coming from that direction, and also distort the pattern of motion of the galaxies as viewed from Earth. So not only did the universe commence with a bang of a quite precise magnitude, it was a highly orchestrated explosion as well, a simultaneous outburst of exactly uniform vigour everywhere and in every direction.

The extreme improbability that such a coherent, synchronized eruption would occur spontaneously is exacerbated by the fact that, in the traditional big bang theory, the different regions of the primeval cosmos would have been causally isolated. The point here is that, on account of the theory of relativity, no physical influence can propagate faster than light. Consequently, different regions of the universe can come into causal contact only after a period of time has elapsed. For example, at 1 s after the initial explosion, light can have travelled at most one light-second which is 300,000 km. Regions of the universe separated by greater than this distance could not, at 1 s, have exercised any influence on each other. But at that time, the universe we observe today occupied a region of space at least 10^{14} km across. It must therefore have been made up of some 10^{27} causally separate regions, all of them nevertheless expanding at exactly the same rate. Even today, when we observe the cosmic heat radiation coming from opposite sides of the sky, we are receiving identical thumbprints from regions of the universe that are separated from each other by ninety times the distance that light could have travelled at the time the heat radiation was emitted towards us.

How is it possible to explain this remarkable degree of co-operation between different parts of the universe that apparently have never been in communication with each other? How have they come to behave so similarly? The traditional response is, yet again, to fall back on special initial conditions. The extreme uniformity of the primeval explosion is simply regarded as a brute fact: "The universe began that way."

The large-scale uniformity of the universe is all the more mysterious on account of the fact that, on a somewhat smaller scale, the universe is *not* uniform. The existence of galaxies and galactic clusters indicates a departure from exact uniformity, a departure which is, moreover, of the same magnitude and scale everywhere. Because gravity tends to amplify any initial clumping of material, the degree of non-uniformity required to produce galaxies was far less during the big bang than it is today. In spite of this, some small degree of irregularity must have been present in the primeval phase or galaxies would never have started to form. In the old big bang theory these early irregularities were also explained away as initial conditions. Thus, we were required to believe that the universe began in a peculiar state of extraordinary but not quite perfect order.

The explanation can be summarized as follows: with gravitational attraction the only cosmic force available, the big bang must simply be accepted as god-given, an event without a cause, an assumed initial condition. Furthermore, it was an event of quite astonishing fidelity, for the present highly structured cosmos could not have arisen unless the universe was set up in just the right way at the outset. This is the genesis paradox.

The Search for Antigravity

Although a resolution of the genesis paradox has been achieved only in the past few years, traces of the essential idea go back far into history, to a time before the expansion of the universe or the big bang theory were known. Even Newton realized that there was a deep puzzle about the stability of the cosmos. How can the stars just hang out there in space unsupported? The universal force of gravity, being attractive, ought to cause the entire collection of stars to plunge in on itself.

To escape from this absurdity, Newton used a curious argument. If the universe collapsed under its own gravity, he reasoned, every star would be obliged to fall towards the centre of the stellar assemblage. But suppose the universe were infinite, with stars distributed on average uniformly throughout infinite space. There would then be no over-all centre towards which the stars could fall; in an infinite universe every region is identical to every other. Any given star would receive gravitational pulls from all its neighbours, but these would average out in their different directions, and so there would be no systematic net force to convey a star towards any particular place of general congregation.

When Einstein replaced Newton's gravitation theory 200 years later, he was equally troubled by the enigma of how the universe avoids collapse. His first paper on cosmology was published before Hubble's famous discovery of the expanding universe and Einstein presumed, like Newton, that the cosmos was static. His solution of the stability problem was, however, much more direct. Einstein believed that to prevent the universe from imploding under its own gravity there had to be another cosmic force to counteract the gravitational force. This new force would have to be repulsive rather than attractive, a pushing force to balance the pull of gravity. In this respect it might be regarded as "antigravity", although "cosmic repulsion force" is a more accurate description. Einstein did not conjure up the cosmic repulsion force in an *ad hoc* way. He found that his gravitational field equations contained an optional term which gave rise to a force with exactly the desired properties.

Although the idea of a repulsive force pushing against the gravity of the universe is simple enough to grasp in broad conception, the actual properties of the force are decidedly odd. It goes without saying that we do not notice any such force on the Earth, nor has any hint of one been found during several centuries of planetary astronomy. Evidently, if a cosmic repulsion force exists, it must have the property that it does not act conspicuously at close range but accumulates in strength over astronomical distances. Behaviour of this sort was contrary to all pre-vious experience of forces, which tend to be strong nearby and to weaken with distance. Electric and gravitational forces, for example, fall steadily towards zero in accordance with the inverse square law. Nevertheless, a force of this somewhat peculiar sort emerged naturally from Einstein's theory.

The cosmic repulsion found by Einstein should not really be thought of as a fifth force of nature. Rather, it is a weird offshoot of gravity itself. In fact the effects of cosmic repulsion can be attributed to ordi-nary gravity if the source of the gravitational field is chosen to be a medium with rather unusual properties. A familiar material medium, such as a gas, will exert a pressure, but the hypothetical cosmic medium being discussed here is required to possess a *negative* pressure, or tension. To get some idea of what is involved, imagine that we could fill a vessel with this conjectured cosmic stuff. Instead of pushing against the walls of the vessel like an ordinary gas, the cosmic medium would try to pull the walls inwards.

We can envisage the repulsion, therefore, either as a sort of adjunct of gravity, or as caused by the ordinary gravity of an invisible fluid medium with negative pressure filling all of space. There is no conflict, incidentally, between the fact that negative pressure would suck on the walls of a vessel, and the fact that the hypothetical medium exerts a repulsion on galaxies rather than an attraction. The repulsive effect is due to the *gravity* of the medium, not its mechanical action. In any case, mechanical forces arise from pressure differences, not pressure as such and the medium is supposed to fill all of space. It could not be confined to a vessel. In fact, an observer immersed in the medium would not perceive any tangible substance at all. Space would look and feel completely empty.

In spite of these rather bizarre features, Einstein duly declared that he had a convincing model of a universe held in equilibrium between the attractive force of gravity and the newly discovered cosmic repulsive force. With the aid of simple arithmetic he calculated the strength needed for the repulsive force to balance the gravity of the universe. Einstein was able to confirm that the repulsion would be so slight within the solar system, and even the galaxy, that we would never have spotted it observationally. For a while it seemed that an age-old puzzle had been brilliantly solved.

Then things began to go wrong. First there was a problem about stability. The essential idea was to match the forces of attraction and repulsion precisely. But like many balancing acts this one turns out to be a delicate affair. If, for example, Einstein's static universe were to expand a fraction, the attractive force of gravity (which diminishes with separation) would go down a bit, while the cosmic repulsion force (which increases with distance) would go up. This would lead to an overbalance, with the repulsion winning out and forcing a still greater expansion, and leading to the eventual runaway distension of the universe under an all-dominating repulsion. On the other hand, if the universe shrank a little, the gravitational force would go up and the repulsion would go down, causing gravity to win out, and the universe would then shrink faster and faster towards the total collapse that Einstein had sought to avoid. Thus, the slightest hiccup, and the carefully balanced equilibrium would fail, spelling cosmic disaster.

Then, in 1927, Hubble discovered the expansion of the universe. All balancing acts were thereby rendered obsolete. It was immediately apparent that the universe avoids *implosion* because it is engaged in *explosion*. Had Einstein not been sidetracked with the repulsive force he would surely have made this deduction theoretically and thus have predicted the expansion of the universe a decade before its discovery by astronomers. That would surely have gone down in history as one of the great theoretical predictions of all time. In the event, Einstein abandoned the cosmic repulsion force in disgust. "The biggest blunder of my life," he was later to bemoan. But that was by no means the end of the story.

Cosmic repulsion was invented by Einstein to solve a non-existent problem, namely how to explain a static universe. But as with all genies, once this one was let out of the bottle nobody could put it back again, and the possibility that the dynamics of the universe is a competition between attractive and repulsive forces lived on. Although astronomical observations do not reveal cosmic repulsion at work, they cannot prove it is non-existent. It may simply be too weak to have shown up yet.

Einstein's field equations, though admitting a repulsive force in a natural way, make no restriction on the *strength* of the force. Einstein was free to postulate, after his bitter experience, that the strength was precisely zero, thus eliminating the repulsion altogether. But there was no compelling reason to do this. Other scientists were happy to retain the repulsion, even though it was no longer needed for its original purpose. In the absence of evidence to the contrary, they reasoned, nobody is justified in setting the force to zero.

The consequences of retaining the repulsion force in the expanding universe scenario are easily worked out. Early in the life of the cosmos, when the universe is compressed, the repulsion can be ignored. During this phase, the effect of the gravitational attraction is to slow the pace of expansion, in the same way that a missile fired vertically is slowed by the Earth's gravity. If it is assumed without explanation that the universe starts out expanding rapidly, then gravity acts to steadily reduce the rate to the value observed today. With time, the gravitational force weakens as the cosmic material disperses. By contrast, the cosmic repulsion grows because the galaxies move farther apart. Eventually, the repulsion force comes to exceed the gravitational attraction, and the expansion rate begins to pick up again, getting faster and faster. Thereafter, the universe is dominated by the cosmic repulsion and spends all of eternity in runaway expansion.

Astronomers have reasoned that this unusual behaviour, in which the universe first slows up and then accelerates again, ought to be evident in the observed motion of the galaxies. Careful astronomical observations have failed to provide any convincing evidence for such a turnabout, though from time to time claims have been made to the contrary.

Curiously, the idea of a universe caught by runaway expansion had already been mooted by the Dutch astronomer Wilhelm de Sitter in 1916, several years before Hubble discovered that the universe was expanding. de Sitter argued that if the universe were devoid of ordinary matter, then the usual attractive force of gravity would be absent, and the cosmos would come under the sole influence of the repulsion. This would make the universe expand. (At the time this was a novel idea.)

To an observer, who would be unable to see the curious invisible fluid medium with negative pressure, it would merely appear as if empty space were expanding. The expansion could be judged by stationing test bodies in various positions and watching them move apart. The idea of expanding empty space was considered little more than a curiosity at the time, although it turned out to be remarkably prophetic, as we shall see.

What can be concluded from this saga? The fact that astronomers do not see a cosmic repulsive force at work does not logically imply that the force is non-existent. It could be that it is too weak to be detected with present instrumentation. All observations contain a level of error, and only an upper limit on the strength of the force can be obtained. Set against this, it could be argued on aesthetic grounds that the laws of nature would be simpler if cosmic repulsion were absent. This inconclusive debate about the existence of "antigravity" had been grinding on for many years when suddenly an entirely new twist occurred that gave the subject an unexpected immediacy.

Inflation: The Big Bang Explained

In the previous section we saw how, if a cosmic repulsive force exists, it must be very weak and far too weak to have had any significant effect on the big bang. But this conclusion rests on the assumption that the strength of the repulsive force does not change with time. In Einstein's day everybody made this assumption because the force was put into the theory "by hand". No one considered the possibility that cosmic repulsion might be *generated* by other physical processes that could change as the universe expands. Had such a possibility been entertained, then the history of cosmology would have been very different, for one could then conceive of a scenario in which, under the extreme conditions of the early universe, cosmic repulsion momentarily dominated gravity causing the universe to explode, before fading into insignificance.

This general scenario is precisely what has come out of recent work on the behaviour of matter and forces in the very early universe. It is now clear that a huge cosmic repulsion is an inevitable by-product of the activities of the superforce. The "antigravity" that Einstein threw out of the door has come back in through the window.

The key to understanding the re-discovered cosmic repulsion is the nature of the quantum vacuum. We have seen how such a repulsion can be produced by a bizarrre invisible medium which looks identical to empty space but which possesses a negative pressure. Physicists now believe that that is exactly how a quantum vacuum would be.

The vacuum must be regarded as a ferment of quantum activity, teeming with virtual particles and full of complex interactions. It is important to appreciate that, at the quantum level of description, the vacuum is the dominant structure. What we call particles are only minor disturbances bubbling up over this background sea of activity.

In the late 1970s it became apparent that the unification of the four forces required a drastic re-appraisal of the physical nature of the vacuum. The theory suggested that all this vacuum energy could arrange itself in more than one way. To put it simply, the vacuum could become excited and adopt a number of states of very different energy, in the same way that an atom can be excited to higher energy levels. These several vacuum states would look identical if we could view them, but they possess very different properties.

First of all, the energy involved leaps by huge amounts from one vacuum state to another. In the grand unified theories, to take an example, the gap between the least and greatest vacuum energy is almost incomprehensibly large. To get some feeling for the enormity of the numbers involved, consider the huge outpouring of energy from the sun, accumulated over its entire lifetime of about 5 thousand million years. Conceive of taking this colossal quantity of energy—the entire output of the sun during its whole history—and compressing it into a volume of space less than that occupied by the solar system. You then begin to approach the sort of energy density contained in a GUT vacuum state.

Alongside these staggering energy differences are equally enormous changes in the pressure of the vacuum states. But here comes the important twist: the pressures are all *negative*. The quantum vacuum behaves exactly like the previously hypothetical medium which produces cosmic repulsion, only this time the number are so big that the strength of the repulsive force is 10^{120} times greater than Einstein needed to prop up a static universe.

The way now lies open for an explanation of the big bang. Suppose that in the beginning the universe found itself in an excited vacuum state (physicists call this a "false" vacuum). In this state the universe would be subject to a cosmic repulsion force of such magnitude that it would cause headlong expansion at a huge rate. In fact, during this phase, the universe would resemble de Sitter's model mentioned in the previous section. The difference is that, whereas de Sitter envisaged a universe sedately expanding over an astronomical time-scale, the de Sitter phase driven by the false quantum vacuum is far from sedate. A typical region of space would double in size every 10^{-34} s or so!

The way in which this hyper-expansion proceeds is distinctive: distances increase in size exponentially fast. This means that every 10^{-34} s every region of the universe doubles its size, and then goes on doubling again and again in a progression. This type of runaway expansion has been dubbed "inflation" by Alan Guth of MIT, who invented the idea in 1980. Under the impact of the exceedingly rapid and accelerating expansion, the universe would soon have found itself swelling explosively fast. This was the big bang.

Somehow, the inflationary phase has to terminate. As with all excited quantum systems, the false vacuum is unstable and will tend to decay. When that happens, the repulsion force disappears. This would have put a stop to inflation, bringing the universe under the control of ordinary, attractive gravity. The universe would have continued to expand, of course, from the initial impetus imparted by the inflationary episode, but at a steadily falling rate. The only trace that now remains of the cosmic repulsion is this dwindling expansion.

According to the inflationary scenario, the universe started out in a vacuum state, devoid of matter or radiation. Even if matter and radiation were present initially, all traces would soon have been eradicated because the universe swelled by such an enormous factor during the inflationary phase. During this incredibly brief phase, the region of space which today forms the entire observable universe grew from one-thousand-millionth of the size of a proton to several centimetres. The density of any pre-existing material would have fallen essentially to zero.

At the end of inflation, then, the universe was empty and cold. As soon as inflation ceased, however, the universe was suddenly filled with intense heat. This flash of heat which illuminated the cosmos owed its origin to the huge reserves of energy locked up in the false vacuum. When the false vacuum decayed, its energy was dumped in the form of radiation, which instantly heated the universe to about 10^{27} K, hot enough for GUT processes to occur. From this point on the universe evolved according to the standard hot big bang theory. The heat energy created matter and antimatter, the universe began to cool, and in a succession of steps all the structure we observe today began to "freeze" out.

The thorny problem of what caused the big bang is therefore solved by the inflationary theory: empty space itself exploded under the repulsive power of the quantum vacuum. But an enigma still remains. The colossal energy of the primeval explosion—the energy that went to generate all the matter and radiation we now see in the universe—surely had to come from somewhere? We will not have explained the existence of the universe until we have traced the source of the primeval energy.

The Cosmic Bootstrap

The universe came into existence amid a huge burst of energy. This energy survives in the background heat radiation and in the cosmic material — the atoms which make up the stars and planets — as "mass" or locked-up energy. It also lives on in the outward rush of the galaxies and in the swirling activities of all the astronomical bodies. The primeval energy wound up the nascent universe and continues to drive it to this day.

Whence came this vital energy which triggered our universe into life? According to the inflationary theory the energy came out of empty space, out of the quantum vacuum. But is this a fully satisfactory answer? We can still ask how the vacuum acquired the energy in the first place.

When we ask where the energy came from we are making an important assumption about the nature of energy. One of the fundamental laws of physics is the law of *conservation* of energy, which says that although you can change energy from one form to another, the total quantity of energy stays fixed. It is easy to think of examples where this law can be tested. Suppose you have a motor and a supply of fuel, and the motor is used to drive an electric generator which in turn powers a heater. When the fuel is expended, its stored chemical energy will have been converted, via electrical energy, into heat energy. If the motor had been used instead to haul a weight to the top of a tower, and the weight were then released, on impact with the ground it would generate the same amount of heat energy as you would have obtained using the heater. The point is that however you move it about or change its form, energy apparently cannot be created or destroyed. It is a law used by engineers every day.

If energy cannot be created or destroyed, how did the primeval energy come to exist? Was it simply injected at the beginning of time, another *ad hoc* initial condition? If so, why does the universe contain the amount of energy that it does? There are about 10^{68} joules of energy in the observable universe; why not 10^{99} or $10^{10,000}$ or any other number?

The inflation theory is one possible scientific (as opposed to metaphysical) answer to this mystery. According to the theory, the universe started out with essentially zero energy, and succeeded in conjuring up the lot during the first 10^{-32} s. The key to this miracle lies with a most remarkable fact about cosmology: the law of conservation of energy *fails* in its usual sense when applied to the expanding universe.

In fact, we have already encountered this point. The cosmological expansion causes the temperature of the universe to fall. The radiant heat energy that was so intense in the primeval phase had dwindled to a temperature close to absolute zero. Where has all that heat energy gone? The answer is, that in a sense it has depleted itself by helping the universe to expand, adding its pressure to the explosive violence of the big bang. When an ordinary fluid expands, its pressure pushes outwards and does work, so using up its energy. This means that if you expand an ordinary gas, its internal energy must fall to pay for the work done. In stark contrast to this conventional behaviour, the cosmic repulsion behaves like a fluid with *negative* pressure. When a negative-pressure fluid is expanded, its energy goes *up* rather than down. This is precisely what happened in the inflationary period, when the cosmic repulsion drove the universe into accelerated expansion. All the while the total energy of the vacuum kept on rising until, at the cessation of the inflationary era, it had accumulated to a huge amount. As soon as inflation stopped, this energy was released in a single great burst, generating all the heat and matter that eventually emerged from the big bang. From then on, the conventional positive-pressure expansion took over, and the energy began to decline again.

The creation of the primeval energy has an air of magic to it. The vacuum, with its weird negative pressure, seems to have a truly incredible capability: on the one hand it produces a powerful repulsive force, bringing about its own accelerating expansion; on the other hand, that very expansion goes on boosting the energy of the vacuum more and more. The vacuum essentially pays itself vast quantities of energy. It has an inbuilt ability to continue expanding and generating unlimited quantities of energy for free. Only the quantum decay of the false vacuum puts a stop to the bonanza.

The vacuum is nature's miraculous jar of energy. There is in principle no limit to how much energy can be self-generated by inflationary expansion. It is a revolutionary result at total variance with the centuries-old tradition that "nothing can come out of nothing," a belief that dates at least from the time of Parmenides in the fifth century B.C. The idea of creation from nothing has, until recently, belonged solely to the province of religion. Christians have long believed that God created the universe out of nothing, but the possibility that all the cosmic matter and energy might appear spontaneously as a result of purely physical processes would have been regarded as utterly untenable by scientists only a decade ago.

For those who feel uncomfortable with the whole concept of something for nothing, there is an alternative way of looking at the creation of energy by the expanding universe. Because gravitational forces are normally attractive, it is necessary to do work to pull matter apart against its own gravity. This means that the gravitational energy of a collection of bodies is negative; if more bodies are added to the system, energy is released and the gravitational energy becomes more negative to pay for it. In the context of the inflationary universe, the appearance of heat and matter could be viewed as exactly compensated by the negative gravitational energy of the newly created mass, in which case the total energy of the universe is zero, and no net energy has appeared after all! Attractive though this way of looking at the creation may be, it should not be taken too seriously because the whole concept of energy has dubious status as far as gravity is concerned.

The antics of the vacuum are reminiscent of the story, much beloved of physicists, about the boy who falls into a bog and escapes by pulling himself up by his own bootstraps. The self-creating universe is rather like this boy since it too pulls itself up "by its own bootstraps": entirely from within its own physical nature, the universe infuses itself with all the energy necessary to create and animate matter, driving its own explosive origin. This is the cosmic bootstrap. We owe our existence to its astonishing power.

Successes of Inflation

Once the basic idea had been mooted by Guth that the universe underwent an early period of extremely rapid expansion, it became apparent that the scenario provides an elegant explanation for many of the previously *ad hoc* features of big bang cosmology.

In an earlier section we encountered several "fine-tuning" paradoxes relating to the way that the primeval explosion was apparently highly orchestrated and precisely arranged. One of these remarkable "coincidences" related to the way in which the strength of the explosion was exactly matched to the gravitational power of the cosmos such that the expansion rate today lies very close to the borderline between re-collapse and rapid dispersal. A crucial test of the inflationary scenario is whether it produces a big bang of this precisely matched magnitude. It turns out that because of the nature of exponential expansion — the characteristic feature of the inflationary phase — the explosive power is indeed automatically adjusted to yield exactly the right value corresponding to the universe just escaping its own gravity. Inflation can give no other expansion rate than the one that is observed.

A second major puzzle relates to the large-scale uniformity of the universe. This too is immediately explained by inflation. Any irregularities initially present in the universe would have been stretched to death by the enormous distension, rather like the wrinkles in a deflated balloon are smoothed out by inflation. With regions of space being expanded by factors of 10^{50}, any prior disorder would be diluted to insignificance.

We have seen, however, that *complete* uniformity would be incorrect, because a small degree of clumping was necessary in the early universe to account for the present existence of galaxies and galactic clusters. The original hope of astronomers was that the existence of galaxies might be explained as a result of gravitational aggregation since the big bang. A cloud of gas will tend to contract under its own gravity and then fragment into smaller clouds, which in turn fragment into still smaller clouds, and so on. It is possible to imagine the gas emerging from the big bang uniformly distributed, but purely by chance accumulations becoming overdense here and there and under-dense elsewhere. Gravity would reinforce this tendency, causing the enhanced regions to grow stronger and suck in more material, and then to shrink and successively fragment, with the smallest fragments becoming stars. One would then end up with a hierarchy of structure, with stars clustered into groups, which in turn cluster into galaxies and galactic clusters.

Unfortunately, the growth of galaxies by this mechanism would take much longer than the age of the universe if there were no irregularities present in the gas at the outset, because the shrinking and fragmenting process is in competition with the expansion of the universe, which tries to disperse the gas. In the old version of the big bang theory it was necessary to assume that the seeds of galaxies were already built into the structure of the universe when it was created. Moreover, these initial irregularities had to be of just the right magnitude: too small and galaxies would never form, too large and the overdense regions would collapse into huge black holes instead. We are at a loss to know why the galaxies are the sizes they are, or why the clusters contain the numbers of galaxies that they do.

It is now possible to conceive of a better explanation for galactic structure based on the inflationary scenario. The essential idea is simple enough. Inflation occurs while the quantum state of the universe is hanging in the unstable "false" vacuum state. Eventually the false vacuum decays, its excess energy going into heat and matter. At this point the cosmic repulsion disappears and inflation ceases. However, the decay of the false vacuum does not occur at exactly the same instant throughout space. As in all quantum processes, there will be fluctuations in the rate at which the false vacuum decays. Some regions of the universe will decay slightly faster than others. In these regions inflation will end sooner. Irregularities will therefore appear in the final state. The hope is that these irregularities can act as seeds or centres for gravitational clumping that eventually lead to galaxies and galactic clusters. The theorists have been modelling the fluctuation mechanism mathematically, though with mixed success. Generally, the effect is too big, the computed irregularities too pronounced. But the models used are crude, and a more refined approach could prove successful. Although the theory is tentative at this stage, it is at least possible to see the sort of mechanism that could give rise to galaxies without the need for special initial conditions.

In Guth's original version of the inflationary scenario, the false vacuum decayed abruptly into the "true" vacuum, the lowest energy vacuum state, which we identify with empty space today. The way in which this change occurred was regarded as similar to a phase transition such as from a gas to liquid, for example. Bubbles of true vacuum were envisaged as forming at random in the false vacuum, and then expanding at the speed of light to encompass greater and greater volumes of space. To enable the false vacuum to live long enough for inflation to work its magic, the two states were separated by an energy barrier through which the system was obliged to "quantum tunnel". This model suffered from a major shortcoming, however: all the energy released from the false vacuum was found to be concentrated in the bubble walls, and there was no mechanism to distribute it evenly through the interior of bubbles. When the bubbles collided and coalesced, the energy would end up in tangled sheets. The resulting universe would contain severe irregularities, and the work of inflation in achieving large-scale uniformity would be ruined.

Improved versions of the inflationary scenario have been devised which circumvent these difficulties. In the new theory there is no tunnelling between the two vacuum states, but instead the parameters are chosen so that the decay of the false vacuum is very slow, giving the universe time enough to inflate. When decay eventually occurs the energy of the false vacuum is released throughout the "bubble", which quickly heats up to 10^{27} K. It is assumed that the entire observable universe is contained within a single bubble. Thus, on an ultra-large scale the universe may be very irregular, but our own region (and much more beyond) lies within a domain of quiescent uniformity.

Curiously, Guth's original reason for inventing the inflationary scenario was to address an altogether different cosmological problem, namely the absence of magnetic monopoles. The standard big bang theory predicts that a superabundance of monopoles would have been created in the primeval phase. It also happens that these monopoles are likely to be accompanied by other bizarre objects known as "strings" and "sheets" which are their one- and two-dimensional analogues. The problem was how to rid the universe of these undesirable entities. Inflation solves the monopole and related problems automatically because the enormous swelling of space effectively dilutes them to zero density.

Though the inflationary scenario remains a partially developed and speculative theory, it has thrown up a set of ideas that promise to change for ever the face of cosmology. Not only can we now contemplate an explanation for why there was a big bang, but we can begin to understand why it was as big as it was, and why it took the form that it did. We can start to see how it is that the large-scale uniformity of the universe has come about at the same time as the controlled smaller-scale irregularities such as galaxies. The primeval explosion that produced what we know as the universe need no longer be regarded as a mystery for ever beyond the scope of physical science.

The Self-Creating Universe

In spite of the great success of inflation in explaining the origin of the universe, a mystery remains. How did the universe arrive in the false vacuum state in the first place? What happened *before* inflation?

A completely satisfactory scientific account of the creation would have to explain how space (strictly spacetime) came to exist, in order that it might then undergo inflation. Some scientists are content to assume either that space always existed, or that its creation lies beyond the scope of science. A few are more ambitious, however, and believe that it is possible to discuss how space in general, and the false vacuum in particular, might have come out of literally nothing as a result of physical processes that are in principle amenable to study.

As already remarked, the belief that nothing can come out of nothing has only recently been challenged. The cosmic bootstrap comes close to the theological concept of creation *ex nihilo*. It is certainly true that in the familiar world of experience objects usually owe their existence to other objects. The Earth was formed from the solar nebula, the solar nebula from the galactic gases, and so on. If we should happen to encounter an object suddenly appearing out of nowhere we should be inclined to regard the event as a miracle: imagine locking an empty safe and then opening it a few moments later to find it full of coins, or cutlery, or candies? In daily life we expect that everything has to come from somewhere, or out of something.

On the other hand, the situation is not so clear cut in the case of less concrete things. Out of what is a painting, for example, created? Brushes and paints and canvas are, of course, needed, but these are tools. The *form* of the painting — the choice of shapes and colours, the texture, the composition — in not created by the paint and brush. It is the result of ideas.

Are thoughts and ideas created out of something? Thoughts surely exist, and perhaps all thoughts need a brain, but the brain is the mode of realization of the thoughts, not their cause. Brains alone do not create thoughts any more than computers create calculations. Thoughts can be created by other thoughts, but that still leaves the origin of thoughts unexplained. Sensations lead to some thoughts; memory also produces thoughts. Most artists, however, would regard their work as a result of *spontaneous* inspiration. If this is so, creating a painting — or at least the idea of a painting — is a form of creation out of nothing.

Nevertheless, can we conceive of physical objects, or even the entire universe, coming into existence out of nothing? One place where such a bold possibility is taken seriously is on the east coast of the United States where there is a curious concentration of theoretical physicists and cosmologists who have been manipulating mathematics in an attempt to divine the truth about creation *ex nihilo*. Among this esoteric coterie is Alan Guth at MIT, Sidney Coleman of Harvard, Alex Vilenkin of Tufts University, and Ed Tryon and Heinz Pagels in New York. All of them believe that in one sense or another "nothing is unstable" and that the physical universe blossomed forth spontaneously out of nothing, driven by the laws of physics. "Such ideas are speculation squared," concedes Guth, "but on some level they are probably right . . . It is sometimes said there is no such thing as a free lunch. The universe, however, is a free lunch."

In all these conjectures it is the quantum factor that provides the key. The central feature of quantum physics is the disintegration of the cause–effect link. In the old classical physics, the science of mechanics exemplified the rigid control of causality. The activity of every particle, each twist and turn, was considered to be legislated in detail by the laws of motion. A body was understood to move continuously in a well-defined way according to the pattern of forces acting upon it. The laws of motion embodied the link between cause and effect in their very definition, so that the entire universe was supposed to be regulated in every minute respect by the existing pattern of activity, like a gigantic clockwork. It was this all-embracing, utterly dependable causality that prompted Pierre Laplace's claim about a powerful calculator being able to compute the entire history and destiny of the cosmos from the operation of mechanical laws. The universe, according to this view, is for ever unfolding along a pre-ordained pathway.

Quantum physics wrecked the orderly, yet sterile Laplacian scheme. Physicists learned that at the atomic level matter and motion are vague and unpredictable. Particles can behave erratically, rebelling against rigidly prescribed motions, turning up in unexpected places without discernible reason and even appearing or disappearing without warning.

Causality is not completely absent in the quantum realm, but it is faltering and ambiguous. If an atom, for example, is excited somehow by a collision with another atom, it will usually return quickly to its lowest energy state by emitting a photon. The coming-into-being of the photon is, naturally, a consequence of the atom's being excited in the first place. We can certainly say that the excitation caused the creation of the photon. In that sense cause and effect remain linked. Nevertheless, the actual moment of creation of the photon is unpredictable; the atom might decay at any instant. Physicists can compute the expected, or average, delay before the photon appears, but they can never know in any individual case when this event will happen. Perhaps it is better to describe such a state of affairs by saying that the excitation of the atom "prompts" rather than causes the photon to come into being.

The quantum microworld is not, therefore, linked by a tight network of causal influences, but more by a pandemonium of loosely obeyed commands and suggestions. In the old Newtonian scheme a force would address a body with the unchallengable imperative. "You will move!"

In quantum physics the communication is more of an invitation than an order.

Why do we find the idea of an object abruptly appearing from nothing so incredible? What is it about such an occurrence that suggests miracles and the supernatural? Perhaps the answer lies with familiarity. We never encounter the uncaused appearance of objects in daily life. When the conjurer pulls the rabbit out of a hat we know we have been duped.

Suppose that we actually lived in a world where objects did from time to time noticeably pop out of nowhere, for no reason, in a completely unpredictable way. Once we had grown accustomed to such events we would cease to marvel at them. Spontaneous creation would be accepted as a quirk of nature. Maybe in such a world it would no longer strain credulity to imagine the entire physical universe bursting into existence from nothing.

The imaginary world described above is not, in fact, so very different from the real world. If we could actually observe the behaviour of atoms directly with our sense organs, rather than through the intermediary of special instruments, we should frequently see objects appearing and disappearing without well-defined reasons.

The closest known instance to the idea of creation out of nothing occurs if an electric field can be made strong enough. At a critical field strength, electrons and positrons start appearing out of nowhere in an entirely random way. Calculations suggest that near the surface of a uranium nucleus the electric field is intense enough to be on the verge of inducing this effect. If nuclei could be made containing about 200 protons (uranium has 92) then the spontaneous creation of electrons and positrons would be observed. Unfortunately, a nucleus with so many protons is likely to be exceedingly unstable, but nobody is sure about this.

The spontaneous creation of electrons and positrons in an intense electric field can be considered as a bizarre type of radioactivity, in which it is empty space — the vacuum — which decays. We have already encountered the idea of one vacuum state decaying into another. Here the vacuum decays into a state containing particles.

Although the decay of space is difficult to achieve using an electric field, an analogous process involving gravity might well occur naturally. Near the surface of black holes, gravity is so intense that the vacuum sizzles with a continual stream of newly created particles. This is the famous black hole radiation discovered by Stephen Hawking. Gravity is ultimately responsible for creating the radiation, but it does not cause it in the old Newtonian sense: no given particle has to appear at any particular place and time as a result of gravitational forces. In any case, gravity is only a warping of spacetime, so we could say that it is spacetime that induces the creation of matter.

The spontaneous appearance of matter out of empty space is often referred to as creation "out of nothing", and comes close to the spirit of the creation *ex nihilo* of Christian doctrine. For the physicist, however, empty space is a far cry from nothing: it is very much part of the physical universe. If we want to answer the ultimate question of how the universe came into existence it is not sufficient to assume that empty space was there at the outset. We have to explain where space itself came from. The idea of *space* being created might seem exotic, yet in a sense it is happening around us all the time. The expansion of the universe is nothing but a continual swelling of space. Every day the region of the universe accessible to our telescopes swells by 10^{18} cubic light-years. Where is all this space "coming from"? A helpful analogy is with a piece of elastic. When an elastic string is stretched you get "more of it." Space is rather like super-elastic in that it can go on stretching for ever (as far as we know) without "snapping".

The stretching and warping of space also resembles elastic inasmuch as the "motion" of space is subject to laws of mechanics in the same way as matter. These are the laws of gravity. Just as the quantum theory applies to the activities of matter, so it applies to space and time. In earlier chapters we have seen how quantum gravity is an indispensable part of the search for the superforce, which suggests a curious possibility: if quantum theory allows particles of matter to pop into existence out of nowhere, could it also, when applied to gravity, allow space to come into existence out of nothing? And if so, should the spontaneous appearance of the universe 18,000 million years ago occasion such surprise after all?

19

ANDREI LINDE*

The Universe: Inflation Out Of Chaos

THE PUZZLE OF the birth and death of the Universe is one of the most exciting problems in science, comparable in importance with the puzzle of the origin of life. According to the hot big bang theory, which is widely accepted by astronomers today, the Universe was born at some time $t = 0$, about 15 billion years ago, in a state of infinitely high temperature and infinite energy density. The fireball expanded and cooled, with its energy being converted into particles that gave rise to the material from which all the stars and planets were built.

Cosmologists have been able to sketch the broad outlines of the evolution of the Universe from the fireball state to the present day. The resulting standard model of the Universe is only some twenty years old: in the mid-1960s, the discovery of the cosmic microwave background radiation finally convinced astronomers and physicists that there really was a big bang. It was only in 1965 that Arno Penzias and Robert Wilson, at the Bell Research Laboratories in New Jersey, discovered this weak hiss of radio noise with a temperature of about 3 K that seems to fill the entire Universe. It was soon explained as a relict of the fireball which the Universe was born out of. But although the outlines of the standard model seemed satisfactory, there were some remaining problems which bothered many cosmologists during the 1970s. The most important of these problems were:

*Reprinted from *New Scientist*, Vol. 105, No. 1446, 7 March 1985, pp. 14–18, by permission of A. Linde.

The Singularity Problem

The state of infinite density and zero volume at time $t = 0$ is called a singularity. But one may wonder, what was there *before* the singularity —or, putting it another way, where did the singularity come from? What is the origin of the Universe? The standard model of cosmology in the 1960s and 1970s made no attempt to answer this question, but started out from a state of very high energy density a fraction of a second *after* the moment of creation.

The Flatness Problem

According to the general theory of relativity, developed by Albert Einstein seventy years ago, the geometry of our Universe may be different from the Euclidean geometry of flat space. The Universe may be open, in which case parallel lines diverge from one another, or it may be closed, in the way that the surface of a sphere is closed, so that parallel lines cross one another, like the meridian lines on a globe of the Earth. All the observational evidence is that our Universe is very close to being flat. Flatness is a special case among the family of possible geometries, dividing the open universes from the closed universes, so why is our Universe so flat?

The Homogeneity Problem and the Problem of Galaxies

Astronomical observations also show that our Universe is homogeneous on very large scales — matter is distributed evenly through the Universe. As well as being homogeneous, the Universe is also isotropic; on the large scale, it looks the same in all directions. The size of the observable Universe is about 10^{28} cm. On this scale, the deviations of the density of matter from a perfectly smooth distribution amount to no more than one part in 10,000.

But on smaller scales, the Universe is not homogeneous. It contains galaxies, made up of stars, and clusters of galaxies. What small disturbances in the early history of the Universe could have produced these minor inhomogeneities in an otherwise very smooth Universe?

The Problem of the Dimensionality of Spacetime

There is a great deal of interest among mathematicians today in the possibility that space may have more than three dimensions. Paul Davies discussed some of these ideas recently in *New Scientist* ("The eleven dimensions of reality", 9 February 1984, p. 31). In the most interesting of these models, space has ten dimensions (the 11th is for time), all but three of which have been "compactified", shrunk into thin tubes. But why should the compactification have stopped with three effective space dimensions, not two, or five, or some other number?

All these problems (and some others, which I shall not go into here) seemed, for a long time, more metaphysical than physical, puzzles for philosophers, not scientists, to debate. Most physicists did not take the problems seriously, accepting that science might never find ultimate answers to such questions, or at least not for a very long time. If the standard model of cosmology could explain 15 billion years of cosmic evolution, there was no great concern that the theory could not explain what happened during the first millisecond. But in recent years, the attitude of physicists towards these metaphysical problems has changed radically. This shift in attitude began when physicists studying the interactions of the elementary particles began to develop theories of the way particles interact under conditions of very high energy density, like those in the big bang.

The beginning of the 1970s saw revolutionary developments in particle physics. Physicists proposed unified theories incorporating the weak and strong nuclear forces, and electromagnetism, within one mathematical framework (grand unified theories, or GUTs, see *New Scientist*, 17 May 1984, p. 14). More recently some theorists have suggested how to include gravity in the equations, to construct a unified theory of *all* the forces of nature. Each of these interactions is described in terms of a field.

The concept of a field was introduced into physics by Michael Faraday and developed by James Clerk Maxwell to explain (or at least to model) the behaviour of electric forces. If two balls are joined by a stretched spring, then there is a force which tends to pull the balls together. The balls feel a force because they are in contact with the spring. In the same way, Faraday argued that an electrically charged object is surrounded by an invisible electric "field". When another charged object is brought nearby, it feels a force because there is a change in the field, equivalent to the stretching or compression of the spring. Instead of thinking of the electric force jumping across from one charged particle to another, each charged particle feels a force because it is in contact with the field, and the field itself is distorted by the presence of charged particles. The idea has since been extended to all the other forces of nature.

An important feature of the unified theories is that they include another kind of field alongside the familiar four fields mentioned above. These "new" fields are called scalar fields, and have some interesting and unusual properties. The electric field is a vector field, and can be thought of as having both a magnitude and a direction at every point in space. A scalar field has only magnitude, and you might think of a property such as the temperature, or density, of a liquid as being represented by a scalar field, a number associated with each point through the volume of the fluid. A uniform homogeneous scalar field of the kind which comes in to the unified theories of physics is almost unobservable; it looks the same to a moving observer as it does to an observer at rest in the field, and mimics the appearance of empty space. This is quite different from the electric field, for example, which feels very different for a moving charged particle than it does for a particle which is stationary compared with the source of the field. But such a uniform scalar field, filling the whole Universe, has an effect on the properties of all the elementary particles. It helps to determine their masses, and the way in which they interact with other particles. And this is why the scalar fields are so useful in constructing unified theories.

Breaking the Forces of Nature Apart

Without any scalar field, there is no difference between, say, the weak nuclear force and electromagnetism. But when an appropriate scalar field fills the Universe, it has the effect of breaking the symmetry between these two forces, making them go their separate ways. In the modern unified theories, there are many scalar fields, each one responsible for breaking one of the original symmetries of this kind. At a state of very high energy (such as the moment of creation) the scalar fields play no part and the forces are unified; but as the energy density falls (as the Universe expands and cools) each scalar field "switches on" in turn.

Each field has a state of minimum potential energy, and each will tend to "roll" down into that state as soon as the temperature (or energy density) of the Universe falls far enough. An often-used analogy is with a marble rolled in to a large hemispherical bowl. The marble settles at the bottom of the bowl, the state of minimum gravitational potential energy, in the same way that the scalar field settles into a state of minimum energy. But the value of that state of minimum energy depends on the temperature of the Universe. My colleague David Kirzhnits pointed out in 1972 that when the temperature of the Universe was very high, the minimum energy state of the scalar field corresponded to zero energy, which is why there was at that time no distinction between the forces of nature. It is only as the Universe cooled that scalar fields with non-zero energy appeared and caused the symmetry breaking. The change from a symmetric state to a state of broken symmetry is a phase transition, and the best analogy to make is with the change that occurs when a liquid crystallises.

A liquid is very homogeneous and isotropic. It has so much thermal energy that molecules cannot stick together. To a physicist, it is very symmetric — whichever way you look at it, it looks the same. But when the liquid cools and begins to crystallise, different regions of the liquid may begin to crystallise with different orientations for their growing crystal lattices. When the different growing crystal lattices meet one another, they join together as best they can, but inevitably produce boundaries, called defects. Within each domain, there is a preferred orientation of the crystal lattice; but adjacent domains, separated by a defect, may have very different orientations. The overall symmetry has been destroyed. (It is perhaps worth noting that the physicist's idea of symmetry is not like the conception in everyday life. In everyday terminology, a crystal is thought of as showing symmetry, because it has a regular shape; but to the physicist this is a limited symmetry, because there are preferred directions in the crystal. A liquid, which looks the same in all directions, is the physicist's idea of perfect symmetry, because you can make a mirror image of any part of the liquid, in any orientation, and get an image that is a replica of the original.)

During the phase transitions of the cooling early Universe, something similar to the crystallisation of a liquid may have happened. In many theories of the interactions of elementary particles the potential energy of a scalar field has many minima of roughly equal depth, but corresponding to different values of the field. If such theories are correct, the scalar field could have settled into any of these minima when the Universe cooled. Like the growing crystals in a cooling liquid, it is most likely that different regions of the Universe would have settled into different minima, producing domains with different laws of physics from one another, separated by domain walls, sheets with very large surface energy. If a domain wall existed in the observable part of the Universe, it would show up very clearly as a region of extreme anisotropy. But no such region is visible.

The grand unified theories pose more problems. According to them, there should be another kind of defect in the Universe. This is like a mathematical point with very large mass (about 10^{16} times the mass of a proton) and carrying magnetic polarity — a magnetic monopole. Several researchers showed, in the late 1970s, that these theories would have catastrophic consequences for cosmology. They predict a profusion of magnetic monopoles, in flat contradiction with observations. The predicted monopoles would effectively speed up the evolution of the Universe and destroy the agreement between observations and the standard model. At the end of the 1970s, therefore, there were clear indications that the new theories of elementary particles and the standard model of the hot big bang were incompatible. The problems have been largely resolved by changing the cosmology, in the context of the inflationary Universe scenario.

The essence of the inflationary hypothesis is that we live in a single domain of the Universe, a region corresponding to one crystal domain, which has expanded so much ("inflated") that the domain walls are far beyond the range of our telescopes. The few monopoles present in the original small volume of the Universe that has been blown up to the scale of 10^{28} cm cannot play a significant role in the evolution of our local bubble of spacetime, so the concept removes the monopole problem too. But how and why did the Universe as we know it inflate in this way?

Alan Guth, of MIT, suggested the first version of the inflationary Universe in July 1980. His scenario was based on the idea of high-temperature phase transitions, which provided the energy for a rapid burst of expansion early in the life of the Universe. Like water giving up its latent heat of fusion as it freezes, those phase transitions, Guth suggested, might give up energy which went to make the Universe expand exponentially for a short time. But as Guth himself pointed out at the time, this early version of inflation predicted an extremely inhomogeneous state for the Universe after the phase transition.

In October 1981, I put forward an improved version of the inflation idea, which, for obvious reasons, became known as the "new inflationary scenario". This resolved some of the difficulties in Guth's original version. Andreas Albrecht and Paul Steinhardt, of the University of Pennsylvania, came up with similar ideas, independently of my work, in January 1982. The new inflationary scenario caused a stir among cosmologists and physicists, and was very widely discussed; Guth and Steinhardt have reviewed it in *Scientific American*, Vol. 250, No. 5, p. 90. New inflation resolved many of the large discrepancies between the predictions of field theory and the observations of the real Universe, and suggested that we were on the right track towards an understanding of the birth of the Universe. But even this variation on the theme proved impossible to reconcile completely with the most realistic theories of elementary particles yet developed. In 1983, however, I was able to resolve most of those remaining difficulties with another variation on the inflationary theme, called chaotic inflation. This abandons the idea that high-temperature phase transitions provided the push behind the inflation in the very early Universe. In my opinion, this scenario is much simpler and more natural than other versions of the inflationary Universe, and so I shall concentrate on chaotic inflation in the rest of this article (details can be found in my paper in *Reports on Progress in Physics*, Vol. 47, p. 925).

Order Out Of Chaos

According to the unified theories of particle physics, the Universe is filled with many types of uniform, homogeneous scalar field. The nature of each field is determined by the position of a minimum in its potential energy function, the field rolling down to this minimum as the Universe cooled. But at very early stages of the evolution of the Universe, when none of the fields had yet had time to roll down into its minimum state, each field could be inhomogeneous and have a different value in different parts of the Universe. In that split second after the moment of creation, there had not been enough time for the field to become homogeneous. This is what I refer to as a "chaotic" distribution of the field, and it has interesting and unexpected consequences.

If the field in one region is initially almost homogeneous and is far from its equilibrium state (that is, it has a large potential energy) then it "rolls down" into the minimum very slowly: in other words, the field's potential energy itself changes very slowly. But as the Universe expands, the energy density of all the everyday particles in the Universe decreases very rapidly. So the total energy density of the cooling Universe quickly becomes equal to the slowly changing potential energy of the scalar field.

According to the general theory of relativity, the rate at which the Universe expands depends on the energy density of the matter that fills the Universe. *If* the energy density is constant (or changes only very slowly) then the equations tell us that the Universe must expand with ever increasing speed, exponentially. Once the energy density of ordinary matter in a region of the expanding Universe has fallen below the energy density of the scalar field in that region, for as long as the scalar field is slowly rolling down to its minimum value this effect operates.

This period of inflation is longer if the field started out further away from its minimum value, because then it takes longer to roll down to the minimum. The simplest theories of the scalar field suggest that during the exponential expansion the size of the Universe was blown up by a factor of $10^{1,000,000}$, and that the largest domain must have grown from the region originally filled with the field that was in a state furthest *away* from its equilibrium value.

When the field rolls down to its minimum value, it oscillates to and fro about the minimum (just like the marble in the mixing bowl). Energy from the oscillating field is converted into elementary particles. By the time the oscillation has damped itself out, the Universe (or a particular domain) has been filled with hot particles, and the subsequent evolution of that domain can be described entirely adequately by the standard model of the hot big bang. The only difference is that there was a phase of exponential expansion, inflating a tiny seed of the Universe by a factor of $10^{1,000,000}$, *before* the outburst from the hot big bang itself. But this small difference leads to very important consequences.

Suppose, for example, that the exponentially expanding domain started out very curved. After expanding $10^{1,000,000}$ times, however, the geometry of space inside such a domain scarcely differs from the Euclidean geometry of flat space, just as the surface of a balloon expanded by a similar amount would look very much like the surface of a flat plane. Similarly, any irregularities are smoothed away by the expansion (inflation) so that the domain becomes very homogeneous and isotropic. Imagine how flat and smooth even the Himalayas would seem if the radius of the Earth grew to $10^{1,000,000}$ times its present size.

If anything, the homogeneity problem is now turned on its head. The puzzle is how galaxies form at all. But it seems that, during the inflation, quantum fluctuations of the field grow in just the right way to produce the relatively small inhomogeneities that we call galaxies.

Like all inflationary scenarios, chaotic inflation removes the monopole problem. No new monopoles are created after the inflation, so any that originally existed are separated from one another by an amount in proportion to the magnitude of the exponential increase in the size of the Universe. The interior of each domain looks like a mini-universe with a typical size much greater than the distance we can see, 10^{28} cm, and for all practical purposes our domain *is* the Universe. But according to this scenario, there are many such mini-universes, separated from each other by domain walls, in which the scalar fields take different values, and in which, therefore, different laws of physics operate. We live in a domain in which the interactions just happen to have been broken into the strong and weak forces and electromagnetism. This has clearly influenced the development of life, as well as the evolution of the Universe as we know it, and life of our type may be impossible in other domains with different laws of physics.

The division of the Universe into many mini-universes also makes it possible to suggest an answer to the question of why our space is three-dimensional. The process of compactification (shrinking and rolling up of some of the original dimensions) may occur differently in domains that are far enough apart from one another. And, once again, life as we know it may only exist in those domains which are three-dimensional. The physicist Paul Ehrenfest pointed out, as long ago as 1917, that the three-dimensionality of space is intimately connected with the way matter behaves.

Both gravitational and electromagnetic forces obey inverse square laws in our Universe and, by generalising the equations that describe these interactions and solving them in other dimensions, mathematicians have shown that in space with n dimensions the result is always an $n-1$ power law. In four dimensions, the laws would both be inverse cubes and, it turns out, there would be no stable orbits for either planets in solar systems or electrons in atoms. The same is true for all higher dimensions. In a two-dimensional Universe, things are no better, because $n-1$ is 1, and neither gravity nor electromagnetism is affected by distance at all. So atoms and planetary systems may only exist together in a domain with three dimensions of space, like our domain of the Universe.

So the chaotic inflation scenario provides a simple solution to most of the problems with the standard big bang model. The one thing I have not yet discussed, of course, is the first and most important of these problems, the singularity problem. A final solution to this problem will be possible only after the development of a complete quantum theory of gravity, but we already have enough of an idea as to how such a theory must develop to sketch the outlines of a description of the moment of creation (see Stephen Hawking's article "The edge of time", *New Scientist*, 16 August 1984, p. 10).

Effects connected with the quantisation of gravity become important at length scales smaller than the Planck length, 10^{-33} cm, and at densities greater than 10^{94} g/cubic cm. The standard big bang model tells us that this density was reached at a time when the size of the Universe was 10^{-4} cm, about 10^{29} times the Planck length. (This is another expression of the flatness problem: why was our Universe so large at this critical density, when the only typical length scales were around the Planck length, much, much less than the size of the Universe?)

In the various inflationary scenarios, the entire observable Universe, some 10^{28} cm across, originated from a region of the size of the Planck length, 10^{-33} cm. So it could have been created from a quantum fluctuation, in accordance with the uncertainty principle. Edward Tryon discussed this idea in *New Scientist* a year ago (8 March 1984, p. 14). The most important point about this possibility is that if our Universe was created by a quantum fluctuation, then it cannot be infinitely large; at the moment of creation the Universe must contain a finite amount of energy, it must be closed (in the same sense that the surface of a sphere is a closed surface), and it must be smaller than 10^{-33} cm across. After aeons of expansion, our domain (and all the others with it) must eventually collapse back into a singularity under the pull of gravity, and disappear once again into the nothing that existed "before" the moment of creation.

The inflationary universe scenario is now only five years old, and is still rapidly changing and developing as new ideas come to the fore. We do not know which parts of the scenario will survive even for the next five years. But already it has proved able to solve about ten major cosmological problems in one simple model. Ideas which would have sounded like fantastic science fiction only a decade ago, such as the creation of all the matter in the observable Universe (10^{50} tons) by gravitational forces operating inside a domain which originally contained less than 10^{-5} g of matter and was less than 10^{-33} cm across, now seem to be necessary ingredients in any complete theory of the Universe.

And how long did all that activity take? I have saved the most startling fact until last. The phase of exponential inflation that is critical to our modern understanding of the Universe probably lasted for less than 10^{-30} seconds.

20

ROBERT SHAPIRO AND GERALD FEINBERG*

Possible Forms of Life in Environments Very Different from the Earth

Introduction

WE CAN MAKE only a brief presentation here of our ideas on the extent of life in the Universe. A much more detailed account is given in our book, *Life Beyond Earth: The Intelligent Earthling's Guide to Life in the Universe.*[1]

In discussions concerning intelligent life elsewhere, the assumption is often made that such life will develop only in circumstances resembling those on Earth. Estimates are then given of the number of Earth-like planets in our galaxy, as suitable locations in which life might arise. Such estimates may vary, according to the pessimism or optimism of the observer, from the very few[2] to a billion or more.[3] Only those planets are considered habitable which fall into a limited zone around each star. In that zone, liquid water can be present on the surface, and carbon compounds will be abundant. If this view were correct, even in the most optimistic form, then life would be a rare phenomenon, confined to only an insignificant fraction of the material in the Universe. From an extreme pessimists' viewpoint, as expressed elsewhere in this conference, life may have originated only on the planet Earth. The idea of the specialness of the Earth is of course an old one, and has been expressed many times in theology.

We represent a very different point of view: that the generation of

*This article appeared as Chapter 13 of *Extraterrestrials: Where Are They?*, edited by Michael M. Hart and Ben Zuckerman, Pergamon Press, New York, 1982. Copyright © 1982 Pergamon Press: reprinted by permission.

life is an innate property of matter. It can take place in a wide variety of environments very different from the Earth. The life forms that evolve will also be very different from those familiar to us, in harmony with the conditions present there.

Because the point of view opposite to our own is widespread, we think it is important to summarize the reasons presented for it. The most obvious one is the basic unity of Earthlife, the only type of life we have encountered. All living things that we are aware of use the same basic set of chemicals to organize their metabolism, with vital roles for proteins and nucleic acids. A person in a Chinese village might similarly be convinced that only the Chinese language existed, as it was the only one spoken by all the people he knew. In fact, no firm conclusion can be drawn at all from cases where only a single example of a phenomenon is at hand, and a good strategy would be to search for additional examples.

Other arguments have been made on the basis of scientific principles, and we have found that their adherents could be grouped into two categories, which we have called "predestinist" and "carbaquist."

The Predestinists

The predestinists hold that the limited set of chemicals that characterize our biochemistry will be the inevitable result of random chemical synthesis, throughout the universe. We can express this in direct quotes: "The implications of these results is that organic syntheses in the Universe have a direction that favors the production of amino acids, purines, pyrimidines and sugars: the building blocks of proteins and nucleic acids. Taken in conjunction with the cosmic abundance of the light elements, this suggests that life everywhere will be based not only on carbon chemistry, but on carbon chemistry similar to (although not necessarily identical with) our own."[4] "The essential building blocks of life — amino acids, nitrogen-bearing heterocycle compounds and polysaccharides — are formed in space. These compounds occur in large quantities throughout the galaxy."[5]

These concepts are imaginative but unfortunately not supported by the facts. The presence of organic compounds in interstellar dust clouds has been demonstrated by spectroscopy.[6] However, the molecules that have been identified definitely are small in size, and do not include those considered to be the essential building blocks of Earthlife. Meteorite analyses provide another source of information about extraterrestrial organic chemistry.[7] Amino acids are present there, but as part of a complex mixture containing many compounds irrelevant to our biochemistry. There is no preference for the synthesis of compounds important to Earthlife. Finally, we can consider prebiotic simulation experiments of the kind initiated by Stanley Miller and Harold

Urey.[8] Good yields of amino acids have frequently been obtained. Although there is considerable doubt that the conditions used do represent those of the early Earth,[9] such experiments do demonstrate that the preparation of amino acids from very simple compounds is feasible. They do not, however, show that the result is inevitable. In fact, the very first effort by Stanley Miller was unsuccessful: "the next morning there was a thin layer of hydrocarbon on the surface of the water, and after several days, the hydrocarbon layer was somewhat thicker."[10] No amino acids were detected at all.

The course of organic synthesis in the universe may on some occasions turn in the direction of the chemicals of Earthlife, but it is clear that it can take other directions as well. We are not the inevitable predestined endpoint of cosmic evolution.

The Carbaquists

A somewhat different point of view is taken by the carbaquists. They feel that life elsewhere in the universe must resemble that present on Earth, because no other basis for life can exist. Our own chemical system, particularly in its use of water, as a solvent, and carbon, as the key building block of large molecules, is uniquely fit for the purpose of sustaining life. The notion of the fitness of our environment was advocated early in this century by the American chemist Lawrence Henderson,[11] and has had a number of advocates more recently. Again, we will quote them directly.

> I have become convinced that life everywhere must be based primarily upon carbon, hydrogen, nitrogen and oxygen, upon an organic chemistry therefore much as on the Earth, and that it can arise only in an environment rich in water.[12]

> . . . so I tell my students: learn your biochemistry here and you will be able to pass examinations on Arcturus.[13]

> The capacity for generating, storing, replicating and utilizing large amounts of information implies an underlying molecular complexity that is known only among compounds of carbon.[4]

Water *does* have certain special properties as a solvent. One is the greater amount of heat that is needed to melt, warm up, or boil a quantity of water, as compared to the heat needed for most other solvents. Bodies of water thus tend to stabilize the climate of their environment. This property may be pleasant, but it is hardly essential to life. Other physical features could work to stabilize a climate. Alternatively, living beings could adapt by many strategies, such as spore formation or migration, to changes in temperature.

Another property of water that is greatly admired by the carbaquists is its polar character. Water is a good solvent for charged substances, and an appropriate medium for the conduct of transformations of such substances. However, an enormous number of reactions have been described by chemists which take place in less polar, or nonpolar solvents. The absence of water is in some cases essential to the course of the reaction. There is no reason why such reactions could not be the basis of a metabolic scheme to sustain life.

The special properties of carbon include its ability to bond to itself in long chains, and to form bonds to four other atoms at one time. An enormous number of compounds containing carbon can therefore exist. It is not necessary for an atom to bond to itself to form long chains, however; the chains could be made of two or more atoms in alternation. Furthermore, it is conceivable that a basis for life could be constructed using an alternative chemistry in which the possibilities were not as vast as those of carbon. The situation can be compared with the problem of information storage in printed form. The English language uses twenty-six capital letters, twenty-six small letters, space, and a number of punctuation marks to do this: about sixty characters in all. The same amount of information can be stored by a computer, using only the two symbols 1 and 0. Six lines must be used to hold the contents of one English line, but the data is stored just the same. In the same way, a less complex chemistry could serve as the genetic basis for life, perhaps with a larger number of components needed in each molecule, cell or other unit.

The carbaquist viewpoint cannot be made convincing by the type of reasoning its adherents have presented, but it also cannot be refuted strictly on the basis of reason and analogy. We can best proceed by searching for alternate life forms. The discovery of one, with a different physical or chemical basis, would quickly settle the issue. Failure to do so, after a number of extraterrestrial life forms had been encountered, would move us toward acceptance of the carbaquist argument.

A Definition, and Some Conditions

In seeking a broader view of the possibilities of life in the universe than that put forward by the carbaquists and predestinists, we have started by framing a definition of life that is independent of the local characteristics of Earthlife:

Life is the activity of a biosphere. A biosphere is a highly ordered system of matter and energy characterized by complex cycles that maintain or gradually increase the order of the system through an exchange of energy with its environment.

An important feature in our definition is the identification of the biosphere as the unit of life. The history of life on Earth then becomes the tale of the continuous survival and evolution of the biosphere from its origin on the prebiotic Earth. Replication, and subdivision into organisms and species have been strategies adopted by our own biosphere to ensure its own survival but they need not be the methods used by an extraterrestrial biosphere.

The association of life with increasing order, and the emphasis on the need of a flow of energy to sustain this, are related to the ideas of the physicists Erwin Schrödinger[14] and Harold Morowitz.[15] Our biosphere has a number of easily recognizable forms of order, all in a very high degree. It contains very large numbers of a few thousand small organic molecules and none (or very few) of millions of other molecules. The presence of only a few distinct types of large molecules in living things is a second type of order. An additional dramatic type is the near identity of the base sequences in the DNA in different cells in a multi-celled organism. If comparable amounts of order (though perhaps of a very different type) were to be found in an extraterrestrial environment, this would be a strong sign of the presence of life.

With the definition in hand, we can now make a list of several conditions that must be met if life is to originate and develop in a particular location.

1. A flow of free energy: Any of a number of different types could suffice, such as light energy and chemical energy, as on Earth, but also other forms of electromagnetic radiation, such as infrared light and X-rays. Other forms of energy such as streams of charged particles, heat differentials, and nuclear energy could also be used.

2. A system of matter capable of interacting with the energy and using it to become ordered: The nucleic acids and proteins of Earth need not be the basis of this order. In fact, it needn't depend on chemical reactions at all but could be based on physical processes such as the movement of particles, or molecular rotations. However, some systems will be superior to others. A liquid or a dense gas is preferable to a solid for the conduct of reactions. Helium is a poor choice as the base for the development of an ordered system based on a multiplicity of chemical compounds.

3. Enough time to build up the complexity that we associate with life: This is a critical question that determines the scope of life in the Universe. The rate of a process, such as the chemical reactions between molecules widely scattered in outer space, may be so slow that the entire lifetime of the Universe to date has been insufficient for appreciable order to develop. In another case, a drastic change in an environment, for example, the conversion of a star to a supernova,

could destroy the base upon which order has been accumulating.

Alternative Bases for Chemical Life

With the requirements in mind, we have tried to generate some speculative suggestions for life forms that would function on a chemical basis different from that on Earth.

1. Life in ammonia: Liquid ammonia, perhaps with some water, would serve as the solvent. This could occur on a planet with temperatures near $-50°C$. Weaker chemical bonds, such as nitrogen, would predominate in metabolism.

2. Life in hydrocarbons: A mixture of hydrocarbons would function as the solvent. A wide range of temperatures could be accommodated, depending on the composition of the mixture. Processes involving charged species would play only a small role. Reductive reactions, such as hydrogenation, could be used as an energy source.

3. Silicate life: Silicates exhibit a rich chemistry with a propensity for forming chains, rings and sheets, as in minerals on Earth. At a temperature above $1000°$, the medium would become liquid, and could serve as a basis for evolving chemical order. This process could occur on a planet quite close to its sun, or in the molten interior of a planet, such as Earth.

Alternative Chemical Life Within Our Solar System

Locations within our own solar system offer the best opportunities for the detection of alternative life forms in the immediate future. Some of the more promising possibilities are listed below:

1. Earth: in interior magma, or within specialized niches on the surface.

2. Mars: if life is present, it is probably based on carbon and water.

3. Jupiter: many possibilities exist in varied environments.

4. Ganymede, Callisto: life within water oceans beneath the crust.

5. Io, Venus: life in liquid sulfur.

6. Titan: ammonia or hydrocarbon based life.

Physical Life

As we suggested earlier, many physical processes may serve for the
storage and increase of order. We have called such systems "physical
life," and list some speculative possibilities below.

1. Plasma life within stars: Such life would be based upon the
   reciprocal influence of patterns of magnetic force and the
   ordered motion of charged particles. It could exist within
   our own Sun. Individual creatures are called "plasmobes."

2. Life in solid hydrogen: This could occur on a planet with a
   temperature of only a few degrees Kelvin. Infrared energy
   would be absorbed and stored in the special arrangement of
   ortho- and parahydrogen molecules.

3. Radiant life: Life would be based upon the ordered patterns
   of radiation emitted by isolated atoms and molecules in a
   dense interstellar cloud. Individual beings, called "ra-
   diobes" could exist.

It may be difficult to think of such systems as being alive, with the
capability in some cases of developing organisms, complex ecologies
and even civilization. We must remember that the association of a
protein with a nucleic acid, when viewed abstractly, also does little to
convey the wonders, such as elephants and Sequoia trees, that ultimately arise from it.

Conclusions

Our examples have not been presented in order to make specific
predictions, but rather to suggest the vast variety of forms that life
elsewhere may take. If we were gifted with a vision of the whole
Universe of life, we would not see it as a desert, sparsely populated
with identical plants which can survive only in rare specialized niches,
but rather as a botanical garden with countless species, each thriving in
its own setting. This garden awaits our exploration.

NOTES

1. Feinberg, G., and Shapiro, R. (1980). *Life Beyond Earth. The Intelligent
   Earthling's Guide to Life in the Universe*, William Morrow Co., New York.
2. Hart, M. H. (1979). *Icarus* 37, 351.
3. von Hoerner, S. (1978). *Die Naturwissenschaften* 65, 553.
4. Horowitz, N. H. (1976). *Accounts of Chem. Research* 9, 1.
5. Hoyle, F., and Wickramasinghe (1977). *New Scientist* (Nov. 17), 174.
6. Gammon, R. H. (1978). *Chemical and Engineering News* (Oct. 2), 21.
7. Lawless, J. G., Folsome, E. E., and Kwenvold, K. A. (1972). *Scientific
   American* 226, 38

8. Miller, S. L. and Urey, H. C. (1959). *Science* **130**, 245.
9. Kerr, R. A. (1980). *Science* **210**, 42.
10. Miller, S. L. (1974). In *The Heritage of Copernicus: Theories Pleasing to the Mind* (editor: J. Neyman), MIT Press, Cambridge, MA, 228.
11. Henderson, L. J. (1913). *The Fitness of the Environment*, Macmillan Co., New York.
12. Wald, G. (1974). In *Cosmochemical Evolution and the Origins of Life*, (editors: J. Oro *et al*.) Vol. I, D. Reidel, Dordrecht, Holland, 7.
13. Wald, G. (1973). In *Life Beyond Earth and the Mind of Man*, (editor: R. Berendzen) NASA Scientific and Technical Information Office, Washington, D.C., 15.
14. Schrödinger, E. (1956). *What is Life?*, Anchor Books, New York.
15. Morowitz, H. (1968). *Energy Flow in Biology*, Academic Press, New York.

21

MICHAEL H. HART*

Atmospheric Evolution, the Drake Equation, and DNA: Sparse Life in an Infinite Universe

I. *Atmospheric Evolution*

DURING THE FOUR and a half billion years of geologic time, the atmosphere of the Earth has changed markedly. Of the many processes which have played a role in that evolution, the most important are listed below.

IMPORTANT PROCESSES IN ATMOSPHERIC EVOLUTION

1. Degassing of volatiles from interior

2. Condensation of water vapor into oceans

3. Solution of CO_2 and NH_3 in seawater

4. Fixing of CO_2 in carbonate minerals (Urey reaction)

5. Photodissociation of water vapor

6. Escape of hydrogen into space

7. Development of life and variations in the biomass

8. Net photosynthesis and burial of organic sediments

9. Chemical reactions between atmospheric gases

*This article appeared as Chapter 17 of *Extraterrestrials: Where Are They?*, edited by Michael H. Hart and Ben Zuckerman, Pergamon Press, New York, 1982. Copyright © 1982 Pergamon Press: reprinted by permission.

10. Oxidation of surface minerals

11. Changes in solar luminosity

12. Changes in albedo (cloud cover, ice cover, etc.)

13. The greenhouse effect

There are good reasons (Brown, 1952) to believe that at some early stage the Earth had almost no atmosphere, having lost whatever gaseous envelope, if any, that it started with. Our present atmosphere is derived from materials degassed from the interior of the Earth; perhaps largely from volcanoes, but also from fumaroles, and by a slow seepage through the crust.

Among the gases released was water vapor, most of which eventually condensed to form the oceans. The history of the other gases is highly complex. Some molecules were broken apart in the upper atmosphere by the action of sunlight. The lightest gases (hydrogen, helium) were able to escape into outer space (Spitzer, 1952). Other gases, such as carbon dioxide, are highly soluble in seawater and were able to react chemically with minerals dissolved in the oceans (Urey, 1951, 1952).

The origin of life, and subsequent biochemical processes (such as photosynthesis) have powerfully affected the composition of the atmosphere, as have various inorganic reactions such as the oxidation of surface minerals. Meanwhile, there have been marked changes in the Earth's surface temperature, caused in part by variations in the sun's luminosity, by variations in the Earth's reflectivity or albedo, and by the greenhouse effect.

In principle, if one knew the exact rate at which all these processes occurred, one could trace on a high-speed computer the entire evolution of the Earth's atmosphere over the past four and a half billion years. In an earlier paper (Hart, 1978), I have described in some detail the formulas which were used and the approximations which were made in constructing such a computer simulation. In view of the various approximations and uncertainties involved, one cannot expect the results of such a computer simulation to be reliable in every detail; but they are consistent with the available observational data, and they probably indicate the general pattern of our atmosphere's evolution fairly well.

According to the computer simulation, the Earth was probably a good deal warmer during the first 2.5 billion years of geologic time than it is today. It cooled down to about its present temperature roughly 2 billion years ago, when free oxygen first appeared in the atmosphere, and when various other gases capable of causing a large greenhouse effect were largely eliminated by oxidation.

Since the early Earth seems to have been quite warm, it is natural to wonder how much hotter it might have been if the Earth were situated somewhat closer to the Sun. It is fairly easy to modify the computer program so as to simulate the effect of a smaller Earth–Sun distance. The results are quite striking: If the Earth's orbit were only 5 percent smaller than it actually is, during the early stages of Earth's history there would have been a "runaway greenhouse effect", and temperatures would have gone up until the oceans boiled away entirely!

This result was not entirely unexpected. A similar conclusion (although based on a less detailed model) had been reached previously by Rasool and de Bergh (1970); and it is widely believed that a runaway greenhouse effect actually occurred on Venus, which is 28 percent closer to the Sun than the Earth is. More surprising, perhaps, were the results of computer runs which simulated the effect of a somewhat larger Earth-Sun distance. Those runs indicate that if the Earth-Sun distance were as little as one percent larger, there would have been runaway glaciation on Earth about 2 billion years ago. The Earth's oceans would have frozen over entirely, and would have remained so ever since, with a mean global temperature of less than $-50°F$. (Similar conclusions, although derived from quite different models, were reached earlier by Budyko [1969] and by Sellers [1969].) Taken together, these computer runs indicate that the habitable zone about our sun is not wide, as Huang (1959, 1960) had suggested, but is instead quite narrow.

What about the habitable zones about other stars? How large are they? Here too, it is possible to modify the original computer program to simulate the effect of the more intense radiation from a larger star, or the weaker radiation from a smaller one. The modifications needed are a bit tricky, since large stars evolve more rapidly than small stars, and their relative luminosities change with time. But the required modifications can be made, and again the results are quite striking. The computer simulations (Hart, 1979) indicate that a star whose mass, M_{star}, is less than $0.83\ M_{sun}$ will have no zone about it which is continuously habitable. If a planet is far enough from such a star to avoid a runaway greenhouse effect in its early years, it will inevitably undergo runaway glaciation somewhat later in its history. Nor, according to the computer results, does a star heavier than 1.2 solar masses have any continuously habitable zone about it.

Similar calculations indicate that the size of the planet itself has a profound effect on the evolution of its atmosphere. Unless a planet has a mass within the range $0.85\ M_{earth} < M_{planet} < 1.33 M_{earth}$ it cannot — regardless of its distance from the Sun — maintain moderate surface conditions for more than 2 billion years.

II. Calculation of N, Using a Modified Drake Equation

The galaxy we are in, the Milky Way Galaxy, contains upwards of 100 billion stars, many of which appear to be quite similar to our Sun, and many of which may have planets orbiting about them. Within range of our large telescopes there are at least 10^9 other galaxies — possibly 10^{11} or more — together totaling at least 10^{20} stars.

In view of this enormous number of stars, it is quite natural to ask two questions: Of this vast multitude of stars, how many have planets near them which are suitable for the evolution of life? And on how many of those planets has life actually arisen? More intriguing still — since we are naturally more interested in *intelligent* life — are the questions: How many advanced civilizations can we expect to exist in the Milky Way Galaxy? How many can we expect in the entire universe?

To estimate N, the expected number of advanced civilizations in a typical galaxy the size of the Milky Way, many writers use as a starting point some version or modification of the well-known Drake equation. The version which I shall use is:

$$N = N_{gal} \cdot f_{popI} \cdot f_{PMR} \cdot f_{PS} \cdot f_{HP} \cdot f_{life} \cdot f_{intel} \cdot f_{tech} \qquad (1)$$

In this equation, N_{gal} denotes the total number of stars in the galaxy; f_{popI} represents the fraction of those which are population type I stars; f_{PMR} denotes the fraction of population type I stars which are within the "proper" mass range (i.e., stars which are neither too large nor too small to have continuously habitable zones about them); f_{PS} represents the fraction of such stars which have planetary systems; f_{HP} denotes the fraction of planetary systems which include a habitable planet (i.e., a planet whose size, composition, and distance from its sun make it suitable for the development of life); f_{life} represents the fraction of habitable planets upon which life actually arises; f_{intel} is the fraction of those planets on which intelligent life forms (i.e., $\gtrsim$ human intelligence) eventually evolve; and f_{tech} denotes the fraction of those which develop and sustain advanced technologies (avoiding destruction by nuclear war, plagues, ecological disasters, etc.)

N_{gal} is usually estimated to be about 2×10^{11}. Of those, about 50 percent should probably be excluded because the gases from which they condensed had too low an abundance of heavy elements for large, solid planets like the Earth to be formed. According to the calculations described in section I, the "proper" mass range is $0.83 \, M_{sun} < M_{star} < 1.2 \, M_{sun}$. Direct star counts in the solar neighborhood indicate that about 10 percent of stars fall within that range.

The value of f_P is still in doubt; suppose we estimate it to be about 10 percent. (As 50 percent or more of stars are members of double or multiple star systems, that can hardly be much of an underestimate. It might, though, be a serious overestimate — after all, as yet there is no reliable observation of a single planet outside our own solar system.)

If the fairly involved calculations described in section I are correct, only about one planetary system in a hundred (even if the central star is in the proper mass range) contains a habitable planet. That would make

$f_{\text{HP}} \sim 10^{-2}$. The value of f_{life} is extremely speculative; for the moment, let us defer trying to estimate it. However, if life ever does arise on a planet, the process of Darwinian evolution should frequently lead to advanced life forms, and f_{intel} may well be as high as 10 percent. For the final factor, f_{tech}, a guess of 50 percent might be in order.

Since the value of f_{life} is so speculative, we might combine all the other factors in equation (1) together, and write it as

$$N = N_{\text{combo}} \cdot f_{\text{life}}. \qquad (2)$$

If we combine the various numerical estimates given above, we obtain the result: $N_{\text{combo}} \sim 5 \times 10^5$. However, as all the factors which go into N_{combo} are highly uncertain, its true value could be very different. Some optimists have estimated N_{combo} to be as high as 10^9, or perhaps even a bit larger; while if very conservative estimates are used for the various factors, N_{combo} could be only 10^1, or even less.

Now if f_{life} has a very low value—for example, 10^{-15}—this uncertainty in N_{combo} is unimportant. For in that case, any plausible value of N_{combo} results in $N \ll 1$. However, if f_{life} has a moderate value—say 10^{-2}—then the uncertainty in N_{combo} renders the "Drake equation approach" virtually useless as a method of deciding whether advanced civilizations are frequent in a typical galaxy, or whether the majority of galaxies do not contain even a single civilization. Nor, given the highly speculative nature of factors such as f_{intel} or f_{tech}, can we expect to obtain a reliable estimate of N_{combo} within the foreseeable future. What method, then, could we use to estimate the value of N?

III. Our Failure to Observe Extraterrestrials

I would suggest that in that case the best way to approach the problem of estimating N would not be by examining the factors which *cause* N to have a certain value, but rather by taking an empirical approach and considering the various *effects* which we might expect to observe if N had a given value.

If, for example, there were 100,000 advanced civilizations scattered about the Milky Way Galaxy, what observable effects might we expect to see? Well, if there were really so many technologically advanced races in our galaxy, then surely at least *one* of them would have explored and colonized the galaxy, just as we humans have explored and colonized this planet. Various estimates (Hart, 1975; Jones, 1976; Papagiannis, 1978) indicate that no more than a few million years would be needed to colonize most of the galaxy. Since that is very much less than the age of our galaxy (≥ 10 years), if N were really as large as 100,000 then the solar system would have been colonized by extraterrestrials a long time ago, and we would see them here today.

But, of course, we do not see any extraterrestrials, either on Earth or anywhere else in the solar system. There is no indication that the solar system was ever visited by extraterrestrials; and, quite obviously, we have not been colonized. It can reasonably be concluded, therefore, that N is *not* equal to 100,000. The same argument, of course, would rule out any other large number. It would not, though, completely rule out the possibility that there were a *small* number of civilizations in our galaxy, none of which were interested in interstellar exploration and colonization (nor ever had been, in all the ages since they first acquired the technological capability).

N, therefore, is a small number, possibly a very small number; and our conclusion, since it has an empirical basis (i.e., the absence of extraterrestrials on Earth) cannot be upset by any unreliable calculations based on the Drake equation. Nevertheless, it would certainly be interesting to know just *how* low N is. I would like to suggest that a realistic calculation of f_{life} indicates that it is an extremely low number, and that N therefore is also extremely low.

IV. Calculation of f_{life}

Before attempting to compute f_{life}, we should perhaps first explain what we mean by the word "life." It is difficult to give an exact definition of this term (see Feinberg and Shapiro [1980] for an interesting and novel approach), but we might roughly say that a living organism is an object which feeds and reproduces. (An object "feeds" if it ingests and chemically transforms material in its environment into chemicals which it is itself composed of.)

The living organisms which we see on Earth are all composed of complex carbon compounds in an aqueous medium. A wide variety of such compounds are found in most organisms, but the two most significant types are: (a) the proteins, which are large, complex molecules consisting of long strings of simpler components called amino acids; and (b) the nucleic acids, which consist of long strings of simpler components called nucleotides. (The most important type of nucleic acid, DNA, contains 4 different nucleotides, each occurring many times in a single molecule of DNA.) The proteins perform a crucial role in catalysing essential biochemical reactions, while the nucleic acids perform an even more vital role of storing the hereditary information which allows organisms to reproduce, and by directing the synthesis of proteins. Nucleic acids are the primary genetic material, and they contain (in coded form) instructions for synthesizing the organism and its components. The code is based on the number of each of the 4 types of nucleotides in a given strand, and on the *order* in which those different nucleotides are arranged.

Now if there is life on other planets in the universe, it is perfectly possible that the organisms on such planets use quite different compounds to perform the tasks which in terrestrial organisms are carried out by the proteins and the nucleic acids. But since those tasks are so difficult, detailed and varied, the compounds carrying them out would of necessity have to be just about as large and as complex in structure as are the proteins and nucleic acid molecules which we find in terrestrial organisms.

How large, then, is f_{life}, which is defined as the probability that life will actually arise on a given planet which has a wholly suitable environment? We may safely assume that on such a planet the surface temperatures are suitably moderate, that liquid water is present in ample quantity, and that simple compounds of carbon, oxygen, hydrogen and nitrogen are abundant. Many experiments (see Miller and Orgel, 1974 for a partial list) have shown that a combination of such chemicals will, in the presence of electric discharges, react to produce a variety of more complex organic molecules, including amino acids. Under suitable conditions, short chains of amino acids have also been produced.

This is an encouraging start. However, in order to have living organisms, some sort of genetic material — such as DNA — must be present also. Experiments simulating primitive Earth conditions have not, to date, resulted in the formation of nucleotides; but simpler compounds related to them have been produced in such experiments, and it is not unduly optimistic to assume that nucleotide molecules too will naturally be formed on a suitable planet.

To induce those molecules to polymerize into nucleic acid strands (under the assumed primitive Earth conditions) is a bit of a problem, but not a hopeless one. It is, though, crucial for the proper functioning of the resulting nucleic acid molecule that the various nucleotides in the strand are arranged in the correct order. Two different nucleic acid strands, even if of exactly the same length, will not normally be biologically equivalent unless they contain the same nucleotide residues arranged in the same order.

The great majority of possible nucleic acid molecules are quite useless (or even harmful) biologically. Most of the others are useful only in an organism which already has many other genes. Let us suppose, however, that there exists a particular DNA molecule — "genesis DNA" — which if introduced into some primitive conglomeration of proteins, lipids, nucleotides, and their building blocks will both replicate properly and perform some useful biological function. In other words, we are supposing that the formation of a single molecule of genesis DNA and its introduction into a suitable environment will suffice to create a viable organism and to get the process of Darwinian evolution started.

To simplify our calculations, let me make a few more assumptions (admittedly, rather optimistic ones): (a) Under the conditions prevailing on a primitive Earth-like planet, not just amino acids but also nucleotides will be readily formed. (b) Those same conditions will favor the polymerization of nucleotides. (c) Uniform helicity of the resulting strands is thermodynamically favored. (d) A strand of genesis DNA is quite short, as genes go, containing only 600 nucleotide residues. (e) There exists some chemical effect which favors the formation of nucleic acid strands of that length. If these assumptions are valid, then a large number of strands of nucleic acid, each consisting of about 600 residues, will be formed spontaneously on any suitable planet. Let us calculate the probability that one of those strands will have its residues arranged in the right order; that is, in the same order as in genesis DNA.

There are only about 2×10^{44} nitrogen atoms near the surface of the Earth, or in its atmosphere. As a single 600-residue strand of nucleic acid includes more than 2000 nitrogen atoms, there could have been no more than about 10^{41} strands of DNA existing together on the primitive Earth at any given moment. If every such strand could split up and recombine with other fragments at a rate of 30 times a second, then in one year (roughly 3×10^7 seconds) a maximum of 10^{50} different strands could be formed, and in 10 billion years a maximum of 10^{60}. (This, obviously, is a strong maximum.)

The number of conceivable arrangements of the four different nucleotides into a strand of DNA 600 residues long is 4^{600}, which is about 10^{360}. The chance that a *particular* one of them would be formed spontaneously — even in 10 billion years — was therefore extremely small, 10^{-300}. However, the chance of forming genesis DNA is not necessarily that low. It has been demonstrated that at some positions in a strand of nucleic acid it is possible to replace one nucleotide residue by another without changing the biological effect of the strand. Let us suppose (very optimistically) that in a strand of genesis DNA there are no fewer than 400 positions where any one of the four nucleotide residues will do, and at each of 100 other positions either of two different nucleotides will be equally effective, leaving only 100 positions which must be filled by exactly the right nucleotides. This appears to be an unrealistically optimistic set of assumptions; but even so, the probability that an arbitrarily chosen strand of nucleic acid could function as genesis DNA is only one in 10^{90}. Even in 10 billion years, the chance of forming such a strand spontaneously would be only $10^{-90} \times 10^{60}$, or 10^{-30}.

There are several reasons why the true value of f_{life} is very much lower than 10^{-30}. In the first place, we have ignored all the difficulties involved in producing nucleotides abiotically, in concentrating them in a small region, of preventing their spontaneous destruction, and in getting them to polymerize in an aqueous environment.

In the second place, a DNA molecule cannot direct protein synthesis unless certain other complex organic molecules called transfer RNA are present; nor can it even replicate itself spontaneously in the absence of certain other organic catalysts (DNA polymerases). Unless these other compounds had already been formed (how?) and were in the immediate vicinity, even if a molecule of genesis DNA happened to be formed it would be unable to function. And in the third place, the assumption that there exists a gene—genesis DNA—which, without any other genes present, can produce a viable organism is highly optimistic. The simplest known organism which is capable of independent existence includes about 100 different genes. For each of 100 different specific genes to be formed spontaneously (in ten billion years) the probability is $(10^{-30})^{100} = 10^{-3,000}$. For them to be formed at the same time, and in close proximity, the probability is very much lower.

V. Probability and Selection

The conclusion reached above, that the probability of life arising on a given planet—no matter how favorable conditions on that planet might be—is less than one in 10^{30}, is perhaps somewhat surprising. If f_{life} is so low, you may ask, what are *we* doing here?

This leads to an interesting philosophical question: If we calculate the probability of an event occurring to be a very low number, and the event then occurs, does it show that our calculation is wrong? For example, a simple calculation shows that the probability of tossing an honest coin 40 times and getting 40 consecutive heads is $(\frac{1}{2})^{40}$, or about one in a trillion. Suppose, though, that you took a particular coin, flipped it 40 times, and got 40 heads. Would you then rush about excitedly, telling everyone about the "almost unbelievable" coincidence which had occurred, and send in a report to a scientific journal? Of course not! You would simply conclude that the coin was not balanced, and that your calculations therefore did not apply.

Suppose, however, that you made not just one set of 40 flips, but 10^{12} different runs, each of 40 flips. And further suppose that one of those runs resulted in 40 consecutive heads. In that case you would conclude that the coin was honest, that your calculations were correct, and that no unbelievable coincidence had occurred.

Similarly, if we were shown an (undoctored) film displaying a run of 40 consecutive heads, we would normally interpret it not as evidence of a remarkable coincidence, but merely as evidence that the coin was unbalanced. However, if we knew that the maker of the film had made and photographed 10^{12} runs, each of 40 flips, but only let us see the film of the one successful run, we would see no reason to doubt the correctness of our calculations.

VI. Life in the Infinite Universe

Why do I suggest such a fanciful possibility? Because the universe we live in is not finite, but infinite! Modern astronomical observations strongly support the so-called "big bang" cosmology, and the majority of the evidence indicates that our universe is open and will continue to expand indefinitely (Gott et al., 1974). Analysis shows that, unless a very unusual topology is assumed, such an open universe must be infinite in extent, with an infinite number of galaxies, an infinite number of stars, and an infinite number of planets. In an infinite universe, any event which has a finite probability—no matter how small—of occurring on a single given planet must inevitably occur on some planet. In fact, such an event must occur on an infinite number of planets. [See Ellis and Brundrit (1979) for an interesting discussion of this point.]

We are therefore in the position of the hypothetical film-viewer described above. There are an infinite number of habitable planets in the universe. On each of these, nature patiently tosses her tetrahedral dice for ten billion years, trying to line up 600 nucleotides in the proper order to make genesis DNA. In the great majority of cases the attempt is unsuccessful; but these "runs", of course, are never seen. Only in that rare case when a run is successful, and life does get started on a planet, is there anyone around to view the film.

The universe, therefore, contains an infinite number of inhabited planets, but the chance that any specific galaxy will contain life is extremely small. Most intelligent races should see no other civilizations in their galaxy; indeed, they should see no others in the entire portion of the universe (including perhaps 10^{22} stars) which they are able to observe with their telescopes. This theoretical prediction is, of course, in complete agreement with our failure to observe extraterrestrials, and with all our other observational evidence.

Conclusion

All of the calculations made above are based on existing theories. No extraordinary assumptions have been made, nor have any unknown effects or processes been postulated. Normally, when theoretical conclusions based on existing theories are in complete accord with the observations the conclusions are readily accepted.

Why, then, are so many people reluctant to believe that N is a low number? I would suggest that this reluctance is primarily a result of wishful thinking: a galaxy teeming with bizarre life forms sounds a lot more interesting than one in which we are alone. But N can be a high number only if $f_{life} >> 10^{-30}$, and that can only be the case if there exists some abiotic process—as yet totally unknown—which lines up nucleotides in a sequence which is biologically useful. Although we cannot absolutely prove that no such process exists, we should certainly be reluctant to postulate an unknown process when all the observed facts can be explained without it.

NOTES

Brown, H. (1952). Rare gases and the formation of the Earth's atmosphere. In *The Atmospheres of the Earth and Planets*, (editor: G. P. Kuiper), 2nd ed., 258–266. University of Chicago Press, Chicago.

Budyko, M. I. (1969). The effect of solar radiation variations on the climate of the Earth. *Tellus* 21, 611–619.

Ellis, G. F. R. and Brundrit, G. B. (1979). Life in the infinite universe. *Quarterly J. Royal Astronomical Soc.* 20, 37–40.

Feinberg, G., and Shapiro, R. (1980). *Life Beyond Earth*. William Morrow and Co., New York, Chap. 6.

Gott, J. R., Gunn, J. E., Schramm, D. M., and Tinsley, B. M. (1974). An unbound universe? *Astrophysical Journal* 194, 543–553.

Hart, M. H. (1975). An explanation for the absence of extraterrestrials on Earth. *Quarterly J. Royal Astronomical Soc.* 16, 128–135.

Hart, M. H. (1978). The evolution of the atmosphere of the Earth. *Icarus* 33, 23–29.

Hart, M. H. (1979). Habitable zones about main sequence stars. *Icarus* 37, 351–357.

Huang, S.-S. (1959). Occurrence of life in the universe. *American Scientist* 47, 397–402.

Huang, S.-S. (1960). Life outside the solar system. *Sci. Amer.* 202, 55–63.

Jones, E. M. (1976). Colonization of the galaxy. *Icarus* 28, 421–422.

Miller, S. L., and Orgel, L. E. (1974). *The Origins of Life on the Earth*, Prentice-Hall, Englewood Cliffs, N.J., 100–102.

Papagiannis, M. D. (1978). Could we be the only advanced technological civilization in our galaxy? In *Origin of Life* (editor: H. Noda), Center Acad. Publ., Tokyo, Japan.

Rasool, S. I., and de Bergh, C. (1970). The runaway greenhouse and the accumulation of CO_2 in the Venus atmosphere. *Nature* 226, 1037–1039.

Sellers, W. D. (1969). A global climate model based on the energy balance of the Earth-atmosphere system. *J. Applied Meteorology* 8, 392–400.

Spitzer, L. (1952). The terrestrial atmosphere above 300 km. In *The Atmospheres of the Earth and Planets* (editor: G. P. Kuiper), 211–247. University of Chicago Press, Chicago.

Urey, H. C. (1951). The origin and development of the Earth and other terrestrial planets. *Geochim. Cosmochim. Acta* 1, 209–277.

Urey, H. C. (1952). On the early chemical history of the Earth and the origin of life. *Proc. Nat. Acad. Sci. U.S.A.* 38, 351–363.

22

G. F. R. ELLIS*

Emerging Questions and Uncertainties

WE CONSIDER IN turn, uncertainty due to observational limits and horizons; problems in testing the nature of fundamental forces; uncertainty about physical origins of the universe; puzzles concerning deep connections (Olber's paradox, Mach's principle, the arrow of time). Then we turn to the fundamental underlying issues, problems arising from the uniqueness of the Universe; and uncertainty at the foundations.

The issues considered here are all limits on what science can achieve *within its own domain of competence.*

1. Observational Limits and Horizons

Our ability directly to determine the geometry and distribution of matter in the Universe is restricted by many observational difficulties [7], including the faintness of the images we are trying to understand. However, there are much more fundamental restrictions on what we can observe.

We can only detect distant matter by means of particles or radiation it emits that travel to us, receiving most of our information from light.[1] There are therefore fundamental limitations on the region of the Universe we can see, because the radiation conveying information travels towards us at the speed of light (and any material particles travel slower than this speed). As we look out to further and further distances, we are necessarily looking fur-

*Reprinted from pages 71–88, 130–36, 142–43 of *Before the Beginning: Cosmology Explained,* by George F. R. Ellis (1997), by permission of Boyars/Bowerdean, London and New York. Copyright © George F. R. Ellis, 1993.

ther and further back in time (for example, the Andromeda galaxy is 1 million light years away; this means we see it as it was 1 million years ago). We are therefore seeing the sources at earlier stages in their evolution. This makes it very difficult to disentangle the effects of physical evolution of the sources observed from geometrical evolution of the Universe. This is the main reason why we are unable to tell directly from observations of the rate of change of redshift with distance if the Universe will recollapse or not.

THE PARTICLE HORIZON

Furthermore, because the Universe has a finite age, light can only have travelled a finite distance since the origin of the Universe. This feature implies that we can only see out to those particles whose present-day distance corresponds to the age of the Universe; the particles beyond cannot be seen by us no matter what detectors we may use (light has not had time to travel to us from them since the creation of the Universe). The effect is the same as the horizon we see when we look at distant objects on the Earth: there are many further objects we cannot see because they lie beyond the horizon. In the case of the expanding Universe, we call the horizon separating those particles[2] that we can have seen (or indeed have had any causal contact with) from those we cannot, the *particle horizon* [7,8,10]. Actually we cannot even see as far as the particle horizon, because the Universe is opaque at early times. In reality we can see only as far as the *visual horizon*, where the universe becomes transparent; this lies inside the particle horizon, and corresponds to looking back as far as matter that emitted the blackbody background radiation.

It is because of these limits that we are able to say very little about the Universe on scales bigger than the *Hubble* size (the distance we can have seen since the beginning of the Universe, roughly 10 thousand million light years). Thus we cannot observationally distinguish between universe models that are strictly homogeneous in the large (implying conditions are the same at a distance 1 million times the Hubble size away from us, as they are here), and those that are not. If the Universe has finite spatial sections, there are at least as many galaxies outside our view as within it; while if it has infinite spatial sections, we cannot see an infinite number of galaxies, so what we can see is an infinitely small fraction of all there is. Any statements we make about the structure of the Universe on a really large scale (that is, many times the horizon size) are strictly unverifiable.

These limitations make it very difficult to tell if an idea such as the chaotic inflationary Universe idea is a true description of the real Universe, or not. In that case, at the present time huge sections of the Universe that are nearly homogeneous (but with different expansion rates, density parameters, etc.) would be separated from each other by very inhomogeneous transition zones, but these zones would not be visible to us.

It is often stated that the inflationary Universe idea solves the horizon problem. This refers to the issue of microwave background radiation isotropy, which runs into severe causal difficulties in an ordinary (noninflationary) universe model, for then regions that could not have been in causal contact with each other appear to be in identical physical states, because they emit radiation that we measure to be at the same temperature. These causal problems in the early Universe are solved by inflation, for there the greatly increased early expansion allows these regions causal contact [2,5,9,14,18]. However, there are still visual horizons in these Universes,[3] so the verification problem remains.

SMALL UNIVERSES

There is one exception to this generally pessimistic situation. It is possible (even if the Universe is a low density Universe) that the large-scale connectivity of space could be different from what we expected, so that the Universe is in fact a *Small Universe,* spatially closed on a scale smaller than the Hubble size. Then if one could go in an arbitrary spatial direction at constant time, one would eventually end up very close to where one began (as in the case of a sphere, torus, or a Möbius strip). If this were the case we would be able to see right round the Universe several times; so we could see each galaxy (including our own) several times through images in different directions in the sky, a relatively small number of galaxies giving a very large number of images [8].

The effect is like being in a room whose walls, floor, and ceiling are all covered with mirrors: you see a huge number of images of yourself fading away into the distance in all directions. Similarly in a Small Universe, despite its small size we would see a large number of images of each galaxy fading away in an apparently infinite universe. In this case (and only in this case) there would be no visual horizon, and we could in principle determine the geometry of the whole Universe by observation, for all the matter that exists would then be accessible to our observation (in contrast to the usually considered situation, where only a small fraction of that matter can be seen). Furthermore, in this case we would be able to study the history of our own Galaxy by optical observations, as we would be able to see it at different times in its history in the different images that would be visible to us.

Now it is possible we live in such a small Universe, but if this were true then proving it by observation would be difficult; and there is no solid evidence that this is indeed the case. Thus the working hypothesis is that we do not live in a small Universe, but we should keep an open mind on this matter.

LIMITS TO VERIFIABILITY

Overall, what we can say with any degree of certainty is strictly proscribed by observational limits [7]. We can in principle observationally determine (a) a great deal about the region we can observe (which lies inside the visual horizon); (b) a little about that which lies outside our visual horizon but inside the particle horizon (we might be able to tell something by use of neutrino or gravitational wave telescopes, someday when technology has developed sufficiently, but this is decades into the future); (c) nothing about that which lies beyond the particle horizon: this region is unobservable by any method. In a Small Universe there are no visual horizons, but the real Universe is probably not like that. The implication is that when our models give predictions of the nature of the Universe on a larger scale than the Hubble radius, these are strictly unverifiable, however appealing they may be.

2. Testing the Nature of Fundamental Forces

In trying to understand the early Universe, we also come up against major limits in terms of our ability to test the predictions of our proposals for physical laws. Even if we could build a super-collider as large as the entire Solar System, we could not reach the kinds of energies that come into play in the very early Universe, so we cannot test the behaviour of matter under the relevant conditions [18]. This puts major limits on our ability to test whether our theories of those times are right or not. For example, while it is commonly believed that inflation took place in the early Universe, we have been unable so far to detect in experiments on Earth the field responsible for inflation, and so cannot confirm that the proposal for the underlying mechanism is correct. Similarly the proposals as to how synthesis of protons from quarks took place in the early Universe cannot yet be confirmed because we have not seen the relevant particles, and measurements of the decay rate of the proton contradicts the simplest theory that could explain the proposed mechanism; we do not know which of the more complex possibilities (if any) may be correct.

Indeed the early Universe is the *only* place where some of the laws of physics come fully into play[4]; consequently the situation is the reverse of what we might hope, in that instead of being able to take known laws and use them to determine what happened in the very early Universe, we may have to proceed the other way round, regarding the early Universe as the only laboratory where those laws can be tested. This has led to an important discovery; comparison of element abundance observations with studies of nucleosynthesis in the early Universe determined that there are only three neutrino types rather than four, before this question had been tested experimentally on Earth. Results from the accelerator at CERN later confirmed this conclusion.

However, this type of reasoning only works when there are a few clear-cut alternative observational predictions, and depends on the assumed cosmological conditions being correct. When we consider the really fundamental questions, whose understanding is the Holy Grail of theoretical physics, even the broad kind of approach to take is not clear. We are concerned here with the unification of our understanding of all the known forces into a single theory. In other words a "theory of everything," combining together the features of gravity, electromagnetism, the weak force, and the strong force in a way compatible with relativity theory and with quantum theory. Various proposals have been made [1,5], of which the most popular recent one is superstring theory [6], representing fundamental particles as string-like rather than as point particles. However, this has not yet been formulated in a fully satisfactory way, and also (despite early hopes that it would turn out to be unique) turns out to be a large family of theories rather than a single theory. This kind of physics probably controls the very earliest phases of the expansion of the Universe; we can reject some of the theories on the basis of their cosmological predictions, but cannot in this way select a particular one as being correct, nor can experiments on Earth distinguish between them. We certainly cannot use this broad class of theories to determine a unique history for the very early history of the Universe. Thus the practical limits of testing of physical laws are major limitations in determining what really happened at very early times (fractions of a second after the Big Bang).

3. Physical Origins

This is a basic problem when we consider the events which occurred at the origin of the Universe which determine the circumstances of present-day existence. The Big Bang theory makes it clear that at very early times there must have been an epoch where the ideas of classical physics simply did not apply; Quantum Gravity (a theory unifying general relativity with quantum theory) would have been the dominant factor at these times [5,18,19]. There are a number of different theoretical approaches to this topic, none of which is wholly satisfactory, so we do not even know for sure what basic approach to use in such theories [5,17,19]; and there is no way we can test these different options by Earth-based experiments. However. it is these theories that underlie what we would really like to know about the nature of the origin of the Universe.

Despite this uncertainty, we can claim that major features of quantum mechanics, such as the underlying wave-like nature of matter, must apply here also; on this basis we can make quantum cosmology models with claims correctly to represent the results of the as-yet unknown theory of quantum gravity, when applied to the very origin of the Universe.

Various such theories have been proposed to explain the origin of the Universe in terms of quantum development from some previous state (a collapsing previous phase, a region of flat space-time, a black hole final state, some kind of 'pre-geometry') [20,21]. Such approaches can provide a whole series of alternative hypotheses for the origin of the Hot Big Bang which has led to our existence, but of course they simply postpone the ultimate issue: for we then have to ask, what was the origin of this previous phase? This remains unanswered.

THE NO-BOUNDARY IDEA

One unique and intriguing proposal side-steps this problem neatly. This is the Hartle-Hawking suggestion [5,21] that the initial state of the Universe could be a region where time did not exist: instead of three spatial dimensions and one time dimension, there were four spatial dimensions. This has a great advantage: it is then possible that there can be a Universe without a beginning, for (just as there is no boundary to the surface of the Earth at the South Pole) there is no boundary to this initial region of the Universe; it is uniform and smooth at all points. Much is made of this proposal in Hawking's book *A Brief History of Time* [12], for it docs indeed describe a Universe without a beginning in the ordinary sense of the word, although time does have a beginning (where there is a transition from this strange 'Euclidean' state to a normal space-time structure).[5] The implications of this proposal will be considered shortly; at present the concern is three-fold, related to the testability of the underlying propositions of such a theory.

Firstly, such proposals presuppose the unravelling of some of the underlying conundrums of quantum theory that have not yet been solved in a fully satisfactory manner–(specifically, the related issues of the role of an observer in quantum theory, and what determines the collapse of the wave function, which is an essential feature of measurement in quantum theory [17,19]). These do not arise as significant problems in the context of laboratory experiments, but become substantial difficulties when quantum theory (which is usually applied to sub-microscopic systems) is applied to the Universe as a whole. Second, we certainly cannot test the Wheeler-de Witt equation which underlies quantum cosmology: we have to accept it as a huge extrapolation of existing physics, plausible because of its basis in established physical laws but untestable in its own right. Even some of the underlying concepts (such as 'the wave function of the Universe') have a questionable status in this context, for they are associated with a probabilistic interpretation which may not make sense when applied to a unique object, namely the Universe.

THE ISSUE OF INITIAL CONDITIONS

Thirdly, and irrespective of our resolution of the previous issues, we are tackling here the problem of *initial conditions for the Universe*: we are trying to use physical theory to describe something which happened once and only once, to which no comparable events have ever occurred (or at least, none that are accessible to our observations). The notion of a law to describe this situation faces considerable difficulties. If a 'law' is only ever applied to one physical object, it is not clear if the usual distinction between a physical law and specific initial conditions makes sense (cf. the following section). That 'law' certainly cannot be subject to empirical test in the same way as other physical laws.

Whatever 'law' we may set up to describe this situation [5,12], we have one and only one test we can do: we can observe the existent Universe and see if it is congruent with the predictions of that 'law'. If it is, this supports that law but not decisively, for there will in general be several laws or underlying approaches that give the same result; these cannot be distinguished from each other on the basis of any experimental tests. We can obtain strong support for one particular view (such as the Hartle-Hawking 'no-boundary' proposal) only by utilising criteria for good theories: for instance, simplicity, beauty, and congruence with the rest of our current body of knowledge.

Whatever explanation we may give for them, unique initial conditions occurred at the origin of the Universe. They determine both the initial structure of space-time, and its matter content.

The matter we see around us today is the remnant of that initial state, after it has been processed by non-equilibrium processes in the early Universe and then in a first generation of stars. Thus we understand the role of initial conditions; however, this analysis does not answer the ultimate issues of origin and existence, in particular why the initial conditions had the form they did.

4. Deep Connections

In developing these questions, it is important to understand the *interconnectedness* of the Universe. As well as determining the initial nature of matter and of the space-time geometry, the choice of initial conditions for the Universe profoundly affects the nature of physics in other ways. We consider here three particular examples, namely Olbers' Paradox, Mach's Principle and The Arrow of Time.

OLBERS' PARADOX

The classic illustration of this interconnectedness is known as *Olbers' Paradox,* and concerns the question: why is the sky dark at night? [10,11].

The point is as follows: if we consider a simple static Universe uniformly filled with steadily shining stars, then while the radiation received per star goes down with the inverse square of the distance from the observer, the number of stars goes up with the square of the distance. When we add up the effect of all the stars, the two factors in the square of the distance cancel, and we conclude that the radiation received becomes unboundedly large as we consider the combined effects of more and more distant stars. Thus the night sky should be infinitely bright, according to this simplest model. If we allow for the fact that nearer matter interposes between the observer and more distant sources, we conclude that (because each direction eventually intersects the surface of a star, and the calculation above shows that the surface brightness of a star is independent of its distance from us) the night sky (and, for that matter, the day sky) should in every direction be as bright as the surface of the Sun.

Now at first you might think the problem is simply that it would be a bit uncomfortable having a bright sky at night; we'd have to keep the curtains closed to get some sleep. Nothing could be further from the truth. If this were the case, Earth could not radiate its waste energy to the sky, which would everywhere be as hot as the surface of the Sun; consequently the Earth would heat up until it was in equilibrium with that temperature. There would be no possibility of life here (the surface of Earth would be molten rock and any organic molecules would be disintegrated by radiant energy). The dark night sky is essential to life on Earth.

Why then is the real sky dark at night? There are three factors not taken into account in this calculation. Firstly, the expansion of the Universe results in the received light from distant galaxies being redshifted; this causes a diminution in the intensity of light received (proportional to the inverse fourth power of the redshift), greatly reducing the expected radiation from distant stars. Secondly, stars cannot shine for an infinite time, because they only have a finite supply of nuclear fuel; so the underlying assumption that stars can shine forever is false. The model ignored conservation of energy. Thirdly, the Universe itself has a finite age, so if we look back far enough into the past we reach an era when stars had not yet turned on; the matter at that time is dark because it has not yet formed stars, and the pre-existing background radiation is nothing other than the cosmic background radiation, which is only of sufficient density to be seen as 3 K radiation today. All three factors reflect the fact that the Universe is not in a state of equilibrium, as this simple model supposed.

Thus the simple model underlying the paradox did not take into account the real nature of the expanding Universe. This is an interesting and important result in its own right,[6] but it also shows us how we cannot ignore the effect of distant matter just because it is so far from us. There is so much of it, that its effects could be very important for daily life.

MACH'S PRINCIPLE

Another famous example of this type concerns the origin of inertia, and is known as *Mach's Principle*. This starts with a simple fact that has puzzled physicists for three hundred years: the fixed stars (in modern terminology, very distant galaxies) stay in fixed positions in the sky, when compared with a non-rotating local reference frame, defined by local dynamical experiments. Specifically, while stars appear to move across the sky relative to the (rotating) Earth, they appear fixed relative to the plane defined by a Foucault pendulum (or its modern equivalent, rapidly rotating gyroscopes, as used for the inertial guidance of submarines and aircraft). The question then is, is this rather striking fact just a coincidence, or is there some underlying causal mechanism that can explain it? [22,23].

Now *inertia* is the property whereby a freely moving body continues in a straight line relative to a non-rotating reference frame, but moves on a curved path relative to a rotating reference frame (due to 'inertial forces', such as the centrifugal force that pushes one towards the side of a car as it turns a corner). Indeed it is just the absence of 'inertial forces' in a non-rotating reference frame which defines it to be non-rotating; so a causal explanation of the puzzle just posed must relate local inertial properties to distant stars. This fits in with the ideas of General Relativity, according to which gravity (a long-range force) and inertia are closely related. Thus Mach's Principle posits that local inertial properties are determined by distant matter; just as in the case of Olbers' paradox, each single star contributes very little, but there are so many of them that the total effect, taking the contribution from every star, is very large. The identity of the local inertial rest frame and the rest frame of distant stars is not a coincidence: it arises because local inertia–which underlies all local dynamics–is *caused* by distant stars.

This is a controversial proposal, and it is difficult even to phrase it in a rigorous way.[7] If it were true, we could envisage the following: suppose the entire Universe contained but one galaxy, instead of the hundred billion galaxies we can see; then the inertia of one kilogram of matter would be very much less than we now measure it to be. (So, for example, if a car ran into a brick wall, the damage would be much less than we presently experience on Earth). If we could slowly remove galaxies from the Universe, the inertia of matter would gradually decrease. Of course, we cannot carry out such an experiment, so the issue remains unresolved: there is no way we can test to see if this is correct or not. However, a related possibility is that as the Universe expands it is possible that the force of gravity gets weaker; this would result in the gravitational constant decreasing with time. Several theories have been proposed in which this is true, and the effect has been looked for experimentally. The proposal has not been confirmed; if it occurs it is below the detection threshold. However, it makes a very important point: it is quite plausible that if the structure of the Universe were totally different, the locally experienced laws of physics might be quite different, too.

THE ARROW OF TIME

Perhaps the most celebrated and continuously vexing of these kinds of issues is the origin of *the arrow of time* [4,19]. It is very easy to get confused about this, for the one-directional nature of time that determines our daily lives is so deeply ingrained in our experience we find it difficult to imagine how things could be otherwise.

The problem is that the *fundamental laws of physics are time symmetric:* they run equally well forwards or backwards in time.[8] Thus the undeniable existence of an arrow of time (the one-way decay associated with entropy growth, for example) is somewhat mysterious; and the more curious feature is that while one can give arguments as to why such an arrow should exist (for example, by using statistical techniques to predict the behaviour of a gas from the forces between the individual molecules), these arguments seem to work equally well both ways: they may be taken to predict the existence of an arrow of time, but cannot tell which direction of time is the future and which is the past! Thus we know that a broken glass cannot re-assemble itself from its fragments into the whole glass, even though the fundamental laws of physics assert that this is a possibility [19].

The problem is compounded in that there are several potentially independent arrows of time (those of quantum mechanics, of thermodynamics, of electrodynamics, of evolutionary biology, for example), and one of the major questions is why they all end up consistent with each other. A vexing problem that relates to this is the question of consciousness and free-will. Assuming we really do have free will, then despite the determinism of classical laws of physics, the future is not predictable from the past,[9] because human intervention can alter it in a way not predicted by the laws of physics alone. This implies an absolutely fundamental asymmetry in the workings of the biological world, which are based on the laws of physics. It may well be related to the fact that although the fundamental laws of physics are time symmetric in their classical version, quantum mechanics (in its ordinary interpretation) has a major time asymmetry in terms of collapse of the wave function [19].

There are two suggestions of an answer to this conundrum: on the one hand, *the direction of the arrow of time may be related directly to the expansion of the Universe* (which would be experienced as a contraction if time ran the other way). If so, the almost inevitable conclusion is that it would be impossible for an observer ever to see a collapsing phase of the Universe; in a Universe which, according to the ordinary view, reaches a maximum size and then starts to recollapse, the direction of time would reverse then. The physical situation would actually be experienced as two expansions in the opposite directions of time, coupled by a period of indeterminacy near the maximum as the arrow of time switched direction: a conclusion so strange as to call the idea into question.

On the other hand, *the arrow of time may be determined by specific boundary conditions for local physical laws at the beginning and end of the Universe,* restricting the physically realised solutions from all possible ones to those that conform to one consistent time direction [19]. Notice here that we cannot simply say that boundary conditions at the beginning of the Universe would suffice to establish this one-way flow, for until that flow is established the beginning and end of the Universe are on an equal footing: there is no intrinsic distinction between them. Thus such conditions have to be set at both the beginning and the end of the Universe.

A key issue here is how initial conditions for some physical field are correlated with each other at the start and end of the Universe. In the past they should be uncorrelated, but in the future they should be correlated. For example [19], after a glass has fallen to the ground and broken, the pieces disperse away from where it has fallen. We cannot simply give the fragments the correct reverse velocities, so as to all come together at the right time and re-assemble the glass; the correlations required are too exact. While this time-reversed motion would certainly also be a solution to the equations, the problem is the incredible degree of coordination required to achieve this. Similar issues arise, for example, in considering why a radio transmission can only be received after it has been broadcast, and not before (this time-reversed situation being a possible solution of the time-symmetric Maxwell's equations, which determine the behaviour of the electromagnetic field). The point is that in the real world, such a solution would require exact correlations of the incoming field in the past, which are unattainable. However, such correlations necessarily occur in the future all the time (the radio signal, after it has been broadcast, arrives in undistorted form in thousands of receivers; the music they all play is therefore highly correlated).

Many see this as the key feature in the arrow of time: *there are different correlations in the future and the past*. However, the question arises in relation to the issue of free will whether this is a *cause* of the arrow of time or merely a *description* of its effects. Penrose has suggested that when one takes into account the contribution of gravity to entropy growth, it is *smoothness of initial space-time structure* that is the key feature distinguishing the beginning of the Universe from irregularity and roughness that characterises its end [8]; but this view is not shared by all. An alternative view, proposed by Prigogine, is that we should aim at a reformulation of the laws of physics to incorporate the arrow of time in its very foundation, contrary to our present understanding of these laws.

Whichever kind of interpretation we may suggest, it is clear that on our present understanding of the nature of physics, the arrow of time is not embedded in the fundamental laws, but is a property of the boundary conditions for physical quantities imposed at the beginning (and probably also at the end) of time. The situation could be quite different in universes with different boundary conditions. Whatever theories we may have about this cannot be tested by any physical experiment; but the conclusion is of the utmost importance for daily life, and indeed for the very existence of life (which could not function without an arrow of time).

THE UNITY OF THE UNIVERSE

Overall these examples point to deep connections and unity of the physical Universe, not merely in terms of effect of microphysical laws on macroscopic structures, as envisaged in the inflationary Universe picture, but also in terms of the very nature and functioning of those laws [23].

Indeed, the examples just given show there may be no clear-cut distinction between boundary *conditions for physical laws* at the beginning of the Universe, and *the nature of local physical laws*; for the boundary conditions for those laws at the beginning of time are given as part of the structure of the Universe, and cannot be changed; but this is the essential feature characterising the physical laws themselves. What from the viewpoint of an ensemble of Universes is just one of a whole set of possible boundary conditions, may critically affect the nature of local physics within a specific Universe in a way that is experienced as absolute and immutable, so that (in that Universe) it is indistinguishable from an immutable physical law. Thus in the cosmological context, the distinction between initial conditions and physical laws can become blurred, or at least these features may be highly interdependent. However, it is these interconnections that provide the setting within which life can exist.

5. *The Uniqueness of the Universe*

What we run up against time and again is the fundamental feature of *the uniqueness of the Universe,* and the problems this gives rise to as we try to unravel its nature [15,16].

Cosmology is the ultimate historical science, for by definition there is only one Universe. In any other historic science there are other similar objects to compare a particular individual object with (in geology, there are many mountains and a number of continents; in astronomy, there are numerous stars and galaxies, and many planets; in evolutionary theory, there are many different species that have related evolutionary histories). Only in the case of cosmology is there nothing whatever we can compare with the subject of study (the Universe). This is the ultimate reason why, when we penetrate to the heart of the matter–the choice of particular physical laws that govern the Universe, and of the particular initial conditions that occurred in the one unique Universe–our theories simply cannot be subject to confirmation in the normal sense.

We cannot perform the kinds of experiments that experimental sciences rely on (there is no way we can alter its initial conditions and see the resultant effects), and we cannot even do the kinds of comparisons with similar objects that underlie the other historical sciences. We can only observe what is there, and compare predictions with observations. In this way we can learn a lot about the physical nature of the Universe and the way it functions, as much of this is based on observation; but we run into problems when we try to answer issues of the kind considered above, particularly those related to initial conditions. In this case we include a theory in a list of possible theories if its conclusions are not in blatant contradiction to the observations. (Small discrepancies can usually be explained in a myriad of ways that maintain the integrity of the main theory: the sources evolved, selection effects occurred, there was an unrecognised interfering factor, and so on.) We then choose between the theories on the basis of (non-verifiable) philosophical criteria.

The conclusion is that

we have to evaluate theories of the Universe knowing that they are testable but intrinsically unverifiable, in the sense just explained.

Because of this,

the choice of competing theories is largely dependent on the philo-sophical stance adopted (whether this is explicitly acknowledged or not); specifically, the crucial feature is the choice of criteria of what is a 'good' theory and what is not.

Cosmology is more dependent on such criteria than any other science precisely because of the uniqueness of its subject matter. Given a choice of such criteria, the evidence will strongly constrain what is acceptable as a theory and what is not, and may even lead almost uniquely to a spe-cific understanding.

Are such criteria themselves subject to experimental test? To a certain extent, in that past evidence shows what has worked well in general as cri-teria for choosing theories in different areas of understanding; and this plays a considerable role in our choice. However, cosmology is different from all other disciplines; in the end an unavoidable choice must be made that is essentially philosophical and not subject to experimental test.

We should use broad criteria that take into account the whole range of human experience, and not just that part which can be scientifically described (though that, of course, must be included as a central feature).

6. Uncertainty at the Foundations

The reader may be beginning to be dismayed by the uncertainties that are apparent at the foundations of fundamental physics and cosmology, despite the hard-won successes of the physical sciences. To complete the picture we must note that, despite what one might think, certainty is not attainable even in the logical sciences.

At a first glance mathematics itself rests on impregnable logical founda-tions. However, determined attempts to prove this failed, and resulted even-tually in the mathematician Kurt Gödel showing the impossibility of proving the consistency of mathematics [13,19]. Computer science cannot help: indeed Turing and Church have shown there is no general algorithm for deciding mathematical questions [19]. Furthermore, the concepts under-lying probability theory, which is required in order to test any physical theory on the basis of real (noisy) data, are also dubious, because the con-cept of a random number is very difficult to pin down [17].

THE LACK OF CERTAINTY

The conclusion is that, within its own domain, there are considerable limi-tations on what science can determine, in respect of verification of laws and confirmation of the nature of reality; these limits prevent us from obtaining many of the desired answers and checking the validity of our theories and models. While some are the result of practicalities and the current state of technology, ultimately some of these limits are absolute; for example (unless the Theory of Relativity is disproved some day), the speed of light is an absolute limit to communication, and consequently the limits on what we can observe in the Universe (in particular, through the existence of the particle and visual horizons) are absolute: no advances in technology will change them. Furthermore, the ability of science to answer foundational questions is strictly limited.

What attitude should we take to all this? I would suggest that it confirms the profound conclusion that *certainty is unattainable at the foundations of understanding in all areas of life,* including fundamental physics and cosmology, as well as philosophy and theology; even the apparently impregnable bastion of mathematics is vulnerable to this comment. This is not the same as saying that anything goes (as some in the arts and social sciences appear to believe), but rather that what we can learn with reasonable confidence *concerning foundational issues* is strictly bounded.[10]

This may seem obvious to you, and you may even find it easy to put into practice. If so you are very modern in your attitude to knowledge and are able to counter a very deep strain of thought over the past centuries. Historically, while people have from time to time shifted the focus of the hoped-for certainty (for example, from theology to science), they have consistently sought for it. Many who claim to be 'rationalist' or 'free-thinking' are just as dogmatic as any fundamentalist theologian or reductionist scientist, nor are the social sciences free from dogmatic stances and closed minds.

This does not mean that we must give up the hope of attaining a good understanding of the way things work; rather, it means that

a mature attitude must take this problem of uncertainty into account, and make it a central feature of the way we approach any understanding of the Universe.

Furthermore, the complexities we have run into, in terms of interdependencies and even the very notion of physical law, confirm that we need to realise explicitly that

the models and theories on which we base our understandings are partial representations of reality, not to be confused with reality itself.

They can be very useful representations of reality in a limited domain, providing excellent understanding of that domain, but cannot rest on a foundation of absolute certainty. They cannot ever be infallible guides to reality, for they are not the same as reality.

Once we have accepted these limitations, giving up the unattainable hope of certainty, we can achieve satisfying and even profound understandings of the Universe and the way it works, provisional without doubt, but nevertheless offering a satisfactory world-view and basis for action.

Notes

1. It is understood that "light" is a generic term for any form of electromagnetic radiation by which we can see distant objects: radio waves, infra-red radiation, ultraviolet radiation, and X-rays as well as ordinary light.

2. Which later will become galaxies.

3. There are also particle (causal) horizons if the inflationary Universe has infinite spatial sections; but they do not exist if it has closed spatial sections (then the particle horizons are broken at very early times, when light has had time to travel right round the Universe).

4. Apart from what happens to matter in the final state of collapse in a black hole; but that is completely inaccessible to observation.

5. While this has originally been developed as a quantum cosmology idea, it is now known there are classical solutions of the Einstein equations with the same property.

6. Updated versions of the calculation determine what background radiation we expect to receive at each wavelength, from very distant matter in the Universe; this can then be compared with observations.

7. Einstein developed his static Universe model (1917) in the hope that it would show General Relativity fully incorporates Mach's principle in its structure. However, de Sitter's universe model (also found in 1917) showed this is not so.

8. There is an exception in the case of some of (the weak interactions; this is difficult to detect, and it seems very unlikely it is the fundamental source of the arrow of time.

9. Quite apart from the issue of chaotic dynamics.

10. We can attain effective certainty in numerous practical matters, controlled by the regular action and effectiveness of physical laws.

References

[1] Barrow, J. *Theories of Everything: The Search for Ultimate Explanation.* Oxford University Press, 1991.

[2] J. Barrow, D. and F. J. Tipler: *The Anthropic Cosmological Principle.* Oxford: Oxford University Press, 1986.

[3] Cooper, L. N. *An Introduction to the Meaning and Structure of Physics.* Harper and Row, 1968.

[4] Coveney, P. and R. Highfield: *The Arrow of Time.* Flamingo, 1990.

[5] Davies, P. C. W. (Ed.). *The New Physics.* Cambridge: Cambridge University Press, 1989.

[6] Davies, P. C. W. and J. Brown. *Superstrings: A Theory of Everything?* Cambridge, 1989.

[7] Ellis, G. F. R. *Cosmology and Verifiability. In Physical Sciences and the History of Physics.* Boston Studies in the Philosophy of Science. Volume 82 Ed. R. S. Cohen and M. W. Wartofsky. Reidel, 1984, 93–114.

[8] Ellis, G. F. R. and R. M. Williams. *Flat and Curved Space-Times.* Oxford:

Oxford University Press, 1989.

[9] Gribbin, J. and M J. Rees. *Cosmic Coincidences*. Black Swan, 1991.

[10] Harrison, Ted. *Cosmology: The Science of the Universe*. Cambridge University Press, 1981.

[11] Harrison, E. R. *Darkness at Night: A Riddle of the Universe*. Harvard University Press, 1987.

[12] Hawking, S. *A Brief History of Time*. Bantam, 1988.

[13] Kline, M. *Mathematics: The Loss of Certainty*. Oxford University Press, 1980.

[14] Krauss, L. *The Fifth Essence: The Search for Dark Matter in the Universe*. London: Vintage, Basic Books, 1989.

[15] McCrea, W. H. *Rep. Prog. Phys.* 16:32 (1953).

[16] Munitz, M. K. *Brit. J. Philos. Sci.* 13:104 (1962).

[17] Pagels, H. R. *The Cosmic Code*. Penguin, 1982.

[18] Pagels, H. *Perfect Symmetry*. Penguin, 1985.

[19] Penrose, R. *The Emperor's New Mind*. Oxford: Oxford University Press, 1989.

[20] Russell, R. J. N. Murphy, and C. J. Isham (Ed.). *Quantum Cosmology and the Laws of Nature: Scientific Perspectives on Divine Action*. Vatican Observatory/CTNS Conference proceedings, 1993.

[21] Russell, R. J. W. J. Stoeger, and G. V. Coyne. *Physics in Philosophy and Theology. A Common Quest for Understanding*. Rome: Vatican Observatory, 1989.

[22] Sciama, D. W. *Physical Foundations of General Relativity*. Heinemann, 1969.

[23] Sciama, D. W. *The Unity of the Universe*. Faber, 1959.

23

JOHN LESLIE*

The Anthropic Principle Today

I. Observational Selection

As FIRST STATED by Brandon Carter, the anthropic principle is "that what we can expect to observe must be restricted by the conditions necessary for our presence as observers."[1] An intelligent living being can observe only a time, a place, and a universe with properties allowing intelligent observership. This sets up the possibility of observational selection effects. It is by no means plain that every time, place, or universe–a time when all stars have burned out, perhaps, or the sun's center, or a universe lasting a mere traction of a second–would be when or where observers could find themselves.

R. H. Dicke had used this idea before, to oppose P. A. M. Dirac. Dirac had suggested that a gigantic ratio between cosmologically important numbers remained the same at all times, which necessitated that gravity was growing weaker. But in a paper of 1961, Dicke held that the only necessity in this area was an observational one.[2] Observers could find themselves only at times when stars were beaming heat and light to planets whose complex elements (carbon in particular) had been produced inside earlier stars. Even without any variation in gravity, the gigantic ratio would hold at those times. Earlier, the universe would be too simple for observers to exist in it. Later on, it would be too cold and dark.

* Reprinted from pp. 163–87 of *Final Causality in Nature and Human Affairs,* ed. R. F. Hassing (1997), by permission of The Catholic University of America Press. Copyright © 1997, The Catholic University of America Press.

As Carter showed, similar reasoning could be used to oppose Eddington, who drew attention to a second gigantic ratio associated with gravity's extreme weakness.[3] Eddington regarded this ratio as confirming a very unconventional physics. Carter instead saw gravity's measured value as essential to long-lasting stable stars. In a universe where gravity's pull was appreciably different, there could be no such stars and so, presumably, nobody to observe that universe.

In effect, the anthropic principle can counterbalance the "Copernican" or "cosmological" principle which states that reality in its entirety is much like what you and I see. Users of the anthropic principle follow in the steps of Hume and Kant who insisted that what we see may be very atypical–something to be borne in mind when we examine the Teleological or Design Argument that God's creative action is revealed by the properties of the universe as observed by us.

Recently all this has taken on considerable significance, for two main reasons. First, physicists and cosmologists have been accumulating much evidence that the observed universe is "fine tuned for producing life" in the following technical sense: tiny changes in its general properties would have made it a universe in which no life-forms could appear. Notice that talk about fine tuning, when understood in this sense, does not beg the question of whether God's hand is revealed here. Which is important because, secondly, physicists and cosmologists have also been developing theories which suggest that reality in its entirety could include greatly many universes and that general properties could vary from universe to universe. Instead, therefore, of introducing God to explain why our universe is so well tuned to life's needs, we might propose an "anthropic" observational selection effect. Among many actually existing universes, we might be observing one of the rare ones in which evolution can produce observers.

Naturally, this makes no sense if *a universe* has to be the whole of reality, by sheer definition. But cosmologists now commonly talk of multiple "worlds" or "universes," meaning huge domains of causally interacting things, domains largely or entirely separated from one another.

The evidence of fine tuning is strong. It is thus important, both to philosophy and to science, to decide whether the only plausible way in which fine tuning could be explained is a teleological/theistic way or whether we could appeal instead to multiple universes and anthropic observational selection.

II. Fine Tuning

An early discovery of apparent fine tuning was inspired by F. Hoyle. Carbon, crucial to all known life-forms, is manufactured abundantly in stars, thanks to how the carbon nucleus just manages to "resonate" appropriately and to how the oxygen nucleus just fails to resonate in a carbon-destroying fashion. Hoyle had confidently predicted the requisite delicate tuning of resonance levels, his confidence stemming from a belief that such matters varied from one huge domain to another. Obviously, he said, "we can exist only where those levels happen to be correctly placed."[4]

S. W. Hawking similarly drew much of his confidence from "anthropic" considerations when he developed the idea that galaxies could not have formed, had the early cosmic expansion rate been different by one part in a million.[5] (Later writers have argued that far smaller rate changes, corresponding to density changes by as little as one part in 10^{60}, would have prevented their formation.) Tiny differences in early expansion rates would quickly have led to huge differences. A universe which had expanded marginally faster would soon have become very cold near-vacuum, while one expanding a trifle more slowly would equally soon have recollapsed. Hawking postulated the actual existence of greatly many universes expanding at different rates. It would then not be surprising that at least one expanded at the right rate for galaxy-formation: given sufficiently many monkeys typing at random, one or other of them would generate a sonnet. And without galactic clouds condensing into stars and planetary systems, we observers could not have evolved. It would thus be no surprise that a universe of galaxies was what we saw.

The list of factors seemingly in need of fine tuning is a long one. It includes the following further items, discussed in detail in the studies listed in the notes to this chapter and especially in Davies, Barrow and Tipler, and Leslie.[6]

i. *Our universe's smoothness.* A Big Bang might be expected to give rise to immense turbulence, resulting in billion-degree temperatures and vastly many black holes, because large regions coming out of the Bang would seemingly not have had time to agree (so to speak) on how they would move. Penrose calculated that God, placing a pin to select our orderly, life-permitting universe from among the possibilities, could have needed precision to one part in 1 followed by 10^{123} zeros.[7]

ii. *Early inflation.* A currently popular claim, rejected by Penrose,[8] is that cosmic inflation at very early times led both to a galaxy-encouraging expansion rate and to cosmic smoothness. The story is that, with the Big Bang a small fraction of a second old, space began to expand exponentially fast, like an exploding rabbit population. After a very brief period, the cosmos had grown by perhaps a factor of $10^{1,000,000}$. Regions which had now become immensely far apart would earlier have been in causal contact so that they could have reached agreement on fairly orderly ways of behaving, and most of any remaining roughness would then have been smoothed out like the wrinkles on an inflating balloon. The inflation made space very "flat" (Euclidean) so that it thereafter automatically expanded at just the speed needed for galaxies to form. However, Davies, Ellis and others argue that such inflation would itself have needed very accurate tuning to occur at all and to leave roughness of just the right amount to lead to galaxies.[9] Two components of an inflation-driving "cosmological constant" might have had to balance each other with an accuracy of better than one part in 10^{50}.

iii. Tiny alterations in the strength of *the nuclear weak force* would have destroyed all the hydrogen which now helps to make water and steadily burning stars.

iv. Tiny changes in *the nuclear strong force,* in *Planck's constant,* or in *the mass difference between the neutron and the proton* would seemingly have blocked the formation of protons, or made suns burn 10^{18} times faster or else unable to burn at all, or turned even small bodies into miniature neutron stars.

v. *The relative strengths of gravity and electromagnetism* may have needed tuning to one part in 10^{40} for there to be stable suns. Moreover, slight strengthenings of electromagnetism would seemingly have destroyed all atoms (by transforming quarks into leptons), or made hydrogen the only element (by making protons repel one another powerfully), or led to rapid decay of the proton, or made chemical changes immensely slow.

vi. *The masses of various superheavy particles* needed to be tuned so that there would be just the right excess of matter over antimatter when the universe cooled and so that protons would be stable enough for life's purposes. Here the risk was of getting a universe consisting almost entirely of black holes or almost entirely of light rays, or having protons which decayed so rapidly that all matter was violently radioactive.

vii. *The electron-proton mass difference* must be great, for there to be solids and chemistry.

viii. A *top-quark mass* only a little above the actual one could cause space to collapse rapidly in a "vacuum instability disaster."

ix. *Space-time's topological and metrical properties* could differ from universe to universe, for reasons suggested by contemporary Unified Theories. Three spatial dimensions and "signature $+++ -$" (in which the minus sign comes from Einstein's $- (ct)^2$) appear essential for stable atoms, stable stars and planetary systems, and even all particle-like states.

III. Multiple Universes

Cosmologists have suggested numerous ways in which greatly many, greatly varied universes could be generated. They include the following (once again, details can be found in the studies listed in the notes, particularly those of Barrow and Tipler, and Leslie[10]).

i. *Oscillations.* J. Wheeler proposed that the cosmos oscillates, Big Bangs being succeeded by Big Collapses and then new Bangs, and that at each moment of greatest compression it "forgets" its properties, new properties then appearing in the next Bang in a probabilistic way.[11] Each oscillatory cycle could be counted as "a new universe."

Some writers have urged that only a single cycle would be possible, or only a few, but their reasoning is controversial. They assume, for example, that the cosmos would in fact "remember" its properties so that entropy would increase from cycle to cycle, and (see Sikkema and Israel[12] for one argument against this second assumption) that there would be no mass increase to dilute the entropy increase. Or they suppose that a Big Collapse would be irreversible because gravity would continue to be an attractive force, not a repulsive one, even at very high densities; yet this is now widely denied. Trying to explain why properties changed probabilistically from cycle to cycle, Wheeler did little more than wave a hand towards the quantum-fuzziness of everything at the tiny dimensions characterizing the start of each new Bang. However, recent studies in quantum cosmology by Hartle and Gell-Mann suggest that most universes growing from such tiny dimensions would indeed be greatly different from ours.[13] These universes would not even contain particles or readily detectable laws since they would be dominated by "chaotic, non-linear" effects and by "non-locality" (the breakdown of the distinction between being near and being far, so that any orderly systems would be disrupted by events which would otherwise be occurring at a safe distance). Further, the now popular "superstring" theories indicate that particle properties and even the dimensionality of space-time might vary from universe to universe according to how *compactification*—a rolling-up of some of a universe's dimensions as its temperature began to fall—chanced to proceed in each case. Finally and most significantly, modern theories of *symmetry-breaking* suggest that particle masses, which in turn help determine the strengths of nature's main forces, reflect the intensities of scalar fields which could vary probabilistically from one huge domain to another. Before the Big Bang cooled sufficiently for the scalar fields to appear, all particles were massless and all forces (with the possible exception of gravity) were "symmetrical," that is, virtually indistinguishable.

In short, modern theorists find it easy to invent mechanisms for making *apparent physics* and *overt properties* differ from one universe to another even when the underlying physics and the most fundamental properties remain always the same.

ii. *A gigantic or infinite space divided into domains.* Several writers, for instance Ellis, have pointed out that if the universe is "open" (instead of being "closed" like the surface of a sphere by gravitational bending), then it probably stretches infinitely and contains infinitely much material.[14] Huge regions could be contracting while others expanded at any of a great range of speeds; degrees of turbulence could vary widely from region to region; and modern theories—particularly of symmetry-breaking as discussed just a moment ago—could explain why particle masses and force strengths differed from region to region, making it more or less inevitable that some regions had properties appropriately tuned for giving rise to living organisms.

The notion that space is open and infinite is nowadays rather unpopular, yet this is due mainly to the popularity of the inflationary method (see above) for producing an almost "flat" cosmos from a tiny region which becomes gigantic while remaining closed. Now, inflation could provide plenty of room for properties to differ from place to place. The volume at present visible to us, of radius about fifteen billion light years (the sort of distance light could have traveled towards us since the Bang), would be a minuscule fragment of the whole. If the cosmos quickly divided into domains with different properties, rather like the differently oriented crystals on a freezing pond, then the inflation theory suggests that even our own domain now stretches far beyond our present horizon. The fact that this domain interacts with others only at its vastly distant edges, and that its characteristics differ from theirs, could encourage us to speak of it as a separate world or small-u universe inside the greater Universe or cosmos.

Perhaps the most interesting variant of this is the "chaotic inflation" of A. D. Linde.[15] Linde's cosmos inflates for ever. Inside it, there constantly develop gigantic regions—universes or, as Russians like Linde often prefer to say, "metagalaxies"—which differ not merely in their particle masses and force strengths but also in their dimensionalities, in their metric signatures, in their "vacuum energy densities" (the intensities of the fields filling even "empty" space), in their "gauge symmetries" (which determine how many forces and types of particle are found in each), and in other ways as well.

iii. *Many-Worlds quantum mechanics.* First developed by Everett,[16] Many-Worlds quantum mechanics supplies a startling mechanism for generating regions separate enough to be called worlds or universes—and, as always, we could appeal to symmetry-breaking, and so on, to give different (overt) properties to those regions, thereby reinforcing our grounds for calling them worlds or universes. Everett started from the puzzle of why quantum theory's basic equations say nothing about wave-function collapse, the supposed process whereby fuzziness and probability are replaced by definiteness and actuality. His solution was that wave-functions never truly collapse. Instead the cosmos at each instant splits into branches, "worlds" (as they are usually named), which thereafter interact hardly at all: they "jostle" one another just sufficiently to set up, for instance, the strange effect seen in a double-slit experiment where *single electrons* appear to pass through *both* slits in a screen and then interact with themselves so as to help build patterns similar to those of wave interference. Observers, like everything else, are constantly splitting into multiple copies of themselves, each confined to one of the newest branches and unable to detect the thoughts and observations of his or her doubles in the other branches. All this might be no more fantastic than the phenomena which quantum theory seeks to explain.

iv. *Quantum-fluctuational universes.* Of the many other suggested mechanisms for generating multiple universes, perhaps the most important ones reflect the ideas of E. P. Tryon.[17] Tryon offers "the modest proposal that our universe is simply one of those things which happen from time to time."[18] Quantum theory portrays even "empty" space as a ferment of particles popping into existence and then vanishing before the energy accounts become more unbalanced than is allowed by Heisenberg's uncertainty principle. The smaller the energy tied up in any such particle, the longer it can survive. Tryon postulates a superspace in which entire universes jump into being and then last indefinitely long because their gravitational energy is (as is standardly the case with the physicist's "binding energies") *negative energy,* an energy balancing the positive energy of material particles and fields. While "vacuum fluctuations on the scale of our universe are probably quite rare," observers "always find themselves in universes capable of generating life, and such universes are impressively large," he comments.[19]

Later variants replace Tryon's superspace by a space-time foam or speak of universes quantum-tunnelling "from nothing" (where, however, the "nothing" has interestingly specific characteristics). People have tried to show that the properties of any such universe would be fairly firmly dictated, yet this now appears mistaken.

IV. Anthropic Reasoning

There is wide misunderstanding of the anthropic principle and of how it can help explain things.

i. The word "anthropic" is frequently taken to mark some special concern with *anthropos*, with the human species. But the anthropic principle's original definer and baptizer, Carter, insists that he had in mind just a "cognizability principle" concerning the prerequisites of observers, *intelligent organisms* of whatever kind—it being assumed that such beings as immaterial angels are to be disregarded.

ii. It is often complained that the anthropic principle is a tautology, so can explain nothing. The answer to this is that while tautologies cannot by themselves explain anything, they can *enter into* explanations. The tautology that three fours make twelve can help explain why it is risky to visit the wood when three sets of four lions entered it and only eleven exited. The tautology that we could not exist in life-excluding conditions could help throw light on why we are not making our observations at the sun's center or at a time very early in the history of the universe.

iii. Carter distinguished a "weak" and a "strong" anthropic principle: the weak principle stated that our spatiotemporal location "is *necessarily* privileged to the extent of being compatible with our existence as observers," while the strong one said that our universe "must be such as to admit the creation of observers within it at some stage."[20] People have often imagined that he was proposing some deep philosophical division here. Their belief has been that the weak anthropic principle just reminds us that our surroundings must be life-permitting, whereas the strong principle declares dramatically that our universe, or absolutely any real universe, is forced to be life-containing. But although so many have had this belief that it may now no longer be wrong (since custom eventually gives respectability to many an error), Carter has repeatedly made clear that he intended nothing of the kind. Carter's weak principle reminds us of the obvious but oft neglected truth that our place and time must, granted that we are in fact there, be a place and time in which observers can exist: they are not, for example, fried immediately, as they would be shortly after the Big Bang. Carter's strong principle similarly reminds us that our universe must—as we do exist in it, don't we?–be a universe whose nature is not observer-excluding: it is not, say, a universe which recollapses a fraction of a second after beginning its expansion so that intelligent life has insufficient time to evolve. The "must" is in both cases like that of "The photo is marked WIFE, so *must* be of a woman." No suggestion that the photo *had to be* of a woman or that it is somehow especially easy to be a woman! The anthropic principle does not state that we live in a "cozy" universe, well-constructed for our comfort, a universe crammed with living intelligence from side to side and from start to finish, or even a universe in which life was almost certain to appear somewhere, some day.

In many cases there is actually quite a problem of deciding whether it is Carter's weak or his strong principle which applies. A spatio-temporal region that one cosmologist calls "just a time and a place," making it fall under the weak principle, is called by another "a world or universe" so that the strong principle covers it. Is each cycle of an oscillating cosmos a mere time or period, or shall we refer to it as a universe? Inside an inflationary cosmos, is a huge spatial volume a universe, or a mere place? It can be a trivial matter of verbal preference, and the distinction between "weak" and "strong" is then equally trivial and verbal.

iv. Correspondingly the anthropic principle, as Carter intended it to be understood, has nothing to do with teleology or theism. Not even Carter's strong principle says that God ensured that the universe's properties permitted or necessitated the evolution of intelligent life. Again, Carter's anthropic principle in no way declares, idealistically, that *to be* is the same as *to be observed,* either for philosophical or for quantum-physical reasons.

Nevertheless one must remember that *the evidence of fine tuning could well be interpreted teleologically or theistically* (or maybe even idealistically) instead of being explained in terms of many, very diverse universes and "anthropic" observational selection.

v. It is sometimes protested that users of the anthropic principle "reason back to front": they make our universe's character a consequence of our existence, whereas even fools should see that it is instead our existence which results from the universe's character. Oddly enough, some of the most vigorous protesters are philosophers. A philosopher ought to know that there are logical consequences as well as causal ones. When Hawking suggested that our observation of a universe whose early expansion rate allowed galaxies to form was "in a sense a consequence of our existence,"[21] he meant the (logical) sense in which being a woman is a consequence of being a wife, not the (causal) sense in which being a wife is a common consequence of being a woman.

vi. Still, users of the anthropic principle are not guilty of *replacing causal explanations by logical ones.* They do not deny that complex causal stories would be essential to full explanation of why a particular universe came to contain living beings. Compare, for a start, how saying that a square peg cannot be fitted into a round hole with the same cross-sectional area is not denying that a long, long story involving quark and electron movements would be needed for any really complete understanding of why any given peg resisted being thrust into any particular hole.

Suppose you want to know why you have managed to catch a fish neither too big for your net, nor so small as to fall through it. Suppose the net is so ridiculously designed that only fish of an extremely limited range of sizes could be caught. Why did the net catch a particular fish at a particular time? A full explanation would include the entire history of this fish from birth onwards. But a useful partial explanation would be that there were very many fish in the lake, fish of very varied sizes, so that it was quite likely that an appropriately sized fish would sooner or later swim by.

"Yet doesn't the partial explanation possess some redundant features? Once we know the complete life-story of the fish which was caught, don't we see that the other fish were irrelevant?" True enough, the life-stories of the other fish might be separate, either totally or in all relevant respects, from that of the caught fish. If *to explain* a fish-catching could only mean *to give its causal history,* then the other fish might indeed fall outside the explanation, the relevant causal tale. Still, we ought to distrust the idea that this tale concerned *the one and only fish in the lake.* The existence of many fish would help make it believable that there was one of the right size. It would throw light on the affair. It would reduce or remove reasons for puzzlement. Now, "an explanation" can mean that sort of thing too.

vii. The explanation would not involve claiming that the lake contained fish of all possible sizes–so it is strange to hear people suggesting that anthropic explanations presuppose that *all possible universes* actually exist. The most that such explanations could need would be *sufficiently many* universes to make it quite likely that observers would evolve inside one of them.

Again, no anthropic explanation of fine tuning need say that absolutely all of our universe's properties are crucial to the presence of life in it. This would be like a fisherman's claim that no fish could be caught by his net unless coming from exactly the right lake.

viii. Users of anthropic reasoning need not claim that the existence of many other universes had somehow *made it more likely that our universe would develop life-permitting properties* when it underwent early probabilistic compactifications or probabilistic symmetry-breakings. This would be like claiming that the existence of many other fish in the lake had made it more likely that the particular fish which was caught *would grow* to precisely the dimensions necessary for it to be caught; or that, in an experiment involving a sleeping man who was to be wakened only when triple-six was thrown with three fair dice, that the existence of many earlier throws of the dice would somehow have made triple-six more likely to occur when it did; or that when a forest is filled with many men, then all the men who were not in fact hit by the randomly flying arrow had somehow made it more likely that the particular man who was hit would be hit–rather than just making it more likely that some man or other would be.

The true situation is instead as follows. First, the presence of greatly many, greatly varied universes could render it unsurprising that one or several universes had life-permitting properties. And second, it would further be unsurprising that any living being would find himself, herself, or itself in one of the life-permitting universes and not in a life-excluding one.

Both of these points are crucial to making the fine tuning unsurprising. It is not enough to appeal just to the second point, saying that if our universe hadn't been appropriately tuned, then *we shouldn't be here to discuss it* and that therefore the fine tuning cannot be a sign of many universes. This would be like your saying that if all fifty riflemen in the firing squad hadn't missed, then you would be dead, unable to consider the matter, and that therefore their failure could show nothing. You would instead need to postulate something like a million firing-squad cases: sufficiently many to make it fairly likely that in at least one case all the bullets would miss. Or else you would need teleology: the riflemen wanted to miss, or God deflected the bullets. What has to be rejected is an inexplicable coincidence between a one and only universe and fine tuned observability.

Likewise, it is not enough to say that a life-permitting universe would quite probably occur somewhere, given sufficiently many, sufficiently varied universes. One needs the further point that *here,* the universe where we find ourselves, cannot (since we find ourselves here) be a life-excluding universe. It has to be life-permitting. Yet remember always that this *does not* mean that it *had to become* life-permitting: that it had, for example, been sure from the very first moment of its existence that the dice of quantum indeterminism *would* fall in such a way that early symmetry-breakings occurred life-permittingly. The universe which became "here" to us may not have been at all likely to become anyone's "here." When it initially came to exist, it might have been highly improbable that it would ever become life-permitting. (It could have been exactly as improbable, no matter how many earlier universes there had been—assuming, that is to say, that the universes were spread out in time, perhaps as cycles of an oscillating cosmos. Even the very first life-permitting universe could then, like the first triple-six thrown with three fair dice, be likely to have occurred *on some occasion or other* which was much later than the earliest possible occasion. Yet this does not say that *particular* later universes, the ninety-five trillionth universe, for example, would have been more likely to be life-permitting than the earliest one.)

ix. It is sometimes held that believers in multiple universes defy the principle that scientific theories (or perhaps all theories which are not utterly meaningless) must be supportable by evidence. How could we ever have actual evidence of the existence of other universes?

The quick answer is that people insisting always on *direct* evidence could nowadays do little science. How could we actually see quarks or superstrings or the situation in the first three minutes after the Big Bang, or the interior of a black hole? Scientists of today work with evidence that is very indirect. We have indirect evidence of something, when the existence of this something would throw light on the things whereof we have direct evidence: the lion is indirectly evidenced by the roaring sounds, and the quark by the elegance which its existence would bring to our understanding of bubble chamber photographs. Now, it is thoroughly question-begging to say that the existence of greatly many, greatly varied universes could not possibly throw light on the fine tuning which we see.

Bear in mind that the story of cosmic inflation is accepted by almost all cosmologists nowadays. It tells of gigantic regions ("worlds," "universes") which cannot possibly be directly observed: they are far beyond our present fifteen-billion-light-year horizon. Most of them may remain beyond the horizon at all future times.

x. It is sometimes protested that to believe in *greatly varied* universes is to defy the principle of induction, which states that we have grounds for belief in situations only when they are interestingly like others we have experienced. How could we ever have reason to accept universes with laws different from those familiar to us?

The answer to this is that, as indicated earlier, it need not be thought that the most fundamental laws differ from universe to universe. Instead *apparent physics,* the physics of derived laws and overt properties, can be what is imagined as varying. One and the same set of fundamental laws and properties could give rise to situations which seemed wildly different (supposing that anyone could experience them) when compactifications, symmetry-breakings, etc. had chanced to occur in different ways.

The same point refutes the following objection: that talk of our universe's improbable, fine tuned character must involve an absurd claim to know how frequently life-permitting universes appear in the field of all logically possible universes. The answer to this is that there is no need to consider so gigantic a field. We can limit our attention to the field of such possible universes as are, in their fundamental laws, recognizably like ours: universes which can have forces and particles and expansion rates, but where the forces have different strengths and the particles different masses, and where the expansion rates differ. While they are often wrong, cosmologists are not just guessing blindly when they suggest, for example, that if our universe had been expanding marginally less quickly, then it would have recollapsed long before life could appear.

Imagine a fly on a wall. Around it, an empty area stretches a yard in each direction. A bullet hits the fly. This can forcefully suggest that many bullets are hitting the wall or that the bullet was carefully aimed. One need not ask whether *distant* areas of the wall are crawling with flies so that almost any bullets hitting there would hit them. What is important is that *the area around this particular fly* is empty.

Rather similarly, a cosmologist arguing "anthropically" for many universes, or a theist concluding instead that God chose our universe's properties like a marksman deciding where to send a bullet, need not claim expertise about the properties of all possible universes, and the proportion of them which would be life-permitting.

xi. It is sometimes protested that there may well be just a single universe, in which case its nature cannot be "improbable" like the throwing of triple-six with fair dice. Probabilities can be estimated only when there are repetitions, or talk of probabilities is utterly meaningless unless there are repetitions.

The answer to this is that it would prove too much. It would show that our universe might well be in no way improbable even if electromagnetism were stronger than gravity by a factor of 112, 012, 100, 202, 100, 021, 011, 211, 021, 112, 100–a figure spelling out MADE BY GOD when its zeros, ones and twos are interpreted as the dots, dashes, and spaces of Morse code.

The truth is that actual repetitions are inessential to the meaning of probability statements. The very most that could be required is that repetitions be conceivable. Even if there in fact exists just the one universe, it sounds bizarre to say there could not conceivably have existed any others or that the nature of this one universe could not possibly have depended on early probabilistic processes. At its earliest moments, our universe appears to have had a density at which quantum effects were greatly important. Quantum mechanics is usually viewed as very fundamentally probabilistic.

xii. It is sometimes said that appeal to multiple universes and anthropic observational selection is the lazy scientist's approach which could be used to "explain" almost anything.

This is unfair. It takes hard work to discover a plausible mechanism for generating many and varied universes and to show how various features of our universe are essential to the evolution of intelligent organisms. Further, great care is often needed to avoid the kind of trap into which Boltzmann fell.[22] Boltzmann pictured a cosmos extending so far spatially and/or temporally that it would be bound to contain domains which had fluctuated into the kind of thermal disequilibrium (low entropy) which is life's prerequisite. He pointed out that observers could find themselves only in such domains. Alas, his theory places us in a fluctuation much larger than is needed to explain our ability to observe things. A much tinier fluctuation, where our brains, bodies, and immediate surroundings were oases in a desert of disorder, would be far more probable, just as coin-tossing will far more probably yield fifty heads in a row, than fifty million.

xiii. Finally, it is often objected that users of anthropic reasoning wrongly assume that intelligent life is in special need of explanation, like a coin's falling heads a thousand times. Yet wouldn't just any universe be "fine tuned" to produce *something*? What is so special about life, rather than rocks or rubies? Indeed, aren't life's prerequisites just the prerequisites of long-lived stable stars, planets, water, carbon, and so forth; so why talk of tuning *for life* rather than for these?

The best reply involves asking why a run of a thousand heads should be thought special. Isn't this exactly as likely as any other observed single sequence of a thousand tosses? Yes, if the coin truly is a fair one instead of being double-headed, and if other sequences could equally easily be observed. But on witnessing even twenty successive heads, wouldn't you suspect double-headedness? Or, dragged into a room to observe twenty coins lying heads, suppose you knew all twenty were fair and had been tossed together. Wouldn't you suspect that the tosser had tossed for a long time before achieving this fine result and dragging you in? What is operating here is the Merchant's Thumb principle: the principle that a main ground for suspecting that something stands in special need of explanation is that a plausible explanation springs to mind. The thumb of a silk merchant cannot fail to be *somewhere,* yet if it covers a hole in the silk, then one suspects he positioned it carefully. A hand of cards which at first seems rubbish, a product of mere chance, can come to seem very special indeed–very much in need of an explanation in terms of cheating–when you recall that the rules of this particular game make this a powerful hand and that a million dollars are at stake.

In the case of the fine tuning we have, so to speak, a hundred factors conspiring to produce a fish of almost exactly 23.2576 inches. What is so special there, when every fish must have some length or other? (What's special in *life-encouraging* force strengths, particle masses, cosmic expansion rates, and so forth? All possible force strengths, masses, speeds, would yield *some* particular effects which slightly different factors would not yield.) Well, the fish comes to seem special, that is, specially in need of an explanation by something other than merest chance, when you discover that your fishing apparatus is exceptionally fussy, able to catch only fish of more or less exactly this length. For then two possible tidy explanations suggest themselves: first, that there are greatly many differently lengthed fish in the lake so that it was likely that the apparatus would catch one for you to observe, and second, that a well-wisher has reared a fish of exactly the right length for you to catch.

The second of these two explanations of course corresponds to the teleological or theistic explanation of the fine tuning. When the next section discusses "anthropic" predictions, bear in mind that sometimes no similar predictions would be made by those who prefer an explanation of the teleological or theistic kind–which is, remember, not anthropic at all, when "anthropic" is used in Carter's sense.

V. Anthropic Predictions

The common claim that the anthropic principle leads to no predictions is based, usually, on recognizing that the principle is a tautology. Isn't it trivially obvious that life's prerequisites are satisfied, granted that we living beings exist? How could this lead to anything new?

Well, just as a tautologous anthropic principle can enter into explanations, as already discussed, so also can it enter into acts of prediction. It can *encourage* predictions without itself making them.

i. Recall that Hoyle felt encouraged to predict delicate tuning of carbon-producing resonance levels; also that Hawking felt encouraged to predict that basic physics did not dictate the universe's early expansion rate, so that in most universes galaxies would not form; and that anthropic considerations encouraged Dicke and Carter to predict that Dirac and Eddington were wrong in their explanations of various gigantic ratios.

ii. You cannot treat our universe's fine tuned characteristics as *observationally selected* unless believing that there actually exist universes with differing characteristics. People aware of the anthropic principle will be specially inclined to predict that at least one mechanism for generating many and varied universes will come to seem highly plausible. They may predict, for example, that the Higgs boson will shortly be found, reinforcing the theory that it is interactions with a Higgs scalar field which give particles their masses, and, that it will next be confirmed that a Higgs field can take various stable or metastable values with almost equal potential energies so that such a field could well have settled down to different values in different domains of a cooling, "crystallizing" cosmos.

Several mechanisms might all contribute to producing variations between universes. Remember, there is no standard way of deciding what should be called a universe and what a huge spatiotemporal region. One mechanism could generate universes in great number; another might then generate vast domains inside them, domains which could themselves be called universes; and yet another might then give birth to still more domains/universes inside each of those. This would be very speculative. Being aware of the anthropic principle can make one more inclined to speculate—to predict tentatively not only that no Nobel prize will be earned for a Theory of Everything which dictates all physical force strengths and particle masses, but even that many mechanisms for making universes will survive detailed investigation.

It is curious to find Pagels arguing that the anthropic principle "never predicts anything" and then, in his next breath, that the principle has been refuted by new findings such as those that support the inflation theory (which allegedly shows why our universe came to expand at a life-permitting rate).[23] If anthropic reasoning cannot help predict anything, then it cannot be refuted by new findings, can it? Besides, inflation may (as already noted) itself require considerable tuning, on which the anthropic principle could throw light. And the inflation theory supplies us with a gigantic cosmos and also with reasons for thinking that it is divided into domains with differing characteristics. In fact, *without* inflation we should be hard pressed to explain why characteristics which had been settled probabilistically came to be settled in the same way right out to our horizon, some fifteen billion light years distant. An important "anthropic prediction" is thus that inflation will be confirmed.

iii. The anthropic principle reminds us that even if intelligent life were hard to achieve, we should find ourselves in a spatiotemporal region in which it had been achieved. This can encourage confidence that it really is hard to achieve and that no exotic life-forms exist in defiance of the alleged need for fine tuning. Life, then, will not be found in frozen hydrogen or at the Earth's or the sun's centre or in neutron stars or interstellar clouds or in the other strange places suggested by Feinberg and Shapiro.[24] It could even well be that carbon, which Hoyle and Dicke thought essential to it, truly is essential. And, once having accepted that observable situations could easily be unrepresentative of reality as a whole, we shall be more inclined to predict that many observed matters, which so far appear unimportant, will in due course be found to be crucial to observership, while other things still to be discovered will again turn out to be crucial.

At the same time, one must not forget that anthropic (observational-selection) explanations can run into the kind of trouble that destroyed Boltzmann's position. Steigman proposed that the observed excess of matter over antimatter reflected chance plus the fact that an excess was needed for observers to evolve.[25] He was wrong not only in fact (since the excess was soon successfully explained in another way) but also in inductive logic—for he should have reflected that the matter excess which we see is actually much greater than needed and, the greater the excess, the more unlikely it is that chance produced it. Weinberg took care not to imitate him when discussing the extremely small value of the cosmological constant.[26] Its smallness is essential to our existence because a universe in which it was large would be expanding or contracting violently. In a closed universe, Weinberg reasoned, this could be the basis of an anthropic explanation. In an open universe, in contrast, such an explanation would fail because slightly larger and apparently much more probable values of the constant would also be life-permitting. Anthropic considerations would thus have led us to expect those values instead.

iv. Clearly, anthropic explanations are very much open to refutation. The associated predictions (for example, that life will not be found in the sun or on waterless planets) may be disproved, or the explanations may be found to be technically faulty—based on wrong physics or on unimaginative biology or (cf. Boltzmann and Steigman) leading us to expect something much less impressive than what we actually see.

Anthropic explanations might even be faulty because various characteristics, which really are remarkably accurately tuned, are so because the universes which exhibit them *reproduce themselves* better like rabbits with wombs superbly formed for multiple gestations. Smohin suggests that the carbon-generating capacities of stars, which Hoyle interpreted anthropically, could equally well be explained by a tie between plentiful production of carbon and later production of numerous black holes.[27] Each black hole gives birth to another universe which tends to inherit the same superb ability to produce stellar carbon and black holes and more universes. (Any universe born from a black hole expands into a space of its own, invisibly to us, so all this is not in obvious conflict with experience. Yet a seemingly simpler way of getting numerous black holes would be to have immense turbulence, so Smohin's story probably needs supplementation by the point that in immensely turbulent universes no observers can evolve.)

In Linde's eternally inflating, chaotic cosmos, where universes are constantly generating more universes, some of the universes have scalar fields so superbly tuned that they inflate enormously.[28] Perhaps only those universes are life-permitting; but even if others were too, living beings could most expect to see the enormously inflated ones since these are so large, so rich in places where living beings could evolve. And if a universe's inflationary prowess could be inherited by its offspring, wouldn't this too help to show that an enormously inflated universe was most likely to be observed? Each such universe would give birth to specially many further universes because there was specially much space inside it, space in which new universes could be born, and these further universes would in turn give birth to specially many.

v. It is tempting to use a "superweak" anthropic principle which reminds us (tautologically, as before) that if intelligent life's emergence, *no matter how hospitable the environment,* always involves very improbable happenings, then all intelligent living beings emerged where such happenings happened. Even if most planets, no matter how well provided with carbon and water, et cetera, remained lifeless because life's first beginnings require very, very improbable molecular combinations, our own planet would be one of the lucky ones, unsurprisingly.[29] Carter uses similar points to help explain why the time human intelligence took to evolve was roughly comparable to the total period available for its evolution, which he took to be the period between Earth's formation and the day of our sun's becoming a red giant. He suggests that it would be only extremely rarely that such high intelligence evolved fast enough–but, of course, our own species must (since we are discussing the matter) have been among those fortunate enough to beat the clock.[30]

Barrow and Tipler extend Carter's reasoning in complex ways, reaching the conclusion that mankind will probably become extinct within forty thousand or so years.[31] But, having criticized their argument elsewhere,[32] let me instead give another argument for a similarly pessimistic conclusion. It was discovered by Carter some ten years ago but first put into print by me and by Nielsen.[33] This "doomsday argument" says that *the risk that the human race will fairly soon become extinct has been systematically underestimated.*

Let us creep up on the doomsday argument by noting that observership's prerequisites are seldom entirely firm. For example, observers *just might* exist in the early universe, coming out of black holes. Black holes radiate particles in a random way so that, given sufficiently many such holes, some would (like monkeys typing sonnets) "emit . . . the works of Proust in ten leather-bound volumes" or even somebody just like Charles Darwin.[34] Still, no observer should expect to find that he or she had originated in this way. And likewise, nobody should expect that his or her race was the very first of many intelligent races to evolve–which suggests that either there are (or have been) many intelligent races besides ours, or else humans are more or less the only intelligent beings there ever will be.

Carter noticed that, very similarly, *one would have strong grounds for expecting not to be very exceptionally early in human population history.* One would not expect, for example, to be among the first 0.0001% of all humans who would ever be born. Now, if the human race were going to end soon then, obviously, we should not be exceptionally early; neither should we be very exceptionally late, since recent population growth means that roughly 10% of all humans who have so far been born are still alive today. If, on the other hand, the human race failed to end soon—if it survived for many more centuries even at its present size, let alone at the size it would soon reach if it started colonizing the galaxy—then we should indeed be very exceptionally early. Carter reasons that this ought to reduce any confidence that our race will have a long future. Compare how, if your name comes very early from a hat, then you have increased reasons for suspecting that the hat did not contain ten thousand names.

Admittedly this argument is weakened if the world is radically indeterministic and if the indeterminism is likely to affect how long the human race will last. Still, it could be powerful against the view that it is altogether probable that the race will last long, because the words "altogether probable" mark a belief that any indeterminism is unlikely to affect the matter.

Do not trust the first objection which springs to mind—for example, that later humans *are not alive yet* to observe their temporal positions; or, that we *know* we live in the 1990s and would be just as sure of this, no matter what our theories about our race's future; or, that genes like ours are common only near the 1990s, so we cannot fail to live then. If trustworthy, these objections would make nonsense not only of the doomsday argument but also of other forms of anthropic reasoning which are fairly obviously strong: for example, Dicke's reasoning starting from how one would most probably find oneself alive before most of the life-giving stars had burned out.

Carter has written to me that he considers the doomsday argument "obviously the most practically important application of the anthropic principle." As the argument is just for a *reduction in confidence* that our species will survive long, it encourages us to take great care with germ warfare, destruction of the ozone layer, et cetera. It does not tell us that the risk of imminent annihilation is exactly as high, no matter what precautions we take. Instead, it can persuade us to treat even seemingly slight dangers seriously, when humankind's survival is in question. Whereas, for example, nuclear bombs could seem able only to depress population figures temporarily, there would be no way in which the human race could survive a vacuum instability disaster brought on by experiments at very high energies, the sudden creation of a bubble which expands at nearly the speed of light arid destroys everything.[35] The doomsday argument can suggest that we should be very careful to avoid *that*.[36]

VI. The Teleological or Theistic Alternative

Let us now examine the teleological or theistic way of accounting for the fine tuning, and the predictions it might encourage. By a teleological approach to our universe, I mean one which explains it by reference to a purpose it fulfils. The most important teleological position is theism, the theory that God's power and goodness are responsible for our universe's existence and for its life-permitting properties.

Theism *is compatible with* universes in great number and great variety, for why should God create just a single universe, or universes of just one kind? Nevertheless, theistic explanations *compete with* explanations that appeal to multiple universes and to anthropic observational selection. If we accept the one kind of explanation for the fine tuning, then there is less need to accept the other, and the two kinds tend to lead to different predictions.

How do things stand with respect to prediction of doomsday? It is unclear that theism affects this. Some would argue that God would have grounds to protect the human race, perhaps by making ours a universe in which no vacuum instability disaster could occur; yet might we instead reason that God would create hugely or infinitely many universes so that there would be no lack of living-space even if one of them came to be uninhabitable? Using the words "anthropic principle" in a way that Carter rejects, Tipler has stated a "final anthropic principle" that conscious life will at no time die out.[37] Dyson and others had pioneered fascinating accounts of how it could survive indefinitely even in an ever-expanding cosmos, a cosmos constantly growing colder and more dilute, arid Tipler's "Omega-point" theory has a Big Collapse reaching a final and timeless state as intelligent information-processing becomes infinite.[38] But while Tipler finds his picture ethically attractive and fully consonant with theism, not everyone would agree. At a papal workshop of 1987, John Polkinghorne condemned it as replacing ultimate fellowship with God by something comparable to a gigantic self-conscious encyclopaedia. (Tipler also offers non-theistic support for his final anthropic principle, associating it with a "participatory anthropic principle" defended by Wheeler.[39] The proposal is that quantum theory be interpreted idealistically: no reality is a reality unless it is observed. A criticism of this approach is that it appears "absurdly circular": it involves saying that observations collapse quantum wave-functions "*which must remain uncollapsed until observations occur* while at the same time the brains and bodies essential to those observations *themselves depend for the details of their evolution on how wave-functions collapse in particular ways.*"[40] However, Wheeler amid Tipler view past, present, and future as tied together so intimately that such a criticism may amount merely to a complaint that their world-model is too complicated.)

With respect to other matters, the position is somewhat more clear. Thus, whether or not they believe in multiple universes, theists too should take an interest in the apparent fine tuning, predicting that further instances of it will be discovered. In fact they often oppose it, yet this seems just a case of their being reluctant to believe in things which might be evidence of God's hand, when doing so got opponents of Galileo and of Darwin into so much trouble. They have insufficiently appreciated that others besides theists can believe in such things. Fine tuning can be interpreted atheistically as well as theistically. Still, they should surely permit themselves some slight preference for interpreting it theistically. Theists should feel less pressure to accept that fine tuned force strengths, particle masses, and so on, are products of chance. Yes, they might perhaps picture God as creating immensely many universes, confident that probabilistic factors (symmetry-breakings or whatever) would sooner or later lead to a life-containing one. But they could at least equally well suppose that God created just one universe, or many universes of just one kind, and that he fine tuned things to suit life's needs–maybe by selection of the right values for force strengths, particle masses, et cetera, but perhaps instead by selecting fundamental laws which dictated the right values.

Atheists, in contrast, should be unwilling to accept that any laws dictated those values, for this would give them two unattractive positions to choose between: (a) One would be that there were greatly many universes obeying different laws and that the fine tuning of our universe was really fine tuning of its laws, laws observationally selected as the anthropic principle suggests–but here it seems right to protest that (unless produced by a deity who wanted variety) such variation in laws would be implausible, much harder to accept than any variation in force strengths and particle masses while the laws remained constant. (b) Yet the other position would be little better, for it would be that all the factors which seemed fine tuned to life's needs *were in point of fact dictated by the only fundamental laws which mathematical consistency allowed.* The idea of tuning a force strength or a particle mass should then be dismissed. It would be like that of "tuning" the ratio of an Euclidean circle's diameter to its circumference. Now, there are two defects in this position. First, it can appear easy enough to conceive universes with different laws, without running into mathematical inconsistency. And second, the position's dismissal of all the seeming evidence of fine tuning sounds far too similar to dismissing what looks like a long, readily intelligible message from extraterrestrials as "just a product of mathematical necessities." You might almost as well suppose that mathematical necessities had written GOD CREATED THE UNIVERSE inside every atom or that this message could be derived in a straightforward way from the first fifty prime numbers.

What could be said for reviving the Design Argument, on the basis of the observed fine tuning? (i) It should by now be evident that very general "refutations" of the Argument are often very unpersuasive. I particularly have in mind those alleged refutations which, if they were valid, would be valid also against all "fine tuning" arguments for multiple universes. It can be unpersuasive to claim, for instance, that probability theory tells us that there could be nothing improbable in fundamental physical laws, not even, for example, if those laws dictated that naturally occurring chain molecules should spell out the ten commandments. (ii) It could seem that making God responsible for the fine tuning was preferable to believing in greatly many universes and in probabilistic variations among them. After all, all multiple-universe theories are highly speculative and some may verge on the fantastic. In his defence of Design, Swinburne is particularly critical of Many-

Worlds quantum mechanics, calling it "an enormous inverted pyramid of theory resting on a vertex of observation."[41] (iii) A force strength or a particle mass often appears to need tuning to its actual value, not just for one reason but for two or three or five. Yet evidently it could not have been tuned first in one way and next in another, to satisfy conflicting requirements. Must we then view it as inexplicable good fortune that the various requirements (for example, of long-lived stable stars, and of complex chemistry) were always in harmony? A better interpretation could seem to be that God selected, from among a great many possible sets of physical laws, one of the rare sets that led to no conflicts.

It is sometimes objected that God's existence could not be supported by any finite evidence, because God is infinite. The objection forgets that an infinite creator could be in a way much simpler than any finite one: compare how it could be simpler to have infinitely many vacuumfluctuational universes rather than six hundred and forty-three. Again, it is sometimes said that making God's mind the ultimate source of the order of the physical world only defers our problem: the question just becomes that of why God's mind is orderly. Yet it is unclear whether God even has a mind in any very ordinary sense; and if God has one, then we can, I think, see how its orderliness might perhaps be explained. My *Value and Existence* defends the doctrine–it has a lengthy history–that the ultimate reason for all actually existing things must lie in the eternal realm of platonic realities, and particularly in an unconditionally real ethical requirement, a requirement *which could itself necessitate* the existence of what is required.[42] Not logically, of course, for ethical requirements are not logical ones; yet not all firm necessitations need be logical necessitations. Contemplating their mere concept from an armchair, we cannot tell that ethical requirements are ever creatively powerful, but neither can we tell that they are always powerless. And the little matter of there existing any world at all, together with the strong semblance of fine tuning, can suggest that they are powerful at times, in cases where they have not entered into conflict with one another. Bear in mind that the standard defence against the Problem of Evil, of why a benevolent deity permits crimes and natural disasters, is that *ethical requirements very often do conflict*. The reason, therefore, why very many ethical requirements are powerless, might be that they have been overruled by other ethical requirements. As developed by Plotinus and Paul Tillich, this line of thought may lead to the conclusion that "God" simply names an ethical requirement which is responsible for the world's existence. But, alternatively, one could follow Ewing, picturing a divine mind as owing its existence and orderliness to its perfection, its supreme ethical requiredness.[43]

NOTES

1. Brandon Carter, "Large Number Coincidences and the Anthropic Principle in Cosmology," pp. 131–139 in this volume.
2. R. H. Dicke, "Dirac's Cosmology and Mach's Principle,"

pp. 127–130 in this volume.

3. Carter, "Large Number Coincidences," pp. 136–139 in this volume.

4. Fred Hoyle, *Galaxies, Nuclei and Quasars* (London: Heinemann, 1965), 159.

5. S. W. Hawking, "The Anisotropy of the Universe at Large Times," in Longair, *Confrontation,* 283–86.

6. Paul Davies, *The Accidental Universe* (Cambridge: Cambridge University Press, 1982). John D. Barrow and Frank J. Tipler, *The Anthropic Cosmological Principle* (Oxford: Clarendon Press, 1986). John Leslie, *Universes* (New York: Routledge, 1989).

7. Roger Penrose, "Singularities and Time-Asymmetry," in *General Relativity: An Einstein Centenary Survey,* ed. S. W. Hawking and W. Israel (Cambridge: Cambridge University Press, 1979), 581–638.

8. Roger Penrose, "Difficulties with Inflationary Cosmology," in *Fourteenth Texas Symposium on Relativistic Astrophysics,* ed. E. J. Fenyves (New York: New York Academy of Sciences, 1989), 249–64.

9. See, for example, Paul Davies, "What caused the Big Bang?" pp. 226–244 in this volume.

10. Barrow and Tipler, *Anthropic Principle,* and Leslie, *Universes.*

11. J. A. Wheeler, "Beyond the End of Time," pp. 213–221 in this volume.

12. A. E. Sikkema and W. Israel, "Black-Hole Mergers and Mass Inflation in a Bouncing Universe," *Nature* (3 January 1991): 45–47.

13. J. B. Hartle, "The Quantum Mechanics of Cosmology," in *Quantum Cosmology and Baby Universes,* ed. S. Coleman, J. B. Hartle, T. Piran, and S. Weinberg (Singapore: World Scientific, 1991), 65–151.

14. See, for example, Barrow and Tipler, *Anthropic Principle,* 434–36.

15. A. D. Linde, *Inflation and Quantum Cosmology* (San Diego: Academic Press, 1990)

16. Hugh Everett, "'Relative State' Formulation of Quantum Mechanics," *Reviews of Modern Physics* 29 (1957): 454–62. B. S. DeWitt and N. Graham, eds., *The Many-Worlds Interpretation of Quantum Mechanics* (Princeton: Princeton University Press, 1973).

17. E. P. Tryon, "Is the Universe a Vacuum Fluctuation?" pp. 222–225 in this volume.

18. Ibid., 224

19. Ibid., 225

20. Carter, "Large Number Coincidences," pp. 133–135 in this volume.

21. C. B. Collins and S. W. Hawking, "Why Is the Universe Isotropic?" *Astrophysical Journal* 180, no. 2 (1 March 1973): 317–34, quotation p. 334.

22. L. Bohzmann, "On Certain Questions of the Theory of Gases," *Nature* 51 (1895): 413–15.

23. Heinz Pagels, "A Cozy Cosmology," pp. 180–186 in this volume.

24. G. Feinberg and R. Shapiro, *Life beyond Earth* (New York: William Morrow, 1980).

25. G. Steigman, "Confrontation of Antimatter Cosmologies with

Observational Data," in Longair, *Confrontation,* 347–56; see esp. 355.

26. S. Weinberg, "The Cosmological Constant Problem," *Reviews of Modern Physics* 61 (1989): 1–23, see esp. 8–9.

27. L. Smolin, "Did the Universe Evolve?" *Classical and Quantum Gravity* 9 (1992): 173–91.

28. Linde, *Inflation,* 21.

29. M. H. Hart, "Atmospheric Evolution, the Drake Equation, and DNA: Sparse Life in an Infinite Universe," pp. 262–232 in this volume.

30. Brandon Carter in *The Constants of Physics,* ed. W. H. McCrea and M. J. Rees, *Philosophical Transactions of the Royal Society, London* A30 (1983): 347–63. Carter, "The Anthropic Principle: Self-Selection as an Adjunct to Natural Selection," in *Cosmic Perspectives,* ed. S. K. Biswas, et al. (Cambridge: Cambridge University Press, 1989), 185–206; see esp. 200–203.

31. Barrow and Tipler, *Anthropic Principle,* 564–67.

32. Leslie, "Anthropic Predictions," *Philosophia* 23 (1994): 117–44; see esp. 134.

33. Leslie, "Risking the World's End," *Bulletin of the Canadian Nuclear Society* (May 1989): 10–15, reprinted in *Interchange* 21 (1990): 49–58. Leslie, "Time and the Anthropic Principle," *Mind* 101 (1992): 521–40. H. B. Nielsen, "Random Dynamics," *Acta Physica Polonica* B20 (1989): 427–68; see esp. 447–59.

34. S. W. Hawking, "The Quantum Mechanics of Black Holes," *Scientific American* (January 1977): 34–40, quotation on 40. S. W. Hawking and W. Israel, eds., *General Relativity* (Cambridge: Cambridge University Press, 1979), 19.

35. J. Ellis, A. Linde, and M. Sher, "Vacuum Stability, Wormholes, Cosmic Rays, and the Cosmological Bounds on Top Quark and Higgs Masses," *Physics Letters* 252B (1990): 203–11.

36. Such points are expanded in John Leslie, *The End of the World: The Science and Ethics of Human Extinction* (London: Routledge, 1996).

37. Brandon Carter, "The Anthropic Selection Principle and the Ultra-Darwinian Synthesis," in *The Anthropic Principle,* ed. F. Bertola and U. Curi (Cambridge: Cambridge University Press, 1989), 33–59; see esp. 35–36. Barrow and Tipler, *Anthropic Principle,* 23 and 659.

38. See S. Frautschi, "Entropy in an Expanding Universe," *Science* 217 (1982): 593–99, and F. J. Tipler, "The Anthropic Principle: A Primer for Philosophers," in *Proceedings of the 1988 Biennial Meeting of the Philosophy of Science Association,* ed. A. Fine and J. Leplin (East Lansing, Mich.: PSA, 1989), 27–48.

39. See, for example, J. A. Wheeler, "Beyond the Black Hole," in *Some Strangeness in the Proportion,* ed. Harry Wolff (Reading, Mass.: Addison-Wesley, 1980), 341–75.

40. Leslie, *Universes,* 88–89.

41. R. Swinburne, "Argument from the Fine-Tuning of the Universe," pp. 160–179 in this volume.

42. John Leslie, *Value and Existence* (Oxford: Blackwell, 1979).

43. A. C. Ewing, *Value and Reality* (London: Allen and Unwin, 1973), chap. 7.

24

PAUL DAVIES*

Our Place in the Universe

IT WAS NEWTON, Galileo and their contemporaries who created science as we know it, three centuries ago. Today we take the scientific method of enquiry so much for granted that few people stop to think how astonishing it is that science works.

Of course, science didn't spring ready-made into the minds of Newton and his colleagues. They were strongly influenced by two long-standing traditions that pervaded European thought. The first was Greek philosophy. Most ancient cultures were aware that the universe is not completely chaotic and capricious: there is a definite order in nature. The Greeks believed that this order could be understood, at least in part, by the application of human reasoning. They maintained that physical existence was not absurd, but rational and logical, and therefore in principle intelligible to us. They discovered that some physical processes had a hidden mathematical basis, and they sought to build a model of reality based on arithmetical and geometrical principles.

The second great tradition was the Judaic world view, according to which the universe was created by God at some definite moment in the past and ordered according to a fixed set of laws. The Jews taught that the universe unfolds in a unidirectional sequence—what we now call linear time—according to a definite historical process: creation, evolution and dissolu-

* This was the acceptance address of Paul Davies upon receiving the Templeton Prize for Progress in Religion on May 3, 1995, in Westminster Abbey, London. It is published with the permission of the Templeton Foundation, Inc.

tion. This notion of linear time–in which the story of the universe has a beginning, a middle and an end–stands in marked contrast to the concept of cosmic cyclicity, the pervading mythology of almost all ancient cultures. Cyclic time–the myth of the eternal return–springs from mankind's close association with the cycles and rhythms of nature, and remains a key component in the belief systems of many cultures today. It also lurks just beneath the surface of the Western mind, erupting occasionally to infuse our art, our folklore and our literature.

A world freely created by God, and ordered in a particular, felicitous way at the origin of a linear time, constitutes a powerful set of beliefs, and was taken up by both Christianity and Islam. An essential element of this belief system is that the universe does not *have* to be as it is: it could have been otherwise. Einstein once said that the thing which most interested him is whether God had any choice in his creation. According to the Judaeo-Islamic-Christian tradition, the answer is a resounding yes.

Although not conventionally religious, Einstein often spoke of God, and expressed a sentiment shared, I believe, by many scientists, including professed atheists. It is a sentiment best described as a reverence for nature and a deep fascination for the natural order of the cosmos. If the universe did not have to be as it is, of necessity–if, to paraphrase Einstein, God did have a choice–then the fact that nature is so fruitful, that the universe is so full of richness, diversity and novelty, is profoundly significant.

Some scientists have tried to argue that if only we know enough about the laws of physics, if we were to discover a final theory that united all the fundamental forces and particles of nature into a single mathematical scheme, then we would find that this superlaw, or theory of everything, would describe the only logically consistent world. In other words the nature of the physical world would be entirely a consequence of logical and mathematical necessity. There would be no choice about it. I think this is demonstrably wrong. There is not a shred of evidence that the universe is logically necessary. Indeed, as a theoretical physicist I find it rather easy to imagine alternative universes that are logically consistent, and therefore equal contenders for reality.

It was from the intellectual ferment brought about by the merging of Greek philosophy and Judaeo-Islamic-Christian thought, that modern science emerged, with its unidirectional linear time, its insistence on nature's rationality, and its emphasis on mathematical principles. All the early scientists such as Newton were religious in one way or another. They saw their science as a means of uncovering traces of God's handiwork in the universe. What we now call the laws of physics they regarded as God's abstract creation: thoughts, so to speak, in the mind of God. So in doing science, they supposed, one might be able to glimpse the mind of God. What an exhilarating and audacious claim!

In the ensuing three hundred years, the theological dimension of science has faded. People take it for granted that the physical world is both ordered and intelligible. The underlying order in nature–the laws of physics—are simply accepted as given, as brute facts. Nobody asks where they come from; at least they don't in polite company. However, even the most atheistic scientist accepts as an act of faith the existence of a lawlike order in nature that is at least in part comprehensible to us. So science can proceed only if the scientist adopts an essentially theological world view.

It has become fashionable in some circles to argue that science is ultimately a sham, that we scientists read order into nature, not out of nature, and that the laws of physics are our laws, not nature's. I believe this is arrant nonsense. You'd be hard pressed to convince a physicist that Newton's inverse square law of gravitation is a purely cultural concoction. The laws of physics, I submit, *really exist* in the world out there, and the job of the scientist is to uncover them, not invent them. True, at any given time, the laws you find in the textbooks are tentative and approximate, but they mirror, albeit imperfectly, a really-existing order in the physical world. Of course, many scientists don't recognize that in accepting the reality of an order in nature, the existence of laws "out there," they are adopting a theological world view. Ironically, one of the staunchest defenders of the reality of the laws of physics is the American physicist Steven Weinberg, a sort of apologetic atheist who, though able to wax lyrical about the mathematical elegance of nature, nevertheless felt compelled to pen the notorious words: "The more the universe seems comprehensible, the more it also seems pointless."

Let us accept, then, that nature really is ordered in a mathematical way—that "the book of nature," to quote Galileo, "is written in mathematical language." Even so, it is easy to imagine an ordered universe which nevertheless remains utterly beyond human comprehension, due to its complexity and subtlety. For me, the magic of science is that we can understand at least part of nature—perhaps in principle all of it—using the scientific method of inquiry. How utterly astonishing that we human beings can do this! Why should the rules on which the universe runs be accessible to humans?

The mystery is all the greater when one takes into account the cryptic character of the laws of nature. When Newton saw the apple fall, he saw a falling apple. He didn't see a set of differential equations that link the motion of the apple to the motion of the moon. The mathematical laws that underlie physical phenomena are not apparent to us through direct observation; they have to be painstakingly extracted from nature using arcane procedures of laboratory experiment and mathematical theory. The laws are hidden from us, and are revealed only after much labour. The late Heinz Pagels—another atheist physicist—described this by saying that the laws of nature are written in a sort of cosmic code, and that the job of the scientist is to crack the code and reveal the message—nature's message, God's message, take your choice, but not *our* message. The extraordinary thing is that human beings have evolved such a fantastic code-breaking talent. This is the wonder and the magnificence of science; we can use it to decode nature and discover the secret laws that make the universe tick!

Many people want to find God in the *creation* of the universe, in the big bang that started it all off. They imagine a superbeing who deliberates for all eternity, then presses a metaphysical button and produces a huge explosion. I believe this image is entirely misconceived. Einstein showed us that space and time are *part of* the physical universe, not a preexisting arena in which the universe happens. Cosmologists are convinced that the big bang was the coming-into-being, not just of matter and energy, but of space and time as well. Time itself began with the big bang. If this sounds baffling, it is by no means new. Already in the fifth century St. Augustine proclaimed that "the world was made with time, not in time." According to James Hartle and Stephen Hawking, this coming-into-being of the universe need not be a supernatural process but could occur entirely naturally, in accordance with the laws of quantum physics, which permit the occurrence of genuinely spontaneous events.

The origin of the universe, however, is hardly the end of the story. The evidence suggests that in its primordial phase the universe was in a highly simple, almost featureless state; perhaps a uniform soup of subatomic particles, or even just expanding empty space. All the richness and diversity of matter and energy we observe today has emerged since the beginning in a long and complicated sequence of self-organizing physical processes. What an incredible thing these laws of physics are! Not only do they permit a universe to originate spontaneously; they encourage it to self-organize and self-complexify to the point where conscious beings emerge, and can look back on the great cosmic drama and reflect on what it all means.

Now you may think I have written God entirely out of the picture. Who needs a God when the laws of physics can do such a splendid job? But we are bound to return to that burning question: Where do the laws of physics come from? And why *those* laws rather than some other set? Most especially: Why a set of laws that drives the searing, featureless gases coughed out of the big bang, towards life and consciousness and intelligence and cultural activities such as religion, art, mathematics and science?

If there is a meaning or purpose to existence, as I believe there is, we are wrong to dwell too much on the originating event. The big bang is sometimes referred to as "the creation," but in truth nature has never ceased to be creative. This ongoing creativity, which manifests itself in the spontaneous emergence of novelty and complexity, and organization of physical systems, is permitted through, or guided by, the underlying mathematical laws that scientists are so busy discovering.

Now the laws of which I speak have the status of timeless eternal truths, in contrast to the physical states of the universe which change with time, and bring forth the genuinely new. So we here confront in physics a re-emergence of the oldest of all philosophical and theological debates: the paradoxical conjunction of the eternal and the temporal. Early Christian thinkers wrestled with the problem of time: Is God within the stream of time, or outside of it? How can a truly timeless God relate in any way to temporal beings such as ourselves? But how can a God who relates to a changing universe be considered eternal and unchangingly perfect?

Well, physics has its own variations on this theme. In our century Einstein showed us that time is not simply "there" as a universal and absolute backdrop to existence, it is intimately interwoven with space and matter. As I have mentioned, time is revealed to be an integral part of the physical universe; indeed, it can be warped by motion and gravitation. Clearly something that can be changed in this manner is not absolute, but a contingent part of the physical world.

In my own field of research–called quantum gravity–a lot of attention has been devoted to understanding how time itself could have come into existence in the big bang. We know that matter can be created by quantum processes. There is now a general acceptance among physicists and cosmologists that spacetime can also originate in a quantum process. According to the latest thinking, time might not be a primitive concept at all, but something that has "congealed" from the fuzzy quantum ferment of the big bang, a relic, so to speak, of a particular state that froze out of the fiery cosmic birth.

If it is the case that time is a contingent property of the physical world rather than a necessary consequence of existence, then any attempt to trace the ultimate purpose or design of nature to a *temporal* Being or Principle seems doomed to failure. While I do not wish to claim that physics has solved the riddle of time–far from it–I do believe that our advancing scientific understanding of time has illuminated the ancient theological debate in important ways. I cite this topic as just one example of the lively dialogue that is continuing between science and theology.

A lot of people are hostile to science because it demystifies nature. They prefer the mystery. They would rather live in ignorance of the way the world works and our place within it. For me, the beauty of science is *precisely* the demystification, because it reveals just how truly wonderful the physical universe really is. It is impossible to be a scientist working at the frontier without being awed by the elegance, ingenuity and harmony of the lawlike order in nature. In my attempts to popularize science, I'm driven by the desire to share my own sense of excitement and awe with the wider community; I want to tell people the good news. The fact that we are able to do science, that we can comprehend the hidden laws of nature, I regard as a gift of immense significance. Science, properly conducted, is a wonderfully enriching and humanizing enterprise. I cannot believe that using this gift called science –using it wisely, of course–is wrong. It is good that we should know.

So where is God in this story? Not especially in the big bang that starts the universe off, nor meddling fitfully in the physical processes that generate life and consciousness. I would rather that nature can take care of itself. The idea of a God who is just another force or agency at work in nature, moving atoms here and there in competition with physical forces, is profoundly uninspiring. To me, the true miracle of nature is to be found in the ingenious and unswerving lawfulness of the cosmos, a lawfulness that permits complex order to emerge from chaos, life to emerge from inanimate matter, and consciousness to emerge from life, without the need for the occasional supernatural prod; a lawfulness that produces beings who not only ask great questions of existence, but who, through science and other methods of enquiry, are even beginning to find answers.

You might be tempted to suppose that any old rag-bag of laws would produce a complex universe of some sort, with attendant inhabitants convinced of their own specialness. Not so. It turns out that randomly-selected laws lead almost inevitably either to unrelieved chaos or boring and uneventful simplicity. Our own universe is poised exquisitely between these unpalatable alternatives, offering a potent mix of freedom and discipline, a sort of restrained creativity. The laws do not tie down physical systems so rigidly that they can accomplish little, nor are they a recipe for cosmic anarchy. Instead, they encourage matter and energy to develop along pathways of evolution that lead to novel variety, what Freeman Dyson has called the principle of maximum diversity: that in some sense we live in the most interesting possible universe.

Scientists have recently identified a regime dubbed "the edge of chaos," a description that certainly characterises living organisms, where innovation and novelty combine with coherence and cooperation. The edge of chaos seems to imply the sort of lawful freedom I have just described. Mathematical studies suggest that to engineer such a state of affairs requires laws of a very special form. If we could twiddle a knob and change the existing laws, even very slightly, the chances are that the universe as we know it would fall apart, descending into chaos. Certainly the existence of life as we know it, and even less elaborate systems such as stable stars, would be threatened by just the tiniest change in the strengths of the fundamental forces, for example. The laws that characterize our actual universe, as opposed to an infinite number of alternative possible universes, seem almost contrived—fine-tuned some commentators have claimed—so that life and consciousness may emerge. To quote Dyson again: it is almost as if "the universe knew we were coming." I can't prove to you that that is design, but whatever it is, it is certainly very clever!

Now some of my colleagues embrace the same scientific facts as I, but deny any deeper significance. They shrug aside the breathtaking ingenuity of the laws of physics, the extraordinary felicity of nature, and the surprising intelligibility of the physical world, accepting these things as a package of marvels that just happens to be. But I cannot do this. To me, the contrived nature of physical existence is just too fantastic for me to take on board as simply "given." It points forcefully to a deeper underlying meaning to existence. Some call it purpose, some design. These loaded words, which derive from human categories, capture only imperfectly what it is that the universe is *about*. But, that it is about something, I have absolutely no doubt.

Where do we humans fit into this great cosmic scheme? Can we gaze out into the cosmos, as did our remote ancestors, and declare: "God made all this for us!" Well, I think not. Are we then but an accident of nature, the freakish outcome of blind and purposeless forces, an incidental by-product of a mindless, mechanistic universe? I reject that too. The emergence of life and consciousness, I maintain, are written into the laws of the universe in a very basic way. True, the actual physical form and general mental make-up of homo sapiens contain many accidental features of no particular significance. If the universe were re-run a second time, there would be no solar system, no Earth and no people. But the emergence of life and consciousness somewhere and somewhen in the cosmos is, I believe, assured by the underlying laws of nature. The origin of life and consciousness were not interventionist miracles, but nor were they stupendously improbable accidents. They were, I believe, part or the natural outworking of the laws of nature, and as such our existence as conscious enquiring beings springs ultimately from the bedrock of physical existence–those ingenious, felicitous laws. That is the sense in which I have written in my book *The Mind of God*: "We are truly meant to be here." I mean "we" in the sense of conscious beings, not *homo sapiens* specifically. Thus, although we are not at the centre of the universe, human existence *does* have a powerful wider significance. Whatever the universe as a whole may be about, the scientific evidence suggests that we, in some limited yet ultimately still profound way, are an integral part of its purpose.

How can we test these ideas scientifically? One of the great challenges to science is to understand the nature of consciousness in general and human consciousness in particular. We still haven't a clue how mind and matter are related, nor what process led to the emergence of mind and matter in the first place. This is an arena of research that is attracting considerable attention at present, and for my part I intend to pursue my own research in this field. I expect that when we do come to understand how consciousness fits into the physical universe, my contention that mind is an emergent and in principle predictable product of the laws of the universe will be borne out.

Secondly, if I am right that the universe is fundamentally creative in a pervasive and continuing manner, and that the laws of nature encourage matter and energy to self-organize and self-complexify to the point that life and consciousness emerge naturally, then there will be a universal trend or directionality towards the emergence of greater complexity and diversity. We might then expect life and consciousness to exist throughout the universe. That is why I attach such importance to the search for extraterrestrial organisms, be they bacteria on Mars, or advanced technological communities on the other side of the galaxy. The search may prove hopeless–the distances and numbers are certainly daunting–but it is a glorious quest. If we are alone in the universe, if the Earth is the only life-bearing planet among countless trillions, then the choice is stark. Either we are the product of a unique supernatural event in a universe of profligate overprovision, or else an accident of mind-numbing improbability and irrelevance. On the other hand, if life and mind are universal phenomena, if they are written into nature at its deepest level, then the case for an ultimate purpose to existence would be compelling.

Among the general population there is a widespread belief that science and theology are forever at loggerheads, that every scientific discovery pushes God further and further out of the picture. It is clear that many religious people still cling to an image of a God-of-the-gaps, a cosmic magician invoked to explain all those mysteries about nature that currently have the scientists stumped. It is a dangerous position, for as science advances so the God-of-the-gaps retreats, perhaps to be pushed off the edge of space and time altogether, and into redundancy.

The position I have presented is radically different. It is one that regards the universe, not as the plaything of a capricious Deity, but as a coherent, rational, elegant and harmonious expression of a deep and purposeful meaning.

25

WILLIAM LANE CRAIG*

"What Place, Then, for a Creator?": Hawking on God and Creation

I. Introduction

SCIENTISTS WORKING IN the field of cosmology seem to be irresistibly drawn by the lure of philosophy. Now Stephen Hawking has followed the lead of Fred Hoyle, Carl Sagan, Robert Jastrow, and P. C. W. Davies in speculating on what philosophical implications current cosmological models have for the existence of God. Although his recent, popular best-seller *A Brief History of Time* (1988) is refreshingly free of the acrimony that characterized the works of some of his predecessors, one still might come away with the impression that Hawking is no more sympathetic to theism than they were. A recent article on Hawking's book in the German tabloid *Stern*, for example, headlined, "Kein Platz für den lieben Gott," and concluded, "In his system of thought there is no room for a Creator God. Not that God is dead: God never existed."[1] This impression is no doubt abetted by the fact that the book carries an introduction by Sagan, in which he writes,

> This is also a book about God . . . or perhaps about the absence of God. The word God fills these pages. Hawking embarks on a quest to answer Einstein's famous question about whether God had any choice in creating the universe. Hawking is attempting, as he explicitly states, to understand

* Reprinted from *The British Journal for the Philosophy of Science*, Vol. 4 (1990), pp. 473-91, by permission of Oxford University Press. Copyright © *The British Journal for the Philosophy of Science*, 1990.

the mind of God. And this makes all the more unexpected the conclusion of the effort, at least so far: a universe with no edge in space, no beginning nor end in time, and nothing for a Creator to do. (p. x)

2. God As Sufficient Reason

But such a characterization of Hawking's position is quite misleading. In point of fact, it is false that there is no place for God in Hawking's system or that God is absent. For while it is true that he rejects God's role as Creator of the universe in the sense of an efficient cause producing an absolutely first temporal effect, nevertheless Hawking appears to retain God's role as the Sufficient Reason for the existence of the universe, the final answer to the question, "Why is there something rather than nothing?" He distinguishes between the questions *what* the universe is and *why* the universe is, asserting that scientists have been too occupied with the former question to be able to ask the latter, whereas philosophers, whose job it is to ask why-questions, have been unable to keep up with the technical scientific theories concerning the origin of the universe and so have shunned metaphysical questions in favor of linguistic analysis. But Hawking himself is clear that having (to his satisfaction at least) answered the question what the universe is, he is still left with the unanswered why-question:

> The usual approach of science of constructing a mathematical model cannot answer the questions of why there should be a universe for the model to describe. Why does the universe go to all the bother of existing? Is the unified theory so compelling that it brings about its own existence? Or does it need a creator, and, if so, does he have any other effect on the universe? And who created him? (p. 174)

Pursuing the question why we and the universe exist is a quest that, in Hawking's view, should occupy people in every walk of life. "If we find the answer to that, it would be the ultimate triumph of human reason—for then we should know the mind of God" (p. 175).

At face value, then, God for Hawking serves as the Sufficient Reason for the existence of the universe. Of course, "the mind of God" might well be a mere *façon de parler*, signifying something like "the meaning of existence,"[2] but, as Sagan noted, Hawking seems very much in earnest about determining the proper role of God as traditionally conceived in the scheme of things. And it is interesting to note that when a reader of an earlier summary draft of Hawking's book in *American Scientist* (Hawking [1984]), complained that Hawking seemed afraid to admit the existence of a Supreme Being, Hawking countered that "I thought I had left the question of the existence of a Supreme Being completely open. . . . It would be perfectly consistent with all we know to say that there was a Being who was responsible for the laws of physics" (Hawking [1985], p. 12).

Now it might seem at first somewhat baffling that Hawking senses the need to explain why the universe exists, since, as we shall see, he proposes a model of the universe according to which the universe is "completely self-contained and not affected by anything outside itself," is "neither created nor destroyed," but just *is* (p. 136). On his analysis, the universe is eternal (in the sense that it has neither beginning nor end and exists tenselessly) and therefore has no temporally antecedent cause. But if the cosmos is eternal and uncaused, what sense does it make to ask why it exists?

Leibniz, however, saw the sense of such a question (Leibniz [1697], [1714a], [1714b]). He held that it is intelligible to ask why it is that an eternal being exists, since the existence of such a being is still logically contingent. Since it is possible that nothing exists, why is it that an eternal cosmos exists rather than nothing? There must still be a Sufficient Reason why there exists something–even an eternal something–rather than nothing. Leibniz concluded that this Sufficient Reason can only be found in a metaphysically necessary being, that is, a being whose nature is such that if it exists, it exists in all possible worlds. Hawking would be interested to learn that analytic philosophy in the past two decades has burst the skins of linguistic analysis and that certain analytic philosophers doing metaphysics have defended Leibniz's conception of God as a metaphysically necessary being (Plantinga [1974], pp. 197–221; Adams [1971], pp. 284–91; Rowe [1975], pp. 202–21). Given the existence of such a being, Hawking need not trouble himself about who created God, since God, being metaphysically necessary and ultimate, can have no cause or ground of being.[3]

Thus, it seems to me that far from banishing God from reality, Hawking invites us to make Him the basis of reality. Indeed, I think Hawking's book may rightly be read as a discussion of two forms of the cosmological argument: the so-called *kalâm* cosmological argument for a temporally First Cause of the universe, which he rejects, and the Leibnizian cosmological argument for a Sufficient Reason of the universe, which he prefers.[4] In this paper, I am not concerned to evaluate the Leibnizian cosmological argument. Like Hawking, I feel the force of Leibniz's reasoning and am inclined to accept it; but unlike Hawking, it seems to me that the *kalâm* argument is plausible as well. Accordingly, we need to ask, has Hawking eliminated the need for a Creator?

3. God As Metaphysically First Cause

Now at one level, the answer to that question is an immediate "No." For Hawking has a theologically deficient understanding of creation. Traditionally creation was thought to involve two aspects: *creatio originans* and *creatio continuans*. The first concerned God's bringing finite reality into being at a point in time before which no such reality existed, whereas the second involved (among other things) God's preservation of finite reality in being moment by moment. Only the first notion involves the idea of a beginning.

Creatio continuans could involve a universe existing from everlasting to ever-lasting, that is to say, a universe temporally infinite in both the past and the future at any point of time. Thus, for example, Thomas Aquinas, confronted on the one hand with Aristotelian and Neo-Platonic arguments for the eternity of the world, and, on the other hand, with Arabic *kalām*-style arguments for the finitude of the past, concluded after a lengthy consideration of arguments both *pro* and *contra* that it can be proved neither that the universe had a beginning nor that it did not, but that the question of the temporal origin of the universe must be decided on the basis of divine revelation, that is, the teaching of the Scriptures (Thomas Aquinas *Summa contra gentiles* 2.32–38; cf. *idem, De aeternitate mundi contra murmurantes*). Given this position, it appears at first paradoxical that Aquinas also held that the doctrine of divine *creatio ex nihilo* can be proved (*Summa contra gentiles* 2.16). But once we understand that creation in the sense of *creatio continuans* involves no notion of a temporal beginning the paradox disappears. To affirm that God creates the world out of nothing is to affirm that God is the immediate cause of the world's existence, that there is no metaphysical intermediary between God and the universe.

Actually, what Hawking has done is fail to distinguish from the *kalām* argument yet a third form of the cosmological argument, which we may call the Thomist cosmological argument, that comes to expression in Thomas's Third Way (*Summa theologiae* 1a. 2. 3) and his *De ente et essentia* 3. According to Aquinas, all finite beings, even those like the heavenly spheres or prime matter which have absolutely no potential for generation or corruption and are therefore by nature everlasting, are nevertheless metaphysically contingent in that they are composed of essence and existence, that is to say, their essential properties do not entail that such beings exist. If these essences are to be exemplified, therefore, there must be a being in whom essence and existence are not distinct and which therefore is uncaused, and it is this being which is the Creator of all finite beings, which He produces by instantiating their essences. Hence, *creatio ex nihilo* does not, in Aquinas's view, entail a temporal beginning of the universe.

Even if we maintain, *pace* Aquinas, that a full-blooded doctrine of creation does entail a temporal beginning of the universe, the point remains that this doctrine also entails much more than that, so that even if God did not bring the universe into being at a point of time as in Hawking's model, it is still the case that there is much for Him to do, for without His active and continual bestowal of existence to the universe, the whole of finite reality would be instantly annihilated and lapse into non-being. Thus, any claim that Hawking has eliminated the Creator is seen to be theologically frivolous.

4. God As Temporally First Cause

But has Hawking succeeded even in obviating the role of the Creator as temporally First Cause? This seems to me highly dubious, for Hawking's model is founded on philosophical assumptions that are at best unexamined and unjustified and at worst false. To see this, let us recall the fundamental form of the *kalâm* cosmological argument, so that the salient points of Hawking's refutation will emerge.[5] Proponents of that argument have presented a simple syllogism:

(1) Whatever begins to exist has a cause.
(2) The universe began to exist.
(3) Therefore, the universe has a cause.

Analysis of the cause of the universe established in (3) further discloses it to be uncaused, changeless, timeless, immaterial, and personal.

4.1. HAWKING'S CRITIQUE

Hawking is vaguely aware of the tradition of this argument in Christian, Muslim, and Jewish thought and presents a somewhat muddled version of it in chapter one (p. 7). But it is interesting that, unlike Davies, Hawking does not attack premise (1); on the contrary, he implicitly assents to it. Hawking repeatedly states that on the classical GTR Big Bang model of the universe an initial space-time singularity is unavoidable, and he does not dispute that the origin of the universe must therefore require a supernatural cause. He points out that one could identify the Big Bang as the instant at which God created the universe (p. 9). He thinks that a number of attempts to avoid the Big Bang were probably motivated by the feeling that a beginning of time "smacks of divine intervention" (p. 46). It is not clear what part such a motivation plays in Hawking's own proposal, but he touts his model as preferable because "There would be no singularities at which the laws of science broke down and no edge of space-time at which one would have to appeal to God or some new law to set the boundary conditions for space-time" (p. 136). On Hawking's view, then, given the classical Big Bang model, the inference to a Creator or temporally First Cause seems natural and unobjectionable.

Hawking's strategy is rather to dispute premise (2). Typically, proponents of *kalâm* supported (2) by arguing against the possibility of an infinite temporal regress of events. This tradition eventually became enshrined in the thesis of Kant's First Antinomy concerning time.[6] Hawking's response to this line of argument is very ingenious. He claims that the argument of the thesis and antithesis "are both based on his unspoken assumption that time continues back forever, whether or not the universe had existed forever," but that this assumption is false because ". . . the concept of time has no meaning before the beginning of the universe" (p. 8). This brief retort is somewhat muddled, but I think the sense of it is the following: in the antithesis Kant assumes that "Since the beginning is an existence which is preceded by a time in which the thing is not, there must have been a preceding time in which the world was not, i.e., an empty time" (Kant [1781],

A427-28/B455-56, p. 397). But on some version of a relational view of time, time does not exist apart from change; therefore, the first event marked the inception of time. Thus, there was no empty time prior to the beginning of the universe. In the thesis, on the other hand, Kant states, "If we assume that the world has no beginning in time, then up to every given moment an eternity has elapsed and there has passed away in the world an infinite series of successive states of things" (Kant [1781], A427-28/B455-56, p. 397). To my knowledge, scarcely anyone has ever thought to call into question this apparently innocuous assumption, but it is precisely here that Hawking launches his attack. Unlike other detractors of Kant's argument, Hawking does not dispute the impossibility of forming an actual infinite by successive addition; rather he challenges the more fundamental assumption that a beginningless universe entails an infinite past. The central thrust of Hawking's book and of his proposed cosmological model is to show that a beginningless universe may be temporally finite. Hence, kalâm-style arguments aimed at proving the finitude of the past need not be disputed, for such arguments do not succeed in establishing (2), that the universe began to exist. Therefore, the universe need not have a cause, and God's role as Creator is circumscribed to that envisioned in the Thomist and Leibnizian versions of the cosmological argument.

This is a highly original, if not unique, line of attack on the kalâm cosmological argument, and it will be interesting to see how Hawking essays to put it through.[7] It Is Hawking's belief that the introduction of quantum mechanics into the GTR-based Big Bang model will be the key to success. Noting that at the Big Bang the density of the universe and the curvature of space-time become infinite, Hawking explains that ". . . there must have been a time in the very early universe when the universe was so small, that one could no longer ignore the small scale effects of . . . quantum mechanics" and that the initial singularity predicted by the GTR "can disappear once quantum effects are taken into account" (pp. 50–51). What is needed here is a quantum theory of gravity, and although Hawking admits that no such theory exists, still he insists that we do have a good idea of what some of its central features will be (p. 133). First, it will incorporate Feynman's sum-over-histories approach to quantum mechanics. According to this approach to quantum theory, an elementary particle does not follow a single path between two space-time points (that is, have a single history), but it is rather conceived as taking all possible paths connecting those points. In order to calculate the probability of a particle's passing through any given space-time point, one sums the waves associated with every possible history that passes through that point, histories represented by waves having equal amplitude and opposite phase mutually cancelling so that only the most probable histories remain. But in order to do this without generating intractable infinities, Hawking explains, one must use imaginary numbers for the values of the time co-ordinate. When this is done, it "has an interesting effect on space-time: the distinction between time and space disappears completely" (p. 134). The resulting space-time is Euclidian.

The second feature which any theory of quantum gravity must possess is that the gravitational field is represented by curved space-time. When this feature of the theory is combined with the first, the analogue of the history of a particle now becomes a complete curved space-time that represents the history of the whole universe. Moreover, "To avoid the technical difficulties in actually performing the sum over histories, these curved space-times must be taken to be Euclidean. That is, time is imaginary and is indistinguishable from directions in space" (p. 135).

On the basis of these two features, Hawking proposes a model in which space-time is the four-dimensional analogue to the surface of a sphere. It is finite, but boundless, and so possesses no initial or terminal singularities. Hawking writes,

> In the classical theory of gravity, which is based on real space-time, there are only two possible ways the universe can behave: either it has existed for an infinite time, or else it had a beginning at a singularity at some finite time in the past. In the quantum theory of gravity, on the other hand, a third possibility arises. Because one is using Euclidean space-times, in which the time direction is on the same footing as directions in space, it is possible for space-time to be finite in extent and yet to have no singularities that formed a boundary or edge. . . .
>   . . . There would be no singularities at which the laws of science broke down and no edge of space-time at which one would have to appeal to God or some new law to set the boundary conditions for space-time . . . . The universe would be completely self-contained and not affected by anything outside itself. It would be neither created nor destroyed. It would just BE. (pp. 135–36)

Hawking emphasizes that his model is merely a proposal. and so far as he describes it, it makes no unique successful predictions, which would be necessary to transform it from a metaphysical theory to a plausible scientific theory. Still Hawking believes that

> The idea that space and time may form a closed surface without boundary . . . has profound implications for the role of God in the affairs of the universe. . . . So long as the universe had a beginning, we could suppose it had a creator. But if the universe is really completely self-contained, having no boundary or edge, it would have neither beginning nor end. What place, then, for a creator? (pp. 140–41)

4.2. Assessment

Unfortunately, Hawking's model is rife with controversial philosophical assumptions, to which he gives no attention. Since Hawking is trying to explain how the universe could exist without the necessity of God's bringing it into being at a point of time, it is evident that he construes his theory to be, not merely an engaging mathematical model, but a realistic description of the universe. On a non-realist interpretation of science, there would be no contradiction between his model and temporal *creatio ex nihilo*. Hence, the central question that needs to be addressed in assessing his model as an alternative to divine creation is whether it represents a realistic picture of the world.

Now to me at least it seems painfully obvious that Hawking faces severe difficulties here. Both quantum theory and relativity theory inspire acute philosophical questions as to the extent to which they picture reality. To begin with quantum theory, most philosophers and reflective physicists would not disagree with the remarks of Hawking's erstwhile collaborator Roger Penrose:

> I should begin by expressing my general attitude to present-day quantum theory, by which I mean standard, non-relativistic quantum mechanics. The theory has, indeed, two powerful bodies of fact in its favour, and only one thing against it. First, in its favour are all the marvelous agreements that the theory has had with every experimental result to date. Second, and to me almost as important, it is a theory of astonishing and profound mathematical beauty. The one thing that can be said against it is that it makes absolutely no sense! (Penrose [1986], p. 129)

Does Hawking believe, for example, that Feynman's sum-over-histories approach describes what really happens, that an elementary particle really does follow all possible space-time paths until its wave function is collapsed by measurement? I think most people would find this fantastic. If he does interpret this approach realistically, then what justification is there for such an interpretation? Why not a Copenhagen Interpretation which eschews realism altogether with regard to the quantum world? Or an alternative version of the Copenhagen Interpretation which holds that no quantum reality exists until it is measured? Why not hold that the uncollapsed wave function is, in Bohr's words, "only an abstract quantum mechanical description" rather than a description of how nature is? A disavowal of realism on the quantum level does not imply a rejection of a critical realism on the macroscopic level. Or why not interpret quantum mechanics as a statistical theory about ensembles of particles rather than about the behavior of any individual particle? On this interpretation, the wave function describes the collective behavior of particles in identical systems, and we could quit worrying about the measurement problem. Or again, what about a neo-realist interpretation along the lines of the de Broglie-Bohm pilot wave? A non-local hidden variables theory, in which a particle follows a definite space-time trajectory, is compatible with all the experiment and evidence for quantum theory, is mathematically rigorous and complete, and yet avoids the philosophical difficulties occasioned by the typical wave functional analysis. Obviously, it is not my intention to endorse any one of these views, but merely to point out that a realistic interpretation of Feynman's sum-over-histories approach on Hawking's part would be gratuitous.

In general, I think we should do well to reflect on de Brogue's attitude to the mathematical formalism of quantum theory. As Georges Lochak notes, "He does not consider that mathematical models have any ontological value, especially geometrical representations in abstract spaces; he sees them as practical mathematical instruments among others and only uses them as such . . ." (Lochak [1984], p. 20). The principle of the superposition of wave functions is a case in point. Simply because a mathematical model is operationally successful, we are not entitled to construe its representations physically. Feynman himself gave this sharp advice: "I think it is safe to say that no one understands quantum mechanics. Do not keep saying to yourself, if you possibly can avoid it, 'But how can it be like that?' because you will go 'down the drain' into a blind alley from which nobody has yet escaped. Nobody can know how it can be like that."[8] One can use the equations without taking them as literal representations of reality.

Now it might be said that Hawking's use of Feynman's sum-over-histories approach may be merely instrumental and that no commitment to a physical description is implied. But it is not evident that such a response will work for Hawking. For his model, based on the application of quantum theory to classical geometrodynamics, must posit the existence of a super-space which is ontologically prior to the approximations of classical space-time that are slices of this super-space. This super-space is no *ens fictum,* but the primary reality. The various 3-geometries surrounding the classical space-time slice in super-space are fluctuations of the classical slice. By "summing the histories" of these 3-geometries one can construct a leaf of history in super-space which can be mapped onto a space-time manifold. Since, as we have seen, Hawking takes the wave function of a particle to be the analogue of a physical space-time that represents the history of the universe, an instrumentalist interpretation of the sum-over-histories approach leads to an equally instrumentalist, non-realist view of space-time, which betrays Hawking's whole intent.

In short, Hawking's wave-functional analysis of the universe requires the Many Worlds interpretation of quantum physics, and in another place Hawking admits as much (Hawking [1983], pp. 192–93). But why should we adopt this interpretation of quantum physics with its bloated ontology and miraculous splitting of the universe? John Barrow ([1988], p. 156) has recently remarked that the Many Worlds interpretation is "essential" to quantum cosmology because without it one is left, on the standard Copenhagen Interpretation, with the question, "Who or what collapses the wave function of the universe?"–some Ultimate Observer outside of space and time? This answer has obvious theistic implications. Indeed, although "the theologians have not been very eager to ascribe to God the role of Ultimate Observer who brings the entire quantum Universe into being," still Barrow admits that "such a picture is logically consistent with the mathematics. To escape this step cosmologists have been forced to invoke Everett's 'Many

Worlds' interpretation of quantum theory in order to make any sense of quantum cosmology" (Barrow [1988], p. 232). "It is no coincidence," he says, "that all the main supporters of the Many Worlds interpretation of quantum reality are involved in quantum cosmology" (Barrow [1988], p. 156). But if we, like most physicists, find the Many Worlds interpretation outlandish, then quantum cosmology, far from obviating the place of a Creator, might be seen to create for Him a dramatic new role. Again, my intention is not to endorse this view, but simply to underscore the fact that a realist construal of Hawking's account involves extravagant and dubious metaphysical commitments, such that his model can hardly be said to have eliminated the place of a Creator.

The impression that Hawking's model is thoroughly non-realist is heightened by his use of imaginary time in summing the waves for particle histories and, hence, in his final model of space-time. But does anyone seriously believe that one has thereby done anything more than perform a mathematical operation on paper, that one has thereby altered the nature of time itself? Hawking asserts, "Imaginary time may sound like science fiction but it is in fact a well-defined mathematical concept" (p. 134). But that is not the issue; the question is whether that mathematical concept has any counterpart in physical reality. Already in 1920, Eddington suggested that his readers who found it difficult to think in terms of the unfamiliar non-Euclidean geometry of relativistic space-time might evade that difficulty by means of the "dodge" of using imaginary numbers for the time co-ordinate, but he thought it "not very profitable" to speculate on the implications of this, for "it can scarcely be regarded as more than an analytical device" (Eddington [1920], p. 48). Imaginary time was merely an illustrative tool which "certainly do[es] not correspond to any physical reality" (Eddington [1920], p. 181). Even Hawking himself maintains, "In any case, as far as everyday quantum mechanics is concerned, we may regard our use of imaginary time and Euclidean space-time as merely a mathematical device (or trick) to calculate answers about real space-time" (pp. 134–35). But now in his model this imaginary time and Euclidean space-time are suddenly supposed to be, not merely conceptual devices, but actual representations (however unimaginable) of physical reality. This "ontologizing" of mathematical operations is not only neither explained nor justified, but, is, to my mind, metaphysically absurd. For what possible physical meaning can we give to imaginary time? Having the opposite sign of ordinary "real" time, would imaginary time be a sort of negative time? But what intelligible sense can be given, for example, to a physical object's enduring for, say, two negative hours, or an event's having occurred two negative years ago or going to occur in two negative years? If we are A-theorists and take temporal becoming as objective and real, what does it mean to speak of the lapse of negative time or the becoming of events in negative time? Since imaginary time is on Hawking's view merely another spatial dimension, he admits that there is no direction to time, even though the ordinary time with which we are acquainted is asymmetric (p. 144). But is the whole of the temporal reality we know (including Hawking's thermodynamic, cosmological, and psychological arrows of time) then illusory? Could anything be more obvious than that imaginary time is a mathematical fiction?[9]

Hawking recognizes that the history of the universe in real (= ordinary) time would look very different than its history in imaginary time. In real time, the universe expands from a singularity and collapses back again into a singularity. "Only if we could picture the universe in terms of imaginary time would there be no singularities . . . . When one goes back to the real time in which we live, however, there will still appear to be singularities" (pp. 138-39). This might lead one to conclude that Hawking's model is a mere mathematical construct without ontological import. Instead, Hawking draws the astounding conclusion,

> This might suggest that the so-called imaginary time is really the real time, and that what we call real time is just a figment of our imaginations. In realtime, the universe has a beginning and an end at singularities that form a boundary to space-time and at which the laws of science break down. But in imaginary time, there are no singularities or boundaries. So maybe what we call imaginary time is really more basic, and what we call real is just an idea that we invent to help us describe what we think the universe is like. (p. 139)

I can think of no more egregious example of self-deception than this. One employs mathematical devices (tricks) such as sum-over-histories and changing the sign of the time co-ordinate in order to construct a model space-time, a model which is physically unintelligible, and then one invests that model with reality and declares that the time in which we live is in fact unreal.

Hawking defends his position by arguing that ". . . a scientific theory is just a mathematical model we make to describe our observations: it exists only in our minds. So it is meaningless to ask: Which is real, 'real' or 'imaginary' time? It is simply a matter of which is the more useful description" (p. 139). But this reasoning is fallacious and relapses into an instrumentalist view of science which contradicts Hawking's realist expressions and intentions. One may adopt a sort of nominalist view of the ontological status of theories themselves, but this says absolutely nothing about whether those theories are meant to describe, in approximate limits, physical reality or are merely pragmatic instruments for making new discoveries and advancing technology. I should like to know on what theory of meaning Hawking dismisses the question concerning physical time as meaningless. We seem to see here the vestige of a defunct positivism, which surfaces elsewhere in Hawking's book (pp. 55, 126). But a verificationist theory of meaning is today widely recognized as being simply indefensible.[10] The question Hawking brushes aside is not only obviously meaningful, but crucial for the purposes of his book, for only if he can prove that imaginary time is ontologically real and real time fictitious has he succeeded in obviating the need for a Creator. Which brings us again to his scientific realism: it seems clear that for Hawking the ontological status of time is not just a matter of the more useful description. He believes that "The eventual goal of science is to provide a single theory that describes the whole universe" and that this goal should be pursued even though the theory "may not even affect our lifestyle" (pp. 10, 13; cf. his remarks in [1982], p. 563). Hawking yearns to understand "the underlying order of the world" (p. 13). Knowing the mind of God is for him not just a matter of pragmatic utility. Thus, he both needs and believes in scientific realism.

To address as meaningful, then, the question posed above, it is evident that imaginary time is not ontological time. This is apparent not only from its physically unintelligible nature, but also from the fact that it transforms time into a spatial dimension, thus confounding the distinction between space and time. According to Hawking, the use of imaginary numbers "has an interesting effect on space-time: the distinction between time and space disappears completely . . . there is no difference between the time direction and directions in space . . . time is imaginary and is indistinguishable from directions in space" (pp. 134–35). This decisively disqualifies Hawking's model as a representation of reality, since in fact time is not ontologically a spatial dimension. Contemporary expositors of the Special Theory of Relativity have been exercised to disassociate themselves from the frequent statements of early proponents of the theory to the effect that Einstein's theory had made time the fourth dimension of space.[11] B-theorists of time have been especially sensitive to the allegation by A-theorists that they have been guilty of "spatializing" time and have pointed to the opposite sign of the time co-ordinate as evidence that the temporal dimension is in fact not a mere fourth dimension of space. By changing the sign, Hawking conflates the temporal dimension with the spatial ones. Hawking apparently feels justified in this move because he, like certain early interpreters of STR, believes that STR itself treats time as a spatial dimension. He writes, "In relativity, there is no real distinction between the space and time co-ordinates, just as there is no real difference between any two space co-ordinates," (p. 24). He justifies this statement by pointing out that one could construct a new time co-ordinate by combining the old time co-ordinate, with one of the spatial co-ordinates.

In spatializing time, Hawking implicitly rejects an A-theory and identifies himself as a B-theorist. His statement concerning the universe as he models it that "It would just BE" is an expression of the tenseless character of its existence. Unfortunately, he provides no justification whatsoever for adopting a B-theory of time. Perhaps he thinks that STR entails a B-theory; but A-theorists have argued repeatedly that the Special Theory is neutral with regard to the issue of temporal becoming, and the most sophisticated B-theorists do not appeal to it as proof of their view.[12] The debate between the A-theory and the B-theory is controversial. But in the absence of some overwhelming proof of the B-theory, I see no reason to abandon our experience of temporal becoming as objective. D. H. Mellor, himself a B-theorist, agrees, commenting, "Tense is so striking an aspect of reality that only the most compelling argument justifies denying it: namely, that the tensed view of time is self-contradictory and so cannot be true" (Mellor [1981], p. 5). Mellor accordingly tries to rehabilitate McTaggart's proof against the objectivity of the A-series, but, to my thinking, to no avail.[13] Moreover, it seems to me (although space does not permit me to argue it here) that no B-theorist has successfully defended that theory against the incoherence that if external becoming is mind-dependent, still the subjective experience of becoming is objective, that is, there is an objective succession of contents of consciousness, so that becoming in the mental realm is real. If an A-theory of time is correct, then Hawking's model is clearly a mere mathematical abstraction.

Whether the opposite sign of the time co-ordinate in the relativity equations is sufficient to establish a "real difference" between time and space dimensions in the Special Theory need not be adjudicated here. If it is not sufficient, that only goes to show that the mathematical formalism of the theory is insufficient to capture the ontology of time and space, but is a useful mathematical abstraction from reality.[14] That time and space are ontologically distinct is evident from the fact that a series of mental events alone is sufficient to set up a temporal series of events even in the absence of spatial events.[15] Imagine, for example, that God led up to creation by counting, "1, 2, 3, . . . *fiat lux!*" In that case, time begins with the first mental event of counting, though the physical universe does not appear until later. Clearly, then, time and space are ontologically distinct.

But what, then, of the oft-repeated claim of Minkowski that, "Henceforth, space by itself, and time by itself, are doomed to fade away into mere shadows, and only a kind of union of the two will preserve an independent reality" (Minkowski [1908], p. 75)? This claim is based on one of the most widespread and persistent errors concerning the interpretation of the Special Theory that exists, namely, the failure to distinguish between what we may call measured or empirical time and ontological or real time. According to Hawking, ". . . the theory of relativity put an end to the idea of absolute time. . . . The theory of relativity does force us to change fundamentally our ideas of space and time. We must accept that time is not completely separate from and independent of space, but is combined with it to form an object called space-time" (pp. 21, 23). Nothing could be farther from the truth. Einstein did not eliminate absolute simultaneity: he merely redefined it. In the absence of a detectable aether, Einstein, under the influence of Ernst Mach's positivism,[16] believed that it was quite literally meaningless to speak of events occurring absolutely simultaneously because there was no empirical means of determining that simultaneity. By proposing to redefine simultaneity in terms of the light signal method of synchronization, Einstein was able to give meaning to the notion of simultaneity, only now the simultaneity was relative due to the invariant velocity of light. In so doing, Einstein established a sort of empirical time, which would be subject to dilation and in which the occurrence of identical events could be variously measured. But it is evident that he did nothing to "put an end" to absolute time or absolute simultaneity.[17] To say that those notions are meaningless is to revert to the dead dogmas of positivism and the verificationist theory of meaning. J. S. Bell asserts that apart from matters of style, it is primarily this philosophical positivism which serves to differentiate the received interpretation from the Lorentz-Larmor interpretation, which distinguishes between empirical, local time and ontological, real time. Bell writes,

> The difference of philosophy is this. Since it is experimentally impossible to say which of two uniformly moving systems is *really* at rest, Einstein declares the notions "really resting" and "really moving" as meaningless. For him, only the relative motion of two or more uniformly moving objects is real. Lorentz, on the other hand, preferred the view that there is indeed a state of *real* rest, defined by the "aether," even though the laws of physics conspire to prevent us identifying it experimentally. The facts of physics do not oblige us to accept one philosophy rather than the other. (Bell [1987], p. 77)

Since verificationism is hopelessly flawed as a theory of meaning, it is idle to talk about STR's "forcing" us to change our fundamental ideas of space and time. Lawrence Sklar concludes, "One thing is certain. Acceptance of relativity cannot force one into the acceptance or rejection of any of the traditional metaphysical views about the reality of past and future" (Sklar [1981], p. 140).

Of course, Hawking might retort that ontological time is scientifically useless and may therefore be left to the metaphysician. Granted, but then the point is surely this: *Hawking is doing metaphysics.* When he begins to speculate about the nature of space and time and to claim that he has eliminated the need for a Creator, then he has, as I said, entered the realm of the philosopher, and here he must be prepared to do battle with philosophical weapons on a broader conceptual field or else retreat within the walls of a limited scientific domain.

What is ironic is that even within that restricted domain there may now be empirical evidence for rejecting the received interpretation of STR. For the experimental results of the Aspect experiments on the inequalities predicted by Bell's Theorem have apparently established that widely separated elementary particles are in some way correlated such that measurements on one result instantly in the collapse of the wave function of the other, so that locality is violated. Even a hidden variables interpretation of the fabled EPR experiment must be a non-local theory. Nor is the violation of locality dependent upon the validity of quantum theory; it can be demonstrated on the macro-level, so that even if quantum theory should be superseded, any new theory will apparently have to include non-locality. But these data contradict the received interpretation of STR, not because non-locality posits super-luminal signals, but rather because it goes to establish empirically relations of absolute simultaneity. Hence, disclaimers that STR is not violated because no signal or information is sent from one particle to another are beside the point. Rather the salient point is that the collapse of the wave function in both correlated particles occurs *simultaneously,* wholly apart from considerations of synchronization by light signals. Karl Popper thus regards the Aspect experiments as the first crucial test between Lorentz's and Einstein's interpretation of STR, commenting,

> The reason for this assertion is that the mere existence of an infinite velocity entails that of an absolute simultaneity and thereby of an absolute space. Whether or not an infinite velocity can be attained *in the transmission of signals* is irrelevant for this argument: the one inertial system for which Einsteinian simultaneity coincides with absolute simultaneity . . . would be the system at absolute rest—whether or not this system at absolute rest can be experimentally identified. (Popper [1984], p. 54)

The establishment of non-local correlations in space-time could thus vindicate even within the scientific domain the validity of Lorentz's distinction between local time and real time in opposition to the positivistic conflation of the two in the received view.

What this lengthy excursus goes to show is that it is metaphysically misguided to identify ontological time as a dimension of space. Since Hawking reduces empirical time to a spatial dimension and conflates empirical time with ontological time, he winds up with a tenselessly existing space-time which he wishes to pass off as reality. Add to these errors the fact that the time involved is imaginary, and the metaphysical absurdity of Hawking's vision of the world seems starkly apparent.

5. Conclusion

There are many other things which one should like to say about Hawking's view (for example, his misuse of the anthropic principle), but I think enough has been said to answer his fundamental question, "What place, then, for a Creator?" We have seen that contrary to popular impression. God plays for Hawking an important role as a sort of Leibnizian Sufficient Reason for the universe. With regard to God's role as Creator, we saw that Hawking failed to distinguish between *creatio originans* and *creatio continuans,* so that even if God failed to play the former role, He may still carry out the latter as a sort of Thomistic ground of being. But finally we have seen that Hawking's critique of God's assuming the office of temporally First Cause as demonstrated by the *kalâm* cosmological argument is rife with unexamined and unjustified philosophical assumptions, assumptions that, when examined, degenerate to metaphysical absurdity. The success of Hawking's model appears to depend on a realist application of Feynman's sum-over-histories approach to the derivation of space-time from an ontologically prior super-space, a construal which is implausible and in any case unjustified. Essential to Hawking's scheme is the identification of imaginary time with physical time, a construal which is again never justified and is in any case physically unintelligible. Hawking's model depends, moreover, on certain question-able philosophical assumptions about relativity theory as well, for example, the identification of time as a dimension of space, a move which is extremely dubious, since time can exist without space. Hawking's appeal to the Special Theory to justify this move rests on an interpretation of that theory which fails to distinguish empirical time from ontological time, an interpretation essentially dependent on a defunct positivistic theory of meaning and now perhaps called into question by empirical facts as well. Any attempt to interpret the temporal dimension as a tenselessly existing spatial dimension betrays the true nature of time.

The postulate of metaphysical super-space, the metamorphosis of real to imaginary time, the conflation of time and space: all these seem extrava-gant lengths to which to go in order to avoid classical theism's doctrine of creatio ex nihilo—which forces us and Hawking to confront squarely a dif-ferent question: What price, then, for no Creator?

NOTES

1. *Stern* (undated photocopy), p. 209. "In seinem Gedankengebäude ist für einen schöpferischen Gott kein Raum. Gott ist nicht einmal tot, Gott hat nie existiert."

2. Cf. the remark by Pagels: "Physicists, regardless of their belief, may invoke God when they feel issues of principle are at stake because the God of the physicists is cosmic order" (Pagels [1982], p. 83).

3. On God as the ground of being for other metaphysically necessary entitles see Morris and Menzel (1986) and Menzel (1987). These bold essays should convince Hawking that the great tradition of metaphysics has been fully restored in analytic philosophy!

4. On these arguments, as well as the Thomist argument, see Craig (1980).

5. For exposition and defense of the *kalâm* argument, see Craig (1979a, b, c), (1985).

6. For discussion, see Craig (1979d).

7. One feels a bit diffident about criticizing someone's views as they are expressed in a popular exposition of his thought rather than in his tech-nical papers. But the fact is that it is only in his popular exposition that Hawking feels free to reflect philosophically on the metaphysical Implica-tions of his model. For example, imaginary time, which plays so critical a role in his thought, is scarcely even mentioned in his relevant technical paper (Hartle & Hawking [1983], p. 2960). In any case, I have in no instance based my criticism on the infelicities inherent in popular exposition of tech-nical subjects.

8. Cited in Herbert (1985), p. xiii.

9. As Mary Cleugh nicely puts it, "What is the wildest absurdity of dreams is merely altering the sign to the physicist" (Cleugh [1937], p. 46).

10. Healey describes the contemporary attitude toward positivism:

> Positivists attempted to impose restrictions on the content of scientific theories In order to ensure that they were empirically meaningful. An effect of these restrictions was to limit both the claims to truth of theoretical sentences only distantly related to observation, and the claims to existence of unobservable theoretical entities. More recently positivism has come under such sustained attack that opposition to it has become almost orthodoxy in the philosophy of science. (Healey [1981], p. vii. For a disinterested and devastating critique of positivism, see Suppe [1977], pp. 62–118)

11. See the interesting citations in Meyerson (1925), pp. 354–555. In his comments on Meyerson's book, Einstein repudiated the "extravagances of the popularizers and even many scientists who construed STR to teach that time is a spatial dimension: time and space are fused into one and the same *continuum,* but this continuum is not isotropic. The element of spatial distance and the element of duration remain distinct in nature . . ." (Einstein [1928], p. 367).

12. For A-theoretic approaches to STR, see Capek (1966), Stein (1968), Denbigh (1978). Whitrow (1980), pp. 283–307, 371, and Dieks (1988), Grünbaum (1968) makes no appeal to STR to defend a B-theory.

13. See refutations in Horwich (1987), pp. 26–27.

14. See helpful discussions in Cleugh (1937), pp. 46–69, and Kroes (1985), pp. 6096.

15. On Minkowski space-time, Wenzl cautions, "From the standpoint of the physicist, this is a thoroughly consistent solution. But the physicist will [doubtless] understand the objection, raised by philosophy, that time is by no means merely a physical matter. Time is, as Kant put it, the form not merely of our outer but also of our inner sense. . . . Should our experiences of successiveness and of memory be mere illusion . . .?" (Wenzl [1949], pp. 587–88)

16. The positivistic foundations of Einstein's STR are widely recognized by historians of science, but are surprisingly rarely discussed by philosophers exploring the philosophical foundations of that theory. For discussion, see Holton (1970), pp. 167–77, Frank (1949), Reichenbach (1949), Bridgman (1949), Lenzen (1949). According to Sklar, "Certainly the original arguments in favor of the relativistic viewpoint are rife with verificationist presuppositions about meaning, etc. And despite Einstein's later disavowal of the verificationist point of view, no one to my knowledge has provided an adequate account of the foundations of relativity which isn't verificationist in essence" (Sklar [1981], p. 141). "I can see no way of rejecting the old aether-compensatory theories, without invoking a verificationist critique of some kind or other" (ibid., p. 132).

17. Cleugh hits the essential point: "It cannot be too often emphasized that physics is concerned with the measurement of time, rather than with the essentially metaphysical question as to its nature . . . however useful 't' may be for physics, its *complete* identification with Time is fallacious" (Cleugh [1937], pp. 51, 30).

References

Adams, R. M. (1971). "Has It Been Proved that All Real Existence Is Contingent?" *American Philosophical Quarterly* 8:284–91.

Barrow, J. (1988). *The World within the World*. Oxford: Clarendon Press.

Bell, J. S. (1987). "How to Teach Special Relativity." In *Speakable and Unspeakable in Quantum Mechanics*. Cambridge: Cambridge University Press, pp. 66–80.

Bridgman P. (1949). "Einstein's Theories and the Operational Point of View." In P. A. Schilpp (ed.), *Albert Einstein: Philosopher-Scientist,* Library of Living Philosophers 7. La Salle, Ill.: Open Court, pp. 335–54.

Capek, M. (1966). "Time in Relativity Theory: Arguments for a Philosophy of Becoming." In J. T. Fraser (ed.), *Voices of Time.* New York: Braziller, pp. 434–54.

Cleugh, M. (1937). *Time and Its Importance in Modern Thought.* London: Methuen.

Craig W. L. (1979a). *The Kalâm Cosmological Argument.* Library of Philosophy and Religion. London: Macmillan.

——. (1979b). "Whitrow and Popper on the Impossibility of an Infinite Past." *British Journal for the Philosophy of Science* 39:65–70.

——. (1979c). "Wallace Matson and the Crude Cosmological Argument." *Australasian Journal of Philosophy* 57, 163–70.

——. (1979d). "Kant's First Antinomy and the Beginning of the Universe." *Zeitschrift für philosophische Forschung* 33:553–67.

——. (1980). *The Cosmological Argument from Plato to Leibniz.* Library of Philosophy and Religion. London: Macmillan.

——. (1985). "Prof. Mackie and the *Kâlam* Cosmological Argument." *Religious Studies* 20:367–75.

Denbigh, K. (1978). "Past, Present, and Future." In J. T. Fraser (ed.), *The Study of Time III.* Berlin: Springer Verlag, pp. 301–29.

Dieks, D. (1988). "Special Relativity and the Flow of Time." *Philosophy of Science* 55:456–60.

Eddington, A. (1920). *Space, Time and Gravitation.* Reprint edition: Cambridge Science Classics. Cambridge University Press, 1987.

Einstein, A. (1928). "Comment on Meyerson's 'La déduction relativiste.' " *Revue philosophique la France et de l'étranger* 105:161–66. Reprinted in M. Capek, *The Concepts of Space and Time.* BSPS 2. Dordrecht: D. Reidel, 1976, pp. 363–67.

Frank, P. (1949). "Einstein, Mach and Logical Positivism." In P. A. Schilpp (ed.), *Albert Einstein: Philosopher-Scientist.* Library of Living Philosophers 7. La Salle, Ill.: Open Court, pp. 271–86.

Grünbaum, A. (1968). "The Status of Temporal Becoming." In R. M. Gale (ed.), *The Philosophy of Time,* pp. 322–54. London: Macmillan.

Hartle, J., and S. Hawking (1983). "Wave function of the Universe," *Physical Review* D 28:2960–75.

Hawking, S. (1982). "The Boundary Conditions of the Universe." In H. A. Bruck, G. V. Coyne, and M. S. Longair (eds.), *Astrophysical Cosmology,* PASSV 48. Vatican City: Pontificia Academia Scientiarum, pp. 563–74.

Hawking, S. (1983). "Quantum Cosmology." Reprinted in L. Z. Fang and R. Ruffini (eds.), *Quantum Cosmology.* Advanced Series in Astrophysics and Cosmology 3. Singapore: World Scientific, 1987, pp. 190–235.

———. (1984). "The Edge of Spacetime." *American Scientist* 72:355–59.

———. (1985). "Letters to the Editor: Time and the Universe." *American Scientist* 73:12.

———. (1988). *A Brief History of Time: From the Big Bang to Black Holes.* With an Introduction by Carl Sagan. New York: Bantam Books.

Healey, R. (1981). "Introduction." In R. Healy (ed.), *Reduction, Time and Reality.* Cambridge: Cambridge University Press.

Herbert, N. (1985). *Quantum Reality: Beyond the New Physics.* Garden City, N.Y.: Doubleday Anchor Books.

Holton, G. (1970). "Mach, Einstein, and the Search for Reality." In *Ernst Mach: Physicist and Philosopher.* BSPS 6. Dordrecht: D. Reidel, pp. 165–99.

Horwich, P. (1987). *Asymmetries in Time.* Cambridge, Mass.: MIT Press.

Kant, I. (1781). *Critique of Pure Reason.* Translated by Norman Kemp Smith. London: Macmillan, 1929.

Kroes, P. (1985). *Time: Its Structure and Role in Physical Theories.* Synthese Library 179. Dordrecht: D. Reidel.

Leibniz, G. W. (1697). "On the Radical Origination of Things." In L. E. Loemker (ed.), *Philosophical Papers and Letters,* Dordrecht: D. Reidel, 1969, pp. 486–91.

———. (1714a). "The Principles of Nature and of Grace, Based on Reason." In L. E. Loemker (ed.), *Philosophical Papers amid Letters,* 2nd edition. Dordrecht: D. Reidel, 1969, pp. 636–42.

———. (1714b). "The Monadology." In L. E. Loemker (ed.), *Philosophical Papers and Letters,* 2nd edition. Dordrecht: D. Reidel, 1969, pp. 643–53.

Lenzen, V. (1949). "Einstein's Theory of Knowledge," In P. A. Schilpp (ed.), *Albert Einstein: Philosopher-Scientist.* Library of Living Philosophers 7. La Salle, Ill.: Open Court, pp. 357–84.

Lochak, G. (1984). "The Evolution of the Ideas of Louis de Broglie on the Interpretation of Wave Mechanics." In A. O. Barut, A. v. d. Merwe and J. P. Vigier, *Quantum, Space and Time.* Cambridge Monographs on Physics. Cambridge: Cambridge University Press, pp. 11–33.

Mellor, D. H. (1981). *Real Time.* Cambridge: Cambridge University Press.

Menzel, C. (1987). "Theism, Platonism, and the Metaphysics of Mathematics." *Faith and Philosophy* 4:365–82.

Meyerson, E. (1925). "On Various Interpretations of Relativistic Time." *La déduction relativiste*. Paris: Payot. Reprinted in M. Capek, *The Concepts of Space and Time*, BSPS 2. Dordrecht: D. Reidel, 1976, pp. 353–62.

Minkowski, H. (1908). "Space and Time." Reprinted in *The Principle of Relativity*. Translated by W. Perrett and G. B. Jeffery. New York: Dover Publications, 1952, pp. 75–91.

Morris T. V. and C. Menzel (1986). "Absolute Creation.' *American Philosophical Quarterly* 23:353–62.

Pagels, H. (1982). *The Cosmic Code*. London: Michael Joseph.

Penrose, R. (1986). "Gravity and State Vector Reduction." In R. Penrose and C. J. Isham (eds.), *Quantum Concepts in Space and Time*. Oxford: Clarendon Press.

Plantinga, A. (1974.) *The Nature of Necessity*. Clarendon Library of Logic and Philosophy. Oxford: Clarendon Press.

Popper, K. (1984). "A Critical Note on the Greatest Days of Quantum Theory." In A. O. Barut, A. v. d. Merwe and J. P. Vigier (eds.), *Quantum, Space and Time*, Cambridge Monographs on Physics. Cambridge: Cambridge University Press, pp. 49–54.

Reichenbach, H. (1949). "The Philosophical Significance of the Theory of Relativity." In P. A. Schilpp (ed.), *Albert Einstein: Philosopher-Scientist*. Library of Living Philosophers 7. La Salle, Ill.: Open Court, pp. 289–311.

Rowe, W. L. (1975). *The Cosmological Argument*. Princeton: Princeton University Press.

Sklar, L. (1981). "Time, reality and relativity." In R. Healey (ed.), *Reduction, Time and Reality*. Cambridge: Cambridge University Press, pp. 129–42.

Stein, H. (1968). "On Einstein-Minkowski Space-Time." *Journal of Philosophy* 65:5–23.

Suppe, F. (1977). "The Search for Philosophic Understanding of Scientific Theories." In F. Suppe (ed.), *The Structure of Scientific Theories*, 2nd edition. Urbana, Ill.: University of Illinois Press, pp. 3–241.

Wenzl, A. (1949). "Einstein's Theory of Relativity, Viewed from the Standpoint of Critical Realism, and its Significance for Philosophy." in P. A. Schilpp (ed.), *Albert Einstein: Philosopher-Scientist*, library of Living Philosophers 7. La Salle, Ill.: Open Court, pp. 583–606.

Whitrow, G. (1980). *The Natural Philosophy of Time*, 2nd edition. Oxford: Clarendon Press.

26

MARTIN REES*

Toward Infinity: The Far Future

The Next Hundred Billion Years

IN ABOUT 5 billion years the Sun will die, swelling up into a red giant, engulfing the inner planets, and vaporizing all life on Earth; it will then settle down as a slowly fading white dwarf. At about the same time (give or take a billion years) the Andromeda Galaxy, already falling toward us, will merge with our own Milky Way. When two galaxies merge, most of the constituent stars are unscathed. The chance of a head-on collision between individual stars is only 1 part in 100 billion. But the motions of all the stars would be severely perturbed, and the galactic "grand design" of disk and spiral arms would be shattered.[1] The outcome would be a single swarm of stars resembling a bloated elliptical galaxy.

What might our entire universe be like when it is 10 times *older* than today—after, say, another 100 billion years? Cosmic expansion is being slowed by the gravitational pull that each galaxy exerts on everything else. If the density doesn't exceed the critical value—if omega is 1 or less—our universe is fated to continue expanding. But if the density were substantially higher, gravity would have decelerated the expansion enough to bring it to a halt; indeed, if omega were as large as 2, everything would, before 100 billion years have passed, have been engulfed in a final crunch.

Most cosmologists would bet that our universe will still be expanding

* Reprinted from pp. 191-207 and 274-5 of *Before the Beginning: Our Universe and Others,* by Martin Rees (1997), by permission of Addison-Wesley. Copyright ©1997 Martin Rees.

100 billion years from now. They now believe that omega is either around 0.2 or else, for theoretical reasons, would guess that omega is almost exactly 1. A show of hands among the participants at a conference in 1995 showed a roughly equal split between these views–though, reassuringly, only a small minority thought this a good way to settle scientific issues!

Theoretical prejudices change. In the early 1970s, observational clues were vaguer than they are now (and, such as they were, suggested that omega was small); but there was nevertheless quite widespread prejudice in favor of a finite, "closed" universe. Such a universe would collapse after a finite time, and would contain only a finite amount of material–the larger it was, the longer the cycle would take. There seemed no particular reason why our universe should be enormously larger than the part we'd already seen. Nor why it should heave itself up to much more than its present size, or go on expanding for much longer than it has done already.

There were also some more philosophical arguments for a closed universe. One was based on the so-called problem of inertia. Galileo recognized that inside a windowless laboratory there is no way of knowing your speed–only your acceleration. But *rotation* seems different. When water in a bucket is spun, its surface deforms–it is depressed at the center and rises toward the edge. Newton noted that this does not depend on whether the bucket itself shares the spin of its contents–the water's surface responds to rotation in some "absolute frame," certainly not relative to the bucket.

Newton gave us the concept of an "inertial" frame of reference– a spinning liquid, a gyroscope, or a pendulum picks out a special frame, and we can test whether our laboratory is spinning relative to it. But it is still mysterious what determines this special nonrotating frame. Even before Newton's time, this was a philosophical issue. Among those who discussed it was the early fourteenth-century French philosopher Jean Buridan (famous for his uncompromisingly logical "ass," which starved indecisively midway between two equally succulent bales of hay): "To celestial bodies ought to be attributed the nobler conditions. . . . But it is nobler and more perfect to be at rest than to be moved. Therefore the highest sphere ought to be at rest."

The nineteenth-century Austrian physicist and philosopher Ernst Mach argued that the inertial frame was actually determined by the average motion of all "celestial bodies": a gyroscope's axis, for instance, would be fixed relative to the distant galaxies. What would happen to a rotating bucket, he speculated, if the rest of the universe were removed? It seemed to him that an inertial frame made no sense in an empty universe. Mach's principle, as it came to be called, has figured prominently in cosmological debates ever since.

Among the universes that satisfy the equations of general relativity, there are some in which the distant galaxies would very slowly move across the sky, relative to the axis of a gyroscope. If Mach were right, some extra "principle" would restrict possible universes more stringently than Einstein's equations do, by ruling out the rotating solutions. Einstein took Mach's principle seriously, and deemed only the finite and closed universes to be truly Machian. I learned this point of view from Wheeler, who argued forcefully that our universe must be dense enough to ensure recollapse.

Another appealing argument for a finite universe was that an ensemble of separate universes would be easier to accept if each member of the ensemble was finite rather than infinite.

Countdown to a Big Crunch?

The closed or recollapsing universe was certainly my favored assumption back in 1969, when I wrote a short paper pretentiously entitled, "The Collapse of the Universe: an Eschatological Study," about what will happen if our universe collapses.

Suppose the present density were twice the critical value (or, in other words, omega were 2). The expansion would stop when the galaxies were twice as far away from each other as they are today. Thereafter, they would fall toward one another, their redshifts being replaced by blueshifts. Space is already punctured by black holes created when massive stars die, or by the runaway collapses in galactic centers that manifest themselves as quasars. But these would then just be precursors of a universal squeeze that eventually engulfs everything.

About 100 million years before the crunch, individual galaxies would merge. Later in the countdown the remaining stars, no longer attached to their parent galaxy, would become dispersed throughout the contracting universe. They'd move faster as the contraction progressed, just as atoms in a box move faster (and the gas heats up) when the box is compressed. Eventually, the stars would be shattered by colliding with each other. I was surprised, though, to calculate that most stars would have been destroyed in another way before they got close-packed enough to collide. The sky, brightened by the blueshifted radiation from all other stars (plus the primordial background radiation, which would itself heat up during the compression), would become hotter than the stars themselves. Stars would get cooked in an oven even hotter than their surfaces, and soak up heat faster than they could get rid of it; they would "puff up" and disperse into gas.

The earliest this could happen would be 50 billion years from now; the breathing space is at least 10 times the remaining lifetime of the Sun. The final outcome would be a fireball resembling that with which our expansion began.

But the collapse would not be *exactly* like the initial big bang with the direction of time reversed. The early universe was smooth and uniform, except for the small ripples that evolved into galaxies and clusters; in contrast, the crunch would be irregular and unsynchronized. Our universe is developing more and more structure as it expands, and this trend would not reverse during the contraction phase. Anything that has fallen into a black hole has already, in effect, experienced the final crunch; even more black holes will form during the contraction, and material will experience violent shearing motions. Roger Penrose believes that this difference between the smooth initial stages and the irregular final stages is crucial in setting the arrow of time. (This is discussed further in Chapter 13.)

Could a collapsing universe rebound phoenixlike into a new cycle? Nothing could stop the density rising to infinity—to a "singularity." Such a singularity was once thought to be an artifact of the special symmetry and uniformity. If, for example, the stars in a cluster were pulled inward by gravity in a uniform and exactly symmetrical fashion, they would clearly all collide in the middle. However, small sideways motions would, in Newton's theory, prevent them from all converging to the same point; they may then miss each other, so that the cluster can reexpand to its original size. Perhaps something analogous could happen to a collapsing universe. But Hawking and Penrose showed that Newtonian intuitions are misleading. Singularities are inevitable even when the collapse is irregular: the kinetic energy itself (since energy is equivalent to mass) exerts extra gravity, so the attraction feeds on itself.

Physical conditions in the "bounce" would transcend the physics we understand, so that nothing could be said about the possibility of a rebound into a new cycle—still less about what memory would be preserved of what had gone before. The concept of an "arrow of time" —what is "before" and what is "after"—breaks down under these extreme conditions.

Perpetual Expansion

What about the other case, when there isn't enough gravitating stuff to halt the expansion? Our universe would then have time to run down to a final heat death. If a cosmologist had to answer the question, "What is happening in our universe?" in just one sentence, a good answer would be: "Gravitational energy is being released, as stars, galaxies and clusters progressively contract, this inexorable trend being delayed by rotation, nuclear energy and the sheer scale of astronomical systems, which makes things happen slowly and staves off gravity's final victory." If our universe expands for ever, there *will* be enough time for all stars, all galaxies, to attain a terminal equilibrium.

The sky would get still blacker as galaxies dispersed ever more thinly through the expanding space. But our universe would darken for another reason as well. Galaxies would get intrinsically dimmer. Their constituent atoms would continue to be recycled through successive generations of stars: hydrogen would be processed into helium (and further up the periodic table). Bright stars cannot be created from already spent fuel. More and more gas would get locked up, either in faint stars of very low mass, or in dead remnants: neutron stars, white dwarfs, or black holes.

Just as our Milky Way will crash into Andromeda, so most galaxies will combine with others in the same group or cluster. Each super-cluster will become one unit: the black holes at the center of each galaxy will sink into the middle of the merged system, surrounded by a swarm of dead stars. The hierarchical clustering that has already led to galaxies, clusters, and super-clusters will continue to still grander scales.[2]

Atoms Are Not Forever

Most of the atoms that went into the making of galaxies will eventually get trapped in black holes or inert stellar remnants; each galaxy will become just a dark swarm of cooled white dwarfs, neutron stars, and black holes. But eventually the atoms will themselves decay: if the baryons of which they are made were absolutely immutable (as we believe the amount of electric charge in our universe is), the excess of matter over antimatter could never have emerged in the ultraearly universe. The eventual decay of protons restores the symmetry between matter and antimatter with which our universe began.

The average lifetime of an atom exceeds the present Hubble time (the present "age" of our universe) by more than 20 powers of 10: even though one ton of material contains about 10^{30} atoms, experimenters would need to watch many tons (maybe even many thousands of tons) to detect even one decay in the course of a year. But, given enough time, white dwarfs and neutron stars would dissolve away; so would any diffuse intergalactic gas. The energy would go into electrons and neutrinos.

Black holes would be unaffected by proton decay. But even they do not live forever. They shed energy by the "quantum evaporation" process. This process could be important—and, indeed, conspicuous—in the present-day universe if "miniholes" were created by the huge pressures of the ultraearly universe. Tiny black holes, weighing as much as a mountain but only the size of an atomic nucleus, radiate intensely; as they lose energy (and mass) they shrink but radiate even more energetically, and may eventually disappear in a final outburst of particles and gamma rays.

Bigger black holes are cooler and radiate more slowly. The holes that form when heavy stars die would take 10^{66} years to evaporate. But an ever-expanding universe provides enough time for this to happen—enough time, even, for evaporation of the ultramassive black holes, each as heavy as millions of stars, that build up in the centers of galaxies or supergalaxies (and which decay much more slowly still). Everything the holes had ever swallowed would thereby be recycled back into radiation.

If even the heaviest black holes eventually evaporated too, nothing would be left but radiation, and electrons and positrons. An electron could annihilate by colliding with a positron. A direct hit is highly improbable; electrons and positrons could nevertheless be brought together by forming a bound pair, orbiting around each other, and then spiraling together. So immensely dilute does everything become that there would eventually, on average, be less than one electron in a volume as large as our present observable universe. Immensely wide binary pairs could form: an electron's motion could be controlled by the electric field of a single positron 10 billion lightyears away, and after enough eons had passed the radiation drag would have brought them closer together.

Can "Life" Survive Forever?

The first thorough discussion of what might happen in an ever-expanding universe came in an article entitled "Time Without End: Physics and Biology in an Open Universe." This article was detailed and scholarly (in contrast to my own earlier one on the collapsing universe), and appeared in the austerely technical journal *Review of Modern Physics* (the adjacent article in the same issue has the more forbidding title "Classical Solutions of SU(2) Yang-Mills Theory"). Its author, Freeman Dyson, combines, to a unique degree among physicists, formal mathematical brilliance with an enthusiasm for wide-ranging speculation. Dyson's scientific eminence dates from 1947, when he was still a student. The theory known as quantum electrodynamics–the most precise and successful theory in the whole of physics–was being developed by Richard Feynman and Julian Schwinger, using quite different approaches (as well as, quite independently, by Sin-itiro Tomonaga in Japan). Dyson showed how the very different mathematical ideas underlying Feynman and Schwinger's approaches could be linked together.

Dyson has spent most of his career as a professor at the Institute for Advanced Study at Princeton. At this unusual institution there are no students: the staff, free of the duties and constraints that encumber anyone working in a normal university or laboratory, are generously supported to pursue any research that takes their fancy. Although he has continued to study "formal" mathematical aspects of physics, Dyson has latterly been more influential through his speculative ideas bordering on science fiction, and his eloquent books and lectures celebrating the diversity and complexity of our world. His career exemplifies the best justification (and it's hard to think of many) for a studentless intellectual haven like the Institute for Advanced Study.

Will our universe expand for ever? Dyson cannot tell us–indeed, we still cannot decide this issue–but he has no doubt which option he wants:

> The end of a closed universe has been studied in detail by Rees. Regrettably I have to concur that in this case we have no escape from frying. No matter how deep we burrow into the Earth to shield ourselves from blue-shifted background radiation, we can only postpone by a few million years our miserable end. . . . It gives me a feeling of claustrophobia to imagine our whole existence confined within a box.

Dyson was writing after Hawking's work on black-hole evaporation, but before the case for proton decay became widely accepted. He therefore considered what might happen if, even after black holes have decayed, there were still white dwarfs and neutron stars. The final heat death would be spun out over a much longer period. But still not forever. A neutron star could form a black hole by quantum tunneling. This immensely improbable event–10^{57} atoms "quantum-jumping" in unison–would not be expected until after a time so enormous that, written out in full, it would require as many zeros as there are atoms in the observable universe! The resultant black holes would then evaporate, in a time that, in this perspective, is almost instantaneous.

But what is the prognosis for some exotic form of intelligent life? Even after the stars have died (precluding any manifestations of life such as might evolve on Earth), can "life" survive and develop intellectually forever, thinking infinite thoughts and storing or communicating an ever-increasing body of information? "Energy reserves" are finite. However, it takes smaller pulses of energy to store or transmit information if this is done at a low temperature. And the universe will cool down as it expands. Instead of being 2.7 degrees above absolute zero, it will, after a trillion years, be below a millidegree. As the background temperature falls, any conceivable form of life or intelligence would have to keep cool, think progressively more slowly, and hibernate for long intervals.

If protons lasted forever, hugely complex but tenuous networks could be fabricated. There are quite general limitations on the size and complexity of organisms (or, indeed, computers) because anything too heavy would be crushed by gravity, and its internal workings would generate too much power to be radiated away. But structures in the far future can transcend both these constraints. Gravity can be suppressed, however massive these constructions are, by making them distended enough. And they can have a large enough surface to radiate and stay almost as cool as the background radiation, whose temperature drops as the expansion proceeds; the minimum energy needed to transmit each item of information gets ever lower. Information processing (or "thinking") would be very slow in a spread-out configuration: the rate is limited by how long a signal takes to cross it, moving at the speed of light. (This is of course why supercomputers are made as compact as possible.) But what is the urgency when eons stretch ahead?

Evolution needn't come to an end, even when all the protons vanish. There could always be black holes, provided that they grew, by coalescence, fast enough to counteract their erosion by evaporation. (Their masses would need to go up as fast as the cube root of time–growing tenfold for each factor 1000 on the cosmic clock.) These holes may concentrate energy enough to create new matter. Even a dilute gas made of electrons and positrons could provide the basis for circuitry controlled by complex magnetic fields and currents pervading the medium. This is reminiscent of the inorganic intelligence depicted in *The Black Cloud,* the first of Fred Hoyle's science fiction novels (and the most carefully crafted and imaginative of them).

Subjective Eternity Before the Crunch?

Even if "physical" time runs on forever, Dyson's reassuring conclusion that an infinite amount of *subjective* time lies ahead shouldn't be dismissed as obvious. The endgame of a perpetually expanding universe is played out more and more slowly: any elemental action—a thought, or the processing of a single bit of information—takes longer and longer. Just as an infinite series of numbers (for instance, $1, \frac{1}{2}, \frac{1}{4}, \frac{1}{8}, \ldots$) can add up to a finite sum, there might have turned out to be a finite bound on "subjective" time.

The "time" that appears as the symbol t in the equations of physics is not necessarily a good measure of the "time" whose passage is marked by a succession of significant events.[3] In a perpetually expanding universe, the pace of activity gets ever slower. Perhaps, conversely, this distinction between subjective and physical time allows us to view a *big crunch* more optimistically.

Time is measured by the ticking of standardized clocks. However, no conceivable clock could survive the final stages of a big crunch; and any clock falling into a black hole would be shredded by tidal forces before encountering the singularity. We might start off measuring time in years, by orbits of planets around stars. But, in the later stages of the countdown to the crunch, each star's surroundings become more crowded: stars would be hurtling so close that no planets could survive undisturbed in their orbits, and we should have to use atomic clocks. And the atoms themselves would be destroyed eventually. As conditions became more extreme, timekeeping would require successively smaller and sturdier clocks. No finite sequence of clocks could record every instant right up to the singularity.

This recalls Zeno's classic paradox on the "impossibility" of motion: before completing a journey, you must get halfway: before that, you must get a quarter of the way . . . and so on; there are an infinite number of things to do in getting started. Though seemingly paradoxical, this claim about a collapsing universe isn't manifestly as fallacious as Zeno's argument. Unlike in our everyday world, there is no natural clock that can be used all the time. Instead, an infinite series of increasingly fast-ticking clocks would need to be used in succession.

Viewed in this perspective, the final singularity seems a remote abstraction, separated from us by an infinite number of intervening events. John Barrow and Frank Tipler have developed this line of thought to its limits. If the crunch were smooth and symmetrical, like the time-reverse of the big bang, there would be no possibility of infinite subjective time. This follows as a corollary of Dyson's line of argument for an ever-expanding universe: Dyson found that finite energy reserves were no constraint, because energy could be used in smaller and smaller quanta as the universe cooled down; in contrast, the required quanta get ever larger (and energy is used less and less efficiently) as the universe compresses and heats up.

Barrow and Tipler claim that the prospects for infinite "subjective time" are better if the collapse occurs in a "skew" or anisotropic fashion. Their argument builds on ideas developed in the late 1960s by Charles Misner, who showed that anisotropic universes display what he termed "mixmaster" behavior: strong shearing motions, such that a contracting universe would be squeezed alternately in different directions. This shearing motion can generate enough energy to supply arbitrarily many quanta, despite the requirement that these quanta must get larger as collapse proceeds. (The intervention of quantum effects on the gravitational field itself, however, may "choke off" this process and preclude any infinite regress.) Tipler speculates that an anisotropic "crunch" offers a propitious environment for complex structures with at least some attributes of life, provided that our universe continues for 10^{15} years before recollapsing, so as to allow enough time to prepare for it!

"Fast Forward" Into The Future

Will our descendants need to follow Dyson's conservationist maxims to survive an infinite future? Or, at the opposite extreme, will they fry in the big crunch a few tens of billion years hence? We shall need to compile a more complete inventory of what is in the universe, by observing in all wavebands, and searching for all forms of possible "dark matter," before we can pronounce a more reliable long-range forecast for the next 100 billion years and beyond.

If you're of an apocalyptic temperament and can't wait 100 billion years, then head for a black hole—you'll there encounter a singularity, created by a local gravitational collapse prefiguring the big crunch. Black holes form when heavy stars die—perhaps after some supernovae and there are many millions of them within our Milky Way. Monster black holes each weighing as much as a billion suns lurk in the centers of some galaxies: these are the relic of a catastrophic quasar phase when the galaxy was young. You should aim, preferably, for one of these monster holes: they are so capacious that, even after passing inside, several free-falling hours would remain for leisured observation before the extreme gravitational stresses near the central singularity shredded you apart. If the black hole is spinning, careful navigation may evade the singularity.

A more prudent course would be to remain just outside the hole. The closest orbits around a rapidly spinning black hole have the remarkable property that the time-dilation can be arbitrarily large. A clock moving in such an orbit would seem, to a distant observer, to be deeply redshifted, and running exceedingly slow. Conversely, someone in such an orbit would get a speeded-up preview of the entire future of the external universe.

Terrestrial And Cosmic Hazards

Our biosphere has taken 4.5 billion years to evolve. But the Solar System has another 5 billion years ahead of it. Our universe, even if it eventually recollapses, still has at least 90 percent of its course to run. And, if it expands forever, there may be infinite time and infinite space in which life can develop. In this cosmic perspective, we are still near the beginning of the evolutionary process. The progression toward complexity and diversity has much further to go. There is time enough for life to spread from our Earth through the entire Galaxy, and even beyond. And it may be, primarily, collective human actions that will determine how, or even if, that process unfolds. If Earth's biosphere were snuffed out, potentialities of truly cosmic proportions would be foreclosed. Being mindful of these potentialities stretches our horizons: it may even deepen our commitment to understanding our world and conserving its web of life.

The Earth has always been vulnerable to catastrophes. Many species may well have succumbed to plagues. Impacts of asteroids and comets have caused worldwide extinctions. There is more than one chance in 100,000 that, within the next 50 years, the Earth will be hit by an asteroid large enough to cause worldwide devastation—ocean waves hundreds of feet high, tremendous earthquakes, and changes in global weather. The mortality risk is low, but no lower (for the average person) than the risk, per year, of being killed in an air crash. Indeed, it's higher than any other natural hazards that most Europeans or North Americans are exposed to.

Added to these is now the risk of manmade catastrophe. The nuclear peril may loom less large than it did during the Cold War, but such dangers could resurface. And there could be biological dangers—in this case not organized warfare, but perpetrated by terrorism, or even accident. We are used to the idea that a software "virus" can spread through a computer network. Perhaps an artificially engineered virus could cause a worldwide epidemic. The risk of all human life being extinguished may be slight. But, with such technology readily accessible to terrorist groups (or, indeed, to innocent experimenters who may unleash catastrophe quite unwittingly), could one confidently assess the risk, during the next century, as less than 10 percent? And what about the century after that?

The *scientific* case for manned spaceflight gets ever weaker as robotic and miniaturization techniques develop. Experiments and planetary exploration are better (and far more cheaply) carried out by fleets of tiny unmanned probes. Even in the heyday of the Apollo program, the scientific justification was slender. We learned as much about the early Solar System from meteorites that crashed into the Earth as from analyzing moon dust. Apollo was driven by superpower rivalry, and the spectator sport dimension. The *last* lunar landing was in 1972. To a whole new generation, "men on the Moon" are scenes in a remote historical episode, driven by motives almost as strange as those that led to the pyramids. The Apollo program was seen as an end in itself, rather than a step toward some inspiring longer-range goal that might have sustained its momentum.

The strongest such case–indeed perhaps the only credible one–is that manned spaceflight offers a global (or even cosmic) insurance policy. The ever-present risk from nature has been augmented since humankind entered the nuclear and biotechnological age. The species will remain vulnerable to these (probably increasing) hazards so long as it is confined here on Earth. Self-sustaining communities away from the Earth could be developed within a century if current momentum in space technology were maintained. But is it realistic to divert resources from more immediate needs to guard against a risk (1 percent? 10 percent?) that humans will become extinct, thereby eliminating a potential that stretches ahead not just for a historical time span, but for as long as we've taken to evolve from protozoa–perhaps, indeed, far longer still? Ecological issues–the fragility of the Earth's biological diversity, and the importance of preserving it–now loom large in public awareness. Perhaps these concerns with the potential and destiny of terrestrial life will engender renewed commitment to manned spaceflights.

Premature Apocalypse?

We need not fret about the collapse of our entire universe: this will happen, if at all, long after the Sun has died. But what if humans could preempt this ultimate natural catastrophe, and inadvertently unleash a disaster that destroyed not just life on Earth, but the entire cosmos? This scenario is a conceivable (though fortunately unlikely) consequence of current concepts about the fundamental forces.

As our universe cools down, space itself–what physicists call "the vacuum"–changes its nature, just as steam does when it condenses into liquid water, and then into ice. The vacuum is the arena in which all the particles and forces interact; when it undergoes a phase transition, the masses of particles and the forces between them alter drastically. According to the generally accepted theory of Salam and Weinberg, such a transition occurred when our universe was about 10^{-12} seconds old. Before that time, the forces of electromagnetism and the so-called weak force (which operates in radioactivity and in reactions involving neutrinos) were combined in a single "electroweak" force; it took a phase transition to give them their present properties. Attempts to extend this unification to embrace the strong (or nuclear) forces as well are still tentative. But these "grand unified theories" predict another still earlier phase transition, when the universe was only 10–36 seconds old, before which the forces governing the microworld (that is to say, all the fundamental interactions except for gravity) would be combined in a single primeval force.

If there have already been two phase transitions, in each of which the vacuum "cooled" to a lower-energy state, could there be more? The Harvard theorist Sidney Coleman conjectured that there could be a third transition, *which may not yet have happened.* The present vacuum could be super-cooled, rather as very pure water can remain liquid below freezing point; a change in the vacuum could then be triggered by some local concentration of energy, just as a speck of dust can induce supercooled water to crystallize suddenly into ice. Could physical laws governing the entire universe be transmogrified, simply by the trigger of a local energetic event?

Creating the greatest possible concentration of energy is the main purpose of the huge machines used by physicists at CERN, Fermilab, and elsewhere: particles are accelerated to high energies, and then crashed into one another. Is there a risk that the next generation of machines could inadvertently tear the fabric of space? This would be the ultimate catastrophe. A bubble of the new vacuum would expand at the speed of light. We would have no advance warning of its approach; we wouldn't know what had hit us. The bubble wall would surge onward until it engulfed our entire universe. Worse still, the "new" universe inside the bubble would be a "stillborn" one in which nothing could evolve: it would behave like the time-reverse of an inflationary universe, squeezing everything toward infinite density.

Before the first nuclear tests were carried out, physicists prudently calculated, with reassuring results, that the deuterium in the world's oceans wouldn't be ignited by a thermonuclear explosion. What Sidney Coleman envisaged would be a cosmic and not merely terrestrial catastrophe.

At Princeton's Institute for Advanced Study, the aura of Freeman Dyson encourages unrestrained speculation. During a visit there, I discussed the risk of such a cosmic catastrophe with Piet Hut, one of Dyson's younger colleagues. Hut had previously studied a nonnuclear kind of terrestrial catastrophe. With some colleagues at Berkeley, he had conjectured that a faint star was trapped in an exceedingly large eccentric orbit around the Sun; every 35 million years or so, the orbit would plunge into the Solar System, perturbing comets and triggering a shower of impacts that wreaked havoc on Earth. (The extinction of the dinosaurs was blamed on such an impact.) There is incontrovertible evidence for (not necessarily periodic) impacts of comets or asteroids: one of these may indeed have wiped out the dinosaurs; in future, we could suffer a similar fate. But this so-called Nemesis theory has now been abandoned—the proposed orbit was interesting, but no star seemed to occupy it.

Could unwary experimenters crash particles together with enough energy to transform the vacuum into a new state, triggering an expanding "bubble" that would destroy our universe? Piet Hut and I did some simple calculations. We wanted to check whether particle accelerators in the laboratory could generate more energetic impacts than have happened naturally. The most energetic natural collisions involve cosmic rays—very fast particles that pervade the entire Galaxy, perhaps even the entire observable universe. These particles have been accelerated, almost to the speed of light, by cosmic explosions even more violent than supernovae explosions: they could come from strong radio sources, which we now think are energized by jets from huge black holes. Or they could come from the sudden release of energy when (for instance) two neutron stars orbiting each other spiral together and coalesce. Their origin is a mystery, but we know from direct measurements that the fastest cosmic ray particles reaching us from space are millions of times more energetic than any that can be artificially accelerated here on Earth. Each of them, just a single atom, carries as much punch as a bullet or a fast-served tennis ball.

Cosmic rays with these extreme energies are so exceedingly rare–an area of 1 square kilometer would intercept only one per century–that no two would ever have actually collided with each other anywhere in our universe. However, we calculated that there would have been many collisions between cosmic rays whose energies, though somewhat less extreme, were still hundreds of times higher than can be attained by the Large Hadron Collider, the world's most powerful accelerator now being built at CERN in Geneva. So any foreseeable laboratory-induced collisions would be relatively gentle compared with those that have occurred repeatedly, without catastrophic consequences, throughout interstellar space.

This wasn't an entirely frivolous calculation. The vulnerability of space to a catastrophic phase transition was admittedly just the figment of a speculative theory. But the possibility is not absurd–in our present state of ignorance about unified theories, we would be imprudent to disregard it. Indeed, caution should surely be urged (if not enforced) on experiments that create energy concentrations that may never have occurred naturally. We can only hope that extraterrestrials with greater technical resources, should they exist, are equally cautious!

Notes

1. In our Galaxy, most stars are in a thin disk, and each follows a near-circular orbit around the Galactic Center; the stars are held in these orbits by the pull of all the other stars (and the dark matter) which collectively balance centrifugal force. When the merger occurs, each star in our own Galaxy will feel just as strong a force from Andromeda. But this latter force, acting obliquely to our own disk, will therefore disorganize the stellar orbits in our Galaxy. Conversely, the Milky Way's gravity will deflect all Andromeda's stars out of its disk.

2. Our present universe is slightly irregular on scales even larger than superclusters. Just as the precursors of galaxies and clusters were small-amplitude ripples in the early universe; so aggregates even larger than superclusters may eventually condense from regions that are now only slightly denser than average. A region 1 percent denser than the average will condense out when the universe has expanded by a further factor of 100; if the overdensity is only 0.1 percent, the universe must expand by a factor of 1000, and so on. We know about these overdensities on very large scales because they cause slight nonuniformities in the microwave background temperature revealed by the COBE satellite. The hierarchy of clus-

tering will grow in step with the age of the universe. The largest superclusters have dimensions that are 1 percent of the Hubble radius (they contain maybe a millionth of the total mass within our "horizon"). When the horizon is bigger, so also will be the largest clusters. If omega is exactly 1, and the ripples are the same on every scale, the biggest clusters will grow in step with the Hubble radius. If the ripples had larger amplitudes on larger scales, the universe may eventually close up on itself, because the scale of the largest structures becomes as large as the horizon. On the other hand, the ripples may get weaker on larger scales, in which case structures could at some stage stop growing and merging. The most drastic difference would occur if there were a cosmological constant lambda. Even if this were too small to affect the cosmic expansion now, it would eventually (unless it were exactly zero) exert a cosmic repulsion that overwhelmed the ever-diluting strength of gravity. An observer on any cluster would see the others disperse with increasing speed, until none at all were left within view.

3. An anonymous graffiti writer at the University of Texas is credited with the insight: "Time is nature's way of stopping things from happening all at once."

SUGGESTIONS FOR FURTHER READING

Do NOT OVERLOOK the works represented in the previous Readings. For instance, *Gravitation*—from which Reading 16 is taken—might almost have been entitled *Cosmology*. Again, the IAU volume—source of Reading 10—has C. B. Collins and S. W. Hawking explaining the cosmic expansion rate anthropically.

General

Bondi, H. *Cosmology*, 2nd ed. Cambridge Univ. Press, Cambridge, 1960. A tidy, philosophically level-headed introduction by a main defender of the Steady State theory. Getting to be of mainly historical importance.

Gamow, George. *The Creation of the Universe*, rev. ed. Viking Press, New York, 1963. Another fine introduction, from one of the main developers of the Big Bang theory. But the subject has moved so fast that 1963 is a very early date.

Gingerich, Owen (ed.). *Cosmology + 1.* W. H. Freeman, San Francisco, 1977. A varied collection from Scientific American, 1957–1977.

Harrison, Edward R. *Cosmology*. Cambridge Univ. Press, Cambridge, 1981. Perhaps the best introduction today. Enthusiasm for the field's scientific wonders, respect for its philosophical guiding principles, a high standard of precision, and a friendly style. Plenty of diagrams and bibliographies. Note Harrison's solution to Olbers' Paradox.

Hoyle, Fred, and Jayant Narlikar. *The Physics-Astronomy Frontier*. W. H. Freeman, San Francisco, 1980. Not afraid to develop idiosyncratic ideas; e.g., that the cosmos is gigantic and many-celled, masses becoming zero at cell boundaries.

John, Laurie (ed.). *Cosmology Now.* Broadwater Press, Welwyn Garden City, 1976. BBC talks by leading figures. Includes D. W. Sciama's "The Influence of the Stars" (on Mach's principle: my car's slow acceleration might in part reflect the action of distant galaxies).

Narlikar, Jayant V. *The Primeval Universe*. Oxford Univ. Press, Oxford, 1988. An excellent introduction, though often quite technical. The later chapters are very speculative and philosophically interesting.

Novikov, Igor D. *Evolution of the Universe*. Cambridge Univ. Press, Cambridge, 1983. A Soviet view of a field in which Soviet writers are among the best. Confident about many hotly disputed matters.

Rowan-Robinson, Michael. *Cosmology*, 2nd ed. Oxford Univ. Press, Oxford, 1981. Introductions, fairly technical but short and readable, to many topics, some very controversial.

Sciama, D. W. *Modern Cosmology*, 2nd ed., Cambridge Univ. Press, Cambridge, 1982. Clear, authoritative, open-minded.

Silk, Joseph. *The Big Bang*. W. H. Freeman, San Francisco, 1980. A likeable introduction to cosmology in general, somewhat simpler than Harrison's.

Note the chapter on alternatives to the Big Bang. Comparison with 1988's revised and updated edition is an interesting exercise.

Weinberg, Steven. *The First Three Minutes*. New edition, with Afterword on cosmology since 1976. Fontana, London, 1983. A good read and deservedly famous. We can know much about early times if things get simpler as they get hotter. The story begins "when the temperature had cooled to a mere hundred thousand million degrees."

Recent Developments

Atkins, P. W. *The Creation*. W. H. Freeman, San Francisco, 1981. A fast-moving, informative, entertaining defence of the view that a life-encouraging universe had to arrive sooner or later through chance.

Barrow, John D., and Frank J. Tipler. *The Anthropic Cosmological Principle*. Clarendon Press, Oxford, 1986. Over 700 pages; a gold mine of scientific and philosophical ideas and references. Extraordinarily wide-ranging; e.g., contains much history of the Design Argument. Complex. At times untidy. Interprets "our universe must contain life" as a teleological statement. But a beautiful book and essential reading.

Carr, B. J., and M. J. Rees. The anthropic principle and the structure of the physical world. *Nature* 278; 12 April, 605–612, 1979. A classic survey of the early literature. At crucial points the argument gets very compressed: more relaxed is Rees, Our universe and others, *Quarterly Journal of the Royal Astronomical Society* 22; 109–124, 1981.

Davies, P. C. W. *The Accidental Universe*. Cambridge Univ. Press, Cambridge, 1982. Also on the Anthropic Principle. More focused than the Barrow–Tipler book and so in many ways better, though less of an epical achievement. Davies writes phenomenally many useful books and articles.

Davies, P. C. W., and S. D. Unwin. Why is the cosmological constant so small? *Proceedings of the Royal Society, London*: A377, 1981, 147–149. An illustration of how a very important constant could vary from one huge region to another not randomly but deterministically.

Ellis, G. F. R. Alternatives to the Big Bang. *Annual Review of Astronomy and Astrophysics* 22; 157–184, 1984. An authoritative, open-minded review paper, very technical in places.

Ellis, G. F. R., and Tony Rothman. The epoch of observational cosmology. *The Observatory* 107; (Feb) 24–29, 1987. Observations may be possible only in an interestingly restricted period; cf. Reading 9.

Ellis, G. F. R., and Tony Rothman. Has cosmology become metaphysical? *Astronomy* 15; [(2) Feb] 6–22, 1987. Scientific and philosophical doubts about Inflation, which itself seems to depend on fine-tuning. ("Inflationists merely swap the flatness problem for the vacuum energy density problem: why is the vacuum energy density so close to zero?") Though this paper makes easy reading, it must not be taken lightly.

Gale, George. The anthropic principle. *Scientific American* 245 [(6) Dec.] 154–171, 1981. An enjoyable introduction by a philosopher.

Gribbin, John. *In Search of the Big Bang*. Bantam Books, New York, 1986. Einstein's universe, the Bang, and recent ideas about the first moments.

Guth, A. H., and P. J. Steinhardt. The inflationary universe. *Scientific American*

250; [(5) May] 116–128, 1984. Although not first discoverer of the theme, Guth caught people's imaginations. This, or his technical paper on pp. 347–356 of *Physical Review D:* **23** [(2) 15 Jan], 1981, is essential reading. Extending immensely beyond our horizon and quite probably split up into huge domains with randomly varying characteristics, the inflationary universe poses a severe challenge to all efforts to revive the theory that the true is the verifiable.

Hawking, Stephen W. *A Brief History of Time.* An intriguing introduction both to the history of cosmology and to Hawking's very important contributions. Alas, those contributions are described far too quickly to be understood.

Hawking, S. W., and W. Israel (eds.). *Three Hundred Years of Gravitation.* Cambridge University Press, Cambridge, 1987. Up-to-date yet often very readable work by eighteen experts. Includes Guth on starting a new Big Bang in the laboratory, Linde on an eternally inflating cosmos, Penrose on reasons for denying that Inflation can explain the cosmic smoothness, and Hawking's comparison of "What did God do before He made Heaven and Earth?" to "What is Earth like to the north of the North Pole?".

Linde, A. D. The inflationary universe. *Reports on Progress in Physics* **47** [(8) Aug] 925–986, 1984. Sometimes extremely technical but crammed with glorious ideas.

Pagels, Heinz R. *Perfect Symmetry.* Simon and Schuster, New York, 1985. A well-told tale, beginning with classical cosmology but soon reaching modern theories (symmetry breaking, etc.).

Rothman, Tony, and others. *Frontiers of Modern Physics.* Dover, New York, 1985. Cosmology, quantum theory, etc., treated speculatively and enjoyably.

Rozental, I. L. Physical laws and the numerical values of fundamental constants. *Soviet Physics: Uspekhi* **23** [(6) June] 296–305, 1980. Very important. Without fine tuning of the constants there would be no galaxies, and probably even no atomic nuclei.

Trefil, James S. *The Moment of Creation.* Macmillan, New York, 1983. Symmetry breaking, Inflation and allied topics. Popular writing at its best.

Tryon, Edward P. What made the world? *New Scientist* **101**: [(1400) 8 March] 14–16, 1984. An updated version of his pioneering "Is the Universe a Vacuum Fluctuation?".

Vilenkin, A. Creation of universes from nothing. *Physics Letters* **117B**:[(1) 4 Nov] 25–28, 1982. Complex. Though Vilenkin says "literally nothing" he may mean only a foamy mess existing before (if we can use such a time word) space and time became well structured; compare his Quantum creation of universes, *Physical Review D* **30**:[(2) 15 July] 509–511, 1984.

Extraterrestrial Life

Bracewell, Ronald N. *The Galactic Club.* Stanford Alumni Assoc., Stanford, 1974. Optimistic about the Club's existence.

Feinberg, Gerald, and Robert Shapiro. *Life Beyond Earth.* William Morrow, New York, 1980. Equally optimistic, largely through willingness to accept life in the sun, neutron star life, frozen-hydrogen life, and so on. Fascinating. But why so scornful about those who think differently?

Goldsmith, Donald (ed.). *The Quest for Extraterrestrial Life*. University Science Books, Mill Valley, 1980. A large, very useful collection of optimism from Lucretius onward, and of the newly fashionable pessimism.

Goldsmith, Donald, and Tobias Owen. *The Search for Life in the Universe*. Benjamin Cummings, Menlo Park, 1979. Combines suggestions about extraterrestrial biology with a first-rate introduction to astronomy and cosmology.

Heppenheimer, T. A. After the sun dies. *Omni* (Aug) pp. 37–40, 1986. A popular treatment of organisms of the far future as imagined by Freeman Dyson and like-minded scientists. Plasmoids? Or positronium beings whose very atoms are larger than our visible universe? Such oddities might come to exist thanks to planning by people like Dyson. For some technical background, see Dyson's Time without end: Physics and biology in an open universe, *Reviews of Modern Physics* **51**: 447–460, 1979.

MacGowan, Roger A., and Frederick I. Ordway, *Intelligence in the Universe*. Prentice-Hall, Englewood Cliffs, 1966. Continues to be worth reading for its ideas; e.g., that intelligent machines are the main life forms in the cosmos.

Regis, Edward (ed.). *Extraterrestrials: Science and Alien Intelligence*. Cambridge Univ. Press, Cambridge, 1985. More emphasis than usual on the philosophy of the subject.

Rood, Robert T., and James S. Trefil. *Are We Alone?* Charles Scribner's Sons, New York, 1981. Excellent as an account of the newly discovered reasons for pessimism.

Shklovskii, I. S., and Carl Sagan. *Intelligent Life in the Universe*. Dell, New York, 1966. Optimistic. An early diamond.

Tipler, Frank J. Extraterrestrial intelligent beings do not exist. *Quarterly Journal of the Royal Astronomical Society* **21**: 267–281, 1980. Not in our galaxy anyway, else their interstellar probes would be here by now. A classic.

Historical and Philosophical

Barbour, Ian. *Issues in Science and Religion*. Prentice-Hall, Englewood Cliffs, 1966. History and philosophy of the interaction between science and religion. Includes discussions of cosmology, physics and biology.

Grünbaum, Adolf. *Philosophical Problems of Space and Time*, 2nd ed., enlarged. Reidel, Dordrecht, 1973. Scientifically expert, philosophically advanced (but very stimulating) treatment of the issues and of some major figures. A monumental achievement.

Jaki, Stanley L. *Science and Creation*. Scottish Academic Press, Edinburg, 1974. Mainly historical, with much about merest myth, but with some treatment of fairly recent theories; e.g., of cosmic oscillations. A writer with strong personal views.

Hoskin, Michael. *Stellar Astronomy: Historical Studies*. Science History Publications, Chalfont St. Giles, 1982. Sound and interesting scholarship. Includes "Newton, Providence and the universe of stars."

Koyré, Alexandre. *From the Closed World to the Infinite Universe*. Harper and Row, New York, 1958. History enlivened by useful extracts, Nicholas of Cusa to Newton.

Layzer, David. *Constructing the Universe*. W. H. Freeman, New York, 1984. A history of cosmology from the ancients to Einstein.

Leslie, John. Various writings are listed at the end of Swinburne's contribution to this volume: *Value and Existence* was too quick in its dismissal of the Multiple-Universes-plus-Selection-Effect approach in favor of a Neoplatonist creation story (most recently defended in *Religious Studies* 22: 325–342, 1986). See also "Probabilistic phase transitions and the anthropic principle," pp. 439–444 in J. Demaret (ed.), *Origin and Early History of the Universe*, Univ. of Liège Press, Liège, 1987; "No inverse gambler's fallacy in cosmology," *Mind* (April) 1988, a reply to an intriguing argument by Ian Hacking in the July 1987 issue; and *Universes*, Routledge, London and New York, 1989.

Lovell, Bernard. *In the Center of Immensities*. Harper and Row, New York, 1978. A quick, elegant, authoritative tour of astronomy and cosmology, past and present, with discussion of man's place in the scheme of things.

The Monist 47: [(1) Fall], 1962. The issue's title is "Philosophical Implications of the New Cosmology"; the papers, by philosophers and scientists, often make points of lasting importance. M. Bunge mounts a philosophical attack on the "magical" appearance of new matter in a Steady State universe; contrast Reading 7.

Munitz, Milton K. *Theories of the Universe: From Babylonian Myth to Modern Science*. Macmillan, New York, 1957. A very helpful collection of historically important writings. A good companion to this volume.

Munitz, Milton K. *Cosmic Understanding: Philosophy and Science of the Universe*. Princeton Univ. Press, Princeton, 1986. Up-to-date work by a leading philosopher of cosmology. (For Munitz's reactions to the situation of the 1950s, see his *Space, Time and Creation: Philosophical Aspects of Scientific Cosmology*, Free Press, New York, 1957.)

North, J. D. *The Measure of the Universe*. Clarendon Press, Oxford, 1965. A history of cosmology in the first half of the century, with seven chapters on philosophical issues.

Peacocke, A. R. *Creation and the World of Science*. Clarendon Press, Oxford, 1979. A sustained attempt to relate cosmology and biology to religious thought. Chapters 2 and 3 are the ones most relevant to this volume.

Polkinghorne, J. C. *One World: The Interaction of Science and Theology*. SPCK, London, 1986. Terse, expert, and filled with sturdy common sense. The author is far better at philosophy than most professional philosophers — but is in fact a physicist who gave up a Cambridge chair to become a priest. See also his *Science and Creation*, SPCK, London, 1988.

Rolston, Holmes. *Science and Religion*. Random House, New York, 1987. Comments as for A. R. Peacocke, right down to the chapter numbers.

Smart, J. J. C. Philosophical problems of cosmology. *Revue Internationale de Philosophie* 169:(1)112–126, 1987. Interesting work by a leading philosopher.

Smith, Quentin. World ensemble explanations. *Pacific Philosophical Quarterly* 67:[(1) Jan.] 73–86, 1987. Assesses various ways of generating multiple worlds/universes with varied properties.

Smith, Robert. *The Expanding Universe: Astronomy's Great Debate, 1900–1931*. Cambridge Univ. Press, Cambridge, 1982. Scholarly treatment of a philosophically interesting period.

Wheeler, John A. Genesis and observership. In Robert E. Butts and Jaako Hintikka (eds.), *Foundational Problems in the Special Sciences*, pp. 3–33. Reidel, Dordrecht, 1977. Greatly intriguing development of the themes touched on in Reading 16.

Whitrow, Gerald J. *The Structure and Evolution of the Universe.* Harper and Row, New York, 1959. Cosmological speculations and their philosophy. See especially the Appendix on why physical space has three dimensions.

Yourgrau, W., and A. D. Breck (eds.). *Cosmology, History and Philosophy.* Plenum Press, New York, 1977. Colloquium papers, several of philosophical interest; e.g., C. W. Misner's "Cosmology and theology."

Miscellaneous

Burns, Jack O. Very large structures in the universe. *Scientific American.* 255 [(1) July] 30–39, 1986. Superclusters alternate with supervoids. May such huge-scale patterns reflect the microphysics of the first instants?

Cameron, A. G. (ed.). *Astrophysics Today.* American Institute of Physics, New York, 1984. Sixty pieces from *Physics Today*, eleven classified as cosmological physics. Of the others, do not miss J. D. Bekenstein's "Black-hole thermodynamics."

DeWitt, Bryce S., and Neill Graham (eds.). *The Many-Worlds Interpretation of Quantum Mechanics.* Princeton Univ. Press, Princeton, 1973. Classic papers discussing a particularly curious way in which multiple worlds/universes might be generated.

Field, George B., and Eric J. Chaisson. *The Invisible Universe.* Birkhauser Boston, Cambridge Mass., 1985. X-rays, infrared light, radio waves, etc., let us see the invisible. So do advances in theoretical physics. (Neoplatonists may rather like p. 149's quantum-physical suggestion that "the potential existence of the world somehow calls it into existence.")

Hawking, S. W. The quantum mechanics of black holes. *Scientific American* 236 [(1) Jan] 34–40, 1977. Hawking's proof that black holes can (in a sense) radiate is an important step toward unifying general relativity, thermodynamics, and quantum mechanics. It might help to explain the bounces of an oscillating cosmos.

Islam, Jamal N. *The Ultimate Fate of the Universe.* Cambridge Univ. Press, Cambridge, 1983. Irreversible collapse, oscillations, or eternal expansion? If the last of these, then astonishing changes could occur sooner or later; e.g., diamond cubes become iron spheres. Yet life might continue for ever.

Kaufmann, William J. *The Cosmic Frontiers of General Relativity: A Layman's Guide to the New Universe.* Penguin Books, Harmondsworth, 1979. A brave effort with many diagrams. But laymen may feel more at home in his shorter *Relativity and Cosmology*, 2nd ed. Harper and Row, New York, 1977.

Kormendy, J., and G. R. Knapp (eds.) *Dark matter in the Universe.* Reidel, Dordrecht, 1987. An IAU Symposium, hence technical. Includes M. S. Turner's "A cosmologist's tour through the new particle zoo (candy shop?)." Invisible particles may help to "close" the universe.

Narlikar, J. V. *Violent Phenomena in the Universe.* Oxford Univ. Press, Oxford, 1982. Supernovae, black holes, white holes, quasars, pulsars, and the Big Bang itself. Specially interesting when defending the unconventional.

Nicolson, Iain. *Gravity, Black Holes and the Universe.* John Wiley, New York, 1981. A very readable introduction to gravitational cosmology.

Turner, Michael S., and Franck Wilczek. Is our vacuum metastable? *Nature* **298**: 12 Aug., 633–634, 1982. If Yes, then the cosmos as we know it might end tomorrow, quantum-unpredictably. (In *Nature* **302**: 7 April, 508–509, 1983, P. Hut and M. J. Rees show that the sudden bubble of stable vacuum, expanding disastrously and at almost the speed of light, will not be produced, thank heaven, in the present generation of particle accelerators.)

GLOSSARY

$10^6 = 1$ followed by six zeros = 1 million. $10^{-6} = 1$ divided by $10^6 = 1$ millionth.In this book, "a billion" always means 10^9, which is one thousand million.A light year, the distance traveled by light in a year, is 9.46×10^{15} m (meters), or 9.46×10^{12} km (kilometers), since there are 10^3 m in 1 km.

10^{14} gm/cm^3, about the density of a neutron star, is one hundred thousand billion grams per cubic centimeter.

"Mega" means a million, and "giga" a billion: the M and the G appear in MeV and GeV, which stand for energies (or temperatures characterized by those energies) measured in millions or billions of electron volts. (1 eV is the energy gained by an electron moving through a 1-volt difference in potential.)

$\sim$ means "is roughly equal to."

Anthropic principle This has "weak" and "strong" forms. The weak is that our region of space and time is, obviously, one in which observers can exist; the strong, that our universe is, equally obviously, one in which observers can exist. (Some people, however, use "anthropic principle" or "strong anthropic principle" to mean that our universe was designed to contain observers, or was for some other reason compelled to contain them.)

Antimatter Matter made of "antiparticles," whose masses are identical with those of the corresponding particles, but which are opposite in electric charge and various other properties. When particles meet antiparticles, the result is pure energy.

Big bang Explosion in which our universe began — or at least, in which the present era of expansion began if our universe oscillates.

Black hole A gravitationally collapsed region from which not even light can escape. However, black holes can in a sense "radiate" thanks to how particles are created by strong gravitational fields. The radiation can make a black hole shrink.

Closed universe Finitely large universe; its space curves around and joins up with itself, as Earth's surface does. A closed universe will collapse sooner or later, it is thought.

Cosmos See **universe.**

Critical density The minimum cosmic density required to make a universe "closed."

Entropy   "Disorder"—in a sense hard to define precisely. The second law of thermodynamics is that the entropy of an isolated system always increases with time.

Fluctuation   Something statistically unusual, but which could be expected sooner or later, somewhere—for instance because quantum theory permits it, as when particles (typically so short-lived that they are called "virtual") appear out of empty space as "vacuum fluctuations." In coin-tossing, a run of twenty Heads could be called a fluctuation.

General (theory of) relativity (GTR)   The theory that Nature is (in some sense even experts find hard to agree on) "the same for all observers," no matter how they move. Goes beyond special relativity by taking account of accelerations and of gravity, which is pictured as making space more curved—this being why planets circle the sun, for instance.

Homogeneity   Being the same everywhere. (Not necessarily accompanied by isotropy.)

Horizons   Limits to what can interact with what. Light travels as fast as anything, and it has traveled only a limited distance since the big bang started, so there is a horizon (continually growing larger) to how far we can see, and to what can have had effects on us. Particles falling into a black hole pass through a horizon of another sort, since no light waves or other influences can reach us from inside the hole.

Inflation   Accelerating expansion at very early times—like the growth of a rabbit population in which the average rabbit gives birth to a dozen others.

Isotropy   Being the same in all directions. (Not necessarily accompanied by homogeneity.)

Neutron star   Collapsed star, immensely dense, made mainly of neutrons.

Nuclear strong force   or strong nuclear force, or "strong force" for short. Binds together the particles of the atomic nucleus. Otherwise known as "the strong interaction."

Nuclear weak force   or "weak interaction." Responsible for various particle decays, and for reactions involving neutrinos.

Olbers' paradox   The difficulty of explaining why, in an infinite (or very large) universe, the sky is dark at night, since you might expect each line of sight to meet a star sooner or later.

Open universe   A universe in which space neither curves around and joins up with itself, nor is perfectly flat. (Perfectly flat space is the space to which Euclid's theorems apply perfectly.) An open universe would expand for ever, people think—though it would always have been infinitely large.

Phase transition   A sudden, marked change in state; for example, the freezing of water. Symmetry breakings are phase transitions.

Photon to baryon ratio   The number of photons (particles of light) to baryons (neutrons and protons, constituents of the atomic nucleus). Roughly a billion to one. Often used as a measure of how disorderly the universe is.

Quantum theory   The theory that particles have wavelike characteristics and behave in ways that are in part random, while waves, in turn, are in some sense made up of particles whose exact times and places of appearance have a random element. Also energies are "quantized"; i.e., appear in whole multiples of fixed amounts. But the theory itself states that times, places, and amounts are never completely precise. Instead they are characterized by uncertainties which are not mere matters of human ignorance.

Quasars   The objects which, if they are as far as their red shifts suggest, are the brightest relative to their sizes. A volume much smaller than any galaxy may none the less emit several billion times as much light as any normal star. Often thought to be intensely violent regions around black holes.

Red shift   When a radiating body begins to recede very fast, its radiation is seen as shifting to lower frequencies: compare how machine-gun bullets would strike you at less frequent intervals if fired from a fast-receding aircraft. (Blue shifting is the reverse, produced when the radiating body approaches.)

Singularity   A spatiotemporal position (perhaps the center of a black hole, or the start of the big bang) at which histories must begin or else end. It was traditionally assumed that some quantity (density, for example) had to be infinite at a singularity, but this is no longer always written into the definition.

Steady-state universe   A universe which, at least on the largest scales, looks the same at every epoch. For such a universe to be an expanding one, matter would have to be created in it continuously.

Supernova   An exploding star, sometimes as bright as a whole galaxy for a short while.

Symmetry breaking   A process in which similarities between forces, particles, spatial directions, etcetera, become distorted. *Example*: When ice crystals form in it, water stops looking the same in all directions.

Unification of forces   At high temperatures and energies, or very short ranges, Nature's four main forces—gravity, electromagnetism, and the nuclear strong and weak forces—may all take on equal strength, becoming only aspects of a single force. Grand Unified Theories or GUTs hold that electromagnetism unites first with the nuclear weak force and then with the nuclear strong force. (In "supergravity" or "supersymmetry" or "totally unified" theories, gravity joins in at still higher temperatures.) The Unified Theory in which electromagnetism unites with the nuclear weak force at about 100 GeV ("electroweak unification") is well established.

Universe   Everything In Existence, ever, anywhere; or else the region we inhabit plus everything that has interacted or ever will interact with this region; or else this region plus everything that has interacted with it by now, or will at least do so in the next few billion years; or else any gigantic system of causally interacting things that is wholly (or very largely) isolated from others; or else any system that might well have become gigantic, etc., even if it in fact recollapsed while still very small; or . . . (Nowadays, the word *cosmos* might be used to refer to Everything In Existence, while *universe* was used in a way permitting talk of several universes inside the cosmos.)